Praise for the Book

'Nisar shows how the traditional capitalist model is transformed in the current ever changing environment of digital social markets. An essential read for anyone wanting to understand how the digital world has forever changed business structures.'

Brandon Randolph-Seng, *Texas A&M University*

'This book addresses key issues in AI applications across digital platforms and social commerce. Nisar draws on extensive research from economics, finance and related fields to support his findings. I encourage readers with an interest in these topics to get a copy of this important book.'

Douglas J. Cumming, *Florida Atlantic University*

'Very interesting.'

John Roberts, *Stanford Graduate School of Business*

'This book wrestles with the challenging issues raised by the digital economy, such as evolving new business relationships, and how AI is transforming the way we work and the capital-labour nexus. Nisar skilfully combines empirical resources with theoretical precision, in a way that students, researchers, and general readers will find invaluable in developing critical thought around an evolving business landscape.'

Jane Parry, *UK Parliament Thematic Research Lead in Business, Economics and Trade*

'As a leading scholar in the social commerce research domain, I highly endorse this groundbreaking book, which meticulously investigates the intricate social and economic forces shaping our contemporary digital landscape. It offers a profound exploration of the technological advancements and innovative market frameworks that influence job seekers, consumers, businesses, and communities alike … The critical examination of the monopoly power held by platforms such as Amazon and Facebook, alongside the pressing issue of data privacy and the exploration of regulatory frameworks, makes this work an essential resource for both academics and practitioners.'

Nick Hajli, *Loughborough University*

Personalization and Digital Social Markets

Disrupting the Capitalist Economy

Tahir M. Nisar

BLOOMSBURY ACADEMIC
LONDON • NEW YORK • OXFORD • NEW DELHI • SYDNEY

BLOOMSBURY ACADEMIC
Bloomsbury Publishing Plc
50 Bedford Square, London, WC1B 3DP, UK
1385 Broadway, New York, NY 10018, USA
29 Earlsfort Terrace, Dublin 2, Ireland

BLOOMSBURY, BLOOMSBURY ACADEMIC and the Diana logo are trademarks of Bloomsbury Publishing Plc

First published in Great Britain 2025

Series design by Grace Ridge
Cover images © cokada and Aleksandra Konoplia via Getty Images

A catalogue record for this book is available from the British Library.

A catalog record for this book is available from the Library of Congress.

ISBN: HB: 978-1-3504-4441-6
ePDF: 978-1-3504-4443-0
eBook: 978-1-3504-4442-3

Typeset by Newgen KnowledgeWorks Pvt. Ltd., Chennai, Ind

To my parents

Contents

Acknowledgements

My sincere thanks to everyone who contributed to the development of the ideas presented in this book. I am particularly grateful for the valuable contributions of my peers and colleagues – Nick Hajli, Derek Eldridge, Peter Abell, Michael Bourlakis, Stefan Roth, Richard Evans, Laura Costanzo, Konstantinos Katsikopoulos, Vijay Viswanathan, Bernard Bempong, Michalis Veliziotis, Khurrum Siddiq, David Cross, Stratos Ramoglou, Lubica Strakova, Dina Alghamdi, Irina Baydarova, Nicholas Clarke, Mina Beigi, Jane Parry, Naveena Prakasam, Faiza Tabassum, Paurav Shukla, Peter Rodgers, and Yehuda Baruch – whose constructive feedback and engaging discussions encouraged me to delve deeper into my research.

My appreciation also extends to the various authors, researchers, and experts whose works I consulted, enriching my book with diverse perspectives and foundational knowledge. A special thank you to my book editor, Nick Wolterman, for his expert guidance, unwavering support, and valuable critiques, which were instrumental at every stage of the writing process. I am also grateful to our team members, especially Nadine Staes-Polet, whose dedication, innovation, and tireless efforts were fundamental to writing this book.

I also wish to acknowledge my family and friends for their unwavering support, encouragement, and understanding throughout the duration of this endeavour, which greatly contributed to my motivation and well-being.

Thank you all for being part of this journey and for playing a pivotal role in successfully completing this project.

Introduction

This book examines the rise of key economic institutions in the digital era, with a focus on personalization and digital social markets. It argues that these emerging forces have the potential to significantly reshape traditional capitalist models of production and market economies. As digital technologies restructure economic institutions, new markets and industries are emerging at an unprecedent pace. The disruptive impact of these technologies on the established economic order is evident in several critical ways:

Emergence of new markets and industries: The emergence of digital technologies has ushered in an era of innovation and disruption, giving birth to entirely new markets and industries. The internet and mobile app economies exemplify this, characterized by low entry barriers and rapid innovation cycles that pose formidable challenges to traditional sectors with stricter requirements and slower adaptation. Technologies like blockchain and cryptocurrencies are accelerating this shift by enabling the development of decentralized platforms that inherently question conventional centralized business models.

Disintermediation: Platforms such as Amazon, eBay, and Expedia have effectively eliminated intermediaries in e-commerce, retail, and travel industries, connecting consumers directly with products and services. This disintermediation not only drives down costs but also compels legacy businesses to evolve or risk becoming obsolete. Furthermore, peer-to-peer technologies are revolutionizing sectors like finance, transportation, and retail by facilitating direct interactions between consumers and service providers, circumventing traditional middlemen.

Automation through robotics and AI: New technologies are leading to the automation of tasks previously performed by humans. The manufacturing sector, for instance, is witnessing an increasing deployment of robots, leading to a shift in labour dynamics. The integration of artificial intelligence (AI) and machine learning into various workplace processes augments task performance and improves productivity and competitiveness. While this transition results in job displacement in certain areas, it simultaneously creates new employment opportunities, such as roles related to AI-driven customer service bots and financial trading algorithms.

Innovative business models: Digital disruption has paved the way for novel business models that prioritize operational efficiency and customer-centricity. Subscription-based services like Netflix and Hulu, which offer extensive content libraries at a fraction of traditional cable costs, are revamping long-standing revenue models and content distribution networks. Similarly, ride-hailing applications like Uber and Lyft are redefining urban mobility, offering new conveniences for users and alternative earning opportunities.

Transformation of work and lifestyle: The digital age is redefining conventional work paradigms and lifestyle choices. The proliferation of remote work and gig economy platforms is restructuring employment models, while social media and other online platforms are reconfiguring social interactions and community engagement. These changes carry significant implications for societal structures and economic practices.

These advancements underscore the significant impact of digital technologies on the capitalist economic structure. By automating processes, introducing innovative business models, and eliminating intermediaries, these technologies are not only creating new markets and industries but also forcing established entities to adapt to rapid changes. To understand these transformative shifts, we now explore the driving forces behind them.

First, the exponential growth of data science and AI-driven approaches is influencing the way firms customize their offerings, enabling them to achieve unparalleled levels of personalization. These factors are leading to deeper, more direct interactions across diverse sectors and platforms, such as recommendation algorithms in e-commerce. This represents a departure from traditional market practices, with a preference for companies that focus on engaging and involving their customers more directly. Furthermore, consumers are increasingly contributing to the creation of products and services, impacting both design through crowdsourcing platforms and production processes through personalized manufacturing options. These critical elements collectively signify a major change in the consumer-business relationship, characterized by more personalized, collaborative, and socially influenced production processes. This evolution challenges established capitalist norms, heralding a new phase of economic engagement that is more dynamic, inclusive, and consumer-centric.

Second, the past couple of decades have seen a change in how society approaches consumption. The individualistic, disposable purchase and usage patterns prevalent throughout the twentieth century are being replaced by an increased emphasis on efficiency, collaboration, and sharing. This is epitomized by the 'sharing economy' and the 'gig economy', which are influencing various industries and markets with their innovative consumption models. In the sharing economy, individuals take on dual roles as both consumers and producers, utilizing digital platforms to share or rent out personal assets, such as cars or accommodation, in peer-to-peer transactions. This model is powered by technological innovations that enable direct connections and resource sharing among individuals, challenging traditional business models. The gig economy complements this by offering flexible, short-term work engagements through platforms like Uber, Airbnb, and Fiverr. This innovation provides people with the opportunity to earn income on-demand, sidestepping conventional employment frameworks and offering a new level of work-life flexibility.

Adding another layer of disruption to traditional economic structures is decentralized finance (DeFi). Built upon blockchain technology, DeFi represents a groundbreaking financial system that allows users to engage in financial activities, including obtaining loans, saving, and investing, without the mediation of traditional financial institutions like banks. This decentralization poses a considerable challenge to the conventional banking sector, offering more direct and potentially more equitable financial solutions. These developments represent a profound move towards more communal and shared economic interactions, underpinned by technological innovations that facilitate new ways of consuming, working, and engaging in financial activities.

Third, the rapid rise of social media as a platform for interactive communication has spurred firms to build extensive social networks and foster online consumer engagement, both within and beyond their organizational boundaries. Social media has ushered in an era of reciprocal interactions between individuals and organizations, turning users from being mere passive receivers of content to active participants who influence and contribute to the narrative and discourse. These platforms have evolved into dynamic hubs for sharing opinions, experiences, and knowledge, encouraging discussions on a wide array of subjects ranging from specific products and services to broader societal matters.

This evolution of social media from a simple entertainment outlet to a powerful tool for information gathering, evaluation, and decision-making has fundamentally changed the digital environment. The centre of influence has moved towards the users, who now actively seek, analyse, and share information, influencing purchasing decisions through their endorsements and word-of-mouth communication. This highlights the increasing power of consumers and brings to light the concept of co-creation, where consumers are not just passive buyers but are actively involved in the creative process of innovation.

From a sociological perspective, this also reflects the embedding of economic activities within the wider social context, as illustrated by Granovetter's influential work in 1985. The concept of social contagion, wherein personal recommendations have more impact than traditional advertising, is crucial in this new context. It emphasizes the importance of social interactions and community-generated content in shaping consumer behaviours and market trends, highlighting the intertwined nature of social networks and economic actions in the digital age.

Fourth, the rapid ascent of e-commerce has paved the way for the emergence of social commerce, a novel domain that merges social networking with online shopping. Social commerce refers to the use of social networking sites to facilitate the buying and selling of products and services. It integrates online purchasing with social media experience, allowing users to directly procure products through social media platforms without having to navigate to another site. This form of commerce leverages user-generated content, online communities, and social interactions to drive sales and enhance the purchasing experience.

As social commerce continues to develop, it is transitioning from a solely transactional approach towards one that prioritizes building meaningful customer connections in digital marketplaces. Businesses are also increasingly moving away from generic strategies, opting instead for experiences devised using sophisticated data analysis and insights. Social commerce platforms facilitate this personalized approach by providing a wealth of opportunities for firms to collaborate with their customers in the creative process, involving them in product development and the narration of the story. This reflects a wider movement in the commercial world towards valuing authentic engagement and community participation. This is changing the conventional dynamics between buyers and sellers into a more participatory and engaging experience, emphasizing the importance of interaction and collaboration in the modern marketplace.

Fifth, the digital intermediation of work, a defining characteristic of gig economy organizations, significantly impacts and moulds both the transactional processes and the interactions between workers and customers. This business model, facilitated by digital platforms, connects freelance workers with customers requiring specific services. Unlike traditional employment structures where companies directly hire and manage workers, gig platforms act as intermediaries, streamlining the process of matching supply (freelance workers) with demand (customers).

This digital mediation fundamentally changes the way work is transacted and relationships are formed. In relation to the transaction process, digital platforms like freelance marketplaces or task management apps simplify the process by minimizing barriers to entry for both customers browsing and selecting services, and workers seeking job opportunities. This immediacy and convenience redefine expectations for both parties. In relation to worker-customer relationships, the long-term employer-employee relationship gives way to short-term, task-specific interactions. Workers present their skills and experience through online profiles, while customer selection and evaluation rely heavily on ratings and reviews. This promotes a performance-driven culture where feedback directly impacts a worker's reputation and future job prospects.

The emergence of new economic institutions, such as the sharing economy, gig economy, and social commerce, invites a re-evaluation of traditional economic theories, particularly those central to capitalism. A key theory in this discourse is Adam Smith's concept of the 'invisible hand'. Smith posited that individuals, by pursuing their self-interests within the marketplace, inadvertently contribute to societal welfare. The premise is that even though transactions are driven by personal gain, they generate broader economic benefits, creating an environment where the market organically adjusts to supply goods and set prices that align with collective needs.

This theory underpins the rationale for free-market economics and laissez-faire policies, which advocate for minimal governmental intervention. Proponents argue that such an economic environment enhances efficiency and productivity as firms and individuals engage in transactions with reduced market frictions, facilitating optimal resource allocation. Supporters of this view maintain that a thriving capitalist system, characterized by successful businesses, yields benefits for workers through better employment opportunities and higher wages, suggesting a mutually beneficial scenario for both capital and labour. Policies favouring privatization and deregulation are often championed, based on the belief that an economy with fewer constraints allows individuals to act in their self-interest, which, in turn, serves the greater good.

However, the terrain of business-consumer interactions is rapidly evolving, driven by technological innovations that move beyond the broad generalizations suggested by classical economic models. Recent innovations in AI automation and big data analytics have significantly enhanced the capability to customize experiences to individual preferences, marking a notable departure from the traditional methods of mass production and consumption.

This move towards personalization is increasingly apparent across various digital platforms. Websites, streaming services, and smart home devices, among others, now offer customized recommendations that cater to the unique tastes and needs of each user. By adopting such personalized strategies, businesses are better equipped to meet the specific desires of their customers, thereby enhancing customer welfare. This trend not only addresses consumer demands more precisely but also cultivates a deeper relationship between firms and their customers, transforming consumer engagement. As a result, the inclination towards sharing personal information for personalized offerings is becoming more pronounced among consumers. They are more willing to exchange their details for products adapted to their exact requirements, encompassing their preferred type, colour, or style. But to satisfy a wider range of customers with diverse needs, it is also necessary to diversify the functions and features of products and services.

Personalization is thus redefining economic participation, moving beyond traditional frameworks. For instance, platforms like Etsy empower individuals to vend their crafts and services directly, catering to niche demands with a personalized touch. This empowerment also facilitates a departure from standard employment models, enabling individuals to carve out unique professional trajectories. Moreover, digital platforms can galvanize collective endeavours aimed at influencing corporate behaviours or tackling societal challenges. Initiatives such as carpooling and bike sharing exemplify collaborative efforts to contest established norms and champion sustainable alternatives. Digital platforms exploit network effects, where the value of the platform increases as more users join, setting them apart from traditional firms. The dynamics of these platforms require an understanding of value creation and distribution in a multi-sided market, where the platform connects different groups of users. This challenges the conventional wisdom of supply and demand in linear markets, where firms produce goods or services that are directly consumed by customers.

Personalization's influence also extends far beyond the business world, becoming increasingly important in health, education, and many other areas. It has the potential to significantly improve services and outcomes. In healthcare, for instance, personalized health recommendations and treatment plans are becoming more common, highlighting the growing significance of personalization. Technologies such as genetic testing are at the forefront of this movement, empowering individuals to make informed decisions about their health based on data-driven insights. The education sector is also capitalizing on personalization through adaptive learning platforms that adjust content to match each student's learning pace and style. This approach enhances student engagement and optimizes learning outcomes.

These developments hold significant implications for Adam Smith's 'invisible hand' theory and the capitalist production systems it informs. In this evolved environment, individuals are no longer mere passive consumers but active agents capable of moulding market trends and dictating outcomes through concerted actions and direct involvement. Technological innovations in data analytics and AI, coupled with the escalating prominence of social commerce, are driving the trend towards personalization, reshaping the mechanisms of creation, consumption, and organization of goods and services. Personalization thus transcends the mere provision of diverse choices. It entails a deep understanding of individual preferences and requirements to furnish experiences that are significantly more customized and relevant.

In simpler terms, personalization refers to tailoring products and services to the unique preferences and needs of each individual. This approach is a major departure from the mass production models of the past, where everything from cars (think Fordism) to administrative processes (think Weberian bureaucracy) was standardized and produced for the masses. However, as we show in this book, personalization in today's market is also about building a deeper connection and understanding between businesses and their customers. Therefore, personalization can be seen as a novel approach to organizing economic transactions, creating a more efficient and productive system that caters to individual needs while simultaneously fostering connections to wider communities.

More broadly, personalization is part of a significant ecosystem transformation, driven by the rapid growth of e-commerce technologies and the emerging opportunities in trade and commerce. This change in the economic environment has culminated in a multifaceted situation. For consumers, it opens up the possibility to effortlessly compare and purchase products and services from around the globe. This unprecedented level of accessibility provides consumers with a wider array of options, more effective price comparisons, and the benefits of transparency and convenience associated with online platforms. Customer expectations have also significantly changed over time. Previously, simply having access to a product was often enough to meet customer needs. Today, the scenario is markedly different. Contemporary consumers desire a mix of individuality and community. They look for products that not only express their personal identity but also connect them to a broader community.

Conversely, this move towards electronic commerce gives businesses access to a wealth of detailed customer data. Every interaction online leaves a trail of digital breadcrumbs that companies can collect and analyse to uncover insights into consumer preferences, behaviours, and trends. This data enables businesses to fine-tune their offerings, improve customer experiences, and refine their marketing efforts. Companies are now more and more dependent on sophisticated algorithms and computing capabilities to sift through vast amounts of data, discern patterns, and predict consumer demands. This proficiency enables them to quickly adapt to market changes, provide highly personalized products and services, and stay competitive in the rapidly evolving digital marketplace.

Personalization, driven by these technological and economic changes, is central to this evolving ecosystem. It represents a move towards more informed, agile, and customer-focused business practices, underscoring the complex relationship between technological innovation, market forces, and consumer expectations in today's digital landscape (Athey et al., 2023a).

This book delves into the pervasive trend of personalization, focusing on the dynamic interplay between firms and consumers in creating innovative transactions. We dissect how companies adopt various personalization strategies to address diverse customer needs, scrutinize the intricacies of implementation, and evaluate the organizational structures essential for successful personalization endeavours. Furthermore, we explore consumer participation in data-driven consumption patterns, enabling firms to align their offerings with individual preferences.

From the perspective of businesses, we examine the various strategies employed to personalize offerings, including both content and product personalization. We analyse the benefits and challenges of each approach, taking into account factors such as product complexity, the intended audience, and the feasibility of operations. We bridge the gap between strategic planning and practical implementation, emphasizing the critical steps involved. The exploration of personalization's practicalities includes data collection and analysis, building the technological infrastructure, and applying appropriate business communication strategies. Moreover, we will examine the organizational structures that support personalization, such as flexible decision-making and a data-driven culture.

Personalization depends crucially on information about consumer preferences and behaviours. Therefore, from the consumer's perspective, we will investigate how this data is furnished, encompassing both direct inputs like product reviews and indirect signals such as browsing history and purchase records. Consumers are also increasingly willing to exchange personal information in return for personalized benefits. The discussion will also consider how these patterns vary with demographic factors, technological proficiency, and privacy concerns. Furthermore, we will examine how consumer data enables firms to adapt their production processes to match individual preferences, which has profound implications for privacy-related practices within firms.

Moving past the simplistic notion of personalization as a mere transactional tactic, the book will also explore the reciprocal relationship between firms and consumers, highlighting how each entity influences and is influenced by the other. Ethical considerations regarding data privacy and responsible personalization practices will also be addressed. Through a comprehensive examination of these diverse perspectives, the book aims to furnish a thorough understanding of the personalization phenomenon.

Personalization often relies on algorithms and machine learning models to generate recommendations and make decisions. In this way, AI and machine learning fuel the personalization trend, enhancing its sophistication and intuitiveness. For example, personalization in augmented reality (AR) and virtual reality (VR) presents new opportunities for immersive and personalized user experiences. Similarly, with the proliferation of smart assistants and biometric systems, personalization is likely to encompass voice patterns, facial recognition, and beyond.

By adopting a holistic approach to personalization, organizations move beyond simply treating users or customers as data points. They cultivate complex relationships, ensuring each individual feels part of the process and understood. They also become integral to the development of a broader ecosystem, where independent marketplaces and third-party transactions play a significant role. Personalization is thus a potent mechanism for enhancing economic value. For digital platforms and their complementors – including advertisers, content creators, and independent sellers – it facilitates more precise targeting of products and services. Such targeted strategies lead to improved conversion rates because the offerings are closely aligned with the specific desires and needs of each user, increasing the likelihood that users will engage with and purchase these customized products or services.

As personalization makes products and services more accessible to individuals with diverse needs and preferences, this is also how personalization democratizes the capitalist markets by making economic transactions more visible.

In the light of these developments, we argue that a new economic system, fundamentally different from traditional capitalist production, is emerging. Current discussions about the growing role of automation and robotics often assume that automation negatively affects jobs and employment. They tend to concentrate narrowly on the automation of various jobs and its implications for employment and organizational structures in companies. However, we contend that AI technologies are transforming the long-standing dynamics between capital and labour by fostering the emergence of new economic and social institutions, diverging significantly from conventional capitalist systems. For instance, workers now have the opportunity to dedicate more time to progressive and strategic tasks, aimed at enhancing services within their organizations. This redirects the focus from capital-intensive technologies to an emphasis on human creativity and knowledge-driven production and market transactions.

In addition, the rise of digital platforms such as Amazon, Alibaba, and Etsy has introduced new complexities that challenge traditional economic models. Conventional economic theory has predominantly focused on analysing individual industrial sectors, where firms operate as engines of economic growth, transforming substantial inputs into mass-produced outputs. This framework, shaped by historical contexts like those described by Alfred Chandler, emphasizes the role of large, vertically integrated firms as central to the Industrial Revolution. These firms typically operated within well-defined, competitive markets, with success dependent on efficient production management and economies of scale. In contrast, digital platforms aggregate and sell products and services across multiple sectors, often blurring the lines between them. This multifunctional nature of digital platforms marks a significant shift from the classic view of firms as standalone entities to one where firms act as facilitators of ecosystems, connecting various stakeholders, including consumers, producers, and service providers. Digital markets, or multi-sided platform marketplaces, thus exhibit unique dynamics that diverge from the assumptions underlying traditional economic models.

The book investigates the social and economic forces that have spurred the development and expansion of this novel economic system. It further situates these discussions within a wider narrative, examining how an array of technological advancements and inventive market frameworks have profoundly impacted job seekers, consumers, businesses, and communities. For example, we examine the role and characteristics of social media and social media-based organizations and communities within this digital ecosystem. While there is much debate about the considerable influence of platforms like Amazon and Facebook, a comprehensive understanding of the sources of their monopoly power remains elusive, particularly given the rapid changes in the fortunes of many other powerful companies. With data privacy a major concern, we have examined various proposals to improve platform governance around data practices.

The book also recognizes the ongoing efforts by regulators and industry experts to more thoroughly assess the impact of these digital giants and to identify the most suitable policy and regulatory approaches. We hope that the concepts and ideas presented in this book will contribute to the advancement of these approaches and promote further exploration into the evolving dynamics of the digital economy.

Part 1

Product and content personalization

In an era defined by rapid technological advancements, global commerce is undergoing a profound metamorphosis. The convergence of Information and Communication Technologies (ICTs) such as the Internet of Things (IoT), cloud computing, and Artificial Intelligence (AI) is catalysing an unprecedented expansion and diversification of production systems' economic capabilities. These digital tools are not merely optimizing transactions; they are unlocking entirely new domains of economic activity. This digital revolution is redefining traditional business archetypes, leading to the emergence of services that are more efficient, scalable, and – most significantly – personalized across a multitude of industries.

To contextualize this transformation, we first examine the entertainment sector. Here, AI-driven algorithms are powering recommendation engines for streaming giants like Netflix. These sophisticated systems analyse user behaviour to align content creation and curation with consumer preferences, thereby enhancing viewer engagement through tailored content delivery. This exemplifies how AI can bridge the gap between mass-market offerings and individual tastes.

Our narrative then shifts to a historical perspective, examining conventional market structures and organizational frameworks that hinge on industrial technologies like mass production. In the past, such systems prioritized cost-efficiency in both production processes and transactional exchanges. We juxtapose this traditional paradigm with the AI-driven revolution in production and sales methodologies, positing that these innovations may render conventional approaches obsolete. This comparison sets the stage for our central theme: the rise of personalization.

The discourse then pivots to economic theory, specifically how technological shifts impact macroeconomic trends and labour markets. We trace the evolution of automation within economic entities, with a particular focus on the burgeoning field of generative AI. This technology is not only automating tasks but also reconfiguring organizational architectures and human resource strategies.

The final sections of this segment are tripartite. We commence by dissecting personalization through the prism of consumer behaviour and preferences. Coordination and control technologies, such as digital platforms, big data analytics, and AI, are pivotal to effective personalization. Subsequently, we conduct an in-depth analysis of content and product personalization, examining how digital technologies are transforming the customization of goods and services to individual needs. This discussion also encompasses the critical issues of data use and privacy. The concluding chapter explores AI's influence on workplace dynamics, from workflow optimization to bespoke employee training programmes, culminating in enhanced overall operational efficiency.

Through this multifaceted examination, we aim to provide a comprehensive understanding of how personalization, powered by AI and related technologies, is not only refining existing business processes but also architecting novel forms of economic interaction and organizational frameworks. The implications are far-reaching, suggesting a future where the line between mass-market and bespoke offerings blurs, and where AI serves as the linchpin in creating value uniquely suited to each individual within the global marketplace.

1

Personalized selling in the entertainment business

After discovering BoxOffice's new personalization features on a podcast, Sophie decides to give it a try. She's greeted with a survey about her preferences upon signing up, where she indicates her love for Thriller, Sci-Fi, Documentaries, and her admiration for directors like Christopher Nolan and actors such as Cate Blanchett. She even imports her watch history from another platform for a full picture of her preferences.

Sophie's mornings start with a twenty-minute yoga session. BoxOffice takes note, recommending short documentaries that match her morning vibe. In the evenings, when she's ready for more substantial content, the platform showcases 'Evening Thrillers' aligned with her usual login time.

A weekend sci-fi series binge triggers BoxOffice to suggest similar genres and even behind-the-scenes content from the series she enjoyed. Through the 'More Like This' feature, Sophie explores international content that aligns with her tastes, expanding her cultural horizons.

When her social media buzzes about a new drama series, BoxOffice, linked to her social accounts, promptly recommends it on her home screen. She's fond of mood-based playlists, like the 'Rainy Day Comfort Films' on a gloomy day, or the '2-Hour Flight Films' playlist, which she finds just in time for her holiday flight, thanks to her synced calendar.

Occasionally, the abundance of sci-fi recommendations feels overwhelming. Sophie uses the 'Less Like This' feature to request more variety. During her monthly feedback session with BoxOffice, she praises some series and critiques others, helping the platform fine-tune her suggestions. On her birthday, BoxOffice surprises her with an exclusive preview of a new thriller series, and when a new film by Christopher Nolan drops, she gets a personalized notification, prompting her to watch it immediately.

Sophie's active engagement with BoxOffice's personalized features not only delivers content that suits her specific tastes but also helps her discover new favourites and connect with like-minded communities. The platform's continuous adaptation to her interactions ensures a constantly refreshing and relevant viewing experience, making each login a new journey in content exploration.

While BoxOffice excels in areas like deeply personalized recommendations, hidden discovery, and engaging community features, can Sophie find a similar experience on other streaming giants like Amazon, Netflix, Disney+, and HBO Max? How could these platforms leverage their diverse content libraries, user interfaces, and unique strengths to provide Sophie with a competitive and personalized service?

We can begin by discussing Amazon Prime Video's approach to live-streaming football games. Amazon Prime Video secured the broadcast rights for NFL Thursday Night Football games in March 2021, undertaking the responsibility of live-streaming matches to over two hundred countries worldwide. This endeavour demands extensive real-time data analysis to continuously refine market segmentation and enhance the company's performance. Maintaining a high level of reliability during such a grand-scale sporting event is paramount, ensuring that not even a second is lost, as any downtime would negatively impact viewers' experience. This level of reliability can only be achieved if Amazon Prime Video provides adequate support and effectively manages traffic using customer data analytics.

DynamoDB serves as a cornerstone component for Amazon Prime Video's streaming infrastructure, as the platform heavily relies on it for various analytics during live-streaming. DynamoDB's utilization contributes to the high scalability and performance of streaming content during live matches across the globe. A live match typically lasts four hours, with millions of concurrent viewers, making it crucial for the platform to swiftly write to and read from databases. Streaming analytics through DynamoDB facilitates this rapid data processing.

Amazon Prime Video experiences surges of over three hundred thousand simultaneous client requests for ad pods and configuration data during commercial breaks. DynamoDB analysis identified that the platform was exceeding its anticipated peak demand per second across multiple regions. By adjusting the DynamoDB configuration, Prime Video was able to handle these demand spikes without service interruption, ensuring a seamless customer experience. With the support of DynamoDB, Amazon Prime Video has successfully live-streamed eleven NFL matches to 18.4 million football fans in 224 countries so far, garnering a remarkable proportion of satisfied viewers due to effective demand management. Through analytics, Amazon Prime Video also gained insights into the demand for multiple language commentary, leading to the provision of commentary in three different languages, catering to the regional preferences of viewers.

Customer data analysis is widely used across different streaming platforms as it benefits the company to improve its performance; Disney+ is another such example. It is important to understand that the usage of streaming analytics or customer data analytics in streaming companies is evidence for its growing use. Disney+ came into the streaming market in 2019 to acquire the market share of the growing streaming video industry by using the Disney Group name. Although Disney already has a huge fan base, Disney+ is a conglomerate media that has a narrow and specific focus, making it different from others. Through the use of customer data analytics, the segmentation is achieved by transcending demographic and mass appeal along with offering something for everyone. Disney+ has come up with this innovative and focused strategy to make an impact within the shorter term without wasting its energies in markets that do not have the potential.

Disney+ has introduced a data-driven personalization to offer a greater and better experience to the viewers through a complete understanding of their needs and wants.

By feeding the behavioural data through streaming analytics into different algorithms, Disney+ has been able to understand the individual preferences that lead to focused targeting by the platform. This involves data such as movies that a viewer repeatedly watches, time of watching the movie, duration, and time of the credit rolls. The data collection and analysis from the perspective of customers on these aspects help to gain a better understanding of the customer segmentation.

Even Disney has gone to the limit of recording the expressions of the viewers during the movies. The collection of data regarding the expressions helps the company to understand their behaviours, bringing deeper insights into the attitudes of the viewers. It also helps the company to remodify the content as per the needs of the viewers, making it more specific and satisfactory for the customer.

Disney's data-driven approach to audience analysis provides a valuable case study for how streaming platforms can employ customer data analytics to enhance user experience, optimize content offerings, and drive growth:

Enhanced customer segmentation: Streaming companies, by analysing customer demographics, interests, and behaviours, can divide their audience into distinct segments, allowing for targeted content curation and marketing strategies.

Heightened personalization: Gaining insights into individual customer preferences enables streaming services to tailor the user experience, offering content recommendations that align with viewer tastes.

Refined content development: Understanding audience preferences aids streaming platforms in creating content that resonates better with their target demographic, increasing the likelihood of success.

Churn minimization: Identifying the factors behind customer churn enables streaming services to devise effective retention strategies, thereby reducing churn rates.

Like Disney+, HBO Max has also used customer data to optimize its content offerings and improve user engagement. In 2016, HBO Max embarked on a six-month campaign to promote viewers' favourite shows, enabling them to watch their preferred content at their convenience. HBO Max has continuously adapted its content, business model, and pricing strategy over the years, guided by data-driven insights gleaned from customer data analytics. With a focus on customer convenience, streaming analytics has empowered the company to organize data effectively, making it effortless for customers to locate and watch their favourite shows and movies. This enhanced discoverability has contributed to the company's positive image building over time.

Similarly, data analytics has enabled HBO Max to identify viewer preferences, shaping content strategies. Data on content preferences and pricing has informed the platform's ongoing evolution, enhancing its market stance. The introduction of HBO Max, driven by insights from customer data, has led to a notable change in the subscriber base and a gradual uptick in platform engagement. The use of artificial intelligence (AI) in marketing strategies has enabled HBO Max to efficiently guide users towards the new service, showcasing the impact of data analytics on performance enhancement. Adapting to the dynamic nature of data to refine operations poses challenges, yet HBO Max acknowledges the value of data-driven decision-making in its growth trajectory.

Furthermore, HBO Max's strategic use of customer data analytics has enabled it to surpass Netflix in performance metrics. With a focus on customer satisfaction, HBO

Max delivers a viewing experience that users find more personalized and superior. The platform has outpaced Netflix in various customer satisfaction metrics, highlighting the pivotal role of customer data analytics. This achievement is rooted in HBO Max's deep insight into viewer preferences and its adeptness at customizing its offerings to meet those needs.

Now, let's turn our attention to the industry leader, Netflix, which has achieved remarkable success and secured a dominant position in the streaming video market. Netflix offers a vast and diverse selection of award-winning TV shows, movies, anime, documentaries, and more, accessible across thousands of internet-connected devices. Founded in the United States in 1997 by Marc Randolph and Reed Hastings, Netflix pioneered the concept of monthly subscription-based DVD rentals. By April 2003, Netflix had amassed one million subscribers. In 2006, Netflix launched the Netflix Prize, a competition offering a $1 million prize to the team that could significantly improve the accuracy of its movie recommendation algorithm. This investment in personalization technology proved instrumental in establishing Netflix's leading position in the streaming industry. In 2007, Netflix introduced streaming video, a revolutionary media format that delivers content directly to computers and mobile devices for real-time playback. Streaming video eventually became Netflix's primary business model. Today, Netflix has expanded its services to a global audience, reaching over 190 countries worldwide.

The company's core competency in AI and data science lies in its ability to provide personalized content recommendations tailored to individual user behaviour. This personalized approach significantly influences visitor activity, making recommendation algorithms a cornerstone of Netflix's success. Netflix also maintains a strong social media presence, wielding significant influence on platforms like Facebook, Instagram, and Twitter. This social media dominance serves as a powerful tool for attracting new users and expanding its reach.

Netflix's meteoric rise as a streaming service can be attributed to its innovative approach to content delivery, filling the void left by traditional DVD rental services like Blockbuster. By offering a virtual and easily accessible platform, Netflix provided customers with the convenience of instant streaming without the hassle of late fees and return deadlines. Content recommendations play a pivotal role in enhancing customer satisfaction by guiding viewers towards their preferred content seamlessly. Netflix's recommendation system leverages user data analytics to generate personalized suggestions, ensuring that each user encounters content that aligns with their unique interests. This personalized approach has proven to be a key driver of engagement, keeping viewers hooked on the platform.

In 2017, Netflix achieved a remarkable renewal rate of 93 per cent for its original TV shows, compared to a mere 35 per cent renewal rate for cable television. This exceptional retention rate can be attributed, in part, to the effectiveness of its Big Data analytics and AI-based personalization system. Netflix strategically uses audience data to identify areas of focus, guiding its content development strategy and attracting new customers. The company then strives to retain every user who has tried its services, further solidifying its leading position in the streaming industry.

A case study: House of cards

Netflix's data-driven approach to content creation is exemplified by its production of the critically acclaimed series *House of Cards*. In a bold move, the company invested a staggering $100 million in two seasons (twenty-six episodes) of the show before seeing a single episode. This unprecedented decision, though seemingly risky, was a calculated move informed by a rigorous data analysis.

Factors potentially guiding Netflix's decision included: Netflix likely utilized viewing data to understand the interest level of its subscriber base in content directed by David Fincher and starring Kevin Spacey. This analysis probably showed a significant interest overlap, indicating a receptive audience for a political drama series featuring these talents. Historical viewing patterns of political dramas on Netflix would have offered insights into the genre's popularity among its subscribers, potentially reinforcing the decision to invest in *House of Cards*. The original UK series *House of Cards* would have served as a valuable reference point. By examining the viewership numbers and critical response to the UK version, Netflix could assess the potential success of an American adaptation.

By taking these diverse data points into account, Netflix mitigated some of the inherent risk associated with such a large upfront investment. While success was never guaranteed, their data-driven approach significantly increased the likelihood that *House of Cards* would resonate with their audience and become a hit.

The reasons behind Netflix's effective data usage

Netflix's success in leveraging data analytics can be attributed to three key factors. The first factor is robust data infrastructure and collection. Netflix boasts a cutting-edge IT infrastructure built for massive data ingestion and analysis. This allows them to collect vast amounts of data points about user behaviour, including viewing history, search queries, location, and device usage. By continuously analysing this data, Netflix builds a detailed picture of user preferences and identifies trends, informing decisions across the platform. The second factor is data-driven decision-making. From content recommendations to seemingly minor interface tweaks like button colours, data is woven into the fabric of Netflix's decision-making process. This ensures every choice optimizes the user experience and caters to their preferences. It is not just about recommending shows; it is about crafting a personalized and engaging journey for each user.

The third factor is content curation and personalization. Netflix goes beyond just aggregating data; they use their insights to strategically curate content and personalize user experiences. This involves adjusting content recommendations to match individual preferences, creating targeted marketing campaigns, and dynamically modifying platform features to enhance user engagement. This ongoing cycle of data analysis and content strategy drives Netflix's growth and maintains high levels of user engagement. As highlighted, a robust data infrastructure lies at the heart of Netflix's recommendation system. This infrastructure collects and analyses vast amounts of customer data, often referred to as Big Data. This data encompasses a variety of variables, including the following:

Location: Understanding user location allows Netflix to identify regional preferences and tailor content recommendations accordingly.

Viewing history: Analysing viewing patterns provides insights into individual preferences, enabling Netflix to recommend similar content that viewers are likely to enjoy.

Search data: Capturing search queries reveals users' interests, allowing Netflix to suggest content related to their specific pursuits.

Viewing time: Tracking viewing time helps Netflix identify content that resonates with viewers, ensuring that recommendations are aligned with their preferences.

By analysing this comprehensive data set, Netflix can categorize users into distinct segments based on their preferences and generate personalized content recommendations for each segment. Furthermore, to ensure every decision stems from reliable insights, Netflix adopts a multi-pronged approach.

They first gather valuable data directly from users' interactions – from binge-watching habits to curious search queries and device preferences. But the raw data is just the first act. Through a meticulous ETL (data extraction, transformation, and loading) process, Netflix wrangles information from diverse sources, cleans and formats it meticulously, and finally loads it into the analytical brains of the platform. This ensures clean, consistent data ready for powerful analysis. The final piece of the puzzle is data profiling – a technique that helps Netflix understand the intricate patterns and trends within their user base. It is like peering into the soul of their audience, uncovering preferences, behaviours, and the nuances of how they interact with the platform. This combination of meticulous data acquisition, rigorous cleaning, and insightful profiling empowers Netflix to make data-driven decisions that resonate with their audience, keeping them glued to their screens and hungry for more.

Netflix exploits a variety of data sources to create personalized recommendations for its users, including: (1) User ratings and reviews: Netflix analyses billions of user ratings and reviews to understand overall preferences and identify patterns in user behaviour. (2) Presentation data and impression data: Netflix tracks how users interact with content recommendations, such as whether they click on a recommendation, watch a trailer, or start watching a video. This data provides insights into user engagement and helps refine recommendation algorithms. (3) Social data and external sources: Netflix employs social data, such as Facebook connections, to further personalize recommendations. Furthermore, the company incorporates external data sources, such as actor popularity and genre trends, to enhance the accuracy of its recommendations. By combining internal and external data sources, Netflix achieves a high level of personalization, ensuring that its recommendations resonate with individual user preferences.

As our analysis above shows, Netflix stands as a testament to the transformative power of audience data analytics. The company's data-driven approach has revolutionized the streaming entertainment industry, providing viewers with a personalized and engaging experience that caters to their unique preferences. Netflix's success serves as a model for businesses across all sectors, highlighting the potential of data analytics to drive innovation and customer satisfaction.

The rise of digital businesses

Digital economy can be defined as one that harnesses technology to enhance the way businesses serve their customers. It is an economy that thrives on digital connections between businesses and customers through internet-enabled devices. The advent of digital businesses, operating without physical storefronts, represents a burgeoning trend in today's marketplace (Wu and Zhou, 2021). The world's largest taxi company, Uber, does not own any vehicles; Airbnb, the world's leading provider of temporary accommodations, does not possess any real estate. These examples illustrate how the rapid growth of the internet has spawned new types of businesses.

The development, convergence, and integration of information and communication technologies have thus fuelled an endless stream of innovative business models. A multitude of enterprises, including Apple, IBM, Amazon, Netflix, Google, eBay, Facebook, and Haier, have achieved remarkable success by leveraging business model innovation. Examining these examples of business model innovation reveals that most are associated with unrestricted access to consumers and cross-border operations, and they are directly or indirectly linked to information digitization technology and the internet. Business model innovation has taken centre stage in enterprise innovation, and Big Data has become the foundation of business model innovation.

Start-ups are capitalizing on low barriers to entry and the ability to more readily construct new data-driven business models. For established companies, this necessitates rethinking their existing business models and how they are influenced by Big Data (Anshari et al., 2019; Samara et al., 2020). Data has permeated every business function across all industries, becoming increasingly critical for production. Moreover, the widespread individual and organizational use of vast data sets ushers in an era with the potential for enhanced productivity and consumer benefit. The data-driven business model has undoubtedly become the frontrunner in business model innovation. It represents the transformation of products, production methods, markets, and industries driven by the availability of new resources and new technologies. This innovation is grounded in the novel concept of data resources, encompassing the rethinking of the value, exploitation, and acquisition of Big Data resources, as well as the rethinking of other resources, capacity expansion, and utilization methods of enterprises affected by Big Data.

This business model has transformed the content and nature of enterprise demand for external resources, altered the manner and path by which companies create and deliver value, reshaped the enterprise business ecosystem, and blurred the boundaries of resources, markets, and contracts for enterprises.

Specifically, the data-driven business model offers the following advantages: First, data is logical and concrete, unlike intuition. By removing the subjective factors that often cloud business decisions, data-driven decisions can enhance the accuracy of management decisions and instil confidence in decision-makers and the company as a whole. Second, with sufficient practice and a large volume of valid historical data, decision-makers and companies can proactively make business decisions, such as identifying business opportunities ahead of competitors or detecting the presence of threats before they become too severe. Third, companies invest in Big Data initiatives for a variety of reasons, seeking to elevate the importance of data as a driving force in their processes, despite varying success rates of these initiatives.

Consequently, data analytics has emerged as a powerful tool, and many digital economy companies are striving to integrate it into their selling strategies. Data analytics can be applied across a wide range of applications. For instance, a shopping website can analyse page views by registered users and purchases to identify the stages in the customer journey that led to the highest drop-off rates. Mobile location data can provide companies with real-time customer insights, enabling them to send targeted emails or push mobile notifications with relevant offers based on contextual factors.

The growing trend among companies to employ Big Data (both external and internal) to innovate or enhance their business models manifests itself in two main categories:

1. Predictive analytics: Companies can use consumer-generated data to forecast future behaviours through historical data analysis, enabling them to provide more tailored services and generate greater profits. For instance, Amazon's product recommendation system relies on sophisticated analysis of customer browsing and purchasing data. This system constitutes a cornerstone of Amazon's value-delivery function, effectively guiding consumers towards preferred products on the company's website. Amazon's success stems from its access to vast and diverse data sets, coupled with its ability to categorize and analyse them effectively.

   Likewise, Zara's fast fashion business model hinges on the diversity and speed of its Big Data system. The company's real-time analysis of popular fashion data from third-party suppliers and customer spending data from its stores empower Zara to consistently offer trendy clothing while maintaining low inventory levels. In the realm of meal delivery software, Blue Apron demonstrates the critical role of understanding customer behaviours and preferences based on historical data. The company provides subscribers with a fixed meal plan for each week, utilizing data analysis to anticipate demand. This historical data aids in improving order completion rates and minimizing food spoilage. Blue Apron employs algorithms that consider various factors categorized into three groups: customer-related functions, cookbook-related functions, and seasonal functions.

   Customer-related features encompass historical data about a user's order frequency, while cookbook-related features focus on a user's past ordering preferences, allowing the company to infer their future meal choices. Seasonality is accounted for by examining buying patterns against the time of year to determine periods of higher or lower order rates. Blue Apron benefits from predictive analytics to better understand its customers, enhance their user experience, track subscriber taste preferences over time, and identify how product formulations influence changing preferences.

2. Real-time data integration: Companies can integrate and analyse real-time data from diverse sources to gain actionable insights and make informed decisions in real time. This approach is particularly valuable in dynamic industries such as airline operations. Lufthansa, a leading airline company, has established its own system and data flow, enabling the extraction, cleaning, and integration of dynamic and static data from worldwide sources, including weblogs and social media. This centralized repository of data from diverse sources is subjected to real-time analysis, and the system's capacity allows for handling large volumes of data stored in the Hadoop system.

Similar to Amazon, Lufthansa has evolved from a ticket sales company to a customer-centric enterprise, prioritizing the optimization of customer experiences. One example is the implementation of the Miles and More customer loyalty programme, which use customer information and external data (including personal data from social media) to maintain customer profiles and identify customer interactions (online or in-person). First-class passengers and frequent fliers are considered high-value customers. Lufthansa employs predictive analytics to identify and anticipate the preferences of these customers, proactively addressing their travel needs and offering convenient channels for real-time customer interactions.

These examples illustrate how companies are increasingly utilizing Big Data to innovate their business models, enhance customer experiences, and gain a competitive edge. Christensen (2022) explores the significant shift digital platforms have introduced to the traditional mechanisms through which products are discovered and consumed. Central to their findings is the observation that these platforms, coupled with the broader wave of digitization, have streamlined the distribution process within content-driven sectors. This evolution has led to a notable decrease in distribution-related costs, effectively democratizing access to a wider array of content. For example, digital platforms enhance the discovery of new content through features like recommendation algorithms and user-generated content. This advancement promotes niche content discovery and exposure to diverse content creators who might previously have been obscure. In this process of facilitating discovery, platforms play an important role by crowdsourcing information and aggregating consumer preferences to guide users towards content they might enjoy.

At the same time, the diversity of available content has surged, catering to an increasingly segmented audience with varied tastes and preferences. An intriguing aspect of this digital transformation is the emergence of positive spillover effects that bridge the digital and physical realms. Specifically, the expansive reach and accessibility of online distribution have been found to complement and even enhance the value and appeal of in-person events. This synergy suggests a nuanced interplay between digital consumption and physical experiences, enriching the overall ecosystem of content consumption. These developments suggest that digital business is fundamentally changing strategic paradigms.

At the forefront of this change, certain enterprises have emerged as early adopters, capitalizing on data to carve out competitive advantages, as suggested by Bresnahan (2018). Initially, these innovators were predominantly rooted in business-to-consumer sectors. Yet, the digital wave is now expanding into business-to-business arenas and sectors traditionally unassociated with platform models. The transition towards embracing and operationalizing platform-based business models is still unfolding, indicating a significant potential for growth and innovation in this domain.

Spotify's Discovery Weekly

To further illustrate personalized selling in entertainment, let's explore Spotify's song recommendation system. Spotify stands out as a leading force in the crowded digital music scene, with its adept use of personalization technology, particularly within its playlist curation. Among its standout offerings is the Discovery Weekly feature, a tailor-made playlist that serves up fresh tracks to users, potentially uncovering new favourites they have not encountered yet. This innovative feature relies on a sophisticated algorithm that delves deep into individual user playlists, examining listening habits to introduce new songs that might resonate.

The process behind Discovery Weekly is both intricate and user-centric. Spotify's algorithm does not just randomly select songs; instead, it conducts a thorough analysis of each user's musical preferences based on their listening history, liked songs, and most-played tracks. By understanding the nuances of each user's taste, the algorithm can identify patterns and similarities in music styles, genres, and artist preferences.

When the system spots a song that aligns well with the user's established preferences but has not been played by them, it considers this track a strong candidate for the Discovery Weekly playlist. This method ensures that each recommendation feels personalized and relevant, increasing the chances of user engagement and satisfaction. Moreover, Spotify continuously refines this feature by tracking how users interact with the recommended songs – whether they skip, save, or play them on repeat. This feedback loop allows Spotify to fine-tune its recommendations further, making Discovery Weekly an ever-evolving and improving aspect of the Spotify experience.

The Freemium model

Music streaming platforms encounter challenges with ad-based revenue models, such as constrained earnings and potential user discontent. As a solution, the freemium model has gained prominence (Gu et al., 2018). This approach combines complementary basic services with enhanced premium features, appealing to a broader audience, including start-ups and entrepreneurs. Notably, Spotify and Pandora have effectively adopted this model to substantially grow their user base. The freemium model's 'free' aspect is especially appealing, drawing in larger audiences and serving as a pathway to premium subscription conversion. However, its success hinges on two critical metrics: the cost of servicing free users and the rate at which they upgrade to premium. Finding the optimal balance between the complementary and paid components is crucial to maximizing the model's effectiveness.

Spotify's initial choice of a hybrid advertising-subscription model was driven by its cost-efficiency relative to traditional methods of media acquisition. Using online advertisements within the free version allowed for rapid expansion of Spotify's user base at a significantly lower expense than conventional marketing strategies, thereby accelerating Spotify's growth. Without this combined approach, achieving similar levels of user engagement would have likely incurred greater costs and taken more time.

The presence of a free version with advertisements serves as an entry point to premium subscriptions. While users can access the essential features of the platform, they also encounter its constraints, especially the disruptions caused by ads. This experience frequently prompts users to consider upgrading to the premium version, which offers an uninterrupted and more comprehensive service. This strategy mirrors the 'first fix for free' approach, where providing an initial free experience encourages users to opt for the paid version. Such a tactic proves particularly effective for platforms like Spotify, where initial user engagement seamlessly transitions into a desire for the superior features of the premium service.

Personalized recommendation systems

Over the past decade, music discovery has increasingly relied on computer algorithms. Services like Pandora and Last.fm have built their business models around effective recommendation systems, offering personalized suggestions due to the vast amount of music available online and through streaming services. Recommender (or recommendation) systems help music fans navigate this abundance, filtering through irrelevant choices to present relevant selections (Zhang and Liu, 2015). A good music recommendation system analyses user preferences, creating playlists that cater to their tastes. Moreover, collaborative filtering plays a vital role in this process. Collaborative filtering leverages the listening habits of similar users to recommend items the individual might enjoy (Zhang and Liu, 2015).

Personalization encompasses several such components that come together to offer individualized experiences to users. By discerning customer preferences and values, organizations can design experiences that resonate and leave an impact. This goal can be realized through multiple strategies, including consultations before purchase, recommendations that are relevant to the user's context, and customized communications after purchase. Table 1 outlines an array of techniques and approaches that can be implemented to execute personalization effectively.

In 2023, nearly 60 per cent of global industry leaders had already implemented generative AI to create product recommendations for in-store associates. Additionally, 39 per cent were considering its adoption (Chevalier, 2024). Furthermore, 55 per cent employed generative AI for developing conversational digital shopping assistants, 52 per cent for creating virtual models on product pages, and 51 per cent for assembling personalized product bundles. AI is increasingly central to crafting personalized shopping experiences for e-commerce retailers. In 2023, 90 per cent of businesses surveyed globally were using AI-driven personalization to drive growth

Table 1 Personalization Approach and Techniques

Personalization approach	
Individual focus	Personalization is centred on understanding and meeting the unique needs and preferences of each individual. It goes beyond generic segmentation and considers the specific circumstances, behaviours, and desires of each user.
Data-driven insights	Personalization relies heavily on data to gain insights into user behaviours, interactions, preferences, and demographics. This data is collected through various sources, such as website interactions, purchase history, social media profiles, and customer feedback.
Dynamic adaptation	Personalization is not a static process; it continuously adapts and optimizes content, recommendations, and experiences based on real-time user interactions and feedback. This dynamic approach ensures that personalization remains relevant and effective for each individual.
Relevance	Personalization aims to deliver content, products, services, and messages that are relevant and significant to each user. Personalization also integrates into a user's social networks and communities. This relevance is achieved by analysing user data and identifying patterns that indicate their preferences and needs.
Techniques and methods	
User profiling	User profiling involves the systematic creation of detailed user profiles, which encompass various aspects such as demographics (age, gender, location, etc.), behaviour (browsing and purchase histories, interaction patterns), preferences (likes, dislikes, interests), and feedback (reviews, ratings, customer service interactions). This comprehensive method allows businesses to tailor their services and products more effectively to meet individual customer needs.
Behavioural tracking	Behavioural tracking refers to the practice of monitoring and analysing user actions online, including clicks, page views, purchases, search queries, and other interactions. This process allows companies to understand and predict user preferences, interests, and potential future behaviours. By gathering and analysing this data, companies can create more accurate and dynamic user profiles, leading to the recommendation of products, services, or content that aligns closely with individual user needs and preferences.
Collaborative filtering	Collaborative filtering is a recommendation system technique that harnesses the power of collective user-item interactions and preferences to offer personalized suggestions. This method operates on two primary principles: finding similarities among users (user-based collaborative filtering) and identifying similarities among items (item-based collaborative filtering).

(Chevalier, 2024). To gauge AI's effectiveness in personalization, businesses focus on the precision and timeliness of real-time data, as well as factors like customer loyalty and the frequency of repeat purchases. As AI technology evolves, the scope for more sophisticated and impactful personalization in e-commerce is set to grow.

AI machine learning technologies are at the forefront of analysing vast data sets to discern patterns, trends, and relationships (Lim and Zhang, 2022). These technologies enable the prediction of user preferences and behaviours with remarkable accuracy. By utilizing diverse algorithms and models, including behavioural tracking and collaborative filtering, AI and machine learning systems can assimilate historical data and user interactions. This allows them to enhance their predictive accuracy and recommendation quality progressively. The scrutiny of past interactions, purchases, and engagement metrics enables companies to create highly accurate predictive analytics models. These models are adept at foreseeing individual customers' future needs and preferences, providing businesses with a strategic advantage in meeting customer expectations.

The insights gained from behavioural tracking enable businesses to deliver a more personalized and engaging user experience. For instance, an e-commerce platform might suggest items that a user is more likely to purchase based on their browsing and buying history. Similarly, a streaming service such as Netflix could recommend movies or TV shows based on a user's viewing habits. This targeted approach not only enhances user satisfaction but also increases the likelihood of conversions and customer retention.

In user-based collaborative filtering, the system identifies users with similar behaviours or preferences to a given user and then recommends items that these similar users have liked or interacted with but the given user has not yet encountered. For example, if User A and User B have similar viewing patterns on a streaming service, and User A watches a new show that User B has not seen, the system might recommend that show to User B. Item-based collaborative filtering, on the other hand, focuses on the relationships between items. If two products tend to be liked or purchased by the same set of users, the system infers that they are similar. Thus, if a user likes one item, the system is likely to recommend the other, similar item.

Collaborative filtering thrives on the concept that users with similar tastes in the past will continue to have similar tastes in the future. This approach allows for more nuanced and tailored recommendations, enhancing user experience by suggesting relevant content or products based on the collective intelligence of user behaviours and preferences. You can read more about CF in Appendix on Recommender Systems.

The nudge effect

The driving force behind personalized recommendation systems is the application of AI machine learning. Zanker et al. (2019) suggest that personalization harnesses these technologies to integrate insights from cognitive and social psychology, thereby crafting unique experiences for every customer. In this context, nudge theory provides a valuable perspective for comprehending these integrations. For example, through the analysis of user data, companies can discern individual preferences, habits, and vulnerabilities, enabling them to adapt their offerings to precisely match what users want or need. This level of personalization enhances user satisfaction and cultivates loyalty. Moreover, companies can utilize targeted advertising to show users ads that are highly relevant to their interests, thus improving the chances of engagement and conversion. Similarly, user data can be used to subtly influence user behaviour, directing decisions through carefully designed recommendations and interface elements towards specific outcomes (Konstan and Riedl, 2012).

Nudge theory, when applied to user decisions, seeks to subtly guide behaviour in a foreseeable way without limiting choice or employing force (Thaler and Sunstein, 2022; Camerer et al., 2007). It acts as a gentle encouragement towards a desired outcome. Design nudges, for instance, enable companies to craft their presentations in a way that subtly guides users towards specific actions. Examples include (placement) arranging healthier food options at eye level in supermarkets to encourage healthier eating habits; (defaults) pre-setting certain choices on forms, like enrolling employees in a pension plan by default to promote savings; and (framing) drawing attention to the beneficial features of an option, such as the exclusivity of a limited-time offer, to enhance its appeal.

In the context of recommendation nudges, firms apply user data and algorithms to suggest actions that align with intended outcomes. For instance, product recommendations involve offering complementary items at the point of purchase; content recommendations entail presenting similar content or services adapted to the user's past interactions, such as streaming platforms suggesting particular shows or movies based on viewing history; and social suggestions involve proposing potential new connections on social networking platforms. Nudges possess key attributes that define their application: subtlety, a positive approach, and choice presentation. Subtlety refers to the design of nudges to be gentle and not perceived as manipulative. A positive approach emphasizes the advantages or makes preferred choices more accessible. Choice presentation pertains to the manner in which options are presented, significantly affecting decision-making.

Understanding nudge theory enhances awareness of the subtle influences employed by companies to shape decisions, enabling more deliberate choices in the digital sphere and daily life.

2

Industrial transformation and AI

The growing demand for personalization enables businesses to meet a broader spectrum of customer needs and preferences, reflecting the manufacturing industry's shift from mass production towards mass customization. This approach enables the creation of products and services designed to meet specific individual requirements, enhancing the overall consumer experience with more personalized offerings. Consequently, firms are expanding the variety and adaptability of their products and services to cater to this growing desire for personalization. This trend is influencing how products and services are conceptualized, developed, and delivered, indicating a larger societal movement towards appreciating uniqueness and personal expression. It also presents a valuable chance for businesses to stand out in competitive markets by providing customers with distinctive, customized experiences.

The transition from mass production to mass customization

Over the years, the manufacturing industry has undergone a significant transformation, evolving from the traditional model of mass production, characterized by the efficient production of large quantities of identical products, to a new paradigm known as mass customization (Koren, 2010). This change reflects a response to evolving consumer demands, technological advancements, and the increasing complexity of global markets.

Mass production, popularized during the Industrial Revolution and epitomized by assembly line systems introduced by Henry Ford, focused on standardization, economies of scale, and cost minimization (Chandler, 1962). It was an era where consumers had limited choices, and the emphasis was on availability and affordability. However, as markets became more saturated and consumer preferences more diverse, the limitations of mass production became apparent. Consumers started seeking products that catered to their specific needs, tastes, and lifestyles, signalling a shift towards a demand for personalized products and services.

Mass customization emerged as a solution to this challenge, enabled by advancements in technology such as digital fabrication, 3D printing, and flexible manufacturing systems. These technologies allow manufacturers to produce goods that are tailored to individual customer specifications without sacrificing efficiency or significantly increasing costs. The move towards mass customization also reflects changes in supply chain management, with companies adopting more agile and flexible strategies to respond quickly to market changes and customer feedback. It has led to more collaborative relationships between manufacturers and customers, where the latter have a say in the design and features of the products they purchase.

Furthermore, mass customization is not only limited to physical products but also extends to services and digital goods, where personalization can often be achieved with even greater flexibility. For instance, software companies can offer customizable features, and service providers can tailor their offerings to meet individual customer needs.

Early capitalist organizations

Taylorism, a pioneering scientific management theory, revolutionized mass production by emphasizing the division of labour, standardization of tasks, and scientific analysis of work movements. While modern car manufacturers like Toyota showcase diverse models and customization options, Taylorism thrived on uniformity and efficiency. Take the iconic Ford Model T, a prime example of Taylorist principles driving mass production. From 1908 to 1927, Ford churned out over fifteen million of these 'Tin Lizzies', a record not toppled until the Volkswagen Beetle in 1972. One key to the Model T's success was standardized parts. Imagine every bolt, screw, and engine component being interchangeable across millions of cars. This simplified production, allowing for easier and cheaper assembly. Replacing a broken part meant grabbing a readily available replacement, not crafting a custom piece.

Another cornerstone of Taylorism was the division of labour. The complex task of building a car was broken down into smaller, repetitive tasks. Each worker focused on a specific step, honing their skills and speed. This reliance on unskilled labour not only streamlined production but also kept wages low. However, it all came at a cost. Critics pointed to the dehumanizing nature of repetitive work, lack of worker autonomy, and potential for fatigue and alienation.

While the Ford Model T exemplifies Taylorism in mass production, its principles extend beyond manufacturing, influencing various service industries as well. Consider a bustling car dealership. Taylorist principles might inform their sales process, aiming to move more vehicles efficiently. Each step, from initial greeting to closing the deal, follows a standardized script, ensuring consistency and minimizing wasted time.

This 'assembly line' approach prioritizes volume over personalized interactions, potentially making the process more efficient for both buyer and seller. These examples scratch the surface of Taylorism's reach. Think about fast-food chains with standardized menus and procedures, call centres with scripted conversations, or even some aspects of education with standardized testing. Exploring these further illustrates the pervasiveness of Taylorism and Fordism and their lasting impact on shaping work structures across various industries.

The allure of order and efficiency also lies at the heart of both Weber's idealized bureaucracy and Orwell's dystopian regime in 1984. While Weber envisioned a highly regulated, rule-based system as the pinnacle of rational organization, its potential pitfalls are laid bare in Orwell's cautionary tale. On the one hand, Weberian bureaucracy offers stability and predictability. Clear-cut rules establish a consistent framework for decision-making, minimizing ambiguity and potential errors. This can be particularly valuable in large organizations where maintaining order and managing complexities are crucial.

However, as Orwell illustrates, such rigidity comes at a cost. An overly narrow focus on rules, without adaptability or consideration for individual circumstances, can stifle creativity and innovation. This inelasticity becomes a critical liability in today's rapidly changing world, where the ability to adapt quickly is often the key to success. Orwell further highlights another vulnerability of rigid systems: information asymmetry. The Thought Police in *1984* wield immense power but remain blind to the inner thoughts and motivations of the populace. This lack of complete information creates an inherent vulnerability, leaving the regime susceptible to subversion and internal contradictions. It is important to note that the relationship between bureaucracy and efficiency is not always clear-cut. While Weber's model offers valuable insights into organization and order, its limitations must be acknowledged. Similarly, Orwell's dystopia serves as a powerful warning against the dangers of unchecked bureaucratic power.

From an economic perspective, the perfect information required for ideal bureaucratic efficiency presents a paradox. In a theoretical model of perfect competition, individuals have complete knowledge and would be indifferent to whether the market or a firm handles transaction coordination, potentially rendering bureaucracy superfluous. However, this viewpoint overlooks the limitations of the rational actor model. Psychology and sociology remind us that *Homo sapiens* is not simply *Homo economicus*, driven solely by rational decisions. Even with perfect information, factors like emotional biases, bounded rationality, and social influences can lead to suboptimal choices. This challenges the assumption that Weber's bureaucracy, with its emphasis on clear-cut rules and procedures, would automatically lead to optimal outcomes.

Therefore, to fully understand the effectiveness of bureaucratic models, it is important to consider not just economic theory but also insights from other disciplines. Examining early forms of capitalist organizations can reveal the historical evolution of such structures and shed light on the interplay between economic, social, and psychological factors that shape organizational efficiency. For example, Joseph Schumpeter argued that the risk-averse nature of bureaucracies stifles entrepreneurial spirit and hinders the creative destruction that drives economic progress. Notably, Schumpeter refers to the redundancy of once-relied-upon technologies and jobs as 'creative destruction' (Schumpeter, 1934). He defines creative destruction as the 'incessant product and process innovation mechanism by which new production units replace outdated ones' and suggests that it is the underlying principle for long-term growth. Subsequently, Schumpeter refers to production rearrangements as 'the essential fact about capitalism', which create the necessarily cyclical behaviour of unemployment. Creating obstacles to the process of creative destruction can have severe long-term consequences.

Within a bureaucratic environment, a subtle change often occurs. The focus on adhering to regulations can eclipse the drive for innovation and risk-taking. Labour get accustomed to fulfilling minimum requirements, losing sight of the bigger picture and neglecting opportunities to improve or explore new avenues. This culture of complacency, compounded by close supervision and a rigid hierarchy, can stifle creativity like a weed choking out vibrant flowers. Schumpeter eloquently compared this phenomenon to diminishing marginal returns: the more rules and regulations pile up, the less likely individuals are to break free from routine and unleash their innovative potential.

The consequences of this stifling environment reach far beyond stifled creativity. As the web of rules expands, individuals can lose their sense of purpose, feeling like cogs in a machine rather than valued contributors. The sheer complexity and opacity of bureaucratic systems can leave employees feeling disillusioned and disconnected from their work and the organization's goals. The benefits of bureaucratic order, if any, are thus easily outweighed by the loss of human drive and innovative spirit. Franz Kafka's haunting novel, *Der Prozess*, paints a chilling picture of this very disillusionment. The protagonist, Josef K., finds himself ensnared in a labyrinthine bureaucratic nightmare. He faces arrest and execution without explanation or due process, reduced to a mere case number lost in the system's cold, uncaring machinery. Kafka's stark portrayal serves as a powerful reminder of the human cost of excessive bureaucracy, a system that can dehumanize and crush the individuality of those caught within its grasp.

Alternatively, Karl Polanyi argues that freedom ought to be one of society's highest aspirations, vigilantly protected and nurtured by a global perspective. According to this perspective, if the quest for 'abundant freedom for all' is consistently prioritized, there is no need to view centralized power or extensive planning as inherent threats. Rather, they can be utilized as means to attain this overarching aim. Polanyi suggests that this represents the true nature of freedom within a complex society – a shared dedication to broadening and protecting individual liberties, offering both security and stability for everyone.

While Schumpeter's proposed solutions sometimes stumble in practice, Polanyi's vision can appear idealistic, suggesting a complete overhaul of existing systems towards a more free-market utopia. This proposition might be a hard sell for established organizations unwilling to radically change their structures. Instead, a more realistic approach might involve navigating a spectrum between the extremes of perfect markets and rigid hierarchies. This could, for example, involve negotiated transactions, exemplified by strategic alliances where firms collaborate for specific goals, sharing expertise and resources without full mergers.

Additionally, organizations must carefully weigh the costs and benefits of vertical integration. This is based on the idea that businesses should integrate when the 'transaction costs' associated with market exchanges exceed the costs of internal coordination (Coase, 1937; Williamson, 2007). This decision goes beyond pure production costs, encompassing transaction costs involved in external market interactions. Highly integrated industries like Ford's River Rouge demonstrate the potential advantages: internalizing production can significantly reduce transaction costs compared to relying solely on external markets. Ford's steel production within the Rouge complex serves as a prime example of this cost-saving strategy.

While heavily integrated firms benefit from internalizing production, others with lower levels of integration incur higher internalization costs and function more like real markets (Gibbons and Roberts, 2013). Take the superstore giant Walmart, for instance, which relies heavily on external suppliers for various goods. Further along the spectrum, we find companies like McDonald's, employing a more nuanced approach known as tapered integration. They replicate market incentives within the organization through a hybrid strategy. McDonald's University and in-house R&D research, for example, function partially within the company and partially rely on external partners, achieving a balance between internal control and external competition.

Modern capitalist economies

Beyond the internal structures of bureaucracy, modern capitalist economies face additional complexities, which are often navigated through principal-agent models, which address the conflicts of interest between principals (owners or shareholders) and agents (managers). These models are grounded in the idea that if the right types of incentives are provided to managers, they will act in the best interests of the shareholders, ensuring that corporations are managed efficiently and productively (Jensen and Meckling, 1976; de Meza and Lockwood, 1998). The principal-agent framework suggests that aligning the interests of managers with those of shareholders through performance-based compensation, stock options, and other incentives can mitigate agency problems and enhance corporate governance.

This theoretical underpinning significantly influenced economic policies and corporate strategies, particularly during the era of liberalization and privatization championed by political leaders such as Ronald Reagan in the United States and Margaret Thatcher in the UK. Beginning in the early 1970s and gaining momentum through the 1980s, there was a widespread shift towards deregulation, reducing government intervention in the economy and privatizing state-owned enterprises. This movement was driven by the belief that market mechanisms, rather than government control, would lead to more efficient allocation of resources and better economic outcomes.

The push towards liberalization and privatization was also supported by the theoretical contributions of economists such as Milton Friedman and Friedrich Hayek, who argued for the superiority of free markets over government planning. These policies were implemented not only in the United States and the UK but also influenced economic reforms globally, particularly in developing countries and transitioning economies. The principal-agent model's emphasis on incentive structures resonated with these neoliberal economic policies. By privatizing state-owned enterprises and introducing performance-based incentives for managers, the aim was to align the interests of corporate executives with those of shareholders, thus driving better corporate performance and contributing to overall economic growth.

However, it is essential to acknowledge that while the principal-agent model has significantly influenced economic policy and corporate governance, it also has its limitations and has led to new challenges (Piketty, 2014; Chang, 2010). Issues such as short-termism, excessive executive compensation, and financial misconduct have emerged as critical concerns. The model assumes that financial incentives are the primary motivators for managers, potentially overlooking other factors such as ethical considerations, corporate culture, and the broader social impacts of corporate actions.

What is new?

Historically, the rise of corporations and centralized economies marked a shift towards organizations (Milgrom and Roberts, 1992). Today, however, the increasing importance of e-commerce, virtual organizations, and accessible information through IT raises the question: will these factors lead to a reconfiguration of economic structures, potentially with a greater role for markets? While the benefits of organizations like social trust and collective bargaining might still be relevant, they may manifest in new forms. Instead of a simple reversal to traditional markets, we might see the emergence of hybrid models, decentralized networks, or even entirely new platforms that leverage the strengths of both organizations and markets in a dynamic and evolving landscape. Indeed, many organizations are now adopting a platform business model that facilitates transactions among various parties, significantly impacting traditional business environments across multiple industries.

Within the realm of work and organizations, AI (Artificial Intelligence) is poised to bring about significant and potentially irreversible changes to how jobs and tasks are executed (Makridakis, 2017). Throughout history, advancements in technology have fundamentally altered human existence. The Industrial Revolution ushered in widespread mechanization, while the digital age, with the emergence of the internet and the online marketplace, has diminished the need for face-to-face interactions. The future holds even greater promise for AI-driven automation, extending its reach into more data-driven and cognitive domains. Just as Taylorism reformed mass production, modern advancements in AI are driving a new era of industrial transformation, allowing for mass customization or personalization on an unprecedented scale. While early capitalist organizations such as Ford relied heavily on efficiency and uniformity, modern AI-driven businesses focus equally on flexibility and uniqueness, meeting the growing societal demand for personalized products.

Previously, automation's impact on jobs has primarily been confined to manual labour tasks like assembly line work. However, AI's capabilities are already affecting areas like data entry, customer service, and even creative industries, requiring adaptation and reskilling efforts across the workforce. While AI could revolutionize data processing capabilities and efficiency in sectors like production and manufacturing, its impact will extend far beyond these traditional areas. Imagine healthcare professionals using AI-powered diagnostic tools, financial analysts relying on AI for complex market predictions, or educators utilizing personalized AI learning platforms. These are just a glimpse into the potential future of work, where humans and AI collaborate in new ways, requiring a re-evaluation of traditional work practices like Taylorism and Fordism that prioritized cost-efficiency over worker well-being.

Similarly, AI has become a powerful catalyst for major technology companies, driving innovations that have reshaped user experiences and business models. E-commerce behemoth Amazon and media streaming giant Netflix have harnessed AI to deliver highly personalized product recommendations, substantially boosting sales and user engagement. Tech titans Google and Facebook have exploited AI's ability to process massive data sets, allowing for precision-targeted advertising that optimizes ad revenue (Bresnahan, 2018; Spulber, 2011). While pioneers like Google in the tech sector and Siemens in manufacturing anticipate a surge in AI adoption, we must acknowledge that the impact will vary. Some jobs will undoubtedly be replaced, while others will evolve, requiring continuous upskilling and retraining.

Consequently, leading organizations are actively adapting, from reskilling workforces to adopting flatter structures that integrate technology. However, a crucial question remains: are these tools genuinely enhancing productivity, or are they exacerbating the constant pressure and disconnection felt by many modern workers?

The answer lies not just in reducing routine tasks and minimizing costs, but in pursuing broader goals (Anderson and Rainie, 2018). AI should ultimately serve to enhance customer value and create opportunities for meaningful work, defined as jobs that provide not only financial security but also autonomy, creative engagement, and a sense of purpose. This requires careful planning, ethical considerations, and a commitment to upskilling and reskilling to ensure that AI becomes a tool for empowering workers and shaping a more fulfilling future of work.

Industrial transformation

The First Industrial Revolution, marked by the transformative impact of steam engines, witnessed the displacement of manual agricultural jobs, such as threshing and reaping, by mechanized farm equipment. The invention of electricity ignited the Second Industrial Revolution, giving rise to mass production through innovations like assembly lines and standardized parts, fuelled by electric power. The Third Industrial Revolution witnessed the advent of digital technology and electronics, employing memory-programmable control (essentially early computer programming) to automate production processes without direct human intervention.

Today, with advancements in AI machine learning (ML), Big Data, robotics, the Internet of Things, and even emerging technologies like quantum computing, the Fourth Industrial Revolution is well underway (Schwab, 2017). These advancements are paving the way for a potential shift towards Industry 5.0. These developments promise a pervasive integration of technology into the digital age, fundamentally reshaping not only how we work (think smart factories and collaborative robots) but also how we live (imagine personalized healthcare with AI-powered diagnostics) and interact (envision immersive virtual reality (VR) experiences).

AI is no longer a futuristic concept but a tangible force reshaping our reality. From healthcare to finance, AI is infiltrating various industries, promising reduced work hours and enhanced efficiency by automating repetitive tasks currently performed by humans. AI's ability to improve predictive capabilities is substantial (Jones and Tonetti, 2020; Agrawal, Gans and Goldfarb, 2022), leading to more informed decision-making. However, prediction is just one aspect of the complex world of decision-making. *Advances related to generative AI* have the potential to revolutionize various aspects of business operations. This includes increasing labour productivity, improving operational planning with regard to external risks, fine-tuning financial planning, and informing investment decisions. Bresnahan's (2018) research indicates the potential for significant productivity growth through AI adoption, highlighting specific AI development trajectories that could pave the way for its widespread implementation.

The future of work is undoubtedly shaped by AI. While challenges like job displacement and inequality exist (WEF, 2020), AI also holds immense potential to create new and better jobs for everyone. By focusing on education, training, and supportive policies, we can navigate this wave of change and unlock a future where humans and machines work together for a more prosperous and equitable world. Using the immense processing power, storage capacity, and vast data availability at our disposal, AI and its associated disciplines are poised for significant progress, potentially exceeding our current expectations based on recent breakthroughs in areas like natural language processing (NLP) and image recognition. This progress will undoubtedly pave the way for emerging occupations and industries, from AI ethics specialists to VR designers, while simultaneously transforming or even rendering obsolete certain existing ones through a process of creative destruction (Schumpeter, 1934).

However, it is important to remember that AI tools depend on human-labelled data for training, and their effectiveness can vary depending on specific contexts. Providing comprehensive training on how to effectively collaborate with AI will be essential for facilitating seamless integration of these technologies, empowering individuals to optimize productivity and accuracy. Firms aiming for future success must focus on equipping their employees with the skills necessary to utilize AI for automation, data analysis, and informed decision-making. This includes enhancing their critical thinking and adaptability to keep pace with evolving job requirements. Despite facing challenges, the conscientious development and application of AI offer substantial opportunities for innovation and progress in technology.

What is AI?

Just as H. G. Wells predicted that statistical thinking would become essential, so too will understanding AI be crucial for informed citizenship in the future. AI has permeated our society beyond belief, shaping how we work, play, and interact with the world, from online shopping and banking to self-driving cars and personalized healthcare.

This transformative technology's origins can be traced back to the 1940s and 1950s, with early efforts dedicated to mimicking human intelligence and enabling computers to perform complex tasks (Marr, 2019; Haenlein and Kaplan, 2019). Today, innovations like ML and deep learning have driven its explosive growth, allowing AI to learn, adapt, and even exhibit some aspects of human-like thinking. The following examples illustrate the point.

Medical diagnosis: AI algorithms can analyse medical scans and data to detect diseases like cancer at early stages, improving patient outcomes.

Self-driving cars: AI systems navigate roads and react to real-time traffic, paving the way for safer and more efficient transportation.

Personalized learning: AI tutors adapt to individual students' needs and learning styles, creating a more engaging and effective educational experience.

The rapid development of AI in recent years is primarily attributed to the substantial growth in digital data, alongside significant increases in computing power and storage capacity. While numerous definitions of AI exist, the core concept remains consistent: using computer systems to perform tasks typically requiring human intelligence. AI is a vast and captivating realm, pushing the boundaries of what machines can do. It is not just about robots or futuristic sci-fi, but a collection of powerful technologies working together to mimic human intelligence and solve complex problems. On Spotify, the app generates daily mixes for users by building on the music they frequently listen to. Similarly, Amazon studies customers' purchasing habits and recommends other products to them.

This pattern analysis is defined as ML. ML forms the foundation of attempts to guide computers to learn and mimic the functions of a human brain. ML is a subset of AI. Samuel (1959) defines ML as the 'field of study that gives computers the ability to learn without being explicitly programmed'. In other words, these programmes would adjust themselves and respond to data they are exposed to.

The other most common approach to teaching computers to imitate a human brain is Artificial Neural Networks (ANNs). ANNs are inspired by the mechanisms of biological neural networks; statistical models, on the other hand, are applied directly and modelled partially. To simplify the association between these two concepts, consider that each neuron in the brain is responsible for solving a minute part of every task. For instance, in terms of biological neural networks, to determine if someone is alive, the person either needs to breathe or have a pulse. An artificial neuron functions similarly to a human brain neuron; it consumes input data and produces an output. If the neuron learns the information that indicates the individual is breathing or has a pulse, then the neuron will encode this information and confirm that the individual is alive. This is essentially a simplified explanation of how ANNs function.

The ability to learn and adapt unlocks incredible possibilities for AI, taking it beyond tasks like basic calculations, as evidenced by the following applications:

Visual perception: AI systems can now recognize objects in images with remarkable accuracy. Facial recognition software, for instance, identifies individuals with ease, and image analysis tools can automatically detect objects in photos and videos.

Language processing: AI can translate languages with impressive fluency, breaking down communication barriers and fostering global understanding. Machine translation tools seamlessly convert text from one language to another, allowing for real-time conversations and document translation.

Creative content generation: AI is even venturing into the realm of creative text formats, composing poems, scripts, musical pieces, and even emails and letters. While not yet replacing human creativity, AI tools can assist in writing and provide unique perspectives.

Chatbots: A chatbot is a computer programme that uses AI and NLP to comprehend customer inquiries and provide automated responses, simulating human conversation. Examples of chatbots include Apple's Siri, Google Assistant, and Amazon's Alexa.

These are just a few of the many capabilities AI is constantly developing. As the field continues to evolve, we can expect even more impressive feats, pushing the boundaries of what intelligent machines can achieve. It is important to remember, however, that AI is a tool, and like any tool, its impact depends on how we choose to use it.

For example, AI offers numerous opportunities for business organizations to enhance their operations and gain competitive advantages. One significant benefit is data-driven decision-making, where AI algorithms analyse large data sets to uncover valuable insights and patterns that might be missed by humans, enabling more informed decisions in areas like product development (Manyika et al., 2017; Barro and Davenport, 2019). Furthermore, AI enables personalized customer experiences through recommendation systems and chatbots, enhancing consumer satisfaction and loyalty by tailoring interactions to individual preferences. AI-powered analytics and recommendation systems further personalize customer experiences by anticipating preferences and behaviours, allowing businesses to adapt products, services, and marketing to target customers (Bughin et al., 2018).

AI-based predictive analytics are also highly useful, helping businesses anticipate problems such as equipment failures or maintenance needs before they occur by analysing sensor data and historical records, thereby enabling proactive maintenance to minimize downtime and optimize asset utilization (Manyika et al., 2017). In supply chain operations, AI technologies like ML and predictive analytics optimize demand forecasting, inventory levels, and logistics efficiency. These insights help businesses anticipate market fluctuations, mitigate risks, and enhance supply chain resilience (Bughin et al., 2018).

AI also significantly benefits fraud detection and risk management. AI-powered fraud detection systems use advanced analytics and ML algorithms to detect anomalies and suspicious activities by analysing transactional data and user behaviour patterns, thereby identifying fraudulent transactions and mitigating risks.

Predictive and generative AI

Predictive AI and generative AI are two prominent branches of AI that have significantly influenced various industries, offering diverse applications spanning business analytics and creative design. While both types of AI leverage advanced ML techniques, they differ in their objectives, methodologies, and outcomes.

Predictive AI

Predictive AI refers to the use of data-driven algorithms to forecast future outcomes based on historical data. It is largely about prediction and classification, making it a critical tool for decision-making in numerous fields such as finance, marketing, healthcare, and more. Predictive AI relies heavily on data, as models are trained on large data sets, learning from past patterns to forecast future events. Commonly used algorithms include regression analysis, decision trees, neural networks, and ensemble methods like random forests and gradient boosting machines.

In general, applications of predictive AI span various industries: in finance, it is used for credit scoring, predicting stock market trends, and detecting fraud. In healthcare, it forecasts disease outbreaks, assesses patient readmission risks, and predicts treatment outcomes. In retail, it assists in demand forecasting, predicting customer churn and enhancing personalized marketing strategies. Predictive models are also used to analyse customer data and behaviour patterns to identify customers who are likely to churn (stop using a service or cancel a subscription). This allows businesses to take proactive measures to retain those customers. In manufacturing and industrial settings, predictive models are used to analyse sensor data and predict when equipment or machinery is likely to fail, allowing for timely maintenance and reducing downtime. Retailers and e-commerce companies use predictive models to forecast future sales based on historical data, seasonal trends, and other factors, helping them optimize inventory and supply chain management.

These applications also appear in many other company operations that exploit this technology. For example, Amazon uses predictive AI for various purposes, including product recommendation engines, demand forecasting, and supply chain optimization. Similarly, online platforms like Netflix and Spotify use predictive models to recommend products, movies, or music based on a user's historical preferences and behaviour. In the transportation industry, Uber employs predictive AI to anticipate demand for rides, optimize driver allocation, and forecast ride times and pricing. Customer Relationship Management (CRM) platforms, such as Salesforce's Einstein employ AI for lead scoring, predicting sales opportunities, and forecasting revenue. Similarly, Zendesk's customer service platform applies AI to efficiently route inquiries, analyse customer sentiment, and suggest relevant knowledge base articles.

Generative AI

While predictive AI is focused on forecasting future events, generative AI takes a different approach by creating new data instances that mimic the training data, including images, videos, music, text, and voice. It plays a vital role in creative and design fields. Unlike traditional AI, generative AI not only analyses data but also generates new content. Key algorithms used in generative AI are Generative Adversarial Networks (GANs), Variational Autoencoders (VAEs), and Transformer models for NLP.

Applications of generative AI are widespread across different industries. In media and entertainment, it is used to create new content such as music, artworks, and video game environments. In design and manufacturing, generative AI facilitates generative design in architecture and the automotive industry to optimize designs. In NLP, it creates realistic human-like text for chatbots, translation services, and content creation. Language models like GPT-4 are used to generate human-like text for various applications, such as content creation, creative writing, and conversational AI. Likewise, generative models like GANs are used to generate realistic synthetic images, which can be useful for applications like game development, virtual environments, and data augmentation for computer vision tasks. Generative AI models can be trained on existing music to generate new compositions or variations of existing pieces, which can be useful for music production and creativity.

Several companies are actively pushing the boundaries of generative AI models and applications. OpenAI, a prominent AI research lab, has made significant contributions with models like GPT-4 for generating realistic text and DALL-E for creating images from scratch. Anthropic, another research leader, prioritizes safety and ethics in generative AI, exemplified by their language models like Claude. Focusing on image and video generation, Stability AI offers products like Stable Diffusion, while Midjourney, an independent research lab, provides a platform for creating images based on textual descriptions. Additionally, Jasper caters to content creators with its generative AI platform that can craft blog posts, marketing copy, and even code snippets. These examples showcase the diverse range of companies propelling generative AI advancements.

Nike's innovative approach to product design with generative AI

Nike is advancing product design by developing its own generative AI model, exploiting exclusive athlete data to create innovative products. This bespoke large language model (LLM) integrates performance data from Nike's laboratories and public data, forming a 'private garden' for AI training. At a recent event in Paris, Nike showcased the Athlete Imagined Revolution (AIR) project, unveiling prototype shoes for thirteen top athletes. By incorporating detailed athlete input into generative AI models, Nike designers refined hundreds of AI-generated images into single concepts using digital techniques like 3D sketching and printing.

This process represents a new method of product creation at Nike, combining athlete insights, Nike's imagination, and emerging technologies. Despite regulatory constraints requiring shoes in competitions to be widely available, Nike adheres to these rules while continuing to innovate. Nike's AI-driven design approach marks a significant advancement in sportswear, enhancing performance and respecting athlete individuality, with the potential to transform the industry.

Applications of AI in various economic sectors

As discussed, AI technology has permeated various sectors of society, including business, industry, government agencies, and even individuals' daily lives (Bryson, 2019; Bundy, 2017; Guo et al., 2011). Moreover, its applications span diverse industries like healthcare, finance, retail, and manufacturing (Roth and Lomas, 2017). As we delve deeper into these specific examples, we will gain a clearer understanding of how AI is shaping the present and paving the way for a future brimming with possibilities.

AI and health sector

AI tools and procedures have emerged as powerful assets in healthcare research, enabling researchers to analyse vast amounts of data and uncover meaningful insights (Freedman et al., 2018; He et al., 2019). By harnessing the power of AI, researchers can unravel disease patterns. AI algorithms can sift through large data sets of patient data, identifying patterns and trends that may have been overlooked by traditional analytical methods. This deeper understanding of disease progression and patient characteristics can inform the development of more effective diagnostic tools and treatment strategies (Sarwar et al., 2019). AI algorithms can process and analyse data at an incredible speed, far surpassing the capabilities of manual methods. This efficiency allows researchers to rapidly gain insights from large data sets, enabling them to make timely discoveries and respond to emerging health challenges.

AI ML can be integrated into medical devices to detect diseases and health risks like strokes. These devices analyse patient data to identify standard patterns and differentiate them from anomalies that may indicate a stroke. With this capability, AI can accurately categorize 88.5 to 90.5 per cent of patients at risk of a stroke. Thus, using AI to diagnose and detect stroke can assist the decision-maker to provide the correct course of treatment while saving time on numerous tests, since AI can process all the given data in its environment. In addition to stroke diagnosis, AI has the potential to revolutionize healthcare in a variety of other ways, including:

Automated patient monitoring: AI can be used to continuously monitor patient data, such as vital signs and medication adherence, and alert healthcare providers of any potential problems.

Personalized treatment plans: AI can be used to analyse patient data and develop personalized treatment plans that are more effective than traditional one-size-fits-all approaches.

Drug discovery and development: AI can be used to accelerate the drug discovery and development process by identifying new drug targets and predicting the effectiveness of potential drug candidates.

AI procedures can be used in analysing X-ray images, for example, mammograms, to support radiologists in making assessments; and it may speed up the process with a greater accuracy. This can help to reduce the time it takes to diagnose cancer and other conditions, and it can also improve the accuracy of diagnoses. AI can assist in diagnosing skin cancer, particularly malignant melanomas, with a high degree of accuracy when used alongside trained medical professionals (Donnelly, 2018; Sarwar et al., 2019). Remote monitoring technology such as apps and medical devices can assess patients' health and care while they are being cared for at home. This can help to identify potential problems early on and it can also provide support to patients who are managing long-term conditions.

AI and the environment

AI has improved business operations in sectors like manufacturing and finance, and its role in addressing global challenges like climate change is equally significant. While the volume of climate data available is greater than ever before, effectively accessing, interpreting, and acting upon this information is critical to managing environmental crises. AI plays a central role in achieving this goal. For example, AI-powered self-driving cars could reduce emissions by up to 50 per cent by 2050 by identifying the most efficient routes. AI applications in agriculture are leading to higher yields; for instance, peanut farmers in India have achieved a 30 per cent larger harvest by using AI technology.

AI, particularly ML, is also playing an increasingly important role in disaster risk reduction (DRR), ranging from projecting extreme events and developing hazard maps to the detection of events in real time, as well as the provision of situational awareness and decision support. AI can provide faster and more accurate analysis of satellite images, enabling the identification of disaster-stricken areas in need of assistance or regions of deforestation.

As AI-driven data analysis can help predict hazardous weather patterns, it will enhance accountability by precisely monitoring whether governments and companies are meeting their emissions targets. Substantial greenhouse gas reductions in urban transport can be achieved through route and traffic optimization, eco-driving algorithms, programmed 'platooning' of cars, and autonomous ride-sharing services. Electric autonomous vehicle (AV) fleets will play a critical role in delivering real gains. The emerging field of 'Climate Informatics' is harnessing AI to revolutionize weather forecasting and improve our understanding of climate change impacts. This field traditionally demands high-performance energy-intensive computing, but deep learning networks can enable computers to run much faster and incorporate more real-world complexity into calculations.

Embracing AI for personalized travel solutions

Several airline groups have established a significant online presence, highlighting their use of AI in various operational areas. From personalized recommendations and customized customer service to predicting flight demands, baggage tracking, and more, these groups are using AI to enhance the passenger experience and optimize their operations. Navigating the complex regulatory landscape of global airlines is a daunting task. Baggage allowances, visa requirements, and other regulations vary significantly depending on routes, passenger status, and nationalities. Faced with this complexity, no single agent can possess all the necessary knowledge to address every passenger's query effectively. To meet their needs, data scientists have worked to develop prototypes for three key use cases:

1. Delay prevention: AI-powered systems can analyse vast amounts of data to predict potential delays and proactively implement mitigation strategies.
2. Boarding time prediction: By analysing passenger data and historical trends, AI can accurately predict boarding times, ensuring smoother and more efficient boarding processes.
3. Queue management: AI can optimize passenger flow and reduce waiting times at check-in counters by predicting passenger traffic patterns and allocating resources accordingly.

The effectiveness of AI models is contingent on the quality and relevance of the data they are trained on. Therefore, there is a need to prioritize customer involvement throughout the AI development process. This early engagement ensures that AI solutions are adapted to specific needs and address real-world challenges faced by the airline industry.

AR and VR: New innovations and consumer behaviour

VR is a computer-generated simulation of a close-to-real-life experience made with an interactive 3D image or environment. Augmented reality (AR) is the result of using technology to superimpose digital elements (such as sounds, images, and text) on the world we see using a tablet, smart glasses, or a smartphone camera. These immersive technologies (including digital twins) come together to give the user a realistic experience of their augmented or virtual surroundings, allowing for a better perception of the environment. For example, by using medical VR, it is possible to replicate a cell environment to show a journey through the bloodstream in a 3D environment. In a simulation of a VR environment, the patient can be immersed inside their body to see how a medication works or reacts with their bloodstream, showing them what happens at the molecular level. A cancer patient can see the changes in the size of a tumour as a result of treatment such as chemotherapy.

AR and VR can create simulations for mental health patients to face fears and learn coping mechanisms. For instance, VR can simulate a public speaking event, aiding individuals with social anxiety in honing their speaking skills. Furthermore, AR and VR offer doctors a real-time view of a patient's condition, facilitating remote medical consultations and assessments. This can lead to faster diagnoses and more effective treatment. For example, surgeons can use AR to overlay a patient's medical images onto their body during surgery, which can help them to navigate the anatomy more precisely. VR-technology-powered assisted surgeries provide a new way for doctors to operate on their patients which may improve outcomes for the thousands of patients who undergo a surgical or keyhole procedure. Using VR may also shorten operating times and reduce the need for multiple surgeries with a greater accuracy.

These techniques can also be used to train medical personnel and, more importantly, to expose patients to information that they need to learn faster and more effectively. For example, AR and VR can be used to create 3D models of the human body, which can help medical students to learn about anatomy. Furthermore, AR and VR can be used to create simulations of medical procedures, which can help patients to learn about their conditions and prepare for upcoming treatments.

Exploring AR and VR applications in law and courtrooms

AR and VR have emerged as effective and valuable tools in the courtroom setting, particularly in recreating crime scenes. With 3D modelling, artists, data scientists, lawyers, and investigators can accurately recreate crime scenes to gain a deeper understanding of various processes and visualize the events that led to the crime. By overlaying digital information onto the physical world, AR provides real-time visualization, enabling judges and jurors to grasp complex evidence and understand the sequence of events in a more immersive and intuitive manner. VR can also be used to create immersive presentations that help the judge and jury understand complex scenarios and visualize evidence in a way that was never before possible.

Whether it is using 3D models to demonstrate a crime scene or showing a virtual walkthrough of a construction site, these technologies offer a new level of clarity and detail that can make all the difference in a case. Future investigations into how people interact with visual and other digital information may form the basis of new tools that can develop effective communication and collaboration across the crime scene to the court process. These technologies hold immense potential for transforming the way crime scenes are investigated, presented, and understood in courtrooms, leading to more informed decisions and a fairer justice system.

AR and VR in online shopping

AR and VR are significantly changing how we interact with products in the online commercial environment. By integrating immersive technologies, companies are creating novel experiences that enhance customer confidence and reduce purchase anxiety. Virtual showrooms, for instance, allow customers to explore curated product collections in simulated 3D environments. This provides a level of detail and interaction not possible through traditional product images, enabling customers to virtually walk through rooms, examine furniture at various angles, and visualize how different items might look in their own spaces.

AR try-on features are also blurring the lines between online and physical shopping. By superimposing digital representations of clothing, glasses, or other accessories onto the user's live camera feed, this technology allows customers to see how these items would look on them in real time. This removes the guesswork from online shopping, boosting confidence and reducing returns due to poor fit or style mismatch. These immersive technologies not only enhance the product discovery process but also open up a new world of possibilities. AR filters can showcase makeup application virtually, enabling customers to experiment with different styles before purchasing; VR furniture placement tools can help customers visualize how specific items would fit within their own homes; and interactive experiences using both AR and VR can gamify the shopping process, further increasing engagement and customer satisfaction.

As AR and VR technologies continue to evolve and become more accessible, their integration into online shopping is certain to grow. These tools represent a major change in the way we interact with products online, promising a more informed, confident, and, ultimately, more satisfying purchasing experience for consumers.

Big Data analytics

Big Data refers to data sets whose size surpasses the capacity of traditional database systems to capture, store, manage, and analyse within a reasonable time frame. It encompasses the vast, challenging-to-handle volumes of data, both structured and unstructured, that inundate organizations on a daily basis (Liebowitz, 2013). Big Data analytics involves applying unconventional analytical techniques to these extensive, diverse data sets comprising various data types.

Numerous studies have explored the status, potential, and challenges associated with Big Data (Mayer-Schonberger and Cukier, 2014). Najafabadi et al. (2015) highlight the significant advantage of Big Data analytics in identifying complex patterns within vast data sets through advanced techniques like deep learning. Hariri et al. (2019) address the uncertainties inherent in Big Data analytics by assessing its opportunities and limitations. They noted that as data's volume, diversity, and velocity increase, so does the ambiguity within it, leading to decreased confidence in the analysis process and its outcomes.

The concept of Big Data centres on the vast and ever-expanding quantity of data generated by ongoing activities within an organizational setting (Madden, 2012). To grasp Big Data, it is fundamental to first understand what 'Data' entails. Data consists of quantities, symbols, or characters processed by computers, capable of being stored and transmitted as electrical signals, and recorded on various storage mediums such as optical, magnetic, or mechanical devices. Madden (2012) describes Big Data as a collection of data that not only is large in volume but also expands exponentially over time. Analysing this extensive data allows for insights and trends that enhance informed decision-making and provide a foundation for strategic business initiatives (McAfee et al., 2012). Big Data transcends being merely a technological by-product; it has become pivotal as the digital landscape continues to surge with an influx of data and an ever-growing array of data sources.

Big Data is characterized by several key attributes, often referred to as the 5Vs: Volume, Variety, Velocity, Variability, and Value.

Volume refers to the sheer size of Big Data sets, which is significant as it directly influences the potential to extract meaningful insights from the data.

Variety pertains to the diverse sources and types of data, encompassing the three forms of data previously discussed. Big Data comes from a myriad of sources in various formats, such as data from smartphones, social media, financial transactions, and more, including information like names, contacts, transaction details, and personal preferences. In a business context, the diversity of data is crucial for comprehending customer profiles and behaviours.

Velocity describes the rapid rate at which data is generated, a hallmark of Big Data analytics and processing that is both swift and incessant.

Variability indicates the fluctuations in data consistency, which can complicate effective management and processing efforts to derive value.

Value is the beneficial outcomes or the significance realized through intensive data management and processing. Big Data embodies potential wealth, including economic and societal benefits, provided that an organization possesses the necessary expertise and capabilities to manage and analyse it effectively.

The Covid-19 pandemic has notably accelerated the adoption of Big Data analytics among organizations, aiding their economic resurgence. Bragazzi et al. note that, in response to the unparalleled economic disruptions caused by the pandemic, businesses are increasingly turning to predictive analytics. This approach involves employing empirical and descriptive analytics to navigate through tough economic conditions. Predictive analytics leverages data visualization and the simplification of complex data sets to unearth valuable insights from vast amounts of data. For example, during the Covid-19 pandemic, Big Data played an important role in assisting governments and health organizations with tasks like tracking the virus's spread, compiling content databases, validating information, connecting expertise for monitoring purposes, and examining infection patterns. Advances in technology have dramatically reduced the costs associated with data storage and processing, making it more feasible and cost-effective to gather extensive data sets.

Challenges of AI in business and market operations

Despite the potential benefits, adopting AI in business and market operations presents several challenges. One primary concern is job displacement due to automation, which can lead to unemployment and income inequality as AI takes over tasks traditionally performed by humans (Acemoglu and Restrepo, 2019; Manyika et al., 2017). Ethical issues, such as algorithmic bias and data privacy, also pose significant hurdles. Biased algorithms can perpetuate discrimination, and data privacy breaches can erode customer trust (Mittelstadt and Floridi, 2016).

The complexity and opacity of many AI systems, especially deep learning models, make it difficult to understand their decisions, impacting trust and accountability in high-stakes industries like healthcare and finance (Adadi and Berrada, 2018). This 'black-box' nature raises concerns about the reliability and robustness of AI in real-world applications. Furthermore, implementing AI requires substantial organizational changes and integration efforts. Businesses must invest in the necessary infrastructure and talent to deploy AI successfully. Organizational agility and flexibility are key to adapting to AI-driven changes (Manyika et al., 2017). Resistance to change and cultural barriers within organizations can impede effective AI implementation, highlighting the need for leadership commitment and readiness to adapt.

Another challenge is the quality and availability of data. AI algorithms depend on accurate and unbiased data, but inconsistent data formats and privacy concerns can hinder effective AI deployment (Mittelstadt and Floridi, 2016). Poor data quality can lead to suboptimal decision-making and various operational issues. Moreover, there is a significant shortage of skilled AI talent. The demand for AI specialists, ML engineers, and data scientists far exceeds the available talent pool. Developing AI expertise requires a combination of technical skills and problem-solving capabilities, making it challenging for businesses to recruit and retain qualified employees.

3

Automation, jobs, and the future of work

Digital disruption

The rapid development of digital technologies is changing the way we live, work, and interact with the world around us. While this digital revolution has ushered in a wave of innovation and new opportunities, it has also introduced a significant challenge: digital disruption.

Digital disruption is the phenomenon by which new technologies, business models, and ways of thinking disrupt the status quo, challenging established industries and forcing companies to adapt or risk obsolescence (Floridi, 2016; Christensen et al., 2015). This disruption is driven by the convergence of factors, including the proliferation of high-speed internet, the rise of 5G networks, the explosion of big data, and the ubiquity of smartphones. Digital transformation can facilitate the involvement of independent organizations in the open innovation endeavours of firms. Christensen et al.'s concept of disruptive innovation highlights how technological advancements lower barriers to entry and create new opportunities for collaboration and competition. By integrating digital technologies, firms can leverage external sources of innovation, such as start-ups, research institutions, and nonprofits. This enables companies to collaborate more easily, share knowledge, and co-create solutions, thereby enhancing their innovation capabilities and staying competitive in rapidly evolving markets.

The impact of digital disruption is far-reaching, affecting industries ranging from transportation and hospitality to retail and media (Hess, 2016; Verhoef et al., 2021). We have witnessed the rise of Uber, which disrupted the traditional taxi industry by offering a more convenient and affordable alternative. Similarly, Netflix and Amazon Prime Video have transformed the way we consume entertainment, challenging the dominance of cable and satellite television providers. The threat of digital disruption is a growing concern for businesses of all sizes. As new technologies and competitors emerge, companies must continuously adapt their strategies to stay ahead of the curve. This requires a deep understanding of digital environments, a willingness to experiment with new approaches, and a commitment to innovation.

To effectively navigate the challenges of digital disruption, it is crucial to understand its underlying dynamics. Digital disruption is not simply about the adoption of new technologies; it is about the emergence of new business models and ways of thinking that challenge the established norms. Digital disruptors thus often have a different approach to value creation, focusing on providing a more personalized, convenient, or cost-effective experience for customers. They may also have a more agile and adaptable organizational structure, allowing them to quickly respond to changing market conditions.

Navigating the digital landscape

Digital disruption has emerged as a notable phenomenon both within societal contexts and as an aspect of disruptive innovation, yet it stands out as a separate area of academic inquiry (Christensen et al., 2015; Moller et al., 2017; Hess, 2016). Moller et al. (2017) connect the origins of digital disruption to the broader concept of disruptive innovation. From this perspective, Skog et al. (2018) delineate three principal attributes of digital disruption, drawing from current empirical evidence. The first is the emergence of digital innovation that can rapidly erode competitive positions. Secondly, digital disruption redefines an individual's system of value creation by altering resource connections, thereby enhancing direct interactions and transactions. Lastly, while digital disruption may be instigated by one or multiple companies, its effects are systemic, influencing both the creation and capture of value on a broader scale.

Two key concepts in disruptive innovation are digitization and digitalization. While similar, they are distinct. Wautelet (2017, p. 2) defines digitization as the 'technical process of embedding digital artifacts into technological objects'. This applies to business processes as well. Digitalization, however, refers to the 'transformation of sociotechnical structures'. This is considered the digitization method. The digitization of business processes, similar to digitalization, has a strong tendency to influence market structures. Digitalization in business processes brings both positive and negative reinforcements, disrupting existing markets while opening new opportunities, as seen in the technologically revolutionary digital society.

To transform themselves and face digital disruption, many firms are now attempting to transform their business by adapting their core business models. They are aligning their operations with the evolving trends in the disruptive market. They are also establishing a 'capabilities exchange' to foster growth by integrating resources from their primary operations into new, disruptive ventures (Karimi and Walter, 2015; Ross et al., 2017). Through these transformation efforts, some businesses are capitalizing on the rapidity and convenience offered by these ventures, drawing in more customers who prefer digital services. Digital transformation is thus a process where businesses across industries adapt their operations to better meet customer needs in the digital age. This can involve converting traditional processes to digital formats, embedding technology throughout the business, and potentially even creating entirely new business models (Verhoef et al., 2021). As digital disruption continues to upend traditional industries, organizations must respond not only by adopting new technologies but by fundamentally rethinking their business models and operations. This process of adaptation is crucial for companies aiming to stay competitive in an increasingly digital landscape.

Economic theories of jobs and employment

Since the Industrial Revolution, economists have been engaged in an ongoing debate about the short-term and long-term implications of this progress on the labour market. While technological progress serves as a catalyst for economic growth (Rosenberg, 1971; Griliches, 1957), it also renders obsolete the ways of the past, leaving in its wake what Keynes termed 'technological unemployment' (Keynes, 1930). In recent times, a broad spectrum of manufacturing and service industries has been impacted by innovations that have either restructured or transformed their operations.

Particularly, new automation technologies have witnessed a rapid surge over the past few decades, with manufacturing companies embracing robotic technology for its myriad benefits. Ever since the introduction of robotic technologies, many economists and industry experts have expressed concerns over the replacement of human workers. Given the accelerated growth of artificial intelligence (AI) in different industrial and service sectors, it is imperative to explore the impacts of this technology on the labour market to assess whether employment is decreasing or increasing within these companies. Previous studies have yielded mixed forecasts on this topic, as labour demands fluctuate and legislation and regulations evolve over time, impacting the adoption of robots.

In his seminal 1930 essay, 'Economic Possibilities for Our Grandchildren', John Maynard Keynes explores the long-term potential of technological advancement to transform the labour market. Keynes's vision extends beyond the immediate effects of change, venturing into the distant future, specifically one hundred years forward, to examine the 'economic opportunities for our grandchildren'. To assess this long-term impact, Keynes begins by examining the historical trajectory of progress, or rather the relative stagnation from the prehistoric era to comparatively modern times. He attributes the dawn of the modern age to the accumulation of capital from the sixteenth century onwards, which, coupled with the power of compound interest, led to the 'age of science and technical innovation'. Keynes asserts that this remarkable technological advancement has led to an overall improvement in living standards, despite a significant growth in population.

Keynes frames the impact of technological change as transitional, a consequence of rapid increases in technical efficiency. He views the pessimism surrounding technological unemployment as a 'wildly mistaken interpretation of what is happening to us' (Keynes, 1930). While acknowledging the disruptive nature of rapid technological advancement, he characterizes the emergence of 'a new disease … technological unemployment' (Keynes, 1930) as a temporary phenomenon. Keynes confidently asserts that 'the standard of life in progressive countries one hundred years hence will be between four and eight times as high as it is to-day' (Keynes, 1930). This remarkable improvement, he believes, will resolve the fundamental struggle faced by all life on Earth: subsistence. However, it can be argued that this measure of living standards does not fully account for the state of employment, as we remain in the period that Keynes termed the 'temporary phase of maladjustment', at risk of further technological unemployment.

Keynes concludes that achieving 'the economic problem' will necessitate far-reaching changes in our social customs and economic practices, particularly in the distribution of wealth. He envisions a future where the pursuit of wealth is no longer the primary focus, replaced instead by the challenge of allocating our newfound abundance of free time. However, he cautions that this utopia is not present but remains in a distant future, emerging only after at least another one hundred years of 'avarice and usury' (Keynes, 1930). Keynes' perspective on technological unemployment, while optimistic, raises concerns about workforce adaptability – an issue that persists in the era of AI and automation, which we will explore in the following sections.

In their 2015 article, Mokyr and colleagues discuss the notion of a transient labour market adaptation in response to technological advancements. Mokyr et al. distinguish between short-term and long-term effects on employment, quoting Sir James Steuart: 'technological unemployment would occur only if the innovation was introduced very suddenly' (Steuart, 1767). They characterize the rise in unemployment as a temporary phenomenon, emphasizing that 'while the advantages of higher productivity would be permanent'.

Subsequently, Mokyr et al. explore the viewpoints of Luddite thinkers, including reactionary figures such as William Midmay, who acknowledged the potential of machinery to 'destroy the necessity of labour'. These thinkers viewed technology adoption as a 'prisoner's dilemma', where non-adoption would harm the local economy, while adoption would 'make everyone worse off'. Mokyr et al. reinforce their point by presenting evidence that even though technological unemployment was present during the Industrial Revolution, it remained temporary. They justify this by examining the product innovations that created 'entirely new sectors for the economy'.

Mokyr et al. recognize that technological advancements directly influence wages, depending on whether the technology is labour-saving or labour-augmenting. While adhering to neoclassical economics, this article offers a more critical perspective on the short-term consequences for the labour market and society before the 'invisible hand' takes over. Mokyr et al. examine historical impacts of technological progress on society, emphasizing that the lower classes, who must adapt to changes in low-skill labour, are most affected. They note that 'middle-skill workers can then end up competing for lower-skill jobs' (Mokyr et al., 2015).

The Luddites: A symbol of resistance against technological change

During the late eighteenth and early nineteenth centuries, Britain underwent a radical transformation known as the Industrial Revolution. This period was characterized by the introduction of new technologies and manufacturing processes that revolutionized the means of production. While these innovations led to increased productivity and economic growth, they also brought about significant social and economic changes that not everyone welcomed.

One of the most notable consequences of the Industrial Revolution was the rise of capitalism on a much larger scale. This shift in economic systems incentivized factory owners to seek ways to reduce production costs, often leading to the replacement of human workers with machines. This automation process, known as technological unemployment, threatened the livelihoods of many skilled artisans, particularly those in the textile industry.

In response to these perceived threats, a group of textile workers in Nottingham, England, took up arms against the new machines that were displacing them. On 11 March 1811, these workers, now known as the Luddites, began destroying knitting machines in fear that they would replace traditional hand-knitters (Conniff, 2011; Malcom, 1970). The Luddites believed that automation was unsustainable and would lead to the downfall of the textile industry. They feared that technological unemployment would create widespread poverty and new inequalities. Their name was derived from Ned Ludd, a mythical textile worker who was rumoured to have started the movement.

The Luddite protests spread across the English countryside for the next two years, but they were eventually suppressed by the government. Despite their relatively short-lived existence, the Luddites became a symbol of resistance against technological progress and the perceived injustices of the Industrial Revolution. The term 'Luddite' is now defined by the Oxford Dictionary as 'a person opposed to increased industrialization or new technology'. While the Luddites' methods were often violent and destructive, their legacy serves as a reminder of the potential negative impacts of technological change and the importance of considering the human costs of progress.

From the story of the Luddites, several key lessons can be drawn that are still relevant in today's rapidly advancing technological environment:

Technological anxiety: The Luddites exemplify the fear that can accompany new technologies, particularly when such technologies disrupt existing economic structures and job markets. Understanding this anxiety is important when introducing new technology, as similar concerns persist in modern contexts, such as automation and AI potentially displacing jobs.

Impact on employment: The Luddite movement underscores the need to consider the influence of technology on employment. It stresses the importance of transition strategies for workers whose jobs may be displaced by technology, including retraining programmes and educational initiatives to prepare the workforce for new roles.

Social and ethical considerations: The resistance by the Luddites underlines the importance of addressing the social and ethical implications of technological advancements. Technology should not only advance productivity and economic growth but also enhance societal well-being.

Balancing progress with preservation: The Luddites were not against technology per se, but against how its rapid and uncontrolled application was affecting their lives. This speaks to the need for a balanced approach to technological progress, one that considers preserving important aspects of current systems, such as worker rights and community welfare.

Regulation and adaptation: The movement shows that regulatory frameworks need to adapt in step with technological advancements to mitigate adverse impacts.

Governments and policymakers must play a proactive role in ensuring that technology serves the public interest, balancing innovation with regulations that protect workers and consumers.

Resilience and adaptation: From a broader historical perspective, the Luddite movement teaches resilience and adaptation. Industries and workers today must be flexible and adaptive to survive and thrive in changing technological environments.

The Luddites remind us that while technological progress is inevitable, it requires careful management to ensure that its benefits are distributed fairly and that societal values are upheld. The transition driven by new technologies must be managed in a way that minimizes disturbance and maximizes opportunities for all segments of society. Just as the Luddites resisted the changes brought by the Industrial Revolution, today's workers face a similar wave of disruption. The rise of AI and automation is influencing industries in ways that are eerily reminiscent of past technological upheavals.

In their paper 'Smart Machines and Long Term Misery', Sachs and Kotlikoff (2012) further examine the impact of technological unemployment on the welfare of future generations. Unlike Neisser (1942), who views technological unemployment as a temporary phase of adjustment, Sachs and Kotlikoff examine the challenges posed by this adjustment process. They argue that automation and innovations are reducing the demand for unskilled labour, as machines are increasingly designed and operated by skilled workers. The movement towards a skilled workforce has led to a faster increase in the incomes of skilled workers compared to those of unskilled workers. This widening income gap 'threatens the welfare of today's and tomorrow's unskilled workers' (Sachs and Kotlikoff, 2012) by limiting the ability of unskilled and therefore poorer families to afford the resources necessary to participate in the redistribution of labour envisioned by neoclassical economists. A limitation of this article is its lack of consideration for the unexpected job-creating effects of innovations, which can lead to the emergence of new employment sectors or new ways for people to make a living. Innovations such as the recent wave of 'on-demand' services like Airbnb, Uber, and many others have created these new opportunities. Overall, these economic theories provide a framework for understanding the broader trends, but it is in the practical application of automation where we truly see its impact. In industries like automative manufacturing and e-commerce, automation has already revolutionized operations, as evidenced by companies like Tesla and Amazon.

How automation is transforming production

As digital disruption continues to reshape industries, automation emerges as one of the key drivers of this transformation. The rise of automation is quietly reforming production across diverse industries (Dirican, 2015). Take Tesla's Gigafactories, where robots handle welding, painting, and assembly of electric vehicles, enabling mass production and cost reduction for consumers. Likewise, Amazon's warehouses buzz with robotic arms, conveyor belts, and sorting systems, ensuring the rapid and accurate delivery of millions of packages.

Aviation, too, embraces automation. Boeing's 787 Dreamliner, lauded for its lightweight efficiency, owes its strength to automated drilling and riveting, resulting in fuel savings and faster production. In Germany, Siemens' Amberg factory fosters a unique collaboration between humans and robots, where robots assist in assembling high-precision turbine blades with enhanced safety, increased output, and unwavering quality standards. Even the familiar cup of coffee is not exempt. Nestle's Swiss factory uses automated roasting machines, vigilant vision systems, and robotic packaging lines to guarantee consistent coffee quality and maximize production, ensuring the morning brew remains perfect.

These examples showcase the multifaceted impact of automation on production, leading to increased efficiency, enhanced quality, and improved safety. Automation can be achieved using various programmable devices and systems such as AI, robots, and computer-controlled machines, which are often used to automate repetitive or hazardous tasks (Groover, 2018). This allows human labour to concentrate on more complex tasks, improving overall operational efficiency.

Different types of automation, such as fixed, programmable, and flexible automation, offer various advantages. Fixed automation is typically associated with high-volume production where changeovers are rare and costly. Programmable automation is suitable for batch production, providing the ability to produce a wider range of products but requiring downtime for changeovers. Flexible automation allows for automatic changeovers, making it adaptable to changes in production demands, and is often connected to networks for remote monitoring or control, enhancing operational flexibility.

Manufacturers employs automation for numerous benefits, including reducing downtime, ensuring predictable maintenance, and improving decision-making through real-time data analysis (Guskova and Nepopushcheva, 2019). Automation also enhances safety by taking over dangerous tasks and improves quality control by minimizing human error. The key for manufacturers is to align automation strategies with specific business goals to maximize the benefits.

For example, Nissan is committed to utilizing advanced driver assistance technologies to diversify transportation and ultimately reduce the number of fatalities in preventable accidents involving Nissan vehicles to virtually zero. The company has launched the 'Seamless Autonomous Mobility' (SAM) system, developed in collaboration with NASA, to realize fully autonomous mobility. SAM combines in-vehicle AI with remote human support to assist driverless autonomous vehicles in making decisions in unpredictable situations, such as obstructions on the road. Nissan has also applied AI and machine learning to enhance test drive conversion rates across a wider range of audiences. This approach has enabled the company to gain a deeper understanding of its digital customers' needs and preferences, from the initial discovery stage to the trial phase.

The PACE digital showroom serves as a central platform for Nissan's data assets, encompassing 190 markets and 105 countries. By utilizing AI and machine learning, PACE analyses global visitor metrics to identify both positive and negative performance anomalies specific to each market. PACE exploits sophisticated algorithms to assist Nissan in identifying and prioritizing projects likely to offer the most significant benefits to customers and the highest investment returns. Consequently, Nissan has observed a significant rise in global test drive conversions, resulting in decreased customer turnover and improved business results.

Developing sophisticated manufacturing automation systems

The growing use of automation in the manufacturing industry is not just about substituting human labour with robots; it represents a strategic approach to leveraging technology for handling complex physical processes with enhanced precision and efficiency. This trend is especially prominent in electronic manufacturing, where components are miniaturized, and production lines demand extreme accuracy. Two key forces are driving this automation revolution:

1. Demand for product personalization: Today's consumers crave unique experiences, and this extends to the products they purchase. Manufacturers need to be agile and adaptable to cater to this growing demand for customized features and options. Automation offers a solution by enabling flexible production lines. These lines can be easily adjusted to create customized variations of a product without sacrificing efficiency. Imagine a smartphone assembly line that can automatically integrate different colour cases or memory configurations based on individual customer orders.
2. Growing product complexity: Modern technology products like smartphones and medical devices are becoming increasingly complex. They contain intricate components with delicate assembly processes. Manual production for such products becomes not only inefficient but also prone to human error. Automation offers a solution by ensuring consistent quality and precision, even at high production volumes. Imagine a sophisticated robot arm precisely placing microscopic components on a circuit board, a task that would be nearly impossible for human hands to perform with such accuracy and consistency.

The need for both customization and complex production has significantly accelerated the development of sophisticated manufacturing automation systems. Modern industrial robots are now equipped with enhanced dexterity and vision capabilities, enabling them to handle delicate components and execute intricate assembly tasks with unprecedented precision. Automated guided vehicles (AGVs) have become adept at navigating factory floors autonomously, transporting materials and products with remarkable efficiency and safety. Picture an AGV effortlessly manoeuvring through a complex network of production lines, delivering components precisely where they are needed. Similarly, collaborative robots, also known as cobots, represent a growing trend in manufacturing automation. Cobots are designed to work alongside human workers, offering a more collaborative and adaptable form of automation. Cobots are particularly well-suited for tasks that require close human-machine interaction, such as assembly and inspection. Their user-friendly design and adaptability make them suitable for organizations of various sizes and technical expertise.

Social robots, on the other hand, are designed to interact with humans in socially meaningful ways, distinguishing them from industrial robots that perform specific tasks in controlled environments. Equipped with sensors, actuators, and AI, these robots can perceive and respond to human emotions, gestures, and language. Often featuring a humanoid appearance, social robots possess emotional intelligence, enabling them to recognize and react to emotions like happiness, sadness, anger, and fear. Through natural language processing, they can engage in conversations, providing companionship, assistance, or entertainment. Examples include Pepper, Jibo, and Nao, which are used in various settings such as retail, healthcare, and education. As technology advances, social robots are expected to become even more sophisticated and widespread across different fields.

Due to these advancements, the extent and level of automation in the manufacturing industry have expanded considerably. Automation now transcends beyond mere repetitive tasks on the assembly line, infiltrating every facet of the production process. This includes material handling, quality control, data analysis, and predictive maintenance. Envision a fully automated factory floor where robots manage the entire workflow, from raw materials to finished products. Integrated sensors and software continuously oversee performance, proactively identifying and addressing potential issues before they arise.

However, due to substantial initial investment, robots can be expensive to purchase and maintain. Robots can also be intricate to programme and operate, necessitating specialized skills. In some situations, robots can displace human workers, potentially leading to job losses and social unrest (Arntz et al., 2016). Despite these challenges, it is anticipated that the use of robots in manufacturing will grow as they become more affordable and programming becomes simpler. Robots are expected to increasingly undertake tasks that are repetitive, dangerous, or necessitate exceptional precision. Conversely, humans will likely remain indispensable for tasks that require creativity, manual dexterity, and complex problem-solving abilities.

The first signs of automated systems

The term 'automation' was coined in 1936 by D. S. Harder while working for General Motors. He defined it as the transfer of work parts between machines in a production assembly, without the intervention of human labour. The objective was to enhance the 'manufacturing efficiency and labour productivity' of companies, thereby stimulating the economy (Autor, 2015).

Addressing automation without delving into the historical context of manufacturing is not feasible. Before automation, machines used in manufacturing were designed to boost productivity and efficiency, incorporating three key components: a prime mover converting one type of energy into mechanical energy, a transmitter that conveyed the driving force to the work site, and the machining unit that performed the mechanical work. The Industrial Revolution marked the onset of machines and increased manufacturing, significantly benefiting the economy. The effects of the Industrial Revolution in the UK were most pronounced from the 1870s onwards (Matthews et al., 1982). During this period, the manufacturing sector witnessed significant growth, with an average annual increase of 2.2 per cent. This expansion was accompanied by a steady rise in manufacturing employment, averaging an annual growth rate of 0.8 per cent. These figures translate to an impressive annual increase in labour productivity of 1.4 per cent. Overall, employment in manufacturing rose by 30 per cent between 1870 and 1913, highlighting the critical role this sector played in Britain's economic boom leading up to the Second World War.

The US Industrial Revolution began in the late 1700s when Samuel Slater, known as the 'Father of the American Industrial Revolution', brought British textile technology to America. In 1793, he established the first successful textile mill in Pawtucket, Rhode Island. This marked the start of American reliance on mechanization, which spread beyond textiles into other sectors (Beckert, 2014). By the mid-twentieth century, the United States emerged as a global industrial leader. The world wars particularly showcased America's industrial capacity, with massive production of military goods. Post-Second World War, the United States continued to lead in technological innovation and manufacturing, transitioning into more advanced sectors such as electronics and aerospace, culminating in the Information Age.

The initial advances in automation

The story of automated systems began nearly two decades after D. S. Harder's contributions to manufacturing. The 1956 ACM-AIEE-IRE (three major computing institutions) conference meeting showcased the first accounting-compatible computer, the 'UNIVAC', which stored data on magnetic tape (Daly, 1956). Developed in the aftermath of the Second World War by John Mauchly and J. Presper Eckert, the 'UNIVAC' computer represented groundbreaking technology. The system automatically prepared, maintained, and made readily accessible various reports such as inventory control, profit and loss, accounts receivable, and accounts payable, showcasing its capabilities for automated information processing and storage. However, it required forty hours to complete payroll calculations, emphasizing the superior efficiency of contemporary software.

The significant breakthrough in automated accounting came with Dan Bricklin's creation of the 'first electronic spreadsheet', designed to work with the Apple II computer. Upon its release in 1979, 'VisiCalc' became an overnight sensation and led to the displacement of hundreds of thousands of accounting clerks, raising concerns about the potential for further job losses as technology advances (Grad, 2007). Its ability to instantly recalculate values in all cells when any one value was changed facilitated its adoption by accountants for repetitive calculations, examining alternative budget plans and analysing so-called 'what-if' scenarios, tasks that were previously challenging to manage using manual methods.

The 'Lotus 1-2-3' software surpassed VisiCalc from 1982, dominating the spreadsheet market for the next five years (Lewis, 1988). This was followed by modern programs such as 'Microsoft Excel'. Nevertheless, VisiCalc pioneered the first spreadsheet programs, setting the foundational principles for contemporary office software. Since the first implementation of automation software in the workplace, it has remained a critical area for technological innovation. Without such developments in automation, processing tasks would continue to be performed manually, resulting in higher expenses due to labour costs. Besides, automated systems are far less prone to errors, making them ideal for repetitive tasks such as updating financial reports. The introduction of VisiCalc, the first automated accounting system, revolutionized the accounting profession by enabling mathematical and systematic tasks to be completed with greater efficiency and cost-effectiveness, reducing processing times from forty hours to near-instantaneous.

Condoor (2004) emphasizes the importance of teaching the history of technology, as it helps individuals learn from previous successes or failures. This is key for businesses, as they can draw upon the experiences of others to identify optimal implementation strategies for automation, recognizing both the potential benefits and hidden pitfalls associated with these new technologies. History has demonstrated a significant risk of job displacement, as evidenced by the 'hundreds of thousands' of office clerks who lost their jobs following the introduction of VisiCalc. Despite these challenges, there are proactive strategies that can help mitigate the adverse effects of automation on the workforce. Reskilling programmes, for example, can equip displaced workers with the tools they need to thrive in new roles shaped by technological advancement.

Cognition and machine learning

Researchers have identified analysing numbers as a central task in accounting and finance (Dikstein and Gurwitz, 2018). Traditionally, this involved algebraic calculations, but finance professionals increasingly use business intelligence and visual analytics to communicate results more effectively.

A key emerging technology is cognitive technology, which allows machines to learn and analyse data in a more human-like way. Machine learning is one capability of cognitive technology, enabling computers to improve their performance over time. Automation powered by cognitive technology will allow for the collection and storage of vast amounts of data. This data can then be analysed in a personalized way, considering both individual circumstances and broader trends. The development of predictive technologies is a significant outcome, supporting data-informed decision-making and potentially reducing the biases inherent in purely emotional choices. This could lead to diminished errors and a lower risk of fraud or manipulation, given that computers are not prone to these human vulnerabilities.

Deloitte, a consulting firm, has analysed the impact of this 'cognitive wave'. They point to the rapid growth of AI systems and the significant investments being made across various sectors (Deloitte, 2015). This also shows the growing importance of Robotic and Cognitive Automation (R&CA) in accounting and finance (Cooper et al., 2019). R&CA combines three key functionalities: robotic automation (handles basic and repetitive tasks, mimicking human hands and legs); desktop automation (manages and guides the robotic automation processes, acting as a central control system); and cognitive technology (analyses data, learns from it, and identifies new opportunities for automation). R&CA can lead to more efficient software structures, reduced workforce costs, and more accurate client service by supporting complex customer needs while controlling expenses (Dikstein and Gurwitz, 2018; PWC, 2017).

How does automation affect 'professions'?

Driven by the demand for custom products adapted to individual consumer preferences and the growing complexity of new product designs, the manufacturing sector has increasingly adopted automation for complex physical tasks. These driving forces have led to the development of sophisticated systems capable of performing a broad spectrum of tasks with high precision and efficiency. As a result, automation has not only expanded the potential to produce more complex and diverse products but has also introduced a more adaptable production line, capable of rapidly responding to market fluctuations. The integration of advanced robotics, along with AI and machine learning algorithms, has empowered these systems to learn from and adjust to novel production challenges in real time, thereby enhancing the efficiency and productivity of manufacturing operations further.

The manufacturing industry thus utilizes automation to a significantly greater extent than the service sector firms (Susskind and Susskind, 2015; Coombs et al., 2020). This is also evident in the abundance of literature focused on 'manufacturing automation', as manufacturing machinery is now employed in a wide range of labour-intensive tasks. This contrasts with the service firm professions, where the mental capabilities of workers are more highly valued than the physical labour required in manufacturing jobs (Cooper et al., 2019). For example, accounting and finance automation processes typically rely on repetitive tasks (Moll and Yigitbasioglu, 2019; Peng and Chang, 2019). The manufacturing industry, in contrast, implements this technology for a broader range of tasks.

Regardless of the industry, the implementation of automation often raises the demand for skilled workers. The complexity of new technologies necessitates higher qualifications from employees (Coombs et al., 2020). One study indicates that 'at least two years of postsecondary vocational training, and in some cases a four-year college degree or more' is required to perform 'middle-skill jobs' (WEF, 2018).

Redefinition of roles and new professions

Many professional roles are being redefined to complement the capabilities of automation, shifting the focus from routine tasks to strategic and human-centric activities. This allows professionals to leverage automation for greater efficiency and effectiveness. In finance, automation handles data processing and analysis, freeing professionals for strategic decision-making and client relations. In healthcare, automation assists with administrative tasks, enabling healthcare providers to focus on patient care and complex diagnostics. In HR, automation streamlines recruitment processes, allowing HR professionals to concentrate on talent development and organizational culture. In customer service, chatbots manage common inquiries, allowing human agents to address complex issues and build stronger client relationships.

Automation also gives rise to new professions that address the complexities and ethical considerations of these technologies. For example, automation strategists identify areas for effective automation implementation, design solutions, and oversee integration into business operations. Data privacy officers ensure compliance with data protection regulations, develop privacy policies, and respond to data breaches.

Robotics engineers design, develop, and maintain robotic systems, ensuring they perform tasks accurately and safely. Machine learning engineers develop algorithms that enable machines to learn and adapt, creating intelligent systems for various industries. Cybersecurity analysts protect automated systems from cyber threats, ensuring the safety and integrity of these processes.

These new and redefined roles highlight the dynamic nature of the professional landscape in the age of automation. Continuous learning and adaptation are essential for the workforce to harness the benefits of automation while addressing its challenges.

Psychological effects of automation enhancement

Beyond the technical innovations, the rise of automation also brings significant social implications, particularly concerning worker displacement and psychological responses to machine integration. Prejudice and its negative effects on individuals are prevalent in modern society. Jackson et al. (2020) conducted six studies to examine how human-to-human prejudice changes when robots are introduced into the workplace. Their research supports the hypothesis that robots can highlight our common human identity and reduce outgroup prejudice, potentially improving relationships within an organization and contributing to increased unity within accounting firms (Jackson et al., 2020). This cohesion could lead to enhanced productivity through more effective communication and increased motivation due to improved morale (Weakliem and Frenkel, 2006).

However, the potential positive impact of automation on human interactions could be outweighed by its negative psychological effects. Waytz and Norton (2014) conducted experiments examining attitudes towards robotic implementation in workplaces, focusing on factors such as emotional responses, comfort levels, and perceived effectiveness. They found a lack of trust between humans and robots, particularly when jobs were emotion-oriented. However, their research also revealed increasing comfort levels when jobs were more cognition-oriented and when robots were designed to exhibit emotional capabilities (Waytz and Norton, 2014). This suggests that as technology advances in business service firms, human trust in robots will gradually increase as advancements in human-like emotion are integrated into robotics.

In summary, the psychological impact of automation is multifaceted. While automation may cause anxiety or job displacement for some, it can also lead to a more efficient work environment for others. Moreover, technology can enhance human interactions by enabling more concentrated and collaborative efforts. As individuals come to appreciate the advantages of AI technology, trust can gradually build, solidifying the partnership between humans and machines.

The AI impact on industry

The recent emergence of AI has necessitated a reinvention of civilization, fundamentally altering the operation of the entire labour market (Ramos, 2019). AI has significantly boosted workplace productivity, but this may not directly translate to benefits for all workers (ICAEW, 2019). As with past automation waves, one concern is job displacement (Brynjolfsson and McAfee, 2014; Frey and Osborne, 2017). The earlier implementation and extensive research on manufacturing automation have led to predictions that 'more than 50% of human labour in developed countries will be replaced by intelligent automation in the near future', emphasizing automation's potential to disrupt employment rates (Arntz et al., 2016). When automation was first introduced in the late 1970s with VisiCalc, many accountants lost their calculation-based jobs (BBC, 2019). The question remains: will history repeat itself?

Prior literature suggests a moderate to high risk of AI-driven automation for certain jobs (Nagarajah, 2018); technology is likely to automate many repetitive, rule-based positions (Deloitte, 2015). However, as WEF (2018) points out, this does not necessarily mean widespread job losses. While some repetitive tasks might be replaced by machines, new roles are likely to emerge, and existing ones may be transformed. Therefore, the 'risk' of automation may not be entirely negative, potentially leading to job creation and adaptation (Autor et al., 2003).

Augmenting the workforce with AI

The integration of AI in workplace processes is widely praised for its remarkable efficiency gains, automating a broad spectrum of tasks. These advanced AI systems excel at handling repetitive duties such as scheduling interviews, identifying promising candidates, and parsing resumes. AI's capability to swiftly analyse extensive volumes of resumes and applications against specific criteria highlights its efficiency. However, while worker productivity traditionally depends on individual skills like efficiency and organization, AI deployment could undermine these qualities by rendering human effort redundant in certain areas.

The true power of AI lies in its collaborative potential. Humans and machines can work together, leveraging their unique strengths. AI excels at data analysis and processing speed, while humans bring creativity, intuition, and domain expertise (Bughin et al., 2018). This synergy allows teams to tackle complex problems and drive business growth. Research suggests that human-AI collaboration fosters innovation and superior outcomes compared to either working alone (Varian, 2014). Interestingly, AI empowers individuals to become entrepreneurs and innovators. AI-powered tools and resources allow them to develop cutting-edge products and services, automate businesses, and analyse market trends more effectively. AI can accelerate innovation by enabling rapid prototyping and testing, fostering a vibrant culture of entrepreneurship (Bughin et al., 2018).

Contrary to replacing human creativity, AI can enhance it. Generative design algorithms and creative platforms can inspire experimentation and stimulate creative thinking (Yampolskiy, 2018). Collaboration with AI systems allows individuals to explore new possibilities, find innovative solutions, and push the boundaries of creativity across various domains. Finally, AI technologies enable flexible work arrangements, promoting a better work-life balance. AI-driven collaboration tools and remote monitoring systems enable seamless communication and collaboration between distributed teams, potentially boosting employee morale (OECD, 2020). Furthermore,

AI-powered scheduling and task management platforms optimize efficiency in areas like resource allocation, empowering individuals to work autonomously and efficiently from anywhere.

Organizational decision-making

There is another area of interest that relates to the intricate dynamics between automation and organizational decision-making structures (Dogan et al., 2024). Dogan et al. examine how the growing accessibility and integration of automation technologies are influencing the way decisions are made within companies. The core discovery of their investigation is that as automation becomes more readily available and is adopted more widely across various operational facets, there is a noticeable move towards the centralization of decision-making processes within organizations.

This trend towards centralization is attributed to several factors. Firstly, automation technologies often aggregate and analyse data more efficiently than human counterparts, leading to insights that can streamline decision-making at higher organizational levels. Secondly, the implementation of automation can standardize procedures and responses to certain scenarios, reducing the need for decision-making at lower levels of the organization. In the end, the centralization trend may also reflect a strategic choice by organizational leaders to maintain control over key decisions as they navigate the challenges and opportunities presented by advanced automation technologies.

Generative AI and employment

The theory of technological unemployment suggests that advancements in AI and automation technologies could lead to widespread job losses, significantly impacting the current job market (Brynjolfsson and McAfee, 2014). While worries about robots displacing all jobs are valid, the prevailing view among experts now suggests a different outcome. Rather than causing extensive job elimination, AI is expected to reshape the nature of work, necessitating novel skills and approaches. The future favours those who perceive AI not as a menace but as a potent collaborator and commit to evolving their knowledge and skills in tandem with technological advancements.

According to the World Economic Forum's Future of Jobs (2023) report, organizations are seeing a shift in automation, with machines taking on an increasing share of tasks. While manual and physical work were initially thought to be most at risk, the focus is now on automating tasks that require cognitive skills. Current estimates suggest that by 2027, automation will handle 35 per cent of these tasks, compared to 65 per cent of information and data processing (WEF, 2023). Interestingly, stronger human skills like reasoning, communication, and coordination, were previously considered less susceptible to automation. However, these areas are now expected to see increased automation in the future. Artificial intelligence is a key driver of this trend, with nearly 75 per cent of surveyed companies planning to adopt AI (WEF, 2023). This adoption will have a mixed impact on jobs, with 50 per cent of organizations expecting it to create new opportunities and 25 per cent anticipating job losses.

Recent developments in generative AI models, like ChatGPT and Midjourney, have also shown a remarkable enhancement in performance, enabling users to undertake diverse tasks effortlessly. They are seen as general-purpose technologies with the capacity to profoundly influence economic and societal landscapes. The implications of these AI advancements for the workforce are still being actively investigated. AI has the potential to augment human productivity (Noy and Zhang, 2023), yet it might also replace certain jobs, leading to displacement and unemployment (Acemoglu and Autor, 2011). Additionally, it could impact wage dynamics within the workforce by either increasing or reducing wage inequality.

Hui et al. (2023) investigate the immediate impact of generative AI on the job market, with a particular focus on the deployment of ChatGPT. They use data from Upwork, a prominent online platform that connects freelancers with temporary projects. The platform's inherent flexibility, as opposed to traditional employment structures, offers an insightful context for examining ChatGPT's immediate repercussions. Their research indicates that freelancers in highly impacted fields tend to see decreases in both job opportunities and income following the advent of generative AI. Freelancers in occupations more susceptible to the influence of ChatGPT saw a notable decline in platform employment, marked by a 2 per cent reduction in monthly job opportunities and a 5.2 per cent drop in monthly earnings, in contrast to those in less impacted fields. The negative impacts were evident in both the likelihood of securing any work in a given month (a 1.2 per cent decrease) and the number of jobs undertaken by those who were employed (a 4.7 per cent decrease), showcasing challenges on both the intensive and extensive margins of employment (Hui et al., 2023).

Upon examining the influence based on freelancers' work history, the study found no clear evidence that a track record of high-quality service lessens the negative impacts on job prospects. Preliminary data even suggests that top-performing freelancers could be more severely affected by AI advancements. These findings imply that, in the short run, generative AI may diminish the demand for knowledge workers across various skill levels, potentially levelling the playing field among workers. Their analysis suggests that generative AI models currently compete with knowledge workers of all calibres, leading to a decrease in their job opportunities and earnings. The notable effect on high-achieving freelancers might indicate that generative AI is closing the performance gap between less skilled and more skilled workers.

In a related study, Brynjolfsson et al. (2023) examine the phased roll-out of a generative AI-based conversational assistant, drawing on data from 5,179 customer support agents. The introduction of the tool notably boosts productivity, with a 14 per cent average increase in issues resolved per hour. The enhancement is particularly striking among novice and less skilled workers, who experience a 34 per cent productivity gain, in contrast to a negligible effect on seasoned and highly skilled employees. This pattern implies that the AI tool may be spreading advanced workers' best practices and aiding newer employees through immediate feedback or by pointing out pertinent resources. Moreover, their findings indicate that AI support not only elevates customer satisfaction but also enhances employee retention and potentially facilitates worker learning. The evidence underscores the significant potential of generative AI to elevate productivity, with the extent of benefits varying according to the workers' skill level.

Balancing education and skills in the age of AI

The advancements in generative AI are shaping the realms of work and technology, heralding an era that emphasizes the collaboration between humans and machines. This change underlines the importance of personalized education and skill development, adapting learning to individual needs to equip the workforce with the specialized skills necessary to leverage generative AI, including data analysis, effective human-AI interaction, and ethical considerations.

To tackle these challenges, it is essential to gain proficiency in sophisticated AI systems, advocate for their ethical use, and integrate AI technologies into current workflows smoothly. Customized education programmes, aligned with personal learning preferences and career ambitions, can arm individuals with the competencies required to innovate and remain agile in this evolving environment. Initiatives aimed at enhancing skills, encompassing both technical acumen and interpersonal abilities, are vital for preparing people to collaborate with advanced AI systems, encouraging creativity, analytical thinking, and problem-solving capabilities.

As AI's role becomes more pronounced, the focus on bespoke learning paths and skill acquisition is critical, offering a strategic response to the intricate challenges and opportunities presented by generative AI. This approach not only aids in overcoming potential obstacles but also facilitates the widespread adoption of AI in various industries, paving the way for a future characterized by increased cooperation and innovation.

4

Data-driven personalization and consumer concept

When a user engages with a streaming service like Netflix, every interaction – be it logging in, choosing a show, or pausing a scene – is meticulously captured, contributing to a rich data set of customer behaviour. This process extends well beyond simple data aggregation; it involves a deep dive into analytics to extract meaningful patterns and insights. Netflix, recognizing the pivotal role of data analytics in its operational success, invests heavily in refining its data analysis capabilities. The service employs advanced algorithms and machine learning techniques to sift through this extensive data, identifying viewing patterns, preferences, and trends. This continuous analysis feeds into Netflix's artificial intelligence (AI)-driven recommendation system, which is fine-tuned in real time to cater to the unique tastes of each viewer.

Personalization is a digital transformation strategy that leverages digital assets like customer purchase history, browsing behaviour, and demographics to customize products and services to meet individual needs. Through examining this diverse range of personal and behavioural data, companies can uncover critical insights into customer preferences (Lim et al., 2022). Yet, personalization is not a unidirectional process; it flourishes with active customer participation, enabling them to play a part in shaping their personalized experiences. This engagement can occur through diverse avenues, including submitting product reviews, sharing purchasing information, or engaging with companies on social platforms. The essence of personalization is thus in the effective utilization of customer data.

Personalization has been linked to positive outcomes such as increased profitability (Khan et al., 2009), improved customer experiences with a sense of control over their privacy and a rise in click-through rates on personalized recommendations (Tucker, 2014), and even enhanced user motivation and performance (Kaiser et al., 2017; Athey et al., 2023b). Recent investigations have also emphasized the impact of personalization on influencing customer attitudes, intentions, and engagement with companies (Smink et al., 2020). Moreover, the value placed on the shopping experience and the demand for personalized services from businesses have significantly increased in recent years.

In 2022, nearly three-quarters (73 per cent) of consumers anticipated that companies would understand their unique shopping needs and preferences, a noticeable increase from the two-thirds who held this expectation in 2020 (Statista, 2023). Over this two-year span, the respondents expecting personalized promotions rose from 52 to

56 per cent. Furthermore, the advancements in personalization and user experience have contributed to a decrease in shoppers feeling like mere numbers to companies (Statista, 2023). However, the effects of personalization on factors like perceived risk, which influence the intention to buy, have not yet been fully explored.

Perceived risk is crucial, particularly when evaluating the intention to purchase services (like telecom service plans) in a digital setting, which often involves many uncertainties. One common type of perceived risk is customer confusion. If customers realize they are confused about an offering, they may view it as risky. Consequently, many industries and firms have embraced personalization as a core strategy to combat customer confusion. This ensures customers receive relevant information that aligns with their interests (Spenner and Freeman, 2012). This focus on relevance translates directly to a higher likelihood of influencing purchase decisions positively (Riegger et al., 2021).

A worldwide survey conducted in 2023 revealed that 70 per cent of business leaders were increasing their investments in personalization strategies (Twilio, 2023). Notably, 80 per cent recognized that personalized customer experiences contributed to higher consumer spending, and 62 per cent highlighted their positive effect on customer loyalty. However, 50 per cent of the leaders also identified obtaining accurate data for effective personalization as an ongoing challenge. While obtaining precise data for personalization has been acknowledged as a challenge by business leaders, this might only represent part of the obstacle. A global survey of retailers in 2023 found that about 60 per cent of participants claimed they could fully exploit customer data for personalization, highlighting the gap between data access and its effective implementation (Statista, 2023a).

These findings suggest that companies need to make an effort to bridge the gap between accessing data and effectively deploying personalization strategies. Moreover, given the rapid pace of technological progress and evolving consumer demands, which influence the volume and complexity of available information and products, it is vital to alleviate customer confusion through strategic personalization. When executed correctly, personalization can significantly increase conversion rates and revenue. However, this strategy demands a thorough analysis to ensure that it fully meets customer needs and preferences. Assessing the impact of personalization across various strategic scenarios is essential to ensure its success and to optimize the benefits it delivers.

The spectrum of personalization objectives

Sunikka and Bragge (2012) define personalization as the process of presenting the appropriate product and service to the right customer, at the opportune time and location. However, personalization goes beyond simply showing the right product at the right time. It is a strategic approach to building relationships and driving value for both consumers and businesses (Murthi and Sarkar, 2003). Below, we provide a breakdown of personalization objectives across a spectrum, ranging from basic browsing improvements to complex customer-centric goals.

Level 1: Enhanced browsing and shopping

Personalization is essentially about providing content that matches each individual's distinct interests and requirements. This includes displaying products likely to appeal to the users, presenting articles related to their previous searches, and offering deals in line with their buying history. The goal is to ensure that each interaction is relevant and meaningful to the user.

Level 2: Building customer relationship

Personalization goes further than just matching content with user interests by suggesting products and content based on past actions and broader preferences, which enhances user engagement and addresses specific needs. It also includes the creation of targeted content and communications, for example, loyalty programme information that suits individual preferences. Furthermore, personalization can augment loyalty programmes by offering varied benefits tied to a user's purchasing history or engagement level, thereby promoting repeat business and reinforcing customer relationships.

Level 3: Customer engagement and value creation

Personalization can also significantly impact product development, leading to the creation of customized products or services that reflect user feedback and preferences. This process involves incorporating consumer insights into the product design process, enabling companies to develop solutions that resonate deeply with their target audience. Personalization helps businesses understand and meet the unique needs of their customers, fostering a stronger connection and improving customer satisfaction. Predictive analytics plays a pivotal role in this personalized approach. By analysing extensive user data, businesses can predict individual customer needs and preferences, often before the customers themselves realize them. This proactive strategy allows companies to recommend products or services at the optimal moment, thereby enhancing the overall customer experience and satisfaction.

Across this range, personalization must consistently provide tangible benefits to the company. This includes higher sales conversions, better customer engagement indicators such as click-through rates or duration spent on the website, and decreased customer turnover. When personalization clearly shows a positive return on investment, it becomes a viable and long-term approach for businesses. Effective personalization thus benefits both consumers and firms, enhancing the overall experience and driving value. Consequently, adapting services, information, and interactions to individual users based on their past and real-time data and technological capabilities has become a prevalent personalization trend in recent years.

How important is personalization to a customer?

The argument presented by Lindecrantz et al. (2020) that personalization in services and products can be considered a 'hygiene factor' is an intriguing adaptation of Frederick

Herzberg's motivator-hygiene theory, originally formulated in 1959. Herzberg's theory, initially intended to analyse job satisfaction among employees, distinguishes between 'satisfiers' (motivators) that contribute to satisfaction and 'hygiene factors' that, when absent, lead to dissatisfaction. Common examples of hygiene factors in the context of employment include working conditions and salaries.

By extending this theory to the realm of customer satisfaction, the assertion that personalization acts as a hygiene factor suggests a fundamental change in customer expectations. In this perspective, the absence of personalization in a service is not merely a missed opportunity for enhanced engagement but a potential source of dissatisfaction that could drive customers to seek alternatives. This reflects a broader trend in consumer behaviour where personalization is no longer seen as an added value but as a baseline expectation. The longitudinal perspective offered by Postma and Brokke (2001) adds depth to this discussion, highlighting the evolving nature of customer engagement with personalization. Initially, customers may be indifferent to personalized elements due to curiosity or novelty. However, as their journey with a service progresses, their responsiveness to personalization increases, making it a critical factor for sustained satisfaction and engagement.

This evolution underscores the importance of understanding customer expectations and the dynamics of satisfaction over time. As e-commerce entities endeavour to offer more targeted shopping experiences, consumers' expectations regarding personalization are also shifting. From 2020 to 2022, there was a noticeable increase in consumers expecting businesses to recognize and cater to their unique buying preferences (Twilio, 2023a). By 2023, around three-quarters of consumers expected enhanced personalization, driven by their willingness to share more data and advancements in technology (Twilio, 2023a).

For businesses, recognizing personalization as a hygiene factor necessitates a strategic approach to customer engagement, where personalization is integrated as a core component of the service offering from the outset. As consumer preferences continue to evolve, the role of personalization as a critical element of customer satisfaction will likely become even more pronounced, shaping the strategies of companies aiming to maintain competitiveness and relevance in their markets.

The evolving concept of personalization

The concept of personalization has evolved across different contexts. Early research focused on modifying a product's outward appearance or function (Mugge et al., 2009). However, technological advancements have directed scholarly attention towards leveraging consumer data for personalized solutions. This stream of research, driven by big data, online platforms, and recommendation systems, explores online behaviours, web data mining, and database technologies (Pappas et al., 2016; Zhang et al., 2011). Past studies often examined the direct impact of actual personalization on consumer reactions. Researchers typically exposed subjects to pre-designed personalized stimuli, recording their reactions like time spent or clicked content (Tam and Ho, 2006). Bang and Wojdynski (2016) conducted an eye-tracking experiment to investigate the effects of personalization in banner advertising on visual attention to the advertisement. They found that participants paid relatively longer and more attention to the personalized compared to non-personalized advertisements.

Instead of treating customers as faceless masses, personalization now recognizes their individual needs and desires. This move from standardized to tailored service has proven its power in building loyalty and satisfaction (Surprenant and Solomon, 1987). Consequently, personalization extends beyond merely offering the best option. This approach not only elevates the perceived value of a service or product but also establishes a foundation of trust and emotional connection, essential for nurturing enduring customer relationships (Mugge et al., 2009). In addition, this strategy holds particular appeal among younger demographics, who tend to prioritize distinctive experiences and demand customization in the offerings they engage with (Aksoy et al., 2021).

In recent years, technological progress has positioned customers at the core of business strategy. Across industries, organizations are also undergoing digital transformations to align their business models with customer experience. These initiatives encompass endeavours such as digitalization, technology integration, and the adoption of innovative business models. In 2023, 57 per cent of retailers worldwide indicated they fully possess the capability to employ customer data for personalized shopper engagement, a figure that is about double that of the previous year (Statista, 2023a). Moreover, 37 per cent reported having moderate proficiency in using data for personalization purposes, and the remaining 6 per cent acknowledged having limited capabilities in this area.

A journey from bespoke products to hyper-tailored experiences

Personalization, the idea of adapting products, services, or experiences to individual preferences and needs, has a rich history that spans across industries, from retail and fashion to technology and media. While the desire to cater to individual needs has existed for centuries, it is the remarkable advancements in technology that have transformed personalization into a scalable and widely applicable practice.

Pre-industrial age: Personalization as an inherent aspect of production

Prior to the Industrial Revolution, personalization was an inherent part of the production process. Craftspeople, such as tailors, furniture makers, and jewellery artisans, meticulously crafted goods to fit the specific needs and desires of their clientele. This bespoke approach ensured that products were not only functional but also reflected the unique preferences of their owners.

The Industrial Revolution ushered in an era of mass production, revolutionizing manufacturing processes and making goods more accessible to the masses. However, this shift towards standardization came at the expense of personalization. As production lines churned out identical products, the level of individual customization dwindled.

Segmentation and catalogues – seeds of modern personalization

The early to mid-twentieth century witnessed the emergence of segmentation in marketing, a strategy that involved dividing the market into distinct groups based on shared characteristics such as age, gender, or location. This targeted approach allowed companies to adapt their advertising messages to specific segments, increasing the likelihood that their messages would resonate with the intended audience. Mail-order catalogues also played a significant role in the evolution of personalization during this period. Retailers began offering a wider variety of products through catalogues, allowing customers to browse and select items that aligned with their personal tastes and preferences.

The late twentieth century marked a turning point in the history of personalization, as the advent of digital technologies opened up new avenues for tailoring experiences to individual users. Database marketing, enabled by computer databases, allowed companies to track customer purchase histories and preferences, enabling them to send targeted selling campaigns and product recommendations. Recommendation systems, pioneered by online retailers like Amazon, introduced algorithms that analysed user behaviour to suggest relevant products. Personal computers, with their ability to adapt software settings to individual preferences, further enhanced the personalization experience.

Rapid technological advancements drive hyper-personalization

The early twenty-first century witnessed a surge of technological advancements that propelled personalization to new heights. Social media platforms, such as Facebook and Instagram, began offering personalized feeds based on user interactions, providing a curated stream of content tailored to individual interests. Big data and analytics tools emerged, enabling companies to process and analyse vast amounts of data to gain deeper insights into customer behaviour and preferences. This newfound understanding facilitated more precise and effective personalization strategies. Mobile technology, with the proliferation of smartphones, introduced location-based personalization, allowing services to adapt their offerings based on real-time user location data. As hyper-personalization becomes the standard, the future of personalization will likely involve even more sophisticated technologies like AI and machine learning, pushing the boundaries of what is possible in adapting customer experiences. Having traced the evolution of personalization from bespoke craftsmanship to AI-driven experiences, it is clear that modern personalization goes beyond products, extending into the customer's overall journey.

Reflection: A journey of customization and privacy

The history of personalization mirrors the broader evolution of society and technology. While the desire to cater to individual needs and preferences has been consistent throughout history, the means and methods of achieving this have changed dramatically. As technology continues to advance, personalization is poised to become even more intricate and nuanced, requiring a continual re-evaluation of the balance between customization and privacy. Ensuring that personalization enhances user experiences while respecting individual rights and privacy will be essential.

The personalization process

Personalization involves learning about customers, matching them with suitable products or services, and delivering those offerings. This nuanced approach to personalization transcends mere arbitrary suggestions, evolving into a dynamic and intelligent recommendation system that intricately understands and caters to individual customer needs. The essence of personalization technology lies in its ability to leverage collected data – every click, search, and browsing session – to deepen its understanding of customer preferences (Vesanen and Raulas, 2006). Through sophisticated algorithms that employ keywords and taxonomy, the system enhances its capabilities in filtering, browsing, and searching, thereby optimizing the recommendation process.

The goal is to deliver the most apt product suggestions at the opportune moment, all aligned with the individual's digital behaviour and preferences. The personalization process is therefore viewed as a cooperative venture in value creation between businesses and their customers. This approach highlights the necessity of acknowledging the diverse aspects of customer profiles, including their values, knowledge, preferences, and relationships, to improve business strategies via personalization. Industry giants like Amazon and Spotify exemplify the power and potential of advanced personalization. Amazon's ability to present a customized homepage that not only reflects past interactions but also anticipates future desires showcases the depth of its recommendation system. Likewise, Spotify's Discovery Weekly feature represents a pinnacle of personalized content delivery.

This cycle of data collection, analysis, and application forms the backbone of modern personalization strategies, turning each customer interaction into an opportunity to enhance satisfaction and loyalty. As companies continue to harness the power of this technology, the potential for creating deeply personalized and engaging customer experiences is boundless, setting new standards in the digital age.

The concept of personalization can thus be envisioned as an ever-evolving learning loop that refines and enhances its approach with each iteration, benefiting from an expanding reservoir of customer data (Adomavicius and Tuzhilin, 2005; Vesanen and Raulas, 2006). Peppers and Rogers (1997) first outlined a four-step process: identifying customers, understanding their needs, engaging with them, and customizing products or services to meet those needs. Over time, this model has been refined. Adomavicius and Tuzhilin (2005) emphasized the importance of measuring the effectiveness of personalization efforts. Vesanen and Raulas (2006) built on this further, highlighting the comprehensive nature of personalization, encompassing the entire journey from collecting data through customer interactions to ultimately delivering personalized products and services. Next, we explore the specific phases of this personalization cycle.

Firstly, the cycle begins with the data gathering and analysis phase, where customer information is amassed from a blend of internal databases, external sources, and direct interactions customers have with the brand. This foundational step is essential for understanding the customer base in depth. Following this, the second phase involves customer profiling. Utilizing the data acquired, customers are segmented into groups that exhibit similar behaviours, needs, wants, and preferences. This segmentation allows for a more targeted and efficient approach in addressing customer requirements.

The third phase involves decisions regarding product offerings, pricing strategies, distribution channels, and promotional activities, tailored to the unique attributes of each customer segment. This customization ensures that the selling efforts are relevant and resonate well with the target audience. Finally, the cycle culminates in the implementation of targeted marketing strategies. These strategies are crafted based on the nuanced profiles developed in earlier phases, ensuring that each customer segment is approached with a marketing strategy that is most likely to be effective and engaging for them. In conclusion, the practical implementation of these data-driven strategies allows businesses to target their offerings, enhancing user engagement and driving customer loyalty.

The challenge of perfect personalization

Imagine walking into a cosy bookstore filled with shelves overflowing with possibilities. But instead of feeling overwhelmed, you are greeted by a friendly bookseller who takes the time to understand your literary tastes. They recommend options never before discovered, introducing new worlds and characters that resonate deeply. That is the power of personalization. It is about creating experiences that feel tailor-made, like stepping into a story where the main character's journey feels intimately familiar.

This example shows how personalization can achieve a high degree of accuracy in understanding a user's desires and requirements. This is important as it has the potential to significantly impact the effectiveness of the personalization system in enhancing the user experience. Theoretically, a company's personalization system should become more accurate as they gather and analyse larger amounts of data.

However, despite advancements in personalization techniques, achieving perfect accuracy remains a significant hurdle. Human emotions and intelligence are a labyrinthine network, and even sophisticated AI may struggle to navigate the intricacies of human sentiment (Purdy et al., 2019; Perez-Vega et al., 2021). This can lead to inaccuracies, misinterpretations, or biased recommendations. As Alan Turing pondered in his seminal work (1936), perfectly replicating human thought processes might be a chimera, forever out of reach. Moreover, machine learning systems can struggle with new situations they have not encountered before. This challenge arises because machine learning mainly works by recognizing and extending patterns, so an unfamiliar scenario might stump a personalization system. If a user has distinctive preferences or views things differently from what the AI has previously processed, the recommendations might not be accurate.

Conversely, for firms serving millions of users, the likelihood of this impacting their system's precision is minimal, as it is rare for such systems to come across completely new situations. Therefore, from a consumer's perspective, perceived accuracy is critical for effective personalization. The lower the perceived accuracy, the less likely users are to engage with or benefit from recommendations. This is because users are more likely to trust and act upon suggestions they believe are relevant and aligned with their interests.

For companies, recognizing the significance of perceived accuracy in personalization should inform future investment decisions. Several techniques can be adopted to improve perceived accuracy, such as: engaging in extensive A/B testing to empirically identify which versions of personalized recommendations most effectively engage users, thereby boosting user satisfaction and engagement (A/B tests involve comparing two versions of a variable to determine which one performs better) (Gomez-Aguilar, 2020); enhancing metadata tagging by enriching items with pertinent keywords and descriptions, helping algorithms to more precisely align items with user preferences; employing web mining techniques to glean valuable insights from user activities online, providing a fuller picture of user interests and preferences (Eirinaki and Vazirgiannis, 2003).

While enhancing perceived accuracy is important, relying solely on technological progress may not be the best tactic. Companies should adopt a balanced strategy that applies AI's capabilities while also drawing on human insight to grasp customer needs and preferences. This might involve incorporating user feedback mechanisms and employing human oversight to ensure personalization reflects the subtleties of human behaviour. This iterative process highlights the understanding that customer needs are dynamic, diverse, and constantly changing. By dedicating themselves to continuous learning and adaptation, firms can more successfully deliver personalized experiences that not only meet but exceed the distinct desires of every customer.

To see how personalized experiences are impacting customer engagement, consider Nike's approach, which demonstrates the power of personalized product recommendations and dynamic customer interaction. Nike's implementation of personalization techniques is a prime example of how companies are employing customized strategies to enhance consumer experiences:

1. NikePlus members receive personalized product recommendations based on their purchase history and browsing behaviour. For example, if a NikePlus member has recently purchased a new pair of running shoes, Nike might recommend other running apparel or accessories to them.
2. The NikePlus app uses data from the user's fitness tracking to provide personalized workouts and training plans. For example, if a user is training for a marathon, the NikePlus app might recommend a training plan that is specifically tailored to their goals.
3. Nike ID allows users to customize their own Nike products with a variety of options, such as colours, materials, and designs. This allows users to create products that are perfectly suited to their individual needs and preferences. For example, a user might customize a pair of Nike running shoes with their favourite colours and add their own initials.
4. Nike stores have trained sales associates who can help customers find the right products for their needs and preferences. For example, a sales associate might help a customer find the right pair of running shoes for their foot type and running style.

The crux of personalization is adapting offerings and experiences to meet individual needs and preferences. This approach moves beyond the limitations of generic solutions, enabling the development of unique variations designed for particular demographics, interests, and even biometrics. Imagine offering fitness trackers that dynamically adjust training programmes based on individual biometrics, or clothing brands providing custom-fit garments through 3D printing technologies.

We can therefore posit that personalization necessitates a profound comprehension of purchasing behaviours, interests, and aspirations. This comprehensive approach can encompass the following:

Analysing purchase history and browsing behaviour: For example, a footwear retailer might suggest new athletic shoes based on analysis of past purchases of sportswear and search history related to athletic gear.

Utilizing social media insights: A travel agency could tailor vacation packages based on travel-related posts on Instagram or activity in travel-focused Facebook groups.

Gathering direct feedback and preferences: A fashion brand might send a survey after a purchase to gauge preferences in terms of fit and style, aiming to refine future recommendations.

Consequently, the extent of personalization can differ based on the nature of the product or service in question. Some businesses offer the option for customers to fully customize their products from the ground up. In contrast, others might concentrate on providing personalized recommendations or targeted promotions.

The personalization decision

The decision to personalize is not simply a business tactic; it is a strategic move in how companies view their customers. At the heart of this change lies the acknowledgement that customization must be thoughtfully considered, recognizing that not all products are amenable to the same degree of personalization. For instance, while bespoke furniture might present logistical and cost challenges, personalizing recommendations for books or music can be more straightforward and cost-effective. The success of personalized product development strategies thus depends on adopting a systematic approach, requiring companies to move from anecdotal insights to comprehensive, data-driven methodologies.

From the preceding discussion, several key lessons can be discerned regarding the implementation of personalization decisions across various business contexts.

(1) **Continuous improvement and refinement**
Personalization is a dynamic, ongoing process rather than a static, one-off decision. It begins with a commitment to adapting experiences to individual preferences and progresses through a series of experimental and flexible steps. This journey involves setting up pilot programmes, monitoring their outcomes, and continually refining strategies based on both quantitative data insights and qualitative customer feedback. The essence of successful personalization lies in maintaining a flexible and responsive approach, constantly updating and evolving strategies to stay aligned with changing customer needs and expectations.

By embracing personalization, businesses embark on a journey towards a more customer-focused approach, in which every interaction is carefully adjusted to meet the specific needs and preferences of each customer. This important change not only strengthens customer relationships and drives business success but also advances the domain of business exploration into an environment where individuals are acknowledged, comprehended, and personally esteemed.

(2) **Personalized new product development in a consumer-centric age**
The conventional approach to new product development, which typically focuses on creating standardized solutions intended for wide-ranging audiences, is being transformed. This change is driven by technological advancements and a shift in consumer preferences towards more personalized experiences. This transition has profound implications for how products are conceived, designed, and launched, heralding the rise of 'me-markets' that specifically address the unique preferences and requirements of individual consumers. This trend towards personalization not only enhances the relevance of products for each consumer but also opens up new avenues for innovation and differentiation in the increasingly competitive market.

(3) **'Reimagining' existing products**
Personalization transcends the simplistic notion of iterative product improvements; it is about crafting bespoke solutions seamlessly integrated into existing offerings, aligning more closely with individual needs and preferences. Imagine fitness trackers that do more than monitor activities, instead dynamically adjusting training programmes based on unique biometrics and personal preferences. Or music streaming services that do not merely play songs but curate playlists that evolve with individual music tastes over time.

This level of detailed customization extends beyond entertainment and fitness, infiltrating even the most routine aspects of life. Picture a food delivery service that offers more than a standard menu, providing personalized meal options designed for specific dietary needs and preferences. Or consider household appliances designed to adjust features to accommodate individual daily routines and habits. Personalization is revolutionizing not just the design of products and services but also their interaction with individuals, transforming every offering into a bespoke experience crafted for individual lifestyles and preferences.

(4) **Niche innovation within established brands**
Personalization does not require the creation of entirely new product categories; rather, it can rejuvenate existing product lines with carefully crafted extensions. Take clothing brands as an example: by harnessing data analytics and 3D printing technologies, they can provide custom-fit apparel, addressing the needs of body shapes that often find limited options in standard, mass-produced lines. In the automotive sector, manufacturers could offer personalized features, such as customized interior designs or specific performance upgrades, appealing

to distinct preferences within their current clientele. This strategy not only enriches the product range but also strengthens loyalty by recognizing and serving the varied tastes and requirements of their diverse customer base.

(5) **Bespoke sub-brands and new ventures**
Personalization has the capacity to move beyond traditional customization efforts within existing product lines, paving the way for the creation of new identities centred around customized experiences. Envision a scenario where an established company creates a sub-entity dedicated to providing curated travel experiences or personalized luxury items. This strategic approach allows the company to connect with particular market segments effectively without diluting its core essence, fostering loyalty among a varied customer base.

Moreover, the drive for personalization can catalyse the establishment of new businesses designed to meet specialized needs. For instance, a fashion brand could emerge with a focus on adaptive clothing, catering specifically to individuals with disabilities, or a tech start-up might concentrate on developing accessibility solutions targeting populations that mainstream offerings have traditionally overlooked. These ventures, rooted in the principles of personalization, not only fill gaps in the market but also champion inclusivity and innovation, enriching the entire industry.

(6) **Driving groundbreaking innovation**
Personalization is not simply about meeting existing preferences; it can also inspire groundbreaking innovations. Imagine a healthcare system where wearable devices not only monitor vitals but also implement sophisticated algorithms to generate personalized health interventions based on a unique data profile. This level of individualization holds immense potential for transformative changes in medicine, education, and other sectors where personal data can be leveraged to create products and services adapted to individual needs and goals.

The personalization gap

Charlotte, filled with anticipation, explored an online store to find an ideal birthday present for her technologically inclined nephew. However, as she continued her search, she became increasingly puzzled. Terms like 'Wireless noise-cancelling headphones', 'Bluetooth earbuds', and 'gaming headsets' appeared on her screen. Descriptions featuring 'latency', 'impedance', and 'active noise reduction' were prevalent, yet their meanings were unclear to her.

Her frustration grew when she encountered a product named 'Xtreme Blasters', which seemed promising due to its attractive price. However, customer reviews highlighted frequent connection problems. Another product, 'Silent Sentinels', offered a lifetime warranty that, upon closer inspection, was limited to manufacturing defects and excluded damage from regular use. Overwhelmed and disillusioned, Charlotte decided to stop her search, feeling deceived and disheartened.

This scenario illustrates a common issue of customer confusion. Companies, in their efforts to appeal to a wider audience, often overlook the fact that not all consumers are familiar with their specific terminology. The presentation of complex information, inconsistent messages, and unclear product descriptions can perplex customers, resulting in lost opportunities, time, and trust. Therefore, recognizing that personalization provides customers with the benefit of reducing confusion by filtering choices to match their preferences is crucial (Murthi and Sarkar, 2003).

Customer confusion

Customer confusion is a psychological state triggered by excessive, overlapping, or unclear information that exceeds a customer's ability to process it (Schweizer et al., 2006). This information overload leads to misinterpretations of product offerings, hindering information processing and, ultimately, decision-making capabilities (Walsh et al., 2007).

Customer confusion is particularly prevalent in high-involvement purchases, where extensive information search, evaluation, and processing become necessary (Vohs et al., 2008; Sweller et al., 2011). The telecommunications industry exemplifies this perfectly. A fiercely competitive landscape leads to a constant barrage of similar offerings, pricing structures, and promotions, often presented in a confusing or ambiguous way (Edward and Sahadev, 2012). Many companies contribute to this overwhelming environment by introducing a multitude of plans with varied pricing options to meet various customer needs. This complexity significantly increases the effort required for customers to make informed decisions, making customer confusion a critical issue to address in different industrial environments. In the context of user-generated content (UGC), as consumers are presented with increasingly more options to choose from or even opportunities to create content themselves, they become vulnerable to a state of 'mass confusion'. This occurs when consumers experience a sense of over-complexity, high effort, and potential risk, making decision-making more challenging.

Customer confusion: A cognitive challenge

When evaluating product offerings, customers rely on their cognitive abilities to process information into manageable pieces for decision-making. However, this processing capacity has limitations. If bombarded with excessive information (information overload), customers may struggle to process it effectively, leading to confusion (Oberauer and Lange, 2008).

Furthermore, the way information is presented can also contribute to confusion. When multiple offerings share similar features (information similarity), it can be difficult for customers to differentiate between them (Sparrow et al., 2011; Sweller et al., 2011; Vohs et al., 2008). Similarly, vague, incomplete, or conflicting information (information ambiguity) increases the effort required for processing and can result in confusion (Mothersbaugh et al., 2002). Ironically, some industries might even intentionally create ambiguity to portray their offerings as well-rounded, but this can backfire and confuse customers (Wang and Shukla, 2013). In essence, information overload, information similarity, and information ambiguity can all play a role in customer confusion.

Social media fatigue

A significant factor influencing social media usage is the potential for information overload. This phenomenon leads to a state known as social media fatigue, defined as 'the user's tendency to withdraw from social media participation when overwhelmed by information' (Bright et al., 2015). Bright et al. (2015) develop a conceptual model of social media fatigue, identifying a positive correlation between privacy concerns and social media fatigue.

Information overload theory posits that when the vast amount of information and distractions present on social media exceed an individual's capacity to process, information overload occurs (Gu et al., 2007), potentially diminishing social support or exacerbating emotional exhaustion (Fu et al., 2020). Research has shown that while social media can serve as a conduit for obtaining social support through crowdsourcing information, it may also lead to a significant drain on psychological resources (Zivnuska et al., 2019). In a similar vein, Dhir et al. (2019) found that privacy concerns 'significantly and positively correlate' with social media fatigue. Their cross-sectional study surveyed 1,552 young social media users, considering factors such as parental control and monitoring. Understanding this factor and its impact on social media usage is crucial for businesses and organizations, as it is essential to know how consumers react to online content and what might be the most effective way to communicate with them.

Personalization and customer confusion

Amidst the noise of endless options, personalization serves as a beacon of clarity. Personalization aims to alleviate customer confusion by presenting information and offerings that align with individual preferences, using data analysis to understand each customer's unique needs. This approach simplifies the decision-making process by filtering the extensive options available, lessening the effort needed to find pertinent information, and decreasing information overload. Besides, personalization makes offerings stand out from standard ones by offering unique choices suited to each customer. Flourishing in environments rich with data, personalization benefits from the growth of the internet and the widespread availability of customer data. Exploiting this data helps to bridge the gap between what is offered and what customers prefer, thereby reducing information ambiguity.

Personalization has been shown to influence both how customers think (cognitive perceptions) and how they feel (affective perceptions), ultimately leading to purchase decisions (Tam and Ho, 2006). Personalization impacts cognitive perceptions through three key constructs: perceived quality, perceived value, and efficient preference building. First, perceived quality refers to how well the personalized offerings match a customer's specific needs. Effective personalization delivers relevant offerings that meet individual customer demands at the right time. Second, customers perceive value when personalization creates benefits such as improved service, a more positive experience, and greater convenience compared to traditional methods. Third, effective personalization facilitates efficient preference building by providing accurate and complete information.

Personalization moves beyond merely satisfying needs; it can also influence customer emotions in positive ways. This is achieved by exceeding expectations and anticipating (or even accommodating) unexpected needs, ultimately creating feelings of delight (Zhou and Jiao, 2013). Research by Pappas et al. (2016) confirms that personalization fosters positive emotions in customers. Appraisal theory sheds additional light on this phenomenon. Personalization can evoke positive affective perceptions through its perceived significance and relevance to the customer (Ellsworth and Scherer, 2003). Customers experiencing positive emotions like contentment, admiration, or relief due to personalization are more likely to make a purchase (DeSteno et al., 2004).

While emotions play a significant role, they are not the sole driver of purchase decisions. Customers may rely on emotions when lacking sufficient knowledge about the offerings. However, even with negative emotions, customers might still purchase if the product's perceived quality is high (Pappas et al., 2016). In the context of personalization, cognitive perceptions (related to how well a product meets needs) are generally considered the primary determinant of purchase decisions. This is because they provide a more objective foundation for evaluation. However, affective perceptions (emotional responses) can still play a significant role, particularly when influencing how customers perceive value and brand trust.

Personalization: Streamlining the customer journey

Personalization aims to simplify the customer experience by presenting relevant information and offerings based on customer data. This targeted approach streamlines the process as follows:

Reducing choice overload: By filtering out irrelevant options, personalization narrows down the field of choices for customers, making the search process less time-consuming and minimizing information overload (Murthi and Sarkar, 2003).

Decreasing information similarity: Personalized offerings deviate from the standard version, making it easier for customers to differentiate between options based on their specific needs (Kwon et al., 2010).

Lowering information ambiguity: Personalization thrives in data-rich environments enabled by the internet (Montgomery and Smith, 2009; Wedel and Kannan, 2016). By analysing customer data, personalization reduces the chance of encountering offerings that are incongruent with customer needs, thereby minimizing information ambiguity (Simon, 2000).

Customer confusion often leads to irrational decision-making, indicative of shallow information processing. Customers who are not actively engaged with information rely on peripheral processing, leading to weaker attitudes and cognitive perceptions.

Ho and Bodoff (2014) further corroborate the link between depth of processing and customer receptivity towards personalization.

Perceived quality

Building on these insights, we can expect that reducing customer confusion within a personalized context will positively affect cognitive perceptions, such as perceived quality, perceived benefit, and perceived message quality. This can be achieved by minimizing information overload, information similarity, and information ambiguity. For example, personalized offerings that resonate with a customer's specific needs are perceived as higher quality, empowering efficient decision-making and ultimately influencing purchase intention (Tam and Ho, 2006). Personalization tackles information overload by pre-selecting relevant options, ensuring the presented choices closely align with customer needs (Riegger et al., 2021).

Perceived benefits

Personalization can provide valuable incentives to customers, such as better service or greater convenience, positively impacting purchase intention (Montgomery and Smith, 2009; Kwon et al., 2010). By filtering out irrelevant options, personalization reduces information overload, allowing customers to focus on what truly matters within their cognitive limits. This translates to a reduction in decision fatigue and fosters a sense of control over the buying process. Furthermore, unique and personalized offerings (low information similarity) contribute to a more engaging shopping experience. Customers feel a greater sense of connection to the products presented. Finally, a data-rich environment that reduces information ambiguity allows customers to feel confident about their selections. This translates to a perception of high value at a lower cost compared to traditional offline stores. In fact, research suggests that personalization in the online environment can deliver even greater value for money than individualization offered in physical stores.

Personalized messages

Clear, concise, and accurate messages, facilitated by reduced information ambiguity, can significantly enhance customer decision-making (Sweller et al., 2011; Vohs et al., 2008). Customers who perceive messages as helpful are more likely to approve of them, ultimately leading to higher purchase intention. Personalization strengthens this effect by minimizing distractions and focusing on relevant information. This increased relevancy fosters deeper message processing and engagement, leading to a perception of higher message quality. Additionally, relevant messages can activate self-schemas, mental frameworks that aid information interpretation and judgement formation, further enhancing perceived message quality.

Moreover, personalized messages that offer unique value propositions (low information similarity) empower customers. They can make informed decisions based on distinct features that cater to their specific needs, contributing to a perception of high message quality. In essence, a data-rich environment that reduces ambiguity allows personalization to deliver clear, concise, and accurate messages. This comprehensiveness and accuracy are key to creating compelling messages that positively influence customer perceptions.

Understanding customer preferences for personalization

The effectiveness of personalization is rooted in a deep understanding of customer preferences. Simonson (2005) proposes a framework that examines the impact of these preferences on the correlation between perceived value (benefits and costs) and the efficacy of personalization efforts. The framework underscores two critical aspects: preference insight, which pertains to the degree to which customers understand their own preferences, and customer preferences, encompassing the stability and evolution of these preferences. Studies by Franke et al. (2009) and Franke and Hader (2014) indicate that these factors significantly influence the relationship between perceived value and the success of personalization strategies. Because personalization is a learning process where preferences are continuously communicated and refined, the impact of personalized offerings will naturally vary depending on how well-developed an individual's preferences are.

For instance, catering to customers with unstable and underdeveloped preferences presents a formidable challenge. These individuals may struggle to clearly define their own needs, rendering them more vulnerable to influence from personalized marketing strategies or customized products. Although they may express initial satisfaction with such offerings, their preferences could inadvertently be moulded by these experiences, which might lead to a misalignment of their actual needs and desires over time.

To understand how the characteristics of customer preferences affect their interaction with personalization initiatives, we categorize customers into four primary groups (Simonson, 2005; Kramer, 2007), based on their levels of preference insight and the nature of their customer preferences:

Group 1 (*Open Explorers*): These customers have unclear preferences and limited understanding of what they truly want. They are more open to discovery and exploration, readily accepting recommendations and trying new things to refine their preferences. Personalized marketing can be a valuable tool for them to discover new possibilities and uncover hidden interests.

Group 2 (*Unconsciously Biased*): While aware of their uncertain preferences, Group 2 customers often base their choices on superficial factors like aesthetics, neglecting their deeper needs. They might misinterpret their motivations and end up with dissatisfying personalized offers. Companies need to educate and guide these customers by offering transparent data insights and helping them understand their underlying preferences.

Group 3 (*Confident Matchmakers*): These customers have strong, stable preferences but lack insight into the 'why' behind their choices. They confidently select what appeals to them, even if it might not perfectly align with their needs. While they appreciate personalized offers that match their existing preferences, reaching them with truly transformative solutions can be challenging.

Figure 1 Consumer preferences and openness to personalization.

Group 4 (*Discerning Experts*): With clear preferences and strong self-awareness, these customers are the toughest critics of personalization. They expect highly accurate recommendations that perfectly match their needs and wants. However, their power to dictate and educate brands about their preferences can sometimes hinder the learning process and limit the potential for deeper understanding.

Recognizing these diverse customer groups and their distinct reactions is essential for developing effective personalization strategies. By adapting communication, recommendations, and engagement for each segment, companies can forge significant experiences that enable customers to explore their needs, hone their preferences, and ultimately achieve greater satisfaction through personalization.

Figure 1 shows the relationship between the clarity of consumer preferences and their openness to personalization across four distinct groups:

Open Explorers are plotted with low clarity of preferences but high openness to personalization. They are eager to explore and discover new products or services due to their unclear preferences.

Unconsciously Biased customers have slightly clearer preferences but moderate openness to personalization. Their choices are often influenced by superficial factors, which may lead to less satisfaction with personalized offers.

Confident Matchmakers show higher clarity in their preferences but exhibit a moderate level of openness to personalization. They trust their choices but might miss out on more suitable alternatives due to a lack of insight into their preferences.

Discerning Experts possess the clearest preferences and are the least open to personalization. Their strong self-awareness and exacting standards make them critical of personalized offers, which must be highly accurate to be accepted.

This visualization helps us understand the varied needs and responses of different customer segments to personalization strategies.

Implications for personalization strategies

The role of preference development is pivotal in shaping effective personalization strategies. For companies to succeed, they must: customize their communication and offerings for different preference groups, emphasizing discovery and exploration over straightforward recommendations. This approach encourages customers to engage with a variety of options and interactive experiences to better understand their preferences; focus on transparency and control, ensuring customers have a clear understanding of how their data is used and the ability to adjust their personalization settings. This is particularly important for individuals with less defined preferences, as it helps build trust and comfort with the personalization process; aim to cultivate long-term relationships with customers through personalization, rather than merely seeking immediate satisfaction. This involves ongoing engagement that helps customers refine and understand their preferences over time, thereby deepening the customer-brand connection.

Challenges and considerations for data-driven personalization

In a world saturated with options, personalization emerges as a guiding light, providing clarity and direction that is carefully adapted to each individual's preferences. The cornerstone of successful digital transformation lies in adopting evidence-based strategies like personalization (Wedel and Kannan, 2016). Therefore, employing data-driven evaluations is essential for honing personalization tactics and improving results. However, like any powerful tool, it requires careful navigation through a labyrinth of challenges and considerations.

Privacy concerns: At the core of personalization is the intricate balance of handling user data. Firms must prioritize user privacy, adhering to data protection regulations and employing transparent practices. Responsible data management, including clear communication about data collection and usage, is paramount in building trust with users, the cornerstone of any successful personalization endeavour.

Data accuracy: The fuel that drives personalization is data, and its quality is paramount. Inaccurate, outdated, or irrelevant data can lead to misguided and potentially detrimental personalization efforts. Companies must implement robust data governance practices to ensure the data used for personalization is accurate, up-to-date, and relevant to the target audience.

Over-personalization: The quest for personalization can become a double-edged sword. Crossing the line from relevant to intrusive can make users feel uncomfortable, encroaching on their privacy and potentially damaging brand perception. Striking the right balance is essential, focusing on personalization that enhances user experience without infringing upon their boundaries.

Unconscious bias: Data, like any human creation, can be susceptible to bias. Algorithms trained on biased data can perpetuate or even amplify these biases, leading to skewed personalization that excludes or disadvantages certain user groups. Regular reviews and updates of personalization algorithms are essential to mitigate this risk and ensure fair and inclusive experiences for all users.

Despite these challenges, the potential of data-driven personalization remains immense. By embracing a nuanced approach that prioritizes user privacy, data quality, and ethical implementation, businesses can harness the power of personalized experiences to foster stronger customer relationships, boost engagement, and, ultimately, achieve sustainable growth.

In essence, data-driven personalization is more of an ongoing journey than a fixed destination – a dynamic interplay between discovering valuable insights about customers and addressing the ethical and practical aspects involved in customizing experiences. By undertaking this journey with transparency, responsibility, and a focus on user well-being, firms can truly harness the power of personalization. This approach not only transforms customer interactions but also positions companies for success in the constantly changing digital realm.

Online privacy

Privacy was initially seen as the legal right to be left alone, as argued in the landmark 1890 law review article 'The Right to Privacy' by Samuel Warren and Louis Brandeis. However, with the rise of the internet and social media, the concept of privacy has evolved due to the vast amount of personal information shared through various online channels (Martin and Murphy, 2017; Hayes et al., 2021). Despite the numerous advantages of this rapid development, online users have expressed concerns about several issues. One of the primary concerns that consumers have raised from the outset is the risk of their personal information being lost or compromised (Liyanaarachchi et al., 2021; Hong et al., 2021). Moreover, since its inception, the primary approach to characterizing online privacy invasion has been the unauthorized collection, disclosure, or other use of personal information as a direct result of electronic commerce transactions.

Consumer awareness of data privacy

Companies employ a variety of data collection methods. Two of the most common are cookies and loyalty cards. These techniques provide companies with direct access to consumer information. However, these methods also gather an overwhelming amount of data, much of which is irrelevant for business purposes. As a result, techniques such as data mining are employed to extract the pertinent information that can be used for targeted commercial campaigns.

Due to rapid advancements in technology, data collection practices have demonstrated remarkable agility and adaptability. These developments outpace the rate at which policies and regulations can be developed and implemented to safeguard consumer privacy. This lag has encouraged debates and controversies surrounding data collection practices. For example, cookies operate in a covert manner, often concealing their operation and potential threats from consumers. On the other hand, loyalty cards offer companies an efficient means of gathering consumer data. Consumers are often willing to relinquish their personal information in exchange for the benefits, such as discounts and offers, provided by the company (Lee et al., 2014). It is also important to acknowledge the existence of numerous other data collection methods employed by companies, including social networking sites, online product purchases, and banking transactions.

Potential benefits and risks to consumers

Various data collection methods can offer consumers potential benefits. Hann et al. (2005) observe that consumers may be willing to participate in data collection practices if it leads to personalized pricing and promotions. Loyalty cards exemplify this concept. By collecting and analysing data from past transactions, supermarkets like Tesco and Waitrose can create detailed consumer profiles. These profiles enable the distribution of targeted offers and deals to individual consumers.

In a 2023 survey conducted in the United States, 14 per cent of consumers indicated they were comfortable with retailers knowing their gender and city of residence if it meant receiving a more personalized customer experience (Statista, 2023b). Furthermore, 11 per cent of respondents were willing to share details about their budget for a purchase and their age. Conversely, only 1 per cent of those surveyed expressed reluctance to share any data with retailers. Personalization has also become a notable trend in the business-to-business (B2B) e-commerce sector. In 2022, B2B entities used various types of personal data to refine and customize the buying experience for their customers. A survey revealed that the most commonly employed data type was the buyer's job role or persona (37 per cent), closely followed by key account segmentation and engagement history, each at 36 per cent (Coppola, 2023).

A potential risk of data collection is the potential for governmental use of personal information. Dinev et al. (2008) note that governments are increasingly employing new technological capabilities to build profiles and acquire knowledge about citizen behaviours. Diney et al. (2008) suggest that governments intend to enhance security and prevent activities such as fraud, crime, and terrorist activity. However, they conclude that despite the perceived benefits of government surveillance, consumers remain uncomfortable with the use of their data for governmental purposes.

Personalization-privacy paradox

Personalization technology delivers targeted recommendations to customers for products they may find appealing. It implements extensive data analysis to produce customized suggestions for individuals visiting a website, based on their clicks and browsing activity. However, as discussed, there is a level of concern among some customers about the data collected by online sellers, stemming from fears that their personal information might be shared with or sold to third parties (Hong et al., 2021).

The release of the Netflix documentary 'The Social Dilemma' in 2020 also sparked an ongoing debate about privacy concerns surrounding social media usage. This documentary revealed that companies like Facebook, Instagram, and X (Twitter) intentionally design their algorithms to 'keep users constantly engaged through infinite scrolling and push notifications; personalized recommendations use data not just to predict but also influence our actions' (Girish, 2020).

A survey found nearly 60 per cent of respondents are anxious about being tracked online and fear data breaches (Deloitte, 2023). Similarly, a significant portion, nearly 68 per cent of consumers worldwide, report feeling somewhat or very concerned about their online privacy (IAPP, 2023). This wariness impacts their trust in companies, organizations, and governments that collect, hold, and use their personal data. Consequently, consumers are taking control by making choices based on their privacy perceptions. In this data-rich world, they navigate by deleting apps, withholding information, and avoiding purchases when they feel their privacy is at risk (IAPP, 2023).

Consumers also struggle to decipher privacy practices. Obscure privacy notices have long been a barrier for consumers trying to understand how companies handle their personal information. Surveys reveal a significant knowledge gap: few consumers feel confident in a company's privacy practices, and the majority lack a clear grasp of what data is collected about them. Globally, a mere 29 per cent report easily understanding a company's data protection measures (IAPP, 2023). There are some complexities. Consumers may prioritize convenience over privacy at times, and awareness of exactly how data is used can be limited. Regulations like GDPR have increased transparency and user control, but navigating privacy settings can be challenging.

The vast accumulation of data has sparked a debate about the fine line between the advantages of personalization and potential privacy infringements. This dilemma is often referred to as the 'personalization-privacy paradox'. It is important to consider this aspect because if users perceive a violation of their privacy, it could negatively impact their online experience. Consequently, this might indicate that a personalization system fails to improve the user experience as intended (Aguirre et al., 2015; Sher and Benchlouch, 2023). The personalization-privacy paradox also encompasses a discussion about the true extent to which users prioritize their privacy. For example, around three-quarters of consumers surveyed expected enhanced personalization in 2023, driven by their willingness to share more data and advancements in technology (Twilio, 2023a).

However, countering this perspective are numerous surveys highlighting that users are, in fact, significantly concerned about their privacy (Kokolakis, 2017, p. 122). This discrepancy underlines the complex nature of user attitudes towards privacy in the digital realm. Organizations can navigate the personalization-privacy paradox effectively by ensuring that the benefits of personalization clearly outweigh privacy concerns. A key strategy in this endeavour is to abandon any hidden data collection practices. While such covert methods might seem advantageous by minimizing disruptions to the user, they can quickly lead to user dissatisfaction and anger (Aguirre et al., 2015; Hayes et al., 2021; Tucker, 2014). Hence, adopting a policy of transparency and openness about data collection could be a way forward. Informing users about the nature of collected data can prevent feelings of deception and help users maintain a sense of control over their personal information.

5

Personalization in product design

Derek, an ardent environmentalist and tech enthusiast, has been keenly tracking the advancements in electric vehicles (EVs) and is now ready to make a purchase. However, he desires a car that reflects his personality and values. He discovers Wheelys, a car manufacturer known for its unique personalization experience.

Wheelys' website features a 3D digital configurator tool, allowing Derek to virtually customize his car in real time, witnessing the impact of different choices on its appearance and price. He selects: a deep forest-green colour, echoing his love for nature; custom alloy wheels with a futuristic design; a roof entirely composed of solar panels to harness solar energy, further reducing his carbon footprint. For his EV's interior, he opts for: seats crafted from recycled ocean plastic, reflecting his environmental consciousness; a personalized dashboard layout, integrating essential controls within easy reach.

A music lover, Derek upgrades to a premium sound system with an eco-friendly bamboo finish. He seamlessly integrates his EV's system with his smart home setup. As he approaches home, the car communicates with the house, activating driveway lights and adjusting the home's temperature if necessary. Derek saves various driving profiles: 'Eco Mode' maximizes efficiency and range; 'Sport Mode' enhances performance for weekend drives; 'City Mode' optimizes for stop-and-go traffic.

Wheelys offers various subscription services. Derek subscribes to: 'Eco-Updates', providing regular software enhancements focused on increasing the vehicle's energy efficiency; 'Tech & Tunes', offering monthly updates of curated playlists and the latest apps for his in-car entertainment. Upon completion of Derek's personalized EV, Wheelys arranges for home delivery. The representative not only delivers the car to his doorstep but also provides a comprehensive introduction to all custom features. Over time, based on Derek's driving habits and preferences, the car suggests minor tweaks to further enhance his driving experience. For instance, it recommends specific ambient interior lighting colours that may relax him during night-time drives.

Derek's customized electric car from Wheelys demonstrates how product personalization is changing the way consumers seek out unique products that reflect their individual style. Similar to Derek's car, Tesla allows customers to customize their vehicles with a variety of options, including exterior paint colour, interior trim, wheel size, and even performance upgrades for increased acceleration and top speed. These developments are not confined to the automobile industry. For example, Dell has effectively capitalized on the demand for personalized computing solutions by offering extensive customization options for their laptops, encompassing processor type, storage capacity, RAM size, graphics capabilities, and various software preferences.

The Covid-19 pandemic significantly affected e-commerce personalization trends. A worldwide study found that in 2017, 44 per cent of consumers were likely to become repeat purchasers following a personalized digital shopping experience (Twilio, 2023). Following the e-commerce boom in 2021, this percentage decreased but still exceeded pre-pandemic figures. By 2023, 56 per cent of consumers surveyed indicated they were motivated to make repeat purchases from retailers that offered online personalization. While consumer conversion rates saw improvements across various e-commerce categories, marketplaces experienced the most notable increase in conversions before and after personalization was implemented. Boudet et al. (2019) show that successful personalization strategies can directly contribute to a 5–15 per cent increase in revenue and a 10–30 per cent improvement in marketing efficiency within a single channel.

In another survey conducted in the second quarter of 2023, about 55 per cent of Gen X online shoppers voiced their wish for e-commerce platforms to enhance seamless payment solutions (Statista, 2023). Furthermore, approximately 45 per cent of Millennials showed a preference for getting personalized product suggestions while shopping online, a sentiment shared by an equal percentage of Gen Z consumers. The fifth edition of Salesforce's State of the Connected Customer report emphasizes the importance of trust, personalization, and digital-first experiences in satisfying customer demands (Salesforce, 2022). Drawing from a worldwide survey of consumers and business buyers, the report illustrates evolving customer expectations and behaviours. It particularly shows the significance of customer experience; a notable 88 per cent of customers now believe that the experience a company offers is as important as its products or services, marking an all-time high.

According to Adomavicius et al. (2022), personalized recommendations, based on individual users' past behaviour, generally have a greater impact on consumer preferences than aggregate ratings, which represent the overall consensus of all users. The study also found that when both types of ratings are presented together, personalized recommendations tend to be more influential in shaping consumer preferences. Personalized experiences not only improve customer satisfaction but also directly impact business growth. Companies that excel in delivering adapted experiences see higher customer retention rates, increased loyalty, and ultimately, greater market share (Athey et al., 2023b).

Thus, the key to success in today's market is designing products and services suited to individuals. This necessitates a personalized approach that involves both businesses and consumers (Montgomery and Smith, 2009; De Keyzer et al., 2022). From the business perspective, companies collect and analyse data on consumer behaviour, preferences, and interactions to adapt their products, services, and marketing messages to meet individual customer needs. On the consumer side, individuals provide data, either explicitly through preferences and feedback or implicitly through their online behaviour and purchase history. This reciprocal interaction between firms and consumers drives the continuous improvement of personalized experiences, benefiting both parties by creating more value and satisfaction.

The concept of personalization thus represents a fundamental shift in how we conceive economic transactions. At its core, it challenges the traditional one-size-fits-all approach that has long dominated mass-market economies. Instead, it posits that the key to creating vibrant, sustainable marketplaces lies in understanding and catering to the unique needs, preferences, and behaviours of each individual participant. As Simon (2000) argues, bounded rationality has significant implications for understanding decision-making processes, which are central to developing effective personalization strategies.

The strategies employed to achieve personalization in digital marketplaces transcend basic product recommendations, instead representing a holistic approach to shaping every facet of the user's journey. These strategies leverage artificial intelligence (AI) to create dynamic, multidimensional user profiles that evolve in real time based on interactions across multiple touchpoints. These profiles capture not just what users buy but why, how, and what motivates their decisions, integrating data from browsing history, purchase context, social interactions, and even external sources like social media or smart home devices.

Armed with these rich profiles, AI algorithms move beyond simple correlations to predict users' future needs based on their life cycle. For example, a recent baby clothes purchase might lead to suggestions for toddler gear, or an increase in fitness activity could result in recommendations for workout gear. This predictive personalization presents products or services at their most relevant moment, often anticipating needs before users recognize them. Personalization extends to the presentation of products, with unique 'store layouts' crafted for each user. Visual merchandising, narrative curation of product descriptions, and interactive elements like augmented reality (AR) try-ons or AI chatbots are all tailored to individual preferences. Even economic terms are personalized, with dynamic pricing, loyalty programmes, and financing options adapted to each user's behaviour and data. The personalized experience continues post-purchase, with delivery options, onboarding materials, and customer service tailored to individual needs and behaviours. Moreover, personalization encourages a two-way dialogue through targeted feedback mechanisms and co-creation opportunities, inviting users to beta-test features or collaborate on product lines.

As firms diversify, personalization spans entire ecosystems. A user's activity on one service informs recommendations on another, and data (with consent) personalizes experiences with company partners, from travel packages to financial advice. This comprehensive, AI-driven personalization strategy transforms digital marketplaces from mere transaction platforms into dynamic, responsive environments that adapt to and anticipate each user's unique needs, creating a more engaging, efficient, and satisfying economic experience.

The intricate tapestry of personalization strategies woven by digital marketplaces creates a synergistic ecosystem that benefits both sellers and buyers. For sellers, the era of scattershot marketing gives way to precision targeting, where AI-driven insights allow them to focus resources on high-potential leads, maximizing ROI and minimizing waste. In addition, the aggregation of personalized data unveils micro-trends, enabling sellers to innovate products that cater to emerging niche demands. This granular market understanding also optimizes inventory management; predictive algorithms foresee demand fluctuations, mitigating risks of overstocking or stockouts.

Perhaps most valuable is the enhancement of customer lifetime value (CLV); by meeting individual needs with laser precision, sellers create deep brand loyalty that translates into repeat purchases and organic growth through word of mouth. Furthermore, sellers can leverage the platform's broader ecosystem, using personalized user data to tap into new markets or forge strategic collaborations.

Buyers, too, reap substantial benefits. Instead of drowning in a sea of options, they experience the joy of discovery, finding products that resonate on a personal level. This curated approach to choice reduces cognitive load and decision fatigue, saving time and mental energy. But personalization extends beyond mere product recommendations; it aligns buyers with services, content, and interactions that resonate with their core values, be it sustainability, social impact, or personal development. Post-purchase, personalized onboarding and support ensure buyers extract maximum value from their acquisitions, fostering satisfaction and skill growth. Perhaps most transformatively, by inviting buyers into co-creation processes, personalization elevates them from passive consumers to active participants in the value chain.

The culmination of these personalized interactions is a self-reinforcing ecosystem built on trust, engagement, and value creation. When every touchpoint feels tailored, buyers develop deep trust in the platform's ability to understand and fulfil their needs. This trust extends to the platform's recommendations, reducing perceived risk and encouraging exploration of new products or sellers. Personalized feedback loops and co-creation opportunities make buyers feel heard and valued, translating into increased platform engagement, richer interactions, and a wealth of data that fuels even more refined personalization.

This virtuous cycle generates powerful network effects. Satisfied buyers attract a diverse array of sellers eager to access this high-value, loyal customer base. More sellers mean a richer, more varied marketplace, which in turn draws more buyers. This self-reinforcing loop accelerates the firm's growth and cements its market position. At the same time, the rich, dynamic data generated by these personalized interactions becomes an invaluable resource for innovation. It unveils unmet needs, emerging trends, and new market opportunities, driving continuous evolution of the firm and its offerings.

Personalization strategies

Firms embrace personalization as a strategy to reduce costs, enhance convenience, and customize products, pricing, promotions, and distribution channels, all aimed at enriching the customer experience (Krishnaraju and Mathew, 2013; Pfiffelmann et al., 2020). As previously mentioned, Adomavicius et al. (2022) explored the effects of personalized recommendations versus aggregate ratings on consumer preferences in online retail environments. They found that both personalized and aggregate ratings significantly influence consumer behaviour, particularly in post-experience preferences. Personalized recommendations, which are based on individual users' past behaviour, generally have a more substantial impact on consumer preferences than aggregate ratings, which reflect the general consensus of all users. The study also revealed that when both types of ratings are presented together, personalized recommendations tend to dominate in influencing consumer preferences. This suggests that consumers are more likely to trust and be influenced by recommendations that appear specifically intended for them, even when aggregate ratings are also available.

Personalization strategies can be directed at individuals, specific segments, or an entire customer base, incorporating three primary methods: pull, passive, and push personalization (Adomavicius and Tuzhilin, 2005). Building on these methods, Wedel and Kannan (2016) propose three corresponding approaches to personalization in products and services: active personalization, passive personalization, and individualized customization. In active personalization, the process is driven by customers themselves, who share their preferences and interests directly with companies. This direct input enables firms to determine how well their offerings match the specific needs and desires of their customers.

Passive personalization takes a more subtle approach, where companies infer preferences and interests by analysing the data generated from customer behaviours and interactions, without requiring any explicit input from the customers. The third approach, individualized customization, focuses on adapting digital content, such as video recommendations or personalized news feeds, to fit the unique tastes and preferences of each user, ensuring a highly customized experience. These methods represent the spectrum of strategies companies can employ to deliver personalized experiences, each utilizing different levels of customer involvement and data analysis; consequently, each of these methods offers a different level of engagement and initiative from the customer's side, ranging from self-directed customization to fully automated personalization.

According to Aksoy et al. (2011), personalization can be categorized into three distinct types: individual-level, social-level, and situation-based. These categories are based on the nature of the information used to customize the customer experience. Effective personalization relies heavily on in-depth customer insights (Li, 2019). Individual-level personalization applies analysis of a customer's digital behaviour, such as past purchases, reviews, ratings, and comments. Social-level personalization involves techniques like social network analysis and collaborative filtering to understand a customer's social connections and preferences. Lastly, situation-based personalization takes into account contextual factors such as location and time to deliver a more dynamic and relevant experience.

Fan and Poole (2006) suggest that personalization can be defined based on three factors: the aspects being personalized (such as functionality, content, interface, or channel), the target of personalization (whether it is intended for an individual or a group), and the initiator of the personalization process (whether it is customer-driven or initiated by the firm). Personalization strategies can then be broadly divided into two main approaches: system-initiated and user-initiated. The system-initiated approach relies on the collection and analysis of data to personalize offerings without direct input from the customer.

As Arora et al. (2008) define it, the system 'pushes' relevant products or services based on what the data suggests about the customer. Intelligent systems and algorithms provide relevant information through recommendation systems, facilitating system-based personalization for individuals. User-initiated approach, on the other hand, actively engages customers in the personalization process, often through co-production or co-design activities. Customers actively contribute their preferences and input to shape the final product or service.

Research suggests that user-initiated strategies can be more effective than system-initiated ones. While user participation can be perceived as 'troublesome' and lead to lower participation rates, studies show that customers value voluntary participation, control over the process, and convenient co-production opportunities (Kwon and Kim, 2012; De Keyzer et al., 2022). Several other studies support this: Simonson (2005) found that when customers participate in personalization, the resulting product or service better aligns with their preferences. Kwon and Kim (2012), referencing user involvement theory, concluded that customer participation and control in personalization can increase overall satisfaction and loyalty. In conclusion, both system- and user-initiated strategies hold significance in the realm of personalization. These perspectives also align with the views of other scholars like Treiblmaier et al. (2004), who differentiated personalization based on whether it is user-driven (explicit) or generated by the system (implicit).

Drawing on these insights, our subsequent discussion will focus more on content personalization, which is more system-initiated, and product personalization, which tends to be more user-initiated. First, we establish the tools and methods that organizations can use to implement personalization.

Building a consumer profile: Data collection strategies

Advanced digital tools analyse customer information, enabling companies to understand what their customers truly need and want (Ricci et al., 2015). By employing this data-driven approach, companies can ensure they provide the most relevant and desired products or services to their customers. Companies collect consumer data from various sources, including websites, phone interactions, and direct mail, aiming to gain a thorough understanding of their customers. Data collection methods can be categorized as either active or passive. Active data collection, or explicit data collection, involves directly soliciting information from consumers through means such as surveys, forms, or loyalty programmes.

Ulta Beauty uses a loyalty programme called 'Ulta Beauty Rewards' (formerly Ultamate Rewards) to personalize the shopping experience for their customers. Members of the programme earn points for their purchases, which can be redeemed for discounts and other rewards. On the other hand, passive data collection, or implicit data collection, entails monitoring consumer behaviour without direct engagement, tracking activities like purchase history, browsing patterns, and online searches. The scope of data gathered spans demographic details (such as age and location), psychographic elements (covering interests and values), and behavioural data (including past purchases and website interactions). This rich, multifaceted data set enables companies to discern customer needs with greater clarity. The vast amounts of customer data collected through digital interactions offer valuable insights, but the true power lies in harnessing AI to turn this data into actionable intelligence. AI-driven tools allow companies to predict future behaviours, offering even more relevant and personalized experiences.

Building a consumer profile: Profiling methods

Data is used to create consumer profiles, which describe who customers are and how they behave. These profiles are crucial for effective personalization. Most personalization systems build profiles by collecting factual data about consumers, including demographics like age, gender, and location. Furthermore, past behaviour is captured, such as preferred product categories or purchase history on a specific website. This information is typically stored in a database, with one record per customer containing various data points. While profiles based on demographics and past behaviour offer value, advanced personalization necessitates more intricate profiling methods that provide a dynamic view of customers. Examples include:

RFM analysis: This method classifies customers based on Recency (time since their last purchase), Frequency (how often they purchase), and Monetary Value (how much they spend on average). It is particularly effective in identifying valuable customer segments that can benefit from tailored marketing strategies and experiences.

Predictive modelling: Exploiting extensive data, algorithms in this approach can predict future behaviours, enabling companies to proactively meet customer needs and recommend relevant products or services. Predictive modelling helps businesses anticipate customer actions based on historical data, enhancing decision-making and strategy development.

Psychographic profiling: This technique explores deeper into consumers' values, interests, and lifestyles, often employing methods such as surveys, social media analysis, or passive data gathering. Passive data gathering might include monitoring browsing habits and content preferences, providing insights that go beyond basic demographic information to enable more nuanced marketing strategies.

Behavioural segmentation: This strategy segments customers based on their digital behaviours, such as website navigation patterns, product interactions, and the duration of engagement with specific areas of a site. Behavioural segmentation allows for personalized marketing efforts that are more closely aligned with how customers interact with a brand, improving engagement and conversion rates.

Dynamic profiling: Unlike static customer profiles, dynamic profiling adapts and updates in real time based on ongoing data collection. For example, a recent purchase or activity on a website can immediately update a customer's profile, allowing for the delivery of real-time, personalized recommendations that reflect the latest interactions and preferences.

Employing these techniques alongside traditional profiling methods enriches customer understanding, paving the way for nuanced personalization that surpasses simple demographic and historical data analysis.

Machine learning is pivotal in predictive modelling, greatly enhancing personalization through advanced profiling techniques and boosting the efficacy of sophisticated methods. Its main advantages include deciphering complex patterns in extensive data sets, uncovering customer preferences and behaviours that traditional approaches might miss; forecasting future behaviours by training models to anticipate customer actions, essential for predictive modelling focused on proactively fulfilling customer needs; and real-time adaptation, continually refining based on new data, which is key for dynamic profiling that immediately responds to the latest customer activities. Consequently, machine learning facilitates a transition from static data analysis to a continuous, adaptive understanding of customer needs, leading to highly personalized user experiences.

Matching profiles to personalized content and services

After constructing consumer profiles, personalization systems employ these profiles to align individuals with suitable content and services. Various technologies facilitate this matchmaking process:

Recommender systems: These systems employ user data such as purchase history and browsing behaviour to forecast user preferences and recommend products or content that align with their interests. Machine learning algorithms frequently enhance the capabilities of these systems, making them more accurate and responsive to user behaviour changes. Recommender systems are commonly used by e-commerce platforms and streaming services to personalize user experiences and increase engagement.

Statistical prediction: This approach employs statistical models to identify patterns in customer behaviour, enabling predictions about future choices. These insights are instrumental in tailoring product suggestions or marketing communications to individual needs. By understanding the likely future actions of customers, companies can better align their offerings with consumer expectations, enhancing satisfaction and loyalty.

Rule-based systems: Operating based on explicit rules set by experts, these systems can suggest actions such as presenting customers who buy a specific product with complementary items. Although they are less adaptable than methods driven by AI, rule-based systems are effective in managing straightforward personalization scenarios. They provide a reliable way to implement personalization where the decision parameters are well-defined and changes are infrequent.

Through these matchmaking methods, personalization systems effectively connect comprehensive customer profiles with the provision of pertinent content and services. Personalization is now expanding its influence from the business-to-consumer (B2C) sector into the business-to-business (B2B) e-commerce arena as well. In 2022, around 60 per cent of B2B e-commerce companies worldwide found personalized site search results to be their most effective personalization tactic (Statista, 2023c). Likewise, over 55 per cent successfully implemented personalized payment or shipping options. Close to 50 per cent of companies reported effectiveness in personalized marketing, product recommendations, and targeted site content. Features such as product recommendations and website analytics have been recognized as effective conversion tools by B2B sellers.

As personalization enhances the customer experience by offering customized products or services, it has become a priority for many B2B organizations. A global survey revealed that about half of B2B e-commerce companies are dedicating resources to improve customer experience, making it the second most cited objective after attracting new customers (Statista, 2023c). Effective online personalization in the B2B sector is impossible without the precise analysis of customer data, which encompasses various specific customer details.

Measuring personalization impact and making adjustments

As companies implement personalized strategies to enhance customer experiences, it is essential to measure their effectiveness. Understanding the metrics that reflect successful personalization efforts allows firms to refine their approaches and maximize returns. Evaluating the effectiveness of personalization and making necessary adjustments is thus an important step in the personalization process. The common method involves using accuracy-based metrics, which assess the degree to which personalization aligns with customer preferences. These metrics usually evaluate customer responses to recommendations, focusing on their perceived precision and relevance. When inquiring about the criteria for evaluating the effectiveness of AI-driven personalization, 47 per cent of global business leaders pinpointed data accuracy as the key metric (Twilio, 2023a). Closely following this were the speed of real-time data processing and customer retention or repeat purchases, each cited by 44 per cent of respondents. Additionally, 42 per cent considered time-saving benefits for the business as a significant indicator of successful personalization efforts.

Despite their utility, accuracy-based metrics might not fully capture the extensive impact of personalization on overall customer satisfaction and long-term value. To overcome this, there is an increasing focus on more inclusive metrics that encompass a broader array of factors, such as:

Customer lifetime value: Represents the total revenue a customer is expected to generate throughout their engagement with the company. This metric helps businesses understand the long-term value of maintaining relationships with customers.

Loyalty value: Measures a customer's likelihood to continue doing business with and advocating for the company. This indicator reflects the strength of the relationship between the customer and the business, often predicting future loyalty and referral potential.

Purchasing and consumption experience: Encompasses the ease and satisfaction customers experience when locating and purchasing needed products or services.

This metric assesses the effectiveness of the buying process from the customer's perspective.

Return on customer investment (ROCI): Calculates the profit resulting from marketing activities directed at a particular customer group. This metric helps companies evaluate the efficiency of their marketing efforts in generating returns from specific customer segments.

Employing both accuracy-based and more encompassing metrics provides firms with a fuller understanding of how well personalization strategies are performing. This dual approach facilitates the identification of areas for improvement and allows for the fine-tuning of personalization tactics to achieve better outcomes. Just as personalized products cater to individual preferences, content personalization ensures that digital platforms present users with targeted experiences based on their unique preferences.

Content personalization

In the context of content, personalization involves delivering information, articles, or media that align with a user's interests and past interactions. This is commonly seen in streaming services, news websites, and social media platforms. For instance, a streaming service might recommend movies or TV shows based on a user's viewing history, similar to what we discussed in Chapter 1, while a news website might personalize articles based on the user's reading preferences. Therefore, Koutsabasis et al. (2008) define content personalization as the adaptation of content, its presentation, and interaction according to individual user characteristics. This personalization can manifest in numerous forms, including customized interface designs, targeted email campaigns, individualized notifications, and personalized recommendations, all designed to cater to the unique preferences and behaviours of each user.

AI machine learning plays a pivotal role in content personalization. This is highlighted by Amazon's characterization of their personalization system as a fully managed machine learning service (AWS, 2021). Machine learning equips technology with the capability to adapt to new situations and to identify and project patterns (Russell and Norvig, 2010, p. 2). All major Subscription Video on Demand (SVOD) platforms integrate user data with metadata tagging. Each film and TV show is tagged with micro-tags, which assist in identifying similarities between a user's viewing history and potential recommendations (Gomez-Aguilar, 2020). Search engines like Google also employ personalization by adjusting search results based on factors such as a person's search history, location, device, and other contextual elements. This ensures that the search results are more relevant and meaningful to the individual user, improving their overall experience.

The delivery of personalized content to users is complex and involves multiple dimensions. For instance, when a user selects a film or show, they are presented with a percentage match indicating compatibility with their past viewing habits. The platform's interface also plays a critical role in personalization; the machine learning algorithms prioritize content they predict the user will enjoy, placing likely choices prominently at the top and to the left of the screen. This prioritization is part of what is known as the navigational modelling system.

Similarly, the platform's marketing strategies include sending personalized recommendations via email and notifications, driven by machine learning insights. Furthermore, the artwork and preview clips for shows are customized for each user, based on predictions of what will resonate most, showcasing the sophisticated use of new digital tools in enhancing user experience.

Online retail personalized website and customer loyalty

In the digital era, where much of our communication and information sharing happens online, website personalization has become a potent means to improve user experience and cultivate customer loyalty. Personalization in this case involves collecting and analysing data from a customer's interaction with a website (Salonen and Karjaluoto, 2016). This data can include browsing behaviour, search history, purchase history, and demographic information. By analysing this data, businesses can gain insights into individual preferences and needs, enabling them to provide personalized product recommendations, content suggestions, and promotions.

To effectively implement website personalization, businesses may consider the following strategies: (1) Gather data from diverse sources like website analytics, customer surveys, and social media engagements to develop a well-rounded understanding of customer preferences and behaviours. (2) Segment customers into distinct groups based on common attributes such as age, gender, location, and buying history, enabling more focused personalization efforts. (3) Apply the collected data to adjust website content, product suggestions, and marketing offers through methods like dynamic content blocks, customized search outcomes, and targeted email campaigns. (4) Implement A/B testing to continuously evaluate various personalization tactics and identify the most effective ones for different customer groups. (5) Maintain transparency about data collection methods and offer customers options to manage their privacy settings. (6) Consistently assess the impact of personalization initiatives and adjust as necessary to enhance outcomes.

Personalization is widely used in e-commerce sites to deliver customized product recommendations and experiences. For instance, online retailers might recommend products that are frequently bought together, similar to items the user has viewed or purchased, or based on the user's browsing history. This approach is exemplified by sites like Amazon and Etsy, which effectively operate personalized product recommendations to enhance user experience and drive sales.

Before becoming the e-commerce giant it is today, Amazon was just an online bookstore. Now, it has grown to be one of the most valuable companies in the world, with a market cap of more than $1.5 trillion. This vast growth has spiralled from the company's adamant mentality towards constant innovation, expansion, and premium customer service. This mentality is portrayed in the company's customer-centric approach, which prioritizes consumers over anything else (Murphy, 2023). This is achieved through various initiatives, such as next-day delivery, 24/7 customer service, a large selection of products and lower prices compared to other retailers. They also use recommendation algorithms to suggest products that customers are likely to be interested in, based on past purchases and browsing behaviour. All these enhance convenience and boost consumer satisfaction.

Amazon's technology employs AI extensively across its vertically integrated operations, from supply chain management to sales enhancement and delivery optimization. Amazon operates with what is described as 'the world's largest fleet of mobile industrial robots' (Amazon Staff, 2023), highlighting the immense scale of its operations and the critical role of technology integration within its production system to meet customer demand. Notably, AI is employed to personalize customer homepages, enabling the display of targeted product recommendations. It also enhances inventory management by employing optimization tools to ensure products are strategically stocked. AI also contributes to Amazon's logistics efficiency by sorting packages for expedited delivery and determining optimal routes for delivery personnel (Amazon Staff, 2023).

Product personalization

Product personalization involves customizing physical or digital products to match a user's preferences. This can encompass a wide range of products, from personalized merchandise and customized software settings to made-to-order items. Consequently, product personalization is considered the process of imbuing an object, typically an artefact, with characteristics that reflect an individual's preferences. This includes aesthetic attributes like appearance, as well as functions and behaviours (Kaneko et al., 2018). Personalization design thus shapes products and services to match an individual's specific capabilities and preferences. For example, a software company might allow users to personalize their software settings to match their workflow.

When asked what personalized benefits they would trade their personal information for, 22 per cent of US consumers expressed interest in a product custom-made for them, fitting their specific preferences in terms of type, colour, or style (Statista, 2023b). Furthermore, 21 per cent were open to sharing personal data in return for a faster, more focused search experience that closely matches their requirements. Deloitte's 2023 consumer survey found that 86 per cent of consumers are interested in personalized products, and 50 per cent are willing to pay more for them (Deloitte, 2023).

HP Hewlett-Packard provides a customizable approach to its printers, catering to the diverse needs and preferences of its customers. This flexibility allows users to select from various features and options, tailoring their printers to fit specific requirements. Customers can choose the size of the printer to ensure it fits well within their workspace, select from a range of colours to match their office or home decor, and decide on connectivity options that best suit their operational needs, whether it is traditional wired connections or more modern wireless capabilities.

Warby Parker allows customers to try on glasses at home for free before they buy them. This helps customers to find the perfect pair of glasses for their face shape and style. Warby Parker also offers a variety of customization options for its glasses, such as custom lens prescriptions and frame colours. These examples demonstrate the widespread adoption of personalization in consumer markets, with the goal of enhancing user experience and engagement.

Personalization and co-creation

Driven by the ever-evolving complexity of human needs, our focus on products has shifted beyond mere attributes like appearance and quality. Today, consumers seek deeper fulfilment, encompassing social aspirations and personal growth. This necessitates a service-dominant logic, where companies prioritize customized consumer engagement to build lasting relationships and cater to diverse desires (Lusch and Nambisan, 2015).

Service-dominant logic is a theoretical framework that reimagines how value is created and exchanged in markets. It positions co-creation at its core, envisioning value as an emergent property arising from collaborative interactions and the integration of resources among participants (Assiouras et al., 2019; Prahalad and Ramaswamy, 2004). In this view, value is not embedded in goods or services themselves but is co-created through the experiences and contributions of all involved, including providers and consumers. Consumers and companies, along with brands, engage in a dynamic dialogue, shaping experiences that resonate with individual needs and preferences. This mutual communication acts as the common denominator in the exchange process, transforming the mere transaction of goods into the co-creation of value, fostering connections that can last. In essence, companies no longer solely sell products. They co-create experiences with their consumers, forging long-term relationships built on shared value and mutual understanding (Zine et al., 2014). By involving customers in the co-creation process, businesses can also gather unique insights into individual preferences, which directly feed into product design personalization, allowing for more customized and user-centric offerings.

Personalization design and user participation

Personalization design involves creating offerings whose functions and features align with each user's abilities and preferences, often requiring adjustments to specifications based on specific customer requirements through direct interaction between designers and customers. Each individual has unique physical and psychological traits, as well as a distinct environment that includes products, services, and social connections. Although personalization providers do not control these individual or environmental factors, they collect insights from them (Zine et al., 2014). With this information, companies design and deliver products and services that specifically meet the individual's needs. Moreover, individuals can evaluate these functions and features, offering feedback to the personalization provider for future improvements. This cycle of user feedback and design updates promotes continuous enhancement, ensuring that personalized products and services stay relevant and address changing user requirements. Kaneko et al. (2018) outline a framework for designing personalization strategies, delineated as follows:

Full-order personalization: Customers specify their desired product features in great detail, reflecting their unique preferences. This is a highly individualized approach, akin to ordering bespoke suits, where each aspect is tailored to the customer's specifications.

Pattern-order personalization: Customers select their preferred attributes from a set of available options, such as in car customization, where choices are made from predetermined alternatives.

Expert diagnosis: Companies assess customers' needs and suggest suitable solutions, based on professional evaluations. This approach is used in scenarios like creating prosthetic limbs, where expert knowledge dictates the customization.

Matching: Companies align prepared products or services with the identified needs of target customers, as seen in webshop recommendations, where items are suggested based on customer profiles.

Upgrading for an individual: Companies introduce new features or enhancements, and customers assess their value, exemplified by the personalized services offered in first-class hotel hospitality.

Personal reconfiguration: Customers add or remove features from a product as per their needs, similar to installing or uninstalling apps on a smartphone, allowing for dynamic personalization.

Data acquisition: Products or services automatically gather and use personal data to refine performance, like the auto-correction feature in text entry, which adapts based on individual typing habits.

Monitoring and advice: Products or services collect user data and offer tailored responses from a range of options, such as integrated fitness apps that provide personalized health and exercise recommendations.

This framework describes various dimensions of personalization, from highly individualized, customer-driven specifications to more standardized, provider-driven options, each with its own context of application.

Personalization design thus emphasizes the need for user involvement throughout the product design process as user-generated content (UGC), particularly customer reviews, has been shown to be more credible than retailer/manufacturer promotional material (Meybaum, 2014). The emergence of Web 2.0 was hailed as a significant technological advancement due to the newfound ability of users to upload their own content to the internet for others to view and engage with. Businesses have now recognized that this vast repository of public opinions can be harnessed to enhance their own popularity and financial success. Hestad (2013) proposes a three-stage framework for product design: inspiration, ideation, and implementation. Each stage necessitates a distinct level of user involvement to ensure product success.

Inspiration stage: There is a need for user consultation during the inspiration stage to identify market gaps and assess the shortcomings of existing products. This type of research is exploratory, utilizing users as a supplementary source of creativity for designers.

Ideation stage: The ideation stage represents a more refined phase in the design process, where a specific niche has been identified. User involvement is limited to those who fit the profile of the target end-user. Users are consulted on current trends, colours, and materials, as well as their anticipated usage patterns. This stage often reveals discrepancies between intended and actual product usage.

Implementation stage: The implementation stage involves less extensive user research, with users primarily engaged in design testing to evaluate usability and identify potential issues before mass production.

Meybaum (2014) argues that user involvement is needed at every stage of the design process. Although specifically referring to the ways in which virtual prototyping can aid in the product design process, Meybaum nevertheless shows how important it is to have both customer and stakeholder feedback at every step, including the initial stages of deciding whether or not there is a place in the market for such a product. Leahy (2013) takes a slightly different stance while still being in broad agreement with both Hestad and Meybaum. Leahy believes that a new format for product design has been developing whereby users produce the 'what' for a new product (i.e. what product is needed) and the designers produce the 'how' (i.e. building the product itself and bringing it to the market). Leahy has gone a step further from both Hestad and Meybaum and suggests that to develop a successful product, both users and designers should fill set roles in the process in order to maximize end satisfaction. In this way, production is as efficient as possible, and the need for multiple rounds of research is kept to a minimum.

A second direction taken by researchers on the positive involvement of users in production design describes the types of user involvement that can be effectively employed in the design process. Broadly speaking, there are two different types of user involvement: user-centred product design and participatory product design or co-creation.

User-centred design involves consulting end-users at each stage of the design process. Moran (2012) focused on the success that user-centred design can bring by highlighting the 4moms case study, where the designer concentrated on consulting with a small focus group of mothers to design a new pram. The ingenuity and originality of the product that resulted have created a growth rate of 200–400 per cent for the company annually, showing just how effective and profitable user-centred design can be. The participatory design process views users not as those asked to approve the ideas of professional designers at each stage, but as continuous partners or co-creators throughout the process (Sanders and Stappers 2008). Sanders and Stappers go on to say that user-centred design cannot cope with the complexity of modern users' needs due to its focus on a specific end-product. Participatory design, however, is more open-ended, and with the involvement of close user-designer collaboration throughout the process, it results in more innovative and successful products.

Further support for the participatory design process comes from Dell'Era and Landoni (2014), who have conducted more in-depth research to suggest why design through co-creation has more advantages than that of user-centred design. Although their work centres around the concept of a 'living lab', a more advanced version of co-creation, they nevertheless state that while user-centred design is able to record and implement the explicit needs of users (i.e. the needs they speak about), the participatory design process is able to record not only the users' explicit needs but also those that are observable, tacit, and latent (accessed from what users say, do, make, and aspire towards). In this way, the process of product design is enhanced: products are produced with the maximum insight into their end use, which makes it certain before production that there will be a successful place in the market for them.

Van Dijck (2009) states that since the 1980s, the term 'prosumer' has been used to denote the way in which more and more power is shifting to the consumer in the digital age to the point where their role is now partly that of the producer also. This is confirmed by the case study on LEGO carried out by Antorini et al. (2012). It states how, once LEGO had become aware of their split target markets (both children and adults), they were able to build a strong online community of fans and put their ideas into production. In this way, the loyal fan base was satisfied by seeing their dream LEGO sets become a reality, and LEGO as a business knew before releasing the product that it would be a hit on the market.

Personalized production

Personalized production is a production method in which products are custom-made to meet the specific needs of individual customers. In today's competitive marketplace, many businesses are finding that personalized production is becoming more important. However, personalized production can be more expensive and time-consuming than mass production. Businesses need to carefully consider their needs and goals before deciding which approach is best for them.

Personalized production uses new technologies, such as 3D printing, laser cutting, and CNC machining, to produce custom goods and services to meet the individual needs of customers. It uses employees' skills and knowledge to create unique products for each customer. The production system builds on Big Data analysis, machine learning, and AI supply chains. This is different from flexible manufacturing systems. A furniture maker may use personalized production to create custom-made furniture for individual customers. The furniture maker may work with each customer to design a piece of furniture that meets their specific needs and style.

3D printing, laser cutting, and CNC machining are all powerful digital fabrication processes that can be used to create a wide variety of personalized products and objects. The best process to use will depend on the specific application. 3D printing is a process of making a three-dimensional solid object from a digital file. The object is created by adding layers of material, such as plastic, metal, or ceramic, until the desired shape is formed. 3D printing is a versatile process that can be used to create a wide variety of products, from toys and jewellery to medical implants and prosthetics. Laser cutting is a process of using a laser to cut through material. The laser is focused on a specific area of the material, causing it to heat up and vaporize. Laser cutting can be used to cut through a variety of materials, including wood, plastic, metal, and glass.

CNC machining is a process of using computer-controlled machines to cut, mill, or drill material. The CNC machine is programmed with a digital file that specifies the desired shape of the object. The machine then follows the programme to cut, mill, or drill the material accordingly. CNC machining is a versatile process that can be used to create a wide variety of products, from parts for cars and airplanes to medical devices and jewellery.

Personalized selling

Drawing on the success of personalized selling in digital businesses, we can gain valuable insights into how this approach can be applied to build stronger relationships with customers and understand their individual needs (Montgomery and Smith, 2009). Salespeople who use personalized selling techniques will adapt their sales pitch to each customer and offer solutions that meet their specific needs. Customers are increasingly demanding personalized experiences, and businesses that can provide this will be more likely to succeed.

Beyond captivating audiences in the content industry, personalized selling also empowers businesses across various other sectors, including:

Financial services: Financial advisers can use personalized selling to help clients achieve their financial goals. The adviser will work with each client to understand their individual needs and develop a financial plan that suits their specific situation.

Custom tailoring: Custom tailors use personalized selling to sell high-quality, custom-made suits. The tailor meets with each customer individually to discuss their needs and preferences. They then take measurements and create a custom suit for the customer. This process is more time-consuming and expensive than mass production, but it allows the tailor to create a suit that is perfectly tailored to the customer's individual needs.

Luxury car dealerships: Luxury car dealerships use personalized selling to sell their high-value vehicles. For example, the dealership may have a team of experienced salespeople who are experts in luxury cars. These salespeople may build relationships with customers and understand their individual needs before making a sales pitch. The goal is to offer each customer a personalized experience and sell them the car that is the best fit for their needs.

Comparing personalized selling with arm's length trade

Arm's length trade is a type of business transaction where the buyer and seller are independent parties who have no prior relationship with each other. The transaction is conducted on a level playing field, with both parties acting in their own best interests. Arm's length trades are typically impersonal and do not take into account the individual needs or preferences of the buyer or seller.

In contrast, personalized selling is a modern commercial approach that uses data and analytics to create personalized experiences for customers. As the focus is on building relationships with customers and understanding their individual needs, this allows businesses to adapt their sales messages and offerings to each customer, which can lead to higher sales and customer satisfaction. The approach is often used by businesses

Table 2 Arm's Length Trade vs Personalization

Feature	Arm's length trade	Personalization
Aims and goals	Transaction-centric – emphasis on exchanging goods or services: The emphasis is on completing the exchange of goods or services for a set price. The buyer and seller act independently, with minimal focus on the specific needs or preferences of the individual involved.	Individual-centric – adapting experiences to customer preferences: The goal is to tailor the experience to the specific needs and preferences of the customer (preferences may also be driven by wider social factors). This might involve offering product recommendations, discounts, or services based on past purchases or browsing history.
Interaction	Limited – minimal effort to build relationships: There's less emphasis on building a relationship with the buyer. The interaction is transactional – you pay, you get the product.	Greater – engaged interactions to foster loyalty: Companies may use targeted selling campaigns, personalized recommendations, or loyalty programmes to build relationships with customers and encourage repeat business.
Offerings	Standardized – uniform products and services: Products and services are typically offered in a standard form with little variation. Think of buying a loaf of bread at the grocery store – it's the same for everyone.	Customized – tailored to individual preferences and needs: Products and services can be adapted to fit individual preferences. For example, online stores may allow customization of clothing or computer builds.
Privacy and intrusiveness	Minimal concerns: Less data collection.	Potential concerns: Increased data collection can raise privacy issues.
Customer experience	Transactional: Efficiency and simplicity.	Long term: Customer satisfaction leading to brand loyalty, higher customer lifetime value, and positive word-of-mouth communication.

that sell customized products or services; for example, digital business platforms have often relied on this selling approach. Arm's length trade and personalized selling are, therefore, two distinct approaches to sales that produce contrasting results. Table 2 summarizes the key differences between arm's length trade and personalized selling.

This table compares the impersonal, transaction-focused nature of arm's length trade with the individualized, relationship-oriented approach of personalization, underlining the differences in aims and goals, interaction, offerings, concerns about privacy, and the overall customer experience.

Personalized promotion

In the contemporary marketing field, personalized marketing signifies a departure from generic marketing techniques, favouring a more personalized interaction that mirrors a direct conversation between brands and individuals. Personalized marketing customizes advertisements to individual online activities, showcasing products or services that align with previous interactions or searches (Kumar et al., 2019; De Keyzer et al., 2022; Pfiffelmann et al., 2020). This customization extends to television advertising, which adapts to consumer viewing patterns to present relevant promotions. Moreover, this era is distinguished by its interactive nature, moving beyond unidirectional communication. Companies now engage in dialogues with consumers through various channels such as emails and chatbots, enhancing the understanding of consumer needs and preferences. Mobile devices have also now become a key tool for marketers to develop highly contextual and personalized marketing campaigns (Tong et al., 2020).

These strategies also influence product development, with companies applying consumer insights to refine existing products and innovate new ones that cater to specific consumer demands. The efficacy of personalized marketing lies in its relevance to the individual, fostering a deeper connection and trust. This targeted approach not only captures attention but also increases the likelihood of consumer engagement and conversion, marking a substantial evolution from conventional marketing practices towards a more engaged and personalized marketing environment.

Personalization and organizational change

Delivering a seamless personalized experience requires more than just technology; it demands a fundamental shift in how companies operate. This change necessitates a reevaluation of organizational structures, fostering agility and adaptability to meet evolving customer expectations. Personalization therefore stands in stark contrast to the standardized, mass-production models of the past, exemplified by Weberian bureaucracy and Fordism. Driven by technological advancements and a shift towards the service economy, personalization represents a fundamental transformation in how goods and services are produced, consumed, and organized. Consequently, personalization is not just about what is offered; it is also about how businesses operate. Companies embracing personalization often become more agile and adaptable. They achieve this through flatter organizational structures, where teams with diverse skills work together. Besides, a culture that encourages experimentation and rapid improvement becomes key. This allows businesses to quickly adjust to changing market trends, customer feedback, and new technologies, keeping them competitive in the digital age.

Personalization also leads to greater efficiency. By automating routine tasks and optimizing workflows, companies can free up valuable resources. This not only reduces costs but also empowers employees to focus on more strategic and creative work, further driving innovation and business growth. In essence, personalization equips businesses with the tools and mindset to excel in the digital economy. It encourages stronger customer relationships through catered experiences and builds a more responsive and efficient internal organization. This two-pronged approach positions businesses for sustainable success in today's dynamic market.

Personalized pricing

Imagine 'NewTech', an online retailer specializing in electronics and tech gadgets. To stay competitive and maximize revenue, NewTech decides to implement a dynamic pricing strategy using advanced algorithms and real-time market data to adjust prices on the fly.

NewTech's venture into dynamic pricing starts with integrating a sophisticated AI-driven system designed to analyse various variables including demand trends, competitor pricing, inventory levels, and customer behaviour patterns. This system is capable of processing real-time data from multiple sources, ensuring NewTech's pricing strategy is continuously informed by the latest market conditions. For example, when launching a new smartphone, NewTech sets competitive prices to attract early adopters. The AI system closely monitors sales velocity, competitor actions, and stock levels. As demand increases and initial stock begins to deplete, the system gradually raises the price, capitalizing on the high demand while monitoring competitor pricing to stay competitive.

Conversely, if a particular laptop model is not selling as expected and a newer model is about to be released, the system recognizes the stagnant inventory and automatically lowers the price to clear out old stock and make room for new arrivals. This dynamic pricing strategy is also responsive to seasonal trends and special events. For instance, during the holiday season when demand for electronics surges, NewTech's system smartly adjusts prices to optimize profits while offering competitive deals. During slower periods, it might provide more aggressive discounts to boost sales.

Moreover, NewTech uses the system to personalize prices for loyal customers through loyalty programmes, offering special discounts based on their shopping history and preferences, thus enhancing customer satisfaction and retention. Throughout this journey, NewTech maintains transparency with its customers about its dynamic pricing, emphasizing benefits like better deals and personalized offers. The company also establishes ethical pricing boundaries to maintain trust and avoid potential backlash.

Price setting is a pivotal design decision for platforms, significantly influencing user engagement, market dynamics, and overall success. The chosen pricing model can determine a platform's trajectory, either driving growth or hindering progress. Platforms typically adopt either centralized or decentralized pricing strategies. Centralized pricing allows platforms to maintain control over pricing, ensuring consistency and optimizing revenue. This model is common in sectors where price uniformity is critical, such as ride-sharing or online retail. On the other hand, decentralized pricing empowers users to set their own prices, attracting a diverse user base, although it can also result in price volatility and consumer confusion. Ultimately, the optimal pricing strategy should align with the platform's mission and growth objectives. By carefully evaluating their pricing models, platforms can make informed decisions that support long-term success in a competitive digital landscape.

The rise of personalized pricing

While personalized marketing draws consumers with targeted messages, personalized pricing takes this a step further by offering prices that reflect individual buying behaviours and preferences. This strategy permits businesses to optimize both customer satisfaction and profitability. Personalized pricing, once limited to high-stakes transactions involving items like suits and vehicles, has now permeated everyday consumer products (Li, Wang, and Nault, 2024; Elegido, 2011; Waldfogel, 2015). This pricing strategy adjusts prices for individual consumers based on various factors and is applied across numerous sectors, including essential services like electricity and fuel, online shopping, sports, entertainment, professional programmes, financial and insurance industries, and informational goods markets (Balmaceda and Soruco, 2008; Waldfogel, 2015). For instance, Coca-Cola has experimented with vending machines that change prices according to seasonal and weather conditions, charging more on hotter days to reflect increased demand.

Algorithmic price discrimination, as described by Bar-Gill (2019), occurs when sellers use consumer data to set personalized prices based on each consumer's willingness to pay (WTP). This form of price discrimination, powered by Big Data, allows sellers to segment their customer base into increasingly specific groups, assigning distinct prices to each. In the Fast-Moving Consumer Goods (FMCG) industry, personalized pricing benefits both consumers and companies by offering more affordable purchases, discounts on preferred products during peak demand, and loyalty rewards such as discounted movie tickets.

The adoption of personalized pricing has the potential to transform daily transactions by allowing prices to respond to distinct scenarios and consumer actions. By leveraging consumer data, personalized pricing models provide targeted experiences through dynamic price adjustments (Fisher et al., 2018). Furthermore, this data-driven approach helps optimize resource allocation by adjusting prices to encourage the sale of products before they expire or their demand season ends, thereby minimizing waste.

This data-driven approach falls under two main categories:

(1) Dynamic pricing, also known as surge pricing, demand pricing, or time-based pricing, involves setting flexible prices for products or services based on current market demands, including consumer demand, market competition, and external factors like weather. This strategy is widely used in sectors such as e-commerce and airlines, supported by advanced algorithmic tools from companies like Amazon and Google (Calvano et al., 2019).

Dynamic pricing involves setting flexible prices for products or services based on real-time supply and demand dynamics. For instance, airline tickets and hotel room rates may increase as availability decreases or drop if demand is low close to the service date. Prices can vary based on the time of day, day of the week, or season e.g., electricity providers might use dynamic pricing to promote energy usage when it is cheaper and more plentiful. Prices may also surge during special events or holidays when demand is exceptionally high, such as sports events, concerts, or New Year's Eve. In addition, companies may adjust their prices in response to competitors' pricing changes to remain competitive in the market.

Hoffreumon et al. (2024) explore the adoption of AI technology by companies, whether through acquiring commercial off-the-shelf software, developing or tailoring solutions internally, or employing a combination of both approaches. Their research reveals that using off-the-shelf software for AI implementation has become a widespread practice, with the interplay between different sourcing strategies being prevalent across various industries.

Companies gather detailed consumer data from digital interactions, including cookies and browsing histories. Such data drives advanced algorithms capable of accurately determining a customer's WTP, enabling firms to align prices with individual preferences (Xu and Dukes, 2019). For example, recognizing a customer's brand loyalty could lead to tailored pricing for certain products.

(2) Personalized pricing, or individualized pricing, is a strategy where businesses use data analytics to set prices based on individual customer characteristics, behaviours, or circumstances (Li, Wang, and Nault, 2024). This includes factors like purchasing history, browsing behaviour, demand sensitivity, location, or the device used. By analysing data from customer interactions, such as past purchases and search history, companies create detailed customer profiles. Advanced algorithms and machine learning models predict how much a particular customer is willing to pay at a given moment, allowing for real-time price adjustments based on new data or changing market conditions. Additionally, personalized pricing can involve targeted discounts, special offers, or incentives designed to convert or retain specific customers.

The effectiveness of personalized pricing depends on customer willingness to share their data, a trend especially notable in the smartphone app industry. Here, negotiating the trade-off between lower prices and privacy becomes pivotal (Kummer and Schulte, 2019; Fisher et al., 2018). For instance, apps may be offered at discounted rates to users consenting to data collection. While personalized pricing can improve consumer welfare through customized discounts, it is important to consider potential downsides. Privacy-concerned individuals may be reluctant to share their data, potentially disadvantaging or excluding them from the market (Bardakci and Whitelock, 2004).

The use of sophisticated algorithms to deduce specific preferences and create highly customized propositions may be seen as intrusive, subtly steering consumers towards decisions without full clarity (Odlyzko, 2003). However, in certain scenarios, consumers might view personalized pricing favourably. Franke and Schreier's (2008) research indicates that consumers who participate in the design or creation process (through co-creation or co-production) tend to see the resulting product as distinctive and are often willing to pay more for it than for standard, off-the-shelf products.

Recent studies also show the potential welfare benefits associated with dynamic pricing. Williams (2022) suggests that dynamic pricing can enhance overall welfare despite creating disparities among winners and losers. In an online marketplace context, where product pricing is determined by third-party sellers' algorithms, Johnson et al. (2023) demonstrate that this setup can intensify competition among algorithms, potentially leading to reduced prices. While personalized pricing, adapted to individual preferences, has the potential to improve consumer welfare, it also poses a risk of alienating those concerned about privacy and reluctant to share data (Kummer and Schulte, 2019; Seele et al., 2019).

Dynamic pricing and food waste: A case study

A recent report from The Telegraph (Ross, 2023) highlights a growing trend among grocery stores to adopt AI to reduce food waste. This innovative approach implements automatic pricing mechanisms to adjust product prices in real time, eliminating the need for traditional manual markdowns with yellow stickers. This method allows customers to more easily notice and purchase discounted items, thereby enhancing the efficiency of reducing food waste. This AI-driven pricing strategy is currently undergoing trials in various supermarkets across the UK, with plans for broader testing. Retail analysts suggest that such dynamic pricing models could lower consumer costs, especially for meat and fresh produce, and potentially increase supermarket profits by as much as 30 per cent by minimizing waste.

Morrisons has taken initial steps by implementing electronic shelf labels (ESLs) in a select number of its existing stores, as well as in two new outlets opened in Chelmsford and Newcastle. Similarly, Asda has concluded a pilot involving twenty-five thousand products and is extending its ESL trial to include both packaged and unpackaged fruits and vegetables at its Middleton branch in Rochdale, Lancashire. Other major retailers like Sainsbury's and Tesco have previously conducted ESL trials, and Waitrose is reportedly considering testing the system. Discount supermarkets such as Lidl, Aldi, and M&S have also adopted ESLs in some of their stores. According to David Kat from the food waste firm Wasteless, ESLs enable retailers to update prices several times throughout the day, providing a flexible and responsive pricing strategy that can significantly contribute to waste reduction efforts.

Surge pricing

Surge pricing is a dynamic pricing model used by Uber to adjust ride prices during periods of high demand and low supply. This system aims to encourage more drivers to become available and to moderate rider requests during peak times. Surge pricing typically occurs during busy hours, such as Friday and Saturday nights, and major events. The pricing is calculated based on factors like the number of ride requests, driver availability, and estimated travel times. When in effect, a multiplier is applied to the base fare, making rides more expensive. For example, a $10 ride could cost $15 with a 1.5×

surge multiplier. Riders are informed of the surge multiplier beforehand and can choose to wait until prices normalize, although this might result in longer wait times.

The advantages of surge pricing for riders include generally affordable transportation and increased driver availability during high-demand periods. Riders can see surge prices in advance, helping them make informed decisions. However, disadvantages include potentially high ride costs during peak times, unpredictability of surge pricing, and perceptions of unfairness when alternatives are limited. For drivers, surge pricing can feel inequitable, especially in consistently low-demand areas. The influx of drivers during surge periods can lead to more traffic and congestion. Additionally, drivers might receive negative feedback from riders unhappy with surge prices.

In summary, surge pricing is a complex issue with benefits and drawbacks for both riders and drivers. While it aims to balance supply and demand and ensure driver availability, it can result in higher costs for riders and contribute to traffic congestion.

Price discrimination: A double-edged sword

In pricing strategies, the concept of price fairness is crucial, as consumer perceptions of fairness significantly influence the acceptance of personalized pricing. These perceptions are shaped by factors such as the variability in prices for different individuals and the violation of social norms. For instance, when consumers discover they are paying more than others or when personalized pricing deviates from accepted social norms – like offering lower prices to new customers – feelings of unfairness or manipulation may arise. This can lead to diminished trust and decreased demand (Koh et al., 2017). To counter fairness concerns, companies may conceal price details to deter comparisons and present personalized pricing as exclusive offers. Presenting personalized prices as unique deals can alleviate fairness issues and boost consumer receptivity.

While it may seem unfair to charge some customers more than others, there are potential benefits for both consumers and companies. One advantage of price discrimination is that it can make a product or service accessible to a wider range of consumers, including those who may not be able to afford the full price. For example, a company that offers a discounted price for students or seniors may be able to attract new customers who would otherwise be priced out of the market. Furthermore, price discrimination can allow companies to charge a higher price to those who are willing to pay more, thereby increasing their overall revenue. This can be particularly beneficial for companies that offer products or services that are highly valued by certain segments of the population.

Rakowski (2004), therefore, argues that price discrimination can offer societal benefits if implemented effectively. He presents the hypothetical example of a country doctor:

> If he charged a uniform $80 for an office visit, only a small number of his potential patients could afford his services, his practice would be too small for him to survive financially, and the community would be unserved. If he charged only $20, his patient base might double; but his revenues would be even less, still less conducive to his survival. But being plugged into the community as he is, he has a good idea of the financial situation of each patient. If he charges the poor patients

as little as $20 (which is, say, his marginal cost) and the rich patients $120, he may be able to serve the entire community at an average price of $70 and ensure his own financial survival. (Rakowski, 2004: 265)

In this scenario, by charging lower prices from low-income patients and higher prices from wealthier patients, the country doctor can increase his overall revenue and serve a wider segment of the community. This approach allows him to cover his costs, maintain a viable practice, and provide essential medical services to those who would otherwise be unable to afford them.

Potential threats to consumers

Although data collection techniques provide advantages to consumers, they simultaneously present significant risks (Kummer and Schulte, 2019). Price discrimination is identified by Odlyzko (2003) as a primary threat to consumers, challenging Rakowski et al.'s (2004) earlier assessment. Spiekermann (2006) provides an example of this, describing how Amazon varied prices for different customers based on their consumer profiles. These profiles were constructed from data Amazon had gathered about them from previous purchases. In response to a strongly negative reaction from consumers, Amazon discontinued this practice from its marketing strategy. Despite consumer concerns associated with price discrimination, many companies continue to engage in this practice as it represents an easy and effective means for businesses to extract higher profits from unsuspecting consumers (Odlyzko, 2003).

Balancing benefits and fairness

While price discrimination can offer societal benefits, it is important to carefully consider its potential drawbacks. Charging different prices to different customers can raise concerns about fairness and transparency, and it may be challenging to implement effectively and equitably. Personalized pricing could worsen economic disparities, with wealthier individuals receiving more advantageous deals. Ensuring fairness requires companies to be transparent about their pricing methods and to communicate clearly with consumers. Implementing personalized pricing depends on collecting and analysing vast amounts of consumer data. Safeguarding this data and ensuring consumers have control over their personal information is paramount. Companies should implement price discrimination strategies with a clear understanding of their market, customer needs, and the ethical implications of their pricing decisions. Transparency in pricing practices and clear communication with customers can help build trust and minimize perceptions of unfairness.

Personalization: A glimpse into a more sophisticated and ethical approach

The trajectory of personalization is set to accelerate, propelled by advancements in AI and machine learning technologies. These innovations will enable more sophisticated, real-time, and context-aware personalization, customizing experiences to individual preferences and behaviours with unprecedented accuracy. However, the realization of this potential is contingent upon addressing ethical considerations, ensuring user control over personal data, and maintaining transparency in data usage practices. These factors are critical in shaping the responsible implementation of personalization technologies in alignment with user expectations.

Likewise, emerging technologies such as augmented reality (AR), virtual reality (VR), and the Internet of Things (IoT) (or a digital twin) are expected to significantly enhance the delivery of personalized experiences across various domains. AR and VR technologies have the capacity to generate highly personalized virtual environments that adapt to individual aesthetic preferences and functional needs. Concurrently, IoT devices can provide real-time insights into users' interactions and environments, enriching the contextual data available for personalization algorithms. The convergence of these technologies promises to revolutionize the integration of personalization into daily life, offering more immersive and satisfying experiences.

In essence, personalization strategies in digital marketplaces are not just about matching products to people. They are about creating an adaptive, learning environment that aligns economic incentives with individual human needs and aspirations. It is a shift from the industrial-age model of standardization and scale to an information-age model of individuation and relevance. This shift has profound implications. It suggests that in the digital age, the most successful firms would not be those that merely aggregate the most users or list the most products. They will be those that excel at understanding and serving the unique 'markets of one' that each user represents. It points to a future where economic success is less about mass appeal and more about mass customization, less about pushing products and more about nurturing relationships.

Moreover, this model of personalization could extend far beyond commerce. It suggests ways that education could be adapted to individual learning styles, healthcare personalized to genetic profiles, or civic engagement customized to personal values and local issues. In this light, digital marketplaces are not just transforming how we buy and sell; they are pioneering a new paradigm of human-centric, data-driven systems that could reshape how we learn, govern, and interact. Naturally, this vision comes with challenges. The data required for such deep personalization raises serious privacy concerns. The algorithms that power these systems could encode biases or be manipulated for profit over user well-being. And there is a risk that hyper-personalization could create filter bubbles, isolating us from diverse viewpoints and products.

But if we can navigate these challenges – through a combination of ethical AI development, robust governance, and user empowerment – the potential is immense. We stand on the cusp of an economic model that does not just maximize transactions but optimizes for human flourishing – a model where technology does not homogenize us into masses but celebrates and serves our uniqueness. In this light, the continuous refinement of personalization strategies in digital marketplaces is not just a business imperative; it is a stepping stone towards a more humane, responsive, and fulfilling economic future.

6

Human creativity and personalizing work experiences

Owen, a finance analyst at a multinational corporation, found himself at a crossroads. While he was comfortable with traditional finance tools and software, the industry's shift towards data-driven decision-making and advanced analytics tools presented him with a challenge. Recognizing the need for employees to keep up with industry trends, Owen's company introduced an AI-driven personalized learning platform for skill development.

Upon starting, the platform conducted an initial assessment to understand Owen's current skill level and learning preferences. Through a series of questions and mini-tasks, the platform assessed Owen's proficiency with traditional tools and identified gaps in areas like Python programming, machine learning basics, and data visualization.

Armed with this information, the platform crafted a sequential learning path specifically designed for Owen's needs. It started with foundational Python for finance, followed by modules on data visualization tools like Tableau. Recognizing Owen's preferred learning style, the system customized his lessons accordingly, blending video explanations with hands-on practical tasks. As Owen worked on a Python exercise, he encountered a particular function that proved to be challenging. The platform, ever vigilant, instantly recommended a supplemental video, helping him grasp the concept better. This real-time support ensured that Owen didn't get stuck and could continue making progress.

The platform also recognized the power of collaborative learning. It introduced Owen to Clara, another finance professional from a different department who was also learning Python. They engaged in peer code reviews and tackled complex problems together, enhancing their collaborative problem-solving skills. This peer-to-peer learning provided Owen with a supportive environment to practice and refine his skills. Once Owen became comfortable with basic Python, the platform offered project-based learning. He was given real-world finance problems to solve using Python, aligning with his job role. This approach ensured that Owen was not just learning theoretically but was also prepared to integrate his new skills into his daily work.

To keep Owen motivated and engaged, the platform incorporated a gamified approach. Every milestone Owen achieved, like completing a module or a project, earned him badges and points. This gamification strategy proved to be effective, as

Owen continued to demonstrate enthusiasm and dedication throughout his learning journey. To bridge the gap between theory and practice, the platform had a feature that integrated with the tools Owen used at work. This allowed him to directly apply what he learned, such as automating a previously manual data extraction process using Python. This work-integrated learning approach ensured that Owen's newly acquired skills had an immediate impact on his productivity.

Over a year, Owen's journey transformed him from being solely a traditional finance analyst to someone who could harness the power of data analytics in decision-making. He created a predictive model that forecasted market trends with 85 percent accuracy, earning him recognition and respect within his company.

Owen's story shows the transformative potential of artificial intelligence (AI)-driven personalized learning in the workplace. By adapting the learning experience to Owen's individual needs and professional goals, the AI-powered platform played an instrumental role in his success story. This symbiotic relationship of upskilling and company growth demonstrates how AI can not only empower employees but also drive organizational success.

One of the most evident benefits that AI could bring to the broader workplace is personalization (Dutta et al., 2022). AI has been successfully employed in recent years to create more customized experiences for users. For instance, a new employee might require training in a specific skill that the company values, and AI could personalize a training programme that focuses on their weaknesses while avoiding areas they already understand. Put differently, AI creates intelligent content tailored to the specific demographics and traits of employees (Gulliford and Parker, 2019). As AI continues to improve the modern workplace, its applications are becoming more varied and impactful. From personalizing learning and development for individual employees to streamlining organizational processes, AI is redefining how we approach work. This chapter explores several ways AI is enhancing the workplace, including personalizing experiences, improving human resource practices, and enabling more efficient business operations.

Introducing the AI technology

AI emerged as a research field in the 1950s with the goal of understanding and replicating human intelligence. AI has changed our daily lives, from voice assistants like Alexa and Siri to personalized recommendations on platforms like Netflix. It is now poised to transform the workplace with its vast potential for performance improvement, as discussed in Chapter 3. The modern workplace demands a shift away from traditional production methods to remain competitive. AI empowers companies to modernize their processes and achieve greater efficiency. Predictive analytics, chatbots, real-time feedback tools, and collaboration tools are just a few examples of how AI can enhance productivity.

Chatbots, for instance, can interact with employees and customers, enabling AI systems to learn patterns and behaviours, record data, and conduct analyses.

Effective communication is crucial in any workplace, and chatbots can enhance employee interactions by making them more interactive and collaborative, leading to an improved employee experience (Brougham and Haar, 2018; Bansal et al., 2023). A recent study by Dutta et al. (2022) shows that AI chatbots can help employees and organizations minimize barriers, thereby enhancing the effectiveness and fairness of employee performance appraisals. AI chatbots serve as a bridge between organizations and employees. Over time, once a climate of trust has developed, these chatbots can improve employee performance by acting as a direct communication channel within the organization, providing employees with personalized work goals based on their specific situations, and tracking the completion of current tasks.

AI can also utilize biometric data to gauge engagement levels. This data enables companies to personalize their relationship management strategies with employees, customers, and other key stakeholders. Employee engagement is a paramount concern for most firms, and the adoption of AI empowers them to effectively evaluate and engage employees using technology. However, it is important to recognize that human interaction remains a critical aspect of engagement, and employee relationship management should continue to incorporate human interaction.

AI possesses the potential to automate aspects of the workforce, including certain human resource activities. Charlwood and Guenole (2022) suggest that AI's most significant impact will be on transactional work, which is a core function of human resources. AI can automate repetitive tasks, allowing management professionals to focus on strategic initiatives. This raises the question of which areas of human resource operations are most susceptible to AI automation (Pan and Froese, 2023). Potential areas include payroll management, applicant tracking systems, résumé sorting, timesheets, and time-off requests.

As management often involves face-to-face human interaction, it is challenging to predict the full extent of AI's advancement in this domain. Nevertheless, AI has the potential to revolutionize management practices through daily application, enhancing work efficiency and highlighting the use of machine learning for workplace policies. Machine learning can be used to continuously improve decision-making, including the analysis of workplace policies. This is beneficial for companies to adopt as it allows them to constantly update and maintain workplace policies that perfectly reflect their organization. Consequently, the use of AI has a positive impact on company performance by relieving staff of an intense workload and allowing them to focus on other more strategic and creative work (Gulliford and Parker, 2019).

AI and organization and management

As organizations increasingly adopt technologies like AI and machine learning to automate existing processes, innovators are going a step further by radically reimagining work architecture to maximize the synergy between human and machine capabilities. This groundbreaking approach is not just about efficiency; it is about reinventing how work is structured and executed, leveraging the strengths of both humans and machines.

Such pioneering work architecture aims to complement human skills with machine precision and endurance, resulting in a collaborative environment where each contributes its best. This can lead to the creation of new roles where human workers oversee, manage, and complement automated systems, turning their attention to tasks that require creativity, emotional intelligence, and strategic thinking – abilities that machines have yet to master.

By redefining roles and tasks, organizations can harness the full potential of their workforce, offering employees the chance to develop new skills and advance their careers in directions aligned with the evolution of technology. As a result, career paths may become more diversified and dynamic, with an emphasis on continuous learning and adaptation. Moreover, this change has the potential to address significant societal challenges such as job displacement due to automation, as it focuses on the human element within the digital transformation. It prompts a reassessment of educational and training programmes to prepare the current and future workforce for an increasingly automated world, where humans and machines collaborate closely.

In essence, the pioneers of work architecture are setting the stage for a future where technology amplifies human potential, and where the definition of work is continuously evolving, leading to a more adaptable, skilled, and future-ready human workforce.

Changes in work architecture

The significant opportunity at hand extends beyond merely redesigning jobs; it involves a fundamental rethinking of 'work architecture'. This process requires deconstructing work into its essential elements, such as assessment, production, problem-solving, communication, and supervision. Subsequently, it includes exploring new ways for machines and humans to collaborate to fulfil these components, each employing their unique strengths. To thoroughly understand the implications of AI on work and company management practices, it thus becomes critical to explore the diverse effects and their impact on business management as a whole (Vrontis et al., 2022; Wilson and Daugherty, 2018).

For example, AI will have a profound impact on business strategy, particularly in the area of strategic analysis. This applies to both current and future strategies. Organizations can use data derived from AI to inform their future strategic planning. It is conceivable that an AI system could suggest the most viable and effective strategy based on past results. Moreover, an AI system could be employed to analyse competitor strategies, which could aid in the development of future strategies.

The implementation of AI will also enhance organizational efficiency and performance. AI systems can undertake tasks that were previously performed by humans, while eliminating the risk of human error. Moreover, AI systems can perform these tasks at a significantly faster pace, potentially increasing output. This output will also be more predictable, as management will have a clear understanding of the system's capabilities, potentially leading to easier and more consistent management. For instance, AI tools are increasingly playing a larger role in performing routine administrative tasks. AI bots can handle repetitive, low-value tasks, allowing human workers to focus on more productive and strategic work. This can save company managers a considerable amount of time and energy. An example of this is the use of bots to create electronic employee helpdesks, where users can ask questions and receive automated responses.

Finally, the impact of AI on company culture is primarily centred on the core intentions of the business. If the management process becomes automated, businesses may become solely focused on profit and the most efficient means of achieving it. This could pose challenges for organizations whose primary goals are not profit-driven, such as nonprofit organizations or charities. It is also important to note that many profit-oriented organizations are now engaging in activities related to social enterprise. AI is thus poised to transform the way businesses operate, influencing various aspects of company management, including strategy, technology, work organization, economics, the environment, culture, and workforce management.

Navigating AI implementation in the workplace

While AI's potential to personalize work is vast, it is crucial to approach its implementation with care (Daugherty and Wilson, 2018). Addressing privacy concerns, potential biases in algorithms, and the risk of over-reliance on technology are essential steps to ensure responsible and beneficial AI integration. However, when implemented thoughtfully, AI can indeed create a more personalized and productive work environment (Gulliford and Parker, 2019; Charlwood and Guenole, 2022). This can be illustrated through the following examples, as detailed below.

Performance feedback: AI can provide real-time feedback on an individual's performance, highlighting areas for improvement and offering personalized coaching and development suggestions. This timely and targeted feedback can empower individuals to identify their strengths, address weaknesses, and continuously enhance their skills.

Personalized content creation: AI can assist with content creation by customizing messages to specific target audiences. This personalization can lead to more effective communication and engagement, ensuring that the right message reaches the right audience at the right time (Dutta et al., 2022).

Time management and prioritization: AI can help individuals manage their time more effectively by analysing their work patterns and suggesting optimal schedules and task priorities. This data-driven approach to time management can reduce distractions, increase focus, and enhance overall productivity.

Personalized customer interactions: In customer-facing roles, AI can analyse customer data to provide personalized recommendations and support, enhancing the quality of interactions and potentially increasing customer satisfaction. This personalization can create stronger customer relationships, build brand loyalty, and drive business growth.

Career path guidance: AI can provide personalized career guidance by analysing an individual's skills, interests, and industry trends. It can suggest career development opportunities and pathways based on the person's goals, aspirations, and unique strengths. This personalized guidance can empower individuals to make informed career decisions, pursue meaningful opportunities, and achieve their professional goals.

Collaboration and team dynamics: AI can help improve team collaboration by analysing individual working styles and preferences, facilitating better communication and task assignment within teams. This data-driven approach can optimize team dynamics, enhance collaboration, and promote collective success.

AI also offers additional ways to improve workplaces. By gauging employee sentiment and preferences, companies can personalize work experiences, leading to increased satisfaction and productivity (Abdullah and Fakieh, 2020; Anderson et al., 2018). Predictive analytics, for instance, can pinpoint elements leading to disengagement, guiding interventions to bolster satisfaction. Tools like chatbots and virtual assistants support ongoing engagement through check-ins and sentiment assessments, offering human resource (HR) valuable insights into the employee experience.

AI can play a role in recognizing employees, automating the acknowledgement of accomplishments. By analysing performance metrics, intelligent systems can spotlight notable efforts, and personalized messages can be sent to commend employees, boosting morale and nurturing a culture of recognition. Furthermore, AI's predictive capabilities extend to forecasting potential staff turnover by evaluating performance, engagement, and market conditions. Identifying employees at risk enables HR to deploy specific retention measures, aiding in talent preservation and workforce stability.

AI also holds the potential to counteract biases in HR practices, particularly within recruitment and performance evaluations. By training machine learning algorithms, unconscious biases in job listings, candidate assessments, and promotion considerations can be identified and mitigated, paving the way for a more inclusive workplace through fair and objective evaluations (Brodley and Friedl, 1999). Moreover, AI can aid in enhancing diversity by pinpointing representation gaps and recommending specific strategies for improvement. By scrutinizing workforce data, AI tools enable HR professionals to devise and execute diversity and inclusion (D&I) initiatives that resonate with the company's overarching objectives and ethos.

In sourcing diverse candidates, AI can analyse extensive data sets to uncover prospective candidates from varied backgrounds, broadening the candidate pool with diverse experiences and viewpoints. This strategic measure assists organizations in cultivating a more diverse recruitment pipeline. AI tools can also scrutinize the language in job descriptions, internal communications, and other HR documents to ensure inclusivity. Through Natural Language Processing (NLP), algorithms can detect and propose modifications to language that might inadvertently exclude specific groups, ensuring organizational communication is inclusive and in harmony with D&I objectives.

In addition, AI can promote fairness and impartiality in performance evaluations, training machine learning algorithms to identify and remove unconscious biases in language and assessment criteria. This ensures performance reviews are grounded in merit and objective standards rather than subjective opinions, fostering a more equitable and inclusive performance management framework.

Entrepreneurship and creative destruction

Traditional entrepreneurship theories emphasize the significance of ideas and creativity, suggesting that entrepreneurship is about generating a business idea that can be implemented and flourish under favourable conditions and resources. Debate exists regarding the origin of such ideas. Schumpeter (1934) proposes that an entrepreneur actively creates new opportunities in a market through innovation, rendering existing businesses obsolete and paving the way for creative destruction. Creative destruction refers to the process where new business concepts render older businesses outdated and replace them, leading to the emergence of new processes and operating methods. Schumpeter's concept underscores the entrepreneurial nature of innovation and its role in forging new markets. However, Schumpeter's portrayal of the entrepreneur's role is challenged by the Kirznerian perspective. Kirzner (1973) advocates that entrepreneurs are opportunistic individuals who identify gaps or niches in the market and exploit them for personal gain. He argues that economies are in disequilibrium due to the lack of market awareness among individuals, with entrepreneurs tasked with restoring equilibrium by identifying and capitalizing on these market gaps.

While these theories shed light on the origins of business ideas, they fail to address the factors that drive entrepreneurs' perseverance and focus. Motivation can be categorized into intrinsic factors, arising from within oneself, and extrinsic factors, stemming from external sources. While motivation is vital for pursuing entrepreneurial endeavours, it alone does not guarantee a business's survival. To enhance the likelihood of success, there must be a genuine market need or demand for the business's offerings. This often manifests in addressing individuals' pain points. Starting a business presents enticing prospects, but it also harbours significant obstacles that can lead to failure if not properly addressed. These challenges include limited financial resources, regulatory hurdles, competition (based on time or demand), and a lack of effective leadership, to name a few. Therefore, it is essential to craft a comprehensive business plan to increase the chances of survival (Shane and Venkataraman, 2000; Buenstorf, 2007; Kirzner, 1997).

AI and creativity

Creativity is a critical element in entrepreneurship and the formation of new ventures (Baron and Tang, 2011; Dimov, 2007). True creativity stems from the depths of human experiences, emotions, culture, and individual perspectives. While AI presents a multitude of avenues to enhance and support human creativity, it is crucial to acknowledge that the human touch will forever remain the cornerstone of authentic creative expression. We now explore how AI can support and enhance aspects of human creativity and contribute to personalized work experiences (Vrontis et al., 2022). With its capability to analyse extensive data sets, identify patterns, and adjust to user behaviour, AI serves as an invaluable resource for aligning work experiences with individual preferences. Below, we provide a list of AI-powered insights for creative professionals:

Trend forecasting and cultural resonance: AI's ability to analyse vast amounts of data in real time makes it a valuable tool for predicting trends. For designers, writers, and artists, understanding these trends can help them create content that resonates with the current cultural milieu. For instance, AI can identify emerging fashion trends, analyse social media conversations to gauge public sentiment, or track changes in consumer behaviour patterns. By staying ahead of the curve, creative professionals can ensure that their work remains relevant and engaging.

Generative design and idea generation: In fields such as architecture or product design, AI tools can provide a variety of designs based on certain parameters. This approach is known as generative design, where the computer generates a range of solutions and the human designer selects or refines from among them. Generative design can be particularly useful for exploring new design possibilities, optimizing designs for specific criteria, or overcoming creative blocks.

AI-powered content creation: AI tools can generate novel art pieces or visual content. These tools can be used to inspire artists or to generate preliminary concepts. For example, AI-driven tools can assist musicians in composing music by suggesting chord progressions, melodies, or even entire compositions. This can be especially useful for beginners or for artists looking for fresh inspiration. AI tools can also help writers by suggesting plot ideas, refining sentence structures, or even generating whole stories or articles. These tools can serve as a foundation upon which human writers can build.

AI-enhanced creativity and expression: AI can upscale images, restore old paintings or photographs, or colourize black and white films, breathing new life into old creations. AI-driven virtual reality (VR) and augmented reality (AR) tools can provide immersive platforms for artists to experiment with new forms of expression and experience. These tools can enable artists to create interactive installations, explore virtual environments, and engage with audiences in innovative ways.

Task prioritization for enhanced productivity: AI can analyse an individual's work patterns, the nature of tasks, and deadlines to help prioritize tasks more effectively. For instance, AI might recognize that an individual is more productive with analytical tasks in the morning and adjust their task list accordingly, optimizing their daily workflow.

Adaptive learning and training for individualized growth: Personalized learning experiences can be created based on an individual's learning style, pace, and past performance. AI can suggest resources or training modules that are most relevant to an individual's role and knowledge gaps, fostering personalized growth and development.

Personalized content delivery for relevant learning: In roles that require regular upskilling or staying updated with industry news, AI can curate and deliver content that's most relevant to the individual's role, interests, and past content consumption patterns. This personalized content delivery ensures that individuals receive the most relevant and timely information to support their continuous learning and growth.

Recommendation systems for enhanced expertise: For professionals like lawyers or doctors, AI can help by recommending relevant case studies, research papers, or solutions based on their current work or challenge. Personalized recommendations can provide professionals with the knowledge and resources they need to make informed decisions and solve complex problems.

AI in accounting and finance education: An example

Recent technological advancements have significantly impacted general business practices and the accounting and finance professions. The Big Four accounting firms (PwC, Deloitte, KPMG, EY) have developed financial robots that can automatically analyse data, input invoices, and export results, reducing routine accounting tasks (Zhang et al., 2020). Traditional training in accounting and finance, which has emphasized theory-based learning supplemented by on-the-job training, is evolving due to these technological advancements. A study by Ren and Weng (2019) found that the repetitive nature of many accounting and finance tasks makes them ideal for automation by AI, reducing human error. Consequently, future accounting and finance professionals will need skills beyond traditional ones, including data analytics, communication, negotiation, and innovative thinking.

Karbon (2024) conducted a survey to explore the impact of AI on accounting professionals. Of the 595 professionals surveyed, 71 per cent believe AI will bring considerable changes to the accounting industry. Nearly half reported finding it challenging to keep up with advancements in AI technologies. Similarly, PWC (2023b) surveyed their employees to gauge attitudes towards AI, revealing an overall positive outlook, with over half of the respondents agreeing with at least one positive statement about AI, such as its potential to increase productivity and help them learn new skills. However, 25 per cent also expressed concerns by selecting at least one negative statement. These insights from a large professional services firm may not be fully generalizable, as larger firms are more likely to invest in AI training and development, potentially leading to more positive attitudes.

A few other studies have examined AI implementation from the professionals' perspective. For example, a survey by Johnston et al. (2021) of accounting professionals in Florida found that most were somewhat interested in and familiar with AI use in accounting, but only a small percentage had actual experience with it. Furthermore, the study found that those with less experience in the field, often younger professionals, were more interested in AI compared to their more experienced counterparts. Ren and Weng (2019) thus advocate for integrating AI-based technologies into accounting and finance curricula to prepare future professionals to use these technologies effectively. AI has the potential to revolutionize financial data analysis, offering young professionals opportunities to enhance their skills in AI and other advanced technologies. This transformation extends to financial data interpretation, enabling more effective data asset management through robust data governance. User-driven innovation is also expected to gain increasing importance, with self-service AI-powered business intelligence tools allowing users to generate insights independently.

The evolving role of financial management professionals

Financial management roles within accounting and finance firms, such as CFO, financial director, and management accountant, have had to adapt to evolving technologies and embrace innovation to stay competitive. Guo (2019) surveyed five hundred accountants and found that 57 per cent felt a significant change in focus within the accounting field, while 33 per cent perceived a moderate shift. Guo argued that the rapid advancement of AI is diminishing the role of financial accounting, transforming it into management accounting. This shift is driven by the expectation that machine learning and robotic process automation (RPA) will automate simple data processing, reducing manual labour and achieving sustainability by streamlining operations and reducing resource consumption. Guo emphasized that accountants should proactively enhance their strategic skills to prepare for this inevitable change.

Wang (2020) supports this view, noting that machine learning will replace simple and repetitive tasks, necessitating that accountants acquire knowledge and expertise in AI and Big Data (BD). As AI and other emerging technologies are adopted, accountants must adapt to their roles, improving performance and contributing more significantly to societal development. Wang also stresses that business decision-makers must understand accounting firms' enterprise development and strategic needs. In conclusion, the accounting and finance profession is undergoing significant transformation due to the swift progress of AI. Future professionals will need to update their skills to incorporate AI-powered tools and methods while maintaining the core principles of the field (Bakarich and O'Brien, 2020).

AI and the augmented workforce

Recruitment and selection

AI has changed recruitment by automating various stages of the process, from candidate sourcing to interview evaluations. In this section, we explore the specific ways AI improves recruitment efficiency and reduces bias. Vrontis et al. (2022) identify several trends in integrating IT technology into HR practices. One such trend is the use of AI assistants like Google Assistant, Alexa, and Siri to help HR professionals manage their daily schedules. Other common AI applications in HR practices include chatbots, task automation software, and screening software (van Esch et al., 2019; Upadhyay and Khandelwal, 2018). In the HR field, the implementation of AI has enhanced the recruitment process by uncovering hidden talents, speeding up application screening, and scheduling interviews with potential candidates, thus boosting the efficiency of HR professionals.

At the interview stage, Wilson et al. (2021) confirm that using AI in voice or video interviews helps analyse information such as a candidate's reactions, tone, and mood, enabling recruiters to make more accurate assessments. Similarly, Kazim et al. (2021) provide evidence that AI-based recruitment technologies significantly reduce recruitment time and costs while also addressing the issue of insufficient candidate information. Kazim et al. (2021) also report that AI recruitment solutions, such as HireVue, provide comprehensive and unbiased information about candidates, allowing employers to better understand them.

Unilever's use of AI in its recruitment and selection process is a practical example. AI systems are capable of collecting, structuring, and analysing large volumes of data more impartially and swiftly than human recruiters, significantly reducing the likelihood of biased evaluations. By employing AI, companies can gain a comprehensive understanding of applicants, aligning candidates with positions that best match their skills and capabilities. Using AI screening tools, Hilton Hotels significantly reduced their hiring process time from forty-two days to just five days (Black and van Esch, 2020), demonstrating the efficiency AI adds to recruitment. Furthermore, AI can enhance candidate evaluations by analysing video interviews for non-verbal cues, sentiment, and personality traits, providing deeper insights into job suitability (Min, 2018).

Siemens, a renowned German electronics and technology corporation, has integrated AI into its recruitment processes to aid the HR department in screening applicants. AI enables Siemens to efficiently analyse and evaluate résumé data, facilitating the identification of suitable candidates for various roles. Marta Brockwell, Talent Acquisition Consultant at Siemens (Evie, 2020), comments on the significant impact of AI, noting that it has enabled her to schedule nearly one hundred interviews monthly. This efficiency saves her 30 per cent of her time, allowing her to focus on more critical tasks and attract better talent to the company. Siemens uses Evie, an AI robot, alongside virtual assistants to interact with applicants and conduct personalized vetting through various questions.

LinkedIn, a leading recruitment platform, has implemented advanced algorithms to match candidates with positions, offering more precise recommendations and a faster screening process. Concurrently, some companies are creating chatbot interview screening programmes that use simulated conversations to initially evaluate a candidate's suitability. The integration of intelligent technologies like smart technology, artificial intelligence, robotics, and algorithms (STARA) into the hiring process is transforming perceptions of the future workplace within companies.

IBM utilizes its AI platform, 'Watson', to refine its recruitment process. By analysing vast amounts of résumé and application data, Watson can swiftly pinpoint the most compatible candidates. This technology not only enhances the efficiency of the hiring process for companies but also necessitates that HR professionals develop proficiency in data analysis and the interpretation of AI outputs (IBM, 2023). Consequently, for HR personnel, this evolution not only transforms their job responsibilities but also heightens their dependency on technology and the demand for specific skills, particularly in data analytics and understanding AI-generated insights.

Other leading firms like JP Morgan and Point72 employ video interview platforms like HireVue, allowing candidates to showcase their experience and qualifications in a dynamic format. The reach of AI recruitment extends beyond resumes. Companies like Accenture and PwC use AI assessments, like Pymetrics tests, to identify candidates who culturally align with the company. This ensures a good fit for both the candidate and the organization. Previously cumbersome pre-screening interviews are getting a makeover with AI. Companies like Goldman Sachs and Amazon use software to analyse interviews and assess candidate compatibility with the role and company culture (Albert, 2019). This reduces bias and expedites feedback, creating a more positive candidate experience.

Consequently, it can be argued that the advantages of e-recruiting powered by AI are undeniable. Studies like Acemoglu et al. (2020) suggest cost reductions of up to 95 per cent compared to traditional methods. Moreover, the recruitment cycle is significantly shortened, boosting operational efficiency. The benefits go beyond finding new talent (Pan and Froese, 2023). AI analytics can predict employee career paths, allowing managers to develop their leadership skills and invest in talent. AI can also simplify onboarding by automating repetitive tasks like account setup and paperwork, freeing HR professionals for strategic initiatives like employee engagement and development (Konovalova et al., 2023). While AI offers clear benefits, wider adoption faces hurdles. A key challenge is the lack of understanding on how to best evaluate and implement AI for optimal results in the recruitment process.

Employee turnover

Research suggests AI-powered HR strategies also hold promise for reducing employee turnover. Machine learning algorithms can be powerful tools. Studies by Marvin et al. (2021) and Kang et al. (2020) show they can analyse individual data to categorize employees at risk of leaving, allowing HR to target interventions and improve retention efforts. AI can also be a valuable asset in identifying signs of burnout, as Grensing-Pophal (2022) highlights with examples of companies using AI to monitor communication patterns for burnout indicators.

AI can be a force for good in promoting a culture of employee well-being. By employing AI for retention, organizations can prioritize employee loyalty and well-being. Cloud platforms like Veriato analyse activity patterns to predict potential departures, allowing for proactive measures to address employee concerns before they reach a tipping point. Additionally, AI can help optimize resource allocation and redeploy employees to areas of need, potentially preventing layoffs, particularly for vulnerable groups.

AI in HR planning and forecasting

In addition to helping retain employees and reduce turnover, AI plays a critical role in managing different functional areas. When it comes to strategic workforce programming and forecasting, AI capabilities can employ predictive analytics. This provides valuable forecasts about future workforce supply, internal workforce training, performance analysis, and market trends. Graßmann and Schermuly (2020) asserted that AI can assist organizations in predicting skill shortages, planning workforce fluctuations, and managing expansions. Furthermore, it can create simulations of different scenarios to assess the outcomes of diverse strategies. By doing so, HR professionals can better develop their workforce plans to align with the organization's strategic initiatives.

Augmented personnel combine the strengths of AI and technology to enrich human performance. Future HR approaches will involve managing AI tools to enhance human capabilities without replacing humans. This is where human factors integrate with technology, developing shared roles that complement their respective strengths. While AI offers significant benefits, it is important to remember it is a tool, not a replacement for human expertise. Ganatra and Pandya (2023) warn against relying solely on AI. Data inaccuracies and programming errors can lead to misjudgements that negatively impact morale and performance evaluations. The most successful approach combines AI's analytical capabilities with human expertise and oversight to ensure fair and effective retention strategies.

Personalized learning and development

The integration of AI into HR management in contemporary enterprises encompasses a broad spectrum of strategies, from precise and efficient talent acquisition to the implementation of innovative, data-driven training initiatives (Bansal et al., 2023). AI integrates immersive technologies like VR and AR to create training programmes that replicate real-life scenarios. For instance, Walmart collaborated with Strivr to develop a VR-based training programme, which has been implemented in supermarkets nationwide. This programme includes realistic simulations enabling employees to practice and prepare for a variety of situations they might encounter in their roles. Walmart's initiative revealed significant benefits: the VR training led to a 30 per cent increase in employee satisfaction and a 10–15 per cent improvement in knowledge retention. Furthermore, it condensed the eight-hour pickup training to fifteen minutes and reduced the four-hour onboarding process to just forty-five minutes, all while eliminating the necessity for trainers to conduct sessions in physical stores (Walmart, 2020).

From an affordance theory perspective (Keller et al., 2019), AI offers opportunities (affordances) for HR to achieve specific training goals. AI can streamline time management and enhance coordination within HR teams, allowing them to deliver training more effectively. However, as Keller et al. (2019) point out, the success of AI-powered training depends heavily on the technology's readiness and the quality of its implementation. In essence, a practical approach is essential. HR needs to ensure AI effectively supports development initiatives by carefully selecting and implementing the right technology for their specific needs.

Such training solutions offer numerous benefits for both employees and businesses (Maity, 2019; Suk, 2023). Employees benefit from personalized, effective training that helps them develop their skills and advance their careers. Businesses benefit from a more skilled, engaged, and productive workforce. AI-powered employee training solutions are changing the way businesses train their workforce, offering numerous benefits such as:

Personalized learning: AI can assess an employee's skills and knowledge gaps and recommend tailored learning programmes or videos based on their specific job requirements. This personalized approach ensures that employees receive the most relevant and effective training, maximizing their learning outcomes.

Automated learning path creation: AI can automatically read documents, analyse an employee's activities, and identify their learning needs. Based on this information, AI can create customized learning paths that align with each employee's individual goals and development needs.

Data-driven training strategies: AI algorithms can analyse vast amounts of data from employee training programmes to identify patterns and trends. This data-driven approach allows AI to recommend the most effective training strategies for each employee, ensuring that they learn faster and more effectively.

Targeted training recommendations: AI can provide HR teams and managers with insights into which employees need training and in what specific areas. This targeted approach ensures that training resources are allocated effectively and that employees receive the training they need to succeed in their roles.

Cost-effective training solutions: AI-powered training programmes are often more cost-effective than traditional training methods. This is because AI can automate many of the tasks involved in training, such as creating personalized learning paths and grading assessments.

Scalable training for large workforces: AI can supervise and train an entire workforce, regardless of size or location. This is a significant advantage for large businesses that may have difficulty providing consistent and high-quality training to a dispersed workforce.

In today's complex business environment, maintaining a highly proficient workforce is vital for a company like Amazon to stay ahead in the competitive e-commerce industry. Amazon employs AI tools alongside its existing training initiatives, such as Upskilling-2025, to further develop its workforce and secure a competitive advantage. A significant application of AI in learning and development is the use of AI-driven learning platforms that provide personalized training experiences. AI can pinpoint employees' knowledge gaps by analysing their performance against set benchmarks (Maity, 2019), determine their preferred learning styles, and suggest targeted training or more advanced resources (Suk, 2023).

This approach is a departure from traditional training programmes, which may not address the varied needs of individuals, thus being less effective. Moreover, Amazon employs gamification and AI in workforce training, making the learning process more engaging and interactive. For instance, AI-powered quiz generators can transform training content into captivating quizzes, facilitating knowledge testing and reinforcement. Gamification elements like points, achievement badges, and leaderboards can tap into employees' competitive nature, fostering a more enthusiastic learning environment and higher completion rates (Spears, 2023). This setup provides instant feedback, enabling employees and HR leaders to monitor progress and pinpoint areas needing further attention. By adopting AI-driven training methods, Amazon significantly enhances workforce development with personalized and interactive learning experiences, thereby strengthening its position in the e-commerce sector.

AstraZeneca, a leading global pharmaceutical company, is enhancing the coaching skills of its field leaders, who oversee a team of over four thousand individuals in the United States. Both managers and sales representatives complete a detailed field coaching form documenting their daily interactions. To glean deeper insights from these forms, AstraZeneca developed a machine learning model. Analysis of the forms revealed that 90 per cent of performance ratings fell between 3 and 4 on a 5-point scale, indicating a potential lack of objectivity and meaningfulness in performance discussions. As part of a broader initiative, AstraZeneca is employing AI to streamline the completion of these forms, which are often seen as cumbersome or challenging for manual processing. The programme has generally been well-received; some managers report that it has enhanced their sales performance, while others appreciate the emphasis it places on problem-solving and reflective practices (Yorks et al., 2022).

AI with remote working

The Covid-19 pandemic has accelerated the adoption of telecommuting, leading to a widespread shift in work practices. AI technology plays an important role in enabling effective remote work by facilitating data monitoring, management, and analysis. AI-powered tools automate document scanning, recording, conversion, and collation of text for virtual meetings, streamlining communication and collaboration among remote workers.

The rise of telecommuting has enabled companies to use intelligent platforms like Microsoft Teams and Zoom to support remote work arrangements. These platforms offer smooth communication, task management, and collaboration tools, enabling employees to work efficiently from any location. If remote work proves to be successful without significantly impacting organizational performance or employee numbers, companies may consider reducing their office space to cut rental costs. This approach can lead to significant savings and allow companies to allocate resources more effectively. At ING Bank, for instance, agile teams operate in co-located workspaces equipped with large whiteboards that display project plans, shared goals, and project statuses. Moreover, telecommuting opens up new opportunities for companies to recruit talent from a global pool, expanding their reach beyond their immediate geographic area. This broader talent pool can bring fresh perspectives, diverse skills, and specialized expertise, contributing to the company's overall growth and innovation.

However, telecommuting also presents certain challenges. One concern is the potential for employees to experience isolation and psychological issues due to a lack of daily in-person interactions. Companies need to prioritize employee well-being by fostering a sense of community and providing support mechanisms for remote workers. Another challenge is the potential loss of direct supervision by managers, which could affect task completion and project management. Companies need to establish clear communication protocols, regularly monitor progress, and exploit technology to track employee performance effectively.

Despite these challenges, telecommuting offers numerous benefits for both employees and employers. For employees, it can reduce commute time, provide a more flexible work-life balance, and make work more accessible for individuals with disabilities. For employers, it can lead to cost savings, access to a wider talent pool, and increased employee engagement.

Limitations of AI in HR processes

Despite its potential benefits, AI in company practice also faces certain limitations. One limitation is that data-driven decisions are not always guaranteed to be understandable, accurate, or beneficial, as some AI systems may not be fully updated to eliminate all workplace biases. For instance, Amazon, a multinational corporation, discovered that gender bias had infiltrated its hiring processes due to the predominantly male-centric data used to train the AI. Consequently, Amazon had to rewrite its algorithms to ensure gender neutrality.

While much of the current literature argues that AI systems used in recruitment can reduce algorithmic bias and eliminate discrimination, some studies suggest that, in certain cases, data may appear algorithmically neutral, yet the results still reflect bias. For example, Haley et al. (2023) found that after analysing a company's candidate pool, many successful couriers came from the same postcode. The algorithm then began to favour applicants from that postcode, which, as it turned out, was 98 per cent white. Although the data seemed neutral based on the postcode, its application in recruitment unintentionally influenced outcomes, revealing an underlying bias.

While AI can enhance efficiency, it depends heavily on data created by humans, which can introduce human biases into the decision-making model. Even though AI reduces bias by not considering factors like race, age, or gender, it may sometimes overlook important traits. It therefore becomes important to carefully review AI algorithms for accuracy to prevent any potential bias. Evidence suggests that algorithms and machine-based decisions could actually perpetuate bias due to flaws in the underlying data or the algorithm itself (Konovalova et al., 2023). Recognizing this potential risk is essential in preventing a new source of bias from entering an organization's hiring or promotion process.

To address this concern, organizational giants like GE and IBM are developing analytical tools that identify 'non-obvious' job candidates. Another challenge with implementing AI in HR processes is managing the vast amounts of data necessary for making precise and relevant decisions. This involves not only collecting and storing large data sets but also ensuring their quality and relevance to derive meaningful insights. However, when properly monitored and implemented, AI can effectively remove bias from assessment, recruiting, and training processes, enhancing the cultural fit and diversity of the workforce. Therefore, when developed correctly, AI has the potential to improve HR practices such as recruitment and selection by screening candidates fairly and preventing bias.

However, the impact of AI in the workplace extends far beyond just picking who gets hired. It has the potential to promote D&I not only in recruitment but also in onboarding and training, and in two key ways:

1. Regulatory pressure for fair AI: As AI becomes more common in HR, governments are increasingly concerned about fairness and worker well-being. In the United States, the Equal Employment Opportunity Commission is actively tackling discrimination in AI-driven hiring and training. Similarly, the EU's new AI Act requires companies to treat employees fairly when using AI data and processes. This pressure encourages companies to adopt inclusive practices across all stages of the employee journey.
2. Personalized learning and growth: As discussed above, AI can help create customized learning programmes for individual needs and backgrounds.

> Imagine an inclusive language learning model, designed by diverse teams, that lets companies offer targeted training based on different languages and experience levels. This opens the door for equal learning opportunities for all, regardless of their starting point.

But to truly unlock AI's inclusive potential, we need to address bias at the foundation. Building diverse teams right from the start of AI development, from engineers to data scientists, can go a long way in minimizing unintentional exclusion. This proactive approach ensures everyone has a fair chance to thrive in the AI-powered workplace of the future. Similarly, organizations now require strong security measures, transparency, and clear communication regarding their handling of employee data to prevent privacy concerns and backlash over potential data misuse.

In conclusion, AI's integration into the workplace is changing the way companies operate, from personalizing learning experiences and improving diversity efforts to streamlining human resource practices and enhancing strategic business decisions. As AI continues to evolve in both its predictive and generative capacities, its role in driving productivity, efficiency, and innovation will only expand, making it an indispensable tool for organizations looking to stay competitive in the modern business environment.

Part 2

Personalization and platform ecosystem

In this section, we delve into the transformative power of personalization within the digital platform economy. Multi-sided platforms have emerged as dominant forces across industries, connecting diverse user groups and generating substantial value. Characterized by large user bases and significant capital investment, these platforms have increasingly harnessed the power of artificial intelligence (AI). Despite their substantial AI investments, however, these platforms have yet to fully leverage AI to create groundbreaking products or markets. We explore AI's potential to reshape digital platforms, focusing on personalization as a key perspective to examine the intersection of these technologies.

Our exploration begins with the burgeoning field of social commerce, a phenomenon that epitomizes the fusion of e-commerce and digital technologies. This confluence has spawned expansive marketplaces that interconnect global networks of buyers and sellers, fundamentally altering the commercial landscape. Central to this transformation are mechanisms such as user-generated content, co-creation, and influencer markets, which serve as catalysts for these trends. Furthermore, we examine how these digital innovations are reshaping fast fashion and propelling the circular economy, sectors that are undergoing significant metamorphosis due to the recent emphasis on sustainable commerce.

Our analysis then broadens to encompass the diverse economic realms where digital platforms operate. We scrutinize FinTech platforms in financial services, the sharing economy, and the gig economy. The sharing economy, in particular, stands out for its disruptive impact on traditional business paradigms, creating fertile ground for entrepreneurial innovation. This model has democratized economic participation, enabling a new cadre of actors to penetrate vast industries.

At the heart of our discourse is the pivotal role of personalization in elevating the efficacy and user experience of these platforms. New entrants, in particular, face the dual challenge of simultaneously attracting buyers and sellers. This dual imperative casts them as both market creators and operators, tasked with the intricate job of initiating and sustaining a vibrant transactional ecosystem.

To navigate this complexity, platforms must craft and iteratively refine personalization strategies. The crux of these strategies lies in making interactions between sellers and buyers more meaningful and adapted to individual preferences and behaviours. This can range from product recommendations based on historical interactions to customized search results and notifications that align with users' specific needs.

For sellers, personalization might manifest as data-driven market insights that enable them to fine-tune their offerings. For buyers, it translates into a curated shopping journey that simplifies decision-making and enhances satisfaction. The implementation of these strategies demands sophisticated algorithms and robust data analytics to effectively process and derive insights from vast data troves. When successfully deployed, these technologies create a dynamic, responsive marketplace where both sellers and buyers discover heightened value and relevance, thereby strengthening trust and engagement.

As we argue throughout, cultivating a thriving, sustainable marketplace through personalization transcends mere user acquisition, leading to enduring user engagement. By continuously adapting to the evolving needs of their user base and broader market dynamics, platforms can maintain their competitive edge in an increasingly saturated digital market. This ongoing evolution and refinement of personalization strategies are not just optional; they are imperative for the long-term viability of these platforms. Moreover, they are crucial for the evolving role these platforms play in architecting and stewarding novel forms of economic production and distribution in our digital age.

7

Social commerce in online marketplaces

Nestled in the verdant landscapes of Elmswood, a small town celebrated for its rich tapestry of textiles, stood 'Verdant Threads', a boutique owned by Emily, a twenty-nine-year-old artisan. Her shop was an emporium of handcrafted fabrics, each piece narrating tales of heritage and artisanship. Emily's unique creations had garnered a loyal following among both locals and tourists, who visited Elmswood to experience its renowned weaving traditions. Despite the popularity, her business remained largely localized, constrained within the town's perimeters.

During a casual interaction with a fellow craftsman at a regional fair, Emily was introduced to Etsy, a global platform dedicated to handmade and vintage items. Initially sceptical, her curiosity soon led her to explore the platform, discovering a vibrant community of creators and the expansive outreach it offered. Inspired by the prospect of showcasing Elmswood's weaving heritage on a global stage, Emily ventured to establish her presence on Etsy.

Enlisting the aid of a friend proficient in photography, she meticulously captured the vivid hues and elaborate designs of her textiles. Emily ensured that each listing on Etsy mirrored the authenticity and craftsmanship of her work. She composed elaborate narratives for each fabric, embedding tales of Elmswood's weaving traditions and the inspirations behind her designs, while optimizing her listings with pertinent keywords.

Emily's entry into the global market was marked by her first order from a client in France, captivated by the craftsmanship and narrative of an Elmswood tapestry. She meticulously packaged the tapestry, adding a personalized note detailing the weaving art of Elmswood. The customer's glowing review underscored the tapestry's elegance and Emily's thoughtful touch, marking a pivotal moment for 'Verdant Threads' and elevating its stature on Etsy.

Buoyed by this initial success and subsequent positive feedback, Emily saw an uptick in international demand. She adopted Etsy's shipping solutions, streamlining her logistics and allowing her to dedicate more time to her craft. Her textiles began reaching enthusiasts worldwide, from the UK to Canada and Australia.

Sensing a growth opportunity, Emily broadened her collection, introducing new designs and partnering with other weavers from Elmswood, enriching Etsy's selection with a diverse range of textiles. This collaborative effort not only spotlighted

Elmswood's artisanal roots but also fostered unity among the local craftsmen, encouraging them to explore the digital marketplace.

'Verdant Threads' emerged as a symbol of quality and heritage, with Emily's endeavours reigniting interest in Elmswood's textiles. Beyond sales, she invested the profits from her flourishing Etsy business into community weaving workshops and initiatives aimed at preserving and propagating the town's weaving techniques, cementing her role not just as a successful entrepreneur but as a custodian of Elmswood's weaving heritage.

Emily's journey from a local artisan to an internationally recognized seller on Etsy not only transformed her business but also played a pivotal role in revitalizing Elmswood's artisanal community, ensuring the survival and appreciation of its weaving heritage in the digital age.

Emily's experience on a social commerce platform reflects a broader shift in the way businesses and consumers interact, highlighting a transformative trend in the realms of production and consumption. This new paradigm encourages a more collaborative institutional environment where both parties actively participate in the creation and consumption process. It illustrates how modern business platforms are redefining traditional roles, encouraging users to not only consume but also influence and contribute to the product and content offerings. This change is emblematic of a larger movement towards a more interactive and interconnected commercial environment, where the lines between producers and consumers are increasingly blurred. We explore these trends in the subsequent discussion.

First, live video shopping is already big in some countries, and it is rapidly gaining traction globally. Platforms like TikTok, Instagram, and YouTube are doubling down on live shopping features, allowing companies and influencers to host interactive sessions, showcase products in real time, and answer customer questions directly. One can expect innovative formats, such as augmented reality (AR) try-ons and gamified shopping experiences, to significantly boost engagement. Furthermore, platforms like TikTok and Instagram Reels are dominating the attention economy, with short-form video content rapidly becoming the preferred way to discover and buy products. Engaging product demos, tutorials, and influencer partnerships within these formats are key to grabbing attention and driving sales.

Second, while celebrity endorsements still hold some weight, companies are increasingly turning to micro-influencers (those with smaller but highly engaged followings) for more authentic and targeted reach. Micro-influencers typically maintain stronger bonds with their communities, which helps in building trust and achieving higher conversion rates. As a result, there may be an increase in collaborations that concentrate on niche content and personalized recommendations.

Third, chatbots and messaging apps are becoming vital sales tools, offering instant product support, personalized recommendations, and seamless purchase journeys within messaging platforms. AI-powered chatbots can answer customer questions, handle orders, and even negotiate prices, creating a frictionless shopping experience. Similarly, AR and virtual reality (VR) technologies are revolutionizing product visualization and trial. Virtual showrooms and AR try-on features allow customers to experience products in their own homes before buying, boosting confidence and reducing purchase anxiety. It is expected that more companies will employ these immersive technologies to improve customer engagement and decision-making processes. With social platforms implementing built-in payment options, checkout processes are also becoming more streamlined. One-click purchases and integration with digital wallets enable frictionless buying experiences, further blurring the line between browsing and buying on social media.

Fourth, by creating direct connections between local service providers and those in need of services, platforms such as TaskRabbit strengthen community ties and promote a sense of mutual support. TaskRabbit exemplifies the sharing economy by utilizing technology to facilitate peer-to-peer transactions, not only optimizing the use of individual skills and time but also creating a more interconnected and supportive community ecosystem. On the other hand, the gig economy model disrupts conventional employment frameworks by highlighting intermediary work structures. Online food delivery services can boost local economies by increasing sales for restaurants and providing income opportunities for drivers.

Fifth, consumers are increasingly conscious of the environmental and social impact of their purchases. Social commerce platforms are incorporating features to highlight sustainable brands, showcase eco-friendly products, and promote ethical shopping practices. One should anticipate that transparency and sustainability will emerge as key differentiators in the social commerce sector. Social commerce thrives on community engagement. Companies are creating specialized online communities on social platforms, encouraging discussions, product reviews, and peer-to-peer recommendations. This builds trust and promotes natural brand support, leading to increased sales and customer loyalty (Ba et al., 2003).

These developments show how social commerce platforms are benefiting from AI and machine learning to personalize product recommendations, offer targeted ads, and customize the experience to individual users. As social commerce evolves, data analysis will become critical for success. Firms will be tasked with closely monitoring social media interactions, evaluating the efficacy of their campaigns, and dissecting consumer behaviours to extract valuable insights. Leveraging this data, companies can fine-tune their product line-ups, enhance their commercial tactics, and cultivate more resilient ecosystem environments, ensuring a dynamic and responsive social commerce experience.

E-commerce

Electronic commerce (e-commerce) employs technology-enabled exchanges to sell goods and services over the internet. E-commerce encompasses a wide range of economic activities, including online retailing, banking, forex transfers, online payments, travel and accommodation booking services, and more. These economic transactions fall into three categories: business-to-business (B2B), business-to-consumer (B2C), and consumer-to-consumer (C2C). The development of mobile applications has enabled online economic transactions to be conducted on mobile devices, tablets, phablets, and smart-wearables.

Digitalization has opened up new possibilities for e-commerce, bringing businesses and consumers closer together. According to a Forbes Advisor article citing 2022 data, global social media commerce spending reached $992 billion and is anticipated to soar to an impressive $8.5 trillion by 2030 (Rizvi, 2022). Moreover, the global subscription e-commerce market will reach $1 trillion by 2025 (McKinsey, 2021). Online purchases can be made through online marketplaces, retailer websites, brand websites, and emerging digital purchase points.

The impact of e-commerce on consumer behaviour

Since its inception in 1995, e-commerce has experienced an extraordinary growth, transforming from a nascent sector into a massive global economic powerhouse. This significant evolution has brought about profound changes in business practices, market dynamics, and consumer behaviours. E-commerce has evolved beyond its original function as an online retail channel, becoming a vibrant platform for media and encouraging the development of distinctive capabilities and services that are absent in the conventional brick-and-mortar realm. Additionally, e-commerce has empowered businesses to bridge geographical boundaries, reaching consumers worldwide, leveraging the unparalleled reach of the internet.

Consumers, in turn, have benefited from e-commerce's expansive reach, gaining access to a broader array of products at more competitive prices. E-commerce has catalysed a change in consumer behaviour, with a growing number of individuals opting for online shopping. In response to this evolving environment, brick-and-mortar stores have also embraced e-commerce, establishing online platforms to remain relevant and competitive. Consequently, businesses have increasingly adopted an omnichannel approach to better connect with their customers, offering enhanced choice and convenience. Sellers have also felt the significant impact of e-commerce, encountering heightened competition as the online marketplaces have become more integrated, bringing a variety of businesses and their products easily within consumers' reach.

A comprehensive overview of the 2023 online shopping trends reveals significant insights (Chevalier, 2024): marketplaces are the primary starting point for online product searches for a majority of global consumers (about 30 per cent), underscoring the appeal of platforms like Amazon and Taobao due to their convenience and wide range of options. Despite the dominance of marketplaces, search engines and brand websites maintain a significant presence (approximately 14 per cent each), suggesting that consumers may employ various methods in their search process. Online shopping is becoming the preferred method globally, though in regions such as Europe, traditional in-store shopping on a weekly basis remains more prevalent.

For certain categories like holiday gifts and entertainment, over 70 per cent of consumers show a strong preference for online shopping. Beyond just search, marketplaces also emerge as the top source for online shopping inspiration worldwide (about 35 per cent). Amazon leads in Europe, the United States, and the UK, while Taobao is preferred in China, and Mercado Libre is popular in Latin America, underlining the prominence of local e-commerce leaders. In summary, the trends indicate a significant move towards online purchasing, with marketplaces playing a pivotal role in the consumer experience. However, choices in shopping venues and product categories still exhibit regional differences and specific preferences.

The online marketplace is notably diverse, offering a variety of platforms catering to both B2B and B2C segments, which mirrors the competitive and varied landscape of e-commerce. As of 2023, online marketplaces remain at the forefront of online purchases globally, underscoring the convenience and broad reach of platforms like Amazon and Alibaba. Although Amazon leads in website traffic with 6.1 billion direct visits in December 2023, it ranks third in Gross Merchandise Value (GMV), behind Chinese giants Taobao and Tmall. Statista's insights into the thriving e-commerce industry for 2024 reveal a clear growth trajectory: retail e-commerce sales are expected to surpass $6.3 trillion globally in 2024, emphasizing the growing importance of online shopping (Statista, 2023d).

Consumer motivations for online shopping

Research suggests that the consumer purchase decision process typically follows a sequence of steps: need awareness, information search, alternative evaluation, purchase decision, and post-purchase behaviour (Cheung et al., 2014; Verhoef et al., 2015). Online shopping provides consumers with advantages over brick-and-mortar stores, primarily due to the enhanced access to information and alternatives. Online shopping offers several benefits that contribute to its popularity:

Ease of comparison: Consumers can easily compare a product across numerous online retailers with just a few clicks. A major aspect of online purchasing poised to benefit from AI improvements is price comparison, as noted by 50 per cent of participants in a 2023 survey (Chevalier, 2024a). This anticipation enhances consumer interest in finding pertinent deals, promotions, and products.

Access to customer reviews: Online shoppers have access to a wealth of customer reviews, enabling them to make informed decisions based on real-world experiences.

Price transparency: Online retailers are less likely to charge exorbitant prices for generic products due to the ease of price comparison.

Convenience and time savings: Online shopping eliminates the need to travel to physical stores, saving time and effort.

Wider product selection: Online retailers often offer a broader range of products compared to physical stores.

Given the increasing demand for convenience, e-retailers must provide quick, efficient, and flexible delivery services to sustain online sales growth. As discussed earlier, convenience is a key driver of online shopping. If e-retailers fail to meet consumer expectations for fast and flexible delivery options, such as next-day delivery or specific time slots, they risk losing customers to competitors who prioritize convenience. The ease of switching between online retailers further underscores the importance of maintaining consumer perceptions of convenience. Consumers can effortlessly compare products and retailers online, making it easy to switch brands if one fails to meet their expectations. To retain customers, retailers must continuously work to enhance convenience and exceed consumer expectations. This approach is evident in the success of companies like Amazon.

Amazon operates in a wide array of markets, including AI and cloud computing services through Amazon Web Services, as well as digital streaming through platforms like Prime Video and Amazon Music. Despite this diversity, its core focus remains on online retail (e-commerce). In the United States, Amazon dominates the retail e-commerce sector, holding a significant market share that far surpasses its competitors. The global rise in online shopping, driven by the convenience of finding and having products delivered to one's doorstep often by the next day, has contributed to Amazon's staggering growth. Capitalizing on the trend of increasing consumer preference for online purchases, Amazon has solidified its status as a leading force in the industry.

Real-time and targeted prediction of online purchasing behaviours

To achieve real-time and targeted prediction of customer online purchasing behaviours, e-commerce platforms require a comprehensive set of prediction model systems. This involves using data mining, machine learning, statistics, and other methods to uncover knowledge and extract data features. Building on this foundation, a knowledge base for knowledge storage and representation serves as a guide, and a system capable of transforming data inputs into behavioural predictions is established. The core elements of this system include: (1) analysing and understanding consumer behaviour patterns using data processing techniques to create detailed profiles based on consumer actions and preferences; (2) developing predictive models to forecast consumer purchasing behaviours, coupled with comprehensive analysis to grasp the factors that influence their buying decisions; (3) investigating the operational mechanisms and key components that form the core of the predictive system, guaranteeing its efficiency in predicting consumer needs.

In addition, personalized purchasing experiences have redefined how consumers interact with products, but social commerce goes even further. By seamlessly blending social interactions with the shopping journey, digital platforms are creating more dynamic, engaging, and community-driven commercial ecosystems.

Social commerce

Social commerce is a rapidly evolving form of e-commerce that exploits the power of social media platforms and online communities to facilitate transactions (Sturiale and Scuderi, 2013). Social media is no longer just a platform for sharing and connecting. It is increasingly becoming a dynamic marketplace where transactions effortlessly intertwine with social interactions. This emerging phenomenon is reshaping how we shop and interact online.

Particularly, social commerce allows users to utilize their social networks for sharing their online shopping journeys and discussing various products and services. This collaboration cultivates a community spirit, enabling users to base their buying decisions on reliable recommendations from their peers. By promoting the sharing of credible information, social commerce helps users compare prices and secure the best deals.

In scholarly discussions, social commerce has been defined through different lenses (Sharma and Crossler, 2014). It is identified as a segment of e-commerce that thrives on community-based and relational interactions in online marketplaces. The integration with social networking sites (SNSs) enables transactions through a wide range of internet technologies (Horng and Wu, 2020). Given the widespread use of SNS platforms, customers can now engage in online communities, sharing their experiences and discussing products and services with peers.

Zhou et al. (2013) describe social commerce as 'the use of internet-based media (SNSs platforms) to enable users to participate in selling, buying, comparing, and sharing of information about products and services in online marketplaces and communities'. This description emphasizes the user participation aspect and the role of SNSs as platforms for interaction. Sturiale and Scuderi (2013), on the other hand, define social commerce as 'an evolution of Web 2.0 online commerce that allows greater interactivity and engagement among customers via blogs, wiki systems, and sharing of articles written by community members'. This statement highlights the focus on user-generated content (UGC) and increased customer engagement facilitated by Web 2.0 technologies. Finally, according to Liang and Turban (2011), social commerce is 'a subset of e-commerce that involves using social media to assist in e-commerce transactions and activities, with a focus on social interaction between customers'. These definitions showcase the core aspects of social commerce: collaboration, information sharing, and a shift towards a more interactive online shopping experience.

Social commerce is thus built on three key pillars: social media, e-commerce functionalities, and Web 2.0 technologies. These Web 2.0 technologies, such as social media platforms and UGC, facilitate the social interactions and information sharing that are essential to social commerce. Social commerce can be broadly categorized into two main approaches:

E-commerce with social features: This category includes established e-commerce websites like Amazon that have incorporated Web 2.0 functionalities. These functionalities allow for UGC, such as product reviews and ratings, and limited social interaction between customers. However, interactions are typically confined to commenting on existing reviews, and features like direct messaging or adding other users as friends may be absent.

Social networks with e-commerce integration: This category consists of social media platforms like Facebook that have integrated e-commerce features. For example, a brand like Armani Exchange might have a Facebook page where customers can browse products, engage with the brand, and even make purchases directly within the platform. This approach allows for a wider range of social interactions (e.g. C2C, B2C), supports various content formats (text, images, videos), and enables both consumers and vendors to contribute content.

Features like Instagram Shopping allow users to explore, shop, and make purchases from within the platform. Some platforms offer discounts to users who buy in groups (i.e. group buying) or share products with their networks, including peer-to-peer selling or community-based commerce within social platforms or groups.

Social commerce: Empowering the consumer

The transition from traditional e-commerce to social commerce has profoundly altered how businesses interact with consumers (Huang and Benyoucef, 2013). While social commerce is a modern phenomenon, its roots can be traced back to earlier forms of e-commerce, where the integration of user interaction with online shopping began to take shape. Two primary changes brought about by social commerce include: First, social commerce strengthens consumers by fostering online communities and promoting the sharing of information (Hajli et al., 2017). The availability of reviews, recommendations, and direct communication among peers equips consumers with the knowledge to make well-informed decisions and potentially secure more favourable terms, thereby transferring some level of bargaining power from sellers to buyers. Second, social commerce elevates the shopping experience beyond mere transactions. It moves the focus of e-commerce from being product-centric to consumer-centric (Huang and Benyoucef, 2013). Through social interaction and UGC, businesses can more effectively customize their products and marketing approaches to align with consumer desires and expectations.

Traditionally, e-commerce and social media have existed in separate spheres. However, social commerce integrates product discovery, purchase, and community engagement into the very fabric of social media platforms. Users no longer need to navigate away from their preferred social networks to complete transactions, creating a frictionless and integrated experience. This fusion is driven by several key elements:

User-generated content: The rise of social commerce is not just about transactions on social platforms; it is about a fundamental change in how consumers engage with products and brands. At the heart of this transformation lies UGC, playing a vital role in shaping purchase decisions and promoting a vibrant online community. UGC encompasses any content created by consumers related to products or brands, encompassing everything from reviews and testimonials to photos, videos, and live-streams. Unlike traditional marketing materials, UGC is authentic, relatable, and often trusted more by potential buyers than polished advertisements (Bahtar and Muda, 2016; Ayeh et al., 2013).

UGC provides consumers with a window into the real-world experience of using products. Seeing real people wearing an outfit, trying out a new gadget, or sharing their honest opinions builds trust and reduces purchase anxiety. Consequently, 'positive' UGC acts as social proof, demonstrating the value of a product to others and influencing their purchase decisions (Cheong and Morrison, 2008). This peer-to-peer recommendation carries more weight than traditional marketing messages, leading to higher conversion rates. UGC also develops a sense of community around shared interests and products. Consumers can connect, discuss products, and discover new items through UGC, creating a more engaging and interactive purchasing experience.

Influencer marketing: Compared to traditional reliance on high-profile celebrities, contemporary marketing is increasingly turning to micro-influencers. These individuals possess engaged, niche followings and offer a more relatable persona than the polished endorsements of the past. Their authenticity and deep connection with their communities foster higher audience engagement and trust, ultimately leading to improved sales conversions. Therefore, companies are prioritizing collaborations focused on personalized recommendations and content that resonates with specific target audiences.

Built-in social functionalities: Live-streams, interactive polls, and seamless checkout processes create a dynamic and engaging environment that encourages both social connection and economic activity. Reminiscent of late-night television infomercials, but reimagined with interactive capabilities and engaging personalities, live-stream shopping has emerged as a novel e-commerce format. Platforms like TikTok, Instagram, and YouTube are now integrating live shopping features, enabling brands and influencers to host dynamic sessions, demonstrate products in real time, and directly address viewer inquiries (Perez, 2020; Cai et al., 2018). This format applies elements such as AR try-on features, flash sales, and exclusive offers, all within a framework that promotes community engagement and excitement.

Social commerce offers convenience by enabling users to discover and purchase products within their social media platforms, reducing the steps needed to make a purchase. Furthermore, integration with social media allows for greater user interaction, engagement, and UGC related to products or service. Firms can also exploit data from social media to target ads more effectively to the right audience, based on their interests, behaviours, and preferences. On the other hand, instant feedback and reviews from users can help companies improve their products or services and address customer concerns promptly. Social commerce is an evolving domain, with platforms continually innovating and adding new features to enhance the social shopping experience, making it an integral component in the broader e-commerce ecosystem.

Developing a social commerce strategy

While companies like Tom's, Samsung, and Armani Exchange have effectively used social commerce for brand promotion, others such as Walmart have encountered obstacles due to customer apprehensions regarding security, privacy, and the reliability of information sharing (Cheung at al., 2014). Establishing trust is fundamental for online retailers, especially within the social commerce domain.

As discussed, social commerce relies heavily on UGC, encompassing reviews, ratings, and social media dialogues. However, the vast amount of UGC, combined with the absence of in-person interactions, complicates the process for consumers to discern authentic feedback from deceptive content. Trust in social commerce does not just involve the retailer; it also extends to confidence in both the seller and the credibility of UGC (Sharma and Crossler, 2014; Hajli et al., 2017;; Lin et al., 2019). This is particularly challenging given the lack of traditional trust-building mechanisms such as direct interaction.

It is thus critical for businesses in the social commerce sector to address issues related to security, privacy, and the authenticity of UGC. Tackling these concerns is

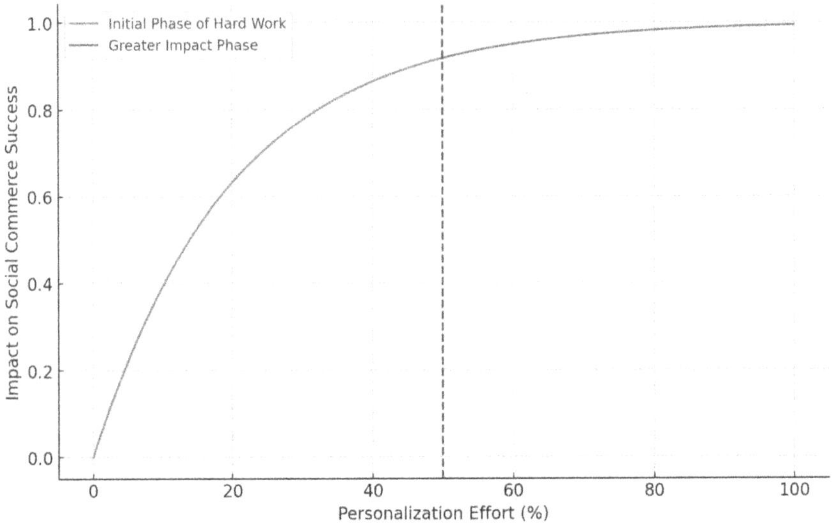

Figure 2 Impact of increasing personalization effort on the success of social commerce.

essential for social commerce firms to create trust and enhance consumer engagement in social commerce transactions.

Figure 2 depicts the critical relationship between personalization efforts and the success of social commerce, beginning with the 'Initial Phase of Hard Work'. In this phase, the benefits to social commerce success gradually increase as personalization efforts intensify. This involves comprehensive strategies such as in-depth user data analysis to understand customer preferences, examining UGC, developing products and services tailored to these preferences, and effectively marketing these personalized offerings to meet individual customer needs.

The curve then advances into the 'Greater Impact Phase', a period where the return on personalization efforts becomes more pronounced. The hard work invested in the initial phase establishes a robust foundation, making subsequent personalization efforts more impactful and efficient. This could include refining algorithms for better recommendation systems, utilizing customer feedback for continuous improvement, and enhancing user experience based on personalized interactions. The transition illustrates that while initial efforts in personalization require substantial investment and may yield gradual results, persistence beyond a certain threshold leads to accelerated benefits, thereby significantly enhancing the success of social commerce initiatives.

Live-streaming commerce

While data analytics forms the backbone of personalization efforts, real-time trends like live-streaming take these strategies a step further. The ability to interact with products and sellers in real-time adds an element of immediacy and engagement that further personalizes the shopping experience. The concept of live-stream shopping, often referred to as 'shopstreaming', has also transformed the way we shop online, especially in the aftermath of the Covid-19 pandemic. Positioned at the intersection of social commerce and the wider e-commerce sector, this engaging shopping approach combines the real-time nature of live-streaming with the functional aspects of e-commerce platforms. It allows viewers to purchase products instantly during a live broadcast, making the shopping experience more interactive and engaging (Cai et al., 2018). This method creates a direct connection between sellers and their audience, enabling live interactions, instant product showcases, and immediate responses to consumer queries.

The increasing consumer desire to incorporate social elements into online shopping signifies a notable evolution in the digital commerce arena. As mentioned, platforms like Instagram have integrated shopping functionalities, making it seamless for users to go from product discovery to purchase within the application. This advancement underscores the transformation of social media from simply being a platform for marketing and communication to becoming an essential sales channel for the future. Alibaba's Taobao, a leading force in the online retail space in China, is at the forefront of this innovative shopping concept with the introduction of Taobao Live. This platform merged the immediacy and engagement of live-streaming with the convenience of online shopping, allowing viewers to make purchases while tuning into live broadcasts. This integration of entertainment and commerce rapidly reshaped the online shopping scene in China, establishing a model that other leading online retailers, including JD, Tmall, and the international powerhouse Amazon, would eventually adopt.

Live-stream shopping stands out for its distinctive characteristics, such as the ability for real-time interactions (simultaneity) and its inherent authenticity, which adds a personal touch to the shopping experience. Typically, participants broadcast using their own devices, such as smartphones or computers with webcams, allowing for a direct and interactive connection with their audience. This interaction is further enriched as viewers can communicate with the hosts in real time, or express their appreciation and support through financial contributions or the purchase of virtual gifts with real currency.

Twitch, founded in 2011, is a live-streaming platform primarily focused on video gaming but has expanded to include various types of content such as music, creative arts, and social interactions. Acquired by Amazon in 2014 for $970 million, Twitch has grown into the leading platform in the live-streaming industry, boasting over 140 million monthly active users as of 2021. Twitch features real-time chat functionality that allows viewers to interact with streamers and other viewers, fostering a strong community atmosphere. It offers monetization options for streamers through subscriptions, Bits (a virtual currency for cheering), and direct donations. Integration with Amazon Prime provides subscribers with free monthly channel subscriptions, in-game loot, and other perks. The platform hosts diverse content categories beyond gaming, including 'Just Chatting', music, art, and more, attracting a broader audience.

Twitch's interactive chat and community features have created a loyal and engaged user base, emphasizing community and personal connection, which differentiates it from other video platforms. It provides various revenue streams for content creators, including subscriptions, Bits, ads, and sponsorships, attracting and retaining top-tier streamers. While gaming remains its core, Twitch's expansion into other categories like music, creative arts, and live talk shows has broadened its appeal. Twitch has become a go-to platform for esports tournaments and live events, further establishing its dominance in the gaming community.

However, managing inappropriate content and maintaining a safe environment for users is a significant challenge due to the vast number of live-streams. Competition from other platforms like YouTube Gaming, Facebook Gaming, and Microsoft's Mixer (before its shutdown) has created a competitive environment. Streamers often critique the revenue-sharing model, pushing Twitch to continuously innovate and offer better incentives.

Twitch has significantly impacted gaming culture and has been a critical platform for the rise of esports and gaming influencers. Its success has driven innovation in live-streaming technology and community engagement, setting industry standards. Twitch's focus on community, diverse content, and strong monetization opportunities for streamers has cemented its position as the leader in live-streaming. Despite challenges, its continuous growth and influence on digital culture highlight its importance in the entertainment and gaming industries.

The motivations behind viewer participation in live-stream shopping have been examined through various theoretical frameworks by researchers. One notable method involves the Elaboration Likelihood Model (ELM), which illuminates the factors influencing consumer behaviour within live-stream shopping contexts (Petty and Cacioppo, 1986). ELM, grounded in the principles of dual-process theories, elucidates how persuasion mechanisms can affect human perception and actions. ELM suggests external information is important in triggering rapid changes in attitudes and subsequent behaviours. Live-stream shopping introduces novel information, encouraging viewers to reassess their pre-existing beliefs, attitudes, and behaviours. Such re-evaluation can result in profound shifts in consumer shopping habits, making ELM an instrumental framework for dissecting the intricate nature of consumer engagement in live-stream shopping settings.

Amazon Marketplace

Amazon enhances the shopping experience for its users in several ways. Its recommendation engine is a critical part of its strategy, suggesting products based on users' browsing and purchase history, and items in their shopping cart. The platform also customizes search results to match individual user behaviour and preferences, ensuring the most relevant products are shown. Personalized marketing efforts include emails, push notifications, and advertisements tailored to the user's purchase history, wish list, and browsing activities, engaging users and encouraging conversions.

Dynamic pricing strategies are employed to offer variable prices to users based on demand, availability, and their behaviour, which can incentivize purchases and maximize revenue.

The user interface of Amazon's website and apps is personalized for each user, with homepages varying to highlight different products, categories, or promotions based on the user's interests and interactions. Amazon Alexa allows for voice shopping, using personalization to understand user preferences and suggest relevant products.

Furthermore, Amazon offers subscription services like Amazon Prime, providing personalized content in the form of movies, music, and books adapted to users' viewing, listening, and reading habits. Amazon's A+ Content feature enables sellers to create enhanced product descriptions with images, videos, and interactive elements, making product presentations more engaging and informative.

Sellers on the Amazon Marketplace collaborate with the company's personalization systems to enhance their listings and advertisements, ensuring they are featured in personalized search and recommendation outcomes. By implementing Amazon's personalization algorithms, sellers have the opportunity to boost their product visibility and sales. Similarly, personalization can improve the purchasing experience by facilitating the discovery of relevant and appealing products. Research reveals that dynamic pricing strategy is already being employed by more than five hundred vendors on Amazon Marketplace (Chen, 2017; Chen et al., 2016). This widespread adoption suggests that sellers are increasingly turning to data-driven strategies to stay competitive in the dynamic e-commerce environment. By employing dynamic pricing, these sellers can instantly respond to market changes, competitor pricing, and consumer demand patterns, ensuring their offerings remain attractively priced and relevant to the constantly evolving preferences of online shoppers.

However, sellers on the Amazon Marketplace also face a variety of challenges. The platform is extremely competitive, with millions of sellers vying for the attention of buyers, making it difficult for new entrants to gain visibility and drive sales. Adhering to Amazon's extensive set of policies and regulations is mandatory, but the complexity and intricacy of these rules can be daunting, with non-compliance risking account suspension or bans. Product reviews are crucial on Amazon; a high volume of negative reviews can significantly damage a seller's reputation and deter potential buyers, making the management of a positive review profile a challenging but essential task.

Moreover, Amazon's search and recommendation algorithms are in a constant state of flux. Keeping up with and adapting to these changes is necessary for maintaining high visibility in search rankings, but it can be a challenging endeavour. Amazon also imposes a range of fees on sellers, including selling fees, advertising fees, and fulfilment fees. These fees can accumulate, especially for sellers of high-volume products, and impact profitability.

Another significant challenge is the presence of counterfeit products on the platform. Sellers can face penalties if associated with counterfeit products, even unwittingly, which can damage a seller's brand reputation. Overcoming these challenges requires a strategic approach, which includes a deep understanding of Amazon's platform, active management of product reviews, staying informed about algorithm changes, careful financial planning to accommodate fees, and implementing measures to guard against counterfeit products.

Despite the hurdles, the Amazon Marketplace presents a lucrative opportunity for sellers. Those who navigate the platform's complexities and effectively manage the inherent challenges can realize substantial growth and success. By mastering Amazon's policies, optimizing product listings for the ever-evolving algorithms, maintaining a strong reputation through positive reviews, and carefully managing financial aspects such as fees, sellers can tap into the vast customer base and diverse market that Amazon offers. Moreover, implementing strategies to safeguard against counterfeit products can protect and enhance brand integrity. Thus, while the Amazon Marketplace is competitive and demanding, it holds the potential for significant rewards for those who adeptly manoeuvre through its challenges.

Etsy, known for its vibrant marketplace featuring handmade and vintage items, operates on a more intimate scale compared to large e-commerce platforms like Amazon but holds a significant position in nurturing independent creativity and entrepreneurship. This platform is distinguished by its focus on unique, often personalized products, making it a hub for artisans, crafters, and vintage sellers seeking to connect with a global audience. Etsy's operational ethos is deeply rooted in values such as creativity, diversity, and sustainability, which are evident not just in the products it hosts but also in its approach to management and community building.

The platform's strategies are also designed to support independent sellers in various ways, from providing them with tools and insights to optimize their online stores to fostering a sense of community among sellers through forums and teams. Etsy's initiatives often encourage sellers to embrace eco-friendly practices, whether in their production methods or packaging, aligning with the company's commitment to sustainability. This focus on sustainability not only appeals to a growing segment of conscious consumers but also helps to differentiate Etsy in the crowded e-commerce environment.

While platforms like Amazon and Etsy have streamlined the way businesses connect with consumers, their influence goes far beyond convenience. These platforms are disrupting traditional economic structures, enabling new forms of entrepreneurship and restructuring industries like retail, finance, and the gig economy.

Business-consumer interactions: From passive consumers to engaged participants

Social media platforms and the evolving digital environment have catalysed a significant change in business-consumer interactions. While the term 'social media' encompasses a broad spectrum of online platforms, at its core, it refers to spaces that actively encourage user participation through content creation, information sharing, and idea exchange (Lin and Kishore, 2021). This interactive nature has fundamentally changed B2C relationships, driving engagement and creating new avenues for communication, innovation, and relationship building.

The rise of social media transcends mere engagement with 'brands'. Its true power lies in the ubiquity and diverse range of uses it offers. Beyond connecting with friends and family, people use these platforms for job seeking, conducting business, engaging with organizations, and participating in communities of interest. This interconnectedness encourages a collective intelligence where every voice contributes to shared knowledge and understanding. Social media also presents an opportunity for co-creation and collaboration unlike anything before. When individuals feel a sense of ownership over a project or initiative they helped shape, it fosters deeper engagement and action. This collaborative spirit extends beyond product development and can be applied to community building, social change initiatives, and more.

Why people socialize?

Socialization is an important aspect of human development, playing a fundamental role in shaping individuals and societies (Chang et al., 2022). It encompasses a dynamic process of learning and adapting to the cultural norms, values, and expectations of a particular society. Through social interaction, individuals acquire essential knowledge, skills, and behaviours that enable them to function effectively within their social environment. Social interactions serve as the building blocks of society, promoting connections and facilitating the exchange of ideas, information, and emotions. They provide opportunities for individuals to develop empathy, cooperation, and a sense of belonging, fostering a cohesive and interdependent social fabric.

Social interactions manifest in various forms, adapting to the evolving nature of human communication and the technological advancements that shape our interactions. Face-to-face interactions, where individuals engage in direct communication through verbal and non-verbal cues, remain a cornerstone of social interaction. However, the rise of technology has paved the way for new forms of social connection, such as online communication platforms, social media networks, and virtual meeting spaces.

Social recommendations and influence theory

One of the main characteristics of social media is the recommendations which occur between users. Social recommendations involve personalized suggestions from peers within a user's social network, effectively aiding individuals in discovering new online products, such as music. According to Onnela and Reed-Tsochas (2010), social influence can shape online human behaviour; in other words, people's online behaviour can be influenced by the actions of others on social media. Social influence through social media can contribute to increased similarities within networks, as suggested by Crandall et al (2008). This phenomenon, known as homophily, involves forming and strengthening connections with existing friends and creating new connections with similar individuals within the network (Ma et al., 2015). However, it is important to note that homophily is likely driven by a combination of factors, including shared interests and values, not solely by social influence.

Social exchange theory, which revolves around the exchange of resources between individuals through interactions, underpins the concept of online network relationships and the social resources derived from them (Cropanzano et al., 2017). Social media act as channels for receiving social support (or mitigating emotional exhaustion), making social media usage a potent factor in facilitating social support (or emotional exhaustion), which plays a pivotal role in influencing consumer purchase behaviours. For instance, platforms like Facebook offer interactive features (such as messaging) that enable users to seek social support from colleagues or bolster intangible resources to address their depletion and fatigue, which are central elements of emotional exhaustion.

The impact of social media on social interactions

Social media has altered the realm of social interaction, providing unmatched opportunities for connecting and sharing information. Social media interactions frequently guide users towards certain behavioural patterns, like commenting or chatting, which can shape their engagement and responses (Shrihari and Srinivasan, 2012; Savci et al., 2021; Lin and Kishore, 2021). Moreover, social media significantly affects knowledge sharing and dissemination through social interactions. These interactions act as channels for exchanging ideas, experiences, and viewpoints, promoting communal learning and innovation.

At their core, social interactions are characterized by reciprocal influence, where individuals mutually impact each other's thoughts, feelings, and behaviours (Cialdini, 2009). This dynamic interplay forms the basis of social relationships, shaping individual and collective actions (Lin and Kishore, 2021). In conclusion, social interactions, encompassing both face-to-face and technology-mediated communication, serve as the foundation for learning, connection, and the exchange of knowledge and information. Understanding the dynamics of social interaction is essential for fostering healthy and thriving societies.

Research indicates that social media serves as an effective platform for fulfilling individuals' need for social approval (Savci et al., 2021; Strickland and Crowne, 1962; Satow,1975). This need, characterized by the desire to gain social recognition from others during social interactions, can be satisfied online with less effort compared to regular face-to-face encounters (Sciara et al., 2023). Contemporary social interactions and communication have now become key factors in establishing trust with customers and gaining social approval. Many companies have showcased their authenticity and integrity, significantly impacting consumer purchasing decisions through this trust. This trust is cultivated through the consistent provision of outstanding and prompt customer service. Likewise, businesses boost customer engagement by presenting distinctive product characteristics, which solidify trust and encourage enduring customer connections. Trust thus plays a pivotal role in shaping consumer purchasing habits, underscoring its essential function in the decision-making process of consumers.

In addition to heightening desire, peer content on social media is believed to influence behaviour through social influence mechanisms (Sciara et al., 2023; Cialdini, 2009). For instance, endorsing products by giving 'likes' on social media or participating in a brand's social media community (Shrihari and Srinivasan, 2012; Lin and Kishore, 2021) has been shown to boost purchasing activity. Beyond the personalized engagement on social media platforms, significant advancements in mobile technology have made such interactions highly mobile-friendly, as people increasingly use mobile devices to stay active on these platforms for extended durations. The rapid spread of smartphones has led to the introduction of numerous mobile applications (apps), revolutionizing how consumers carry out various daily activities, including shopping, bill payments, locating local businesses, gaming, communicating with friends, and obtaining driving directions.

The power of peers: eWOM and the megaphone effect

In the online space, electronic word-of-mouth (eWOM) has become a key factor influencing opinions and decisions (Gvili and Levy, 2023; Bond et al., 2019; Thoumrungroje, 2014). Recommendations and insights shared by everyday users on social media hold immense weight, often surpassing traditional marketing messages

(Lisjak et al., 2021). This 'peer-to-peer' influence thrives because people trust their fellow individuals more than faceless corporations. The megaphone effect further amplifies this influence (Sunstein, 2003). Certain individuals, whose tastes and preferences resonate with others, emerge as powerful voices. These social media 'megaphones' can shape trends, drive behaviour, and even create their own mini-communities.

People create content for a variety of reasons, from self-expression and entertainment to fostering communities and sharing knowledge. This diverse range of content adds authenticity and engagement to social media platforms, blurring the lines between professional media and user-driven narratives. Social media holds tremendous promise for both individuals and communities, yet it comes with its set of challenges (Savci et al., 2021; Pittman, 2015; Naylor et al., 2012). Issues like fake news, misinformation, and concerns about privacy demand vigilant monitoring. Nonetheless, by engaging with social media through a lens of critical thinking, prioritizing authentic connections, and dedicating oneself to responsible use, we can tap into its extensive capacity to cultivate meaningful relationships, influence our environment, and pave the way for a more enlightened and interconnected future.

Social commerce in action

Social commerce is evolving beyond passive scrolling and tapping 'like'. Organizations are now crafting immersive experiences that actively engage their audience, blurring the lines between browsing, interacting, and buying (Lu et al., 2016).

The power of the SMI: Authenticity, expertise, and engagement

One prominent trend is the rise of social media influencers (SMIs). Representing a new breed of independent third-party advocates who influence audience opinions through online posts and media, SMIs provide companies with a potent means to connect with and engage their target audiences. From fitness instructors and foodies to beauty bloggers and beyond, SMIs use platforms like Instagram to share their (paid and sometimes unpaid) perspectives on products and services. Recognizing the persuasive potential of SMIs, companies have developed systems to identify and monitor those most relevant to their goals. These efforts often rely on key performance indicators (KPIs) such as daily post reach, content reposts, and follower count (Ki and Kim, 2019; Lowe-Calverley and Grieve, 2021). Furthermore, companies have begun segmenting SMIs into two distinct categories: micro-influencers with smaller followings and macro-influencers with larger reach.

Among various social commerce tactics, celebrity and influencer endorsements remain the most popular for building brand image (Lee and Watkins, 2016). By partnering with well-liked and recognized figures, companies can tap into their established audiences and gain significant reach. Moreover, when consumers see a trusted personality endorsing a product, they may associate the brand with that individual's positive qualities, leading to increased credibility and purchase intent (Hovland and Weiss, 1951). Similarly, research on influencer marketing highlights the importance of authenticity. Ye et al. (2021) find that users are increasingly discerning, seeking influencers who genuinely believe in what they promote.

SMIs have risen as a powerful force in personalized selling, and their influence goes far beyond traditional celebrity endorsements (Boerman, 2020; Ye et al., 2021). Below, we explore the key characteristics that contribute to the impactful influence of SMIs.

Authenticity: In an environment overwhelmed by sleek advertisements, there is a growing desire among consumers for authentic interactions. SMIs provide a much-needed alternative. They are not remote celebrities but approachable figures who share their experiences and viewpoints in a manner that resonates as genuine and credible. This fosters a community atmosphere and a sense of inclusion, rendering their endorsements more influential than traditional celebrity promotions.

Expertise: Modern consumers are in pursuit of knowledgeable recommendations from individuals who genuinely grasp their interests. SMIs frequently specialize in distinct niches, establishing themselves as authoritative figures within their domains. Their profound understanding and enthusiasm for their specialty imbue their advice with authenticity and worth, positioning them as essential allies for businesses aiming to engage with particular demographics.

Engagement: SMIs transcend the role of mere content producers; they are engaged communicators, encouraging a dialogue with their audience. Through comments, direct messaging, and live Q&A sessions, they cultivate a sense of community and allegiance. This continuous engagement nurtures trust and a collective identity, rendering their endorsements more relatable and potent compared to traditional, one-directional advertising messages.

Authenticity, expertise, and engagement are not just buzzwords; they are the cornerstones of the SMI's influence. By understanding these core strengths, companies can use the power of SMI partnerships to build meaningful connections with their target audience, drive brand loyalty, and ultimately achieve their marketing goals in the dynamic world of social commerce.

Micro-influencers: Authenticity redefines influence

In social commerce, the spotlight has now moved from mega-celebrities to a new breed – micro-influencers. These individuals, with their engaged and niche followings, offer a refreshing alternative to the polished endorsements of the past. Their relatable persona and deep connections within their communities encourage a higher level of engagement and trust, ultimately leading to improved sales conversions.

Companies are increasingly forging collaborations with micro-influencers, utilizing their authenticity and targeted reach (Boerman, 2020; Brooks et al., 2021). These partnerships focus on personalized recommendations and content that resonates deeply with specific audiences, fostering a sense of genuine connection and promoting brand loyalty. In contrast to the broader reach of mega-celebrities, micro-influencers offer a more targeted and impactful approach, allowing firms to directly engage with their ideal customer segments. This move towards authenticity and personalized experiences is shaping the future of social media engagement, and micro-influencers are poised to play a leading role in this transformation.

Influencers and social media play a critical role in formulating consumer perceptions and behaviours. However, it is not just about who is delivering the message - it is also about how consumers are responding. In the next section, we explore the psychology behind consumer decision-making in the digital age and how social commerce is significantly impacting these processes.

Promoting co-creation and value beyond products

As argued in Chapter 5, co-creation enables businesses to incorporate consumers directly into their innovation processes. This aligns with sociological research highlighting the embeddedness of economic behaviour within social contexts (Granovetter, 1985). Social contagion plays a significant role, with word-of-mouth recommendations from peers holding immense sway over purchase decisions.

Communication is the bedrock of meaningful co-creation, and social media platforms have emerged as powerful facilitators in this process. Compared to traditional media, their reach, interactivity, and ability to bridge the online and offline worlds make them ideal for promoting dialogue, influence, and collaboration between businesses and consumers. Furthermore, social media platforms serve as vibrant repositories of user-generated knowledge about products and services. This shared information empowers consumers to participate in co-creation through various means, including:

UGC such as reviews, blogs, and social media posts creates valuable resources for both companies and other consumers, shaping perceptions and influencing purchase decisions;

online discussions in interactive forums and comments sections facilitate knowledge sharing, idea exchange, and collaborative problem-solving between consumers and businesses;

real-time feedback through instantaneous responses and reviews provide invaluable insights for product and service improvement, enabling companies to adapt and iterate quickly;

community relationship networks formed on social media foster a sense of belonging and shared purpose, allowing consumers and businesses to co-create experiences and build lasting relationships.

Co-creation transcends the conventional boundaries of production and consumption, engaging consumers in 'co-production' activities such as applying their knowledge and insights to improve or innovate products and services, and openly sharing information and feedback to help companies identify improvement opportunities and refine their offerings. Within sustainable development, the lines between consumer and producer roles blur, making co-creation a reciprocal process where both sides actively contribute to and gain from their interactions and participation. On social media platforms, this dynamic is exemplified by consumers helping each other in 'constructing' the objects of their consumption, a process

Table 3 Social Commerce, Personalization, and Co-creation Strategies across Various Industries

Industry	Social commerce strategy	Personalization approach	Co-creation outcome
Automotive	Conduct social media contests for designing the next car model, engaging automotive enthusiasts.	Offer customizable car features based on social media feedback and engagement.	Launch a new car model designed with direct input from the brand's social media community.
Electronics	Run interactive social media campaigns where users can suggest and vote on upcoming gadget features.	Introduce gadgets that can be personalized with features chosen by social media voters.	Release electronic products that incorporate the most requested features and customizations from social media feedback.
Beauty and cosmetics	Collaborate with beauty influencers to create social media buzz around customizable makeup palettes.	Provide personalized beauty recommendations and custom product bundles based on social media interactions.	Introduce a new line of cosmetics co-created with the brand's social media followers, reflecting current beauty trends.
Clothing brand	Use social media platforms to showcase limited edition designs and solicit customer design submissions.	Create made-to-order clothing based on customer designs and preferences shared on social media.	Offer a special collection of clothing designed through collaboration with the brand's social media audience.
Travel and hospitality	Engage with followers on social media to share their dream vacation ideas and preferred travel amenities.	Design travel packages that include personalized experiences based on social media suggestions and trends.	Provide tailored travel experiences co-created with potential travellers, enhancing customer satisfaction and loyalty.

known as use value or experience value, which thrives on continuous engagement and interaction.

Co-creation can be used to develop a wide variety of products, including:

Physical products: Lego Ideas, Xiaomi Mi Community, and Nespresso Vertuo are all examples of co-creation physical products.

Digital products: Software companies often use co-creation to develop new features and products. For example, the software company Atlassian uses co-creation to develop new features for its Jira and Confluence products.

Services: Co-creation can be used to develop new services. For example, the airline company JetBlue uses co-creation to develop new in-flight services.

Co-creation and social commerce

Social commerce and co-creation naturally complement each other. Social commerce offers a venue for businesses and brands to engage with their customers and gather their input (Horng and Wu, 2020). Using social commerce and co-creation, companies can enhance their products and services and forge deeper connections with their clientele. Customization, or adapting products and services to fit individual tastes, plays a significant role in social media engagement. Personalization, however, takes it a step further by infusing a unique, personal touch, fostering a closer bond and, as a result, greater trust in the brand. Empirical evidence consistently supports the superiority of personalized social media engagement tactics over generic, wide-reaching strategies (Jain et al., 2021).

Table 3 shows the integration of social commerce, personalization, and co-creation within different industries, showing how they execute social media to engage customers, adapt products and services to their preferences, and incorporate their ideas into the final offerings, enhancing the customer experience and encouraging loyalty. Envision offering products that not only reflect a customer's past choices but also anticipate their future needs. By examining browsing habits and social media inclinations, businesses can propose items that truly align with each customer's unique interests and aspirations. Advanced AI algorithms now enable businesses to categorize audiences by demographics, preferences, and online behaviours, facilitating offers that are highly pertinent and engaging.

Embracing the evolving dynamics of social commerce through co-creation extends beyond just boosting sales; it is about nurturing robust bonds with the audience (Chevalier, 2024b; Jain et al., 2021). Concentrating on authenticity, engagement, and active community involvement lays the foundation for a supportive brand ecosystem in the digital age. It is essential to recognize that adapting experiences to match the distinct preferences and interests of individuals is key to achieving enduring success in this rapidly changing environment.

8

Fast fashion and circular economy

In the environmentally conscious city of Greenford, a groundbreaking start-up named 'EcoCycle Solutions' emerged, driven by a mission to transform the fashion industry through a circular economy model. Founders Bushra and Hanif, motivated by the detrimental environmental impacts of fast fashion, aimed to offer a sustainable alternative that minimized waste and promoted resource reuse. EcoCycle Solutions unveiled a line of high-quality, sustainable apparel crafted from recycled materials and designed to last.

The business model of EcoCycle was anchored in the three fundamental principles of the circular economy: Reduce, Reuse, and Recycle. The start-up focused on sustainable sourcing, collaborating with suppliers committed to eco-friendly practices, and utilizing materials like recycled plastic bottles and organic cotton. Their dedication to sustainability was also evident in their minimalist design philosophy, which promoted timeless, versatile clothing to encourage consumers to buy less but of higher quality, enhancing the longevity of each garment.

To build a community centred around sustainability, EcoCycle organized monthly clothing swap events, both virtually and at their Greenford base. These events enabled customers to exchange their previously worn EcoCycle garments for others' pre-loved items. Alongside, the company offered complementary repair services, greatly prolonging the life of their products and discouraging the constant buying of new items. EcoCycle also introduced a take-back programme, providing discounts on future purchases to customers who returned their old EcoCycle clothes. These returned items were either refurbished for resale or recycled into new materials, fostering a closed-loop system. The company invested in research and development, focusing on pioneering recycling techniques for complex materials like blended fabrics and dyes, aiming for a zero-waste production cycle.

Technological innovation was a key part of EcoCycle's strategy to reinforce its circular practices. They developed an innovative app that allowed customers to track the life cycle of their garments – from the sourcing of materials to the recycling options available – enhancing transparency and engaging consumers. The app also supported the clothing swap programme and offered repair tutorials, encouraging active participation in the circular economy. EcoCycle's commitment quickly resonated with eco-conscious consumers in Greenford and expanded to wider audiences. The company's success led local policymakers to consider incentives for businesses that adopt circular economy practices, sparking a city-wide initiative to boost sustainability across various sectors.

By integrating sustainable sourcing, promoting reuse, and spearheading recycling innovations, EcoCycle Solutions not only reduced its environmental impact but also cultivated a community of informed consumers and set a precedent for sustainable practices in the broader fashion industry.

Building on the principles of circular economy established by EcoCycle Solutions, the broader e-commerce sector is also experiencing a shift towards more sustainable practices.

Prioritizing sustainability: Ethical and eco-conscious consumption in e-commerce

The rise of social commerce has brought a growing awareness of the ethical and environmental implications of our purchases. Consumers are increasingly prioritizing sustainability, seeking products that align with their values and minimize their environmental footprint. This translates into a demand for transparency, traceability, and social responsibility within the social commerce environment. For example, social platforms are facilitating increased transparency, enabling sellers to showcase their sustainability practices, production processes, and sourcing materials. This allows consumers to make informed choices, supporting sellers who align with their ethical and environmental standards. For example, platforms can introduce badges or labels highlighting sustainable products, fair trade practices, or carbon-neutral offerings.

Furthermore, consumers are demanding greater traceability throughout the supply chain, wanting to understand the origin and journey of the products they purchase. Social commerce platforms can offer features that allow users to track the production chain of an item, from raw materials to finished product. This empowers consumers to make conscious choices about sellers who prioritize ethical labour practices and responsible sourcing. Social commerce also presents an opportunity to highlight sellers who promote social good and community engagement. Platforms can showcase sellers who support local communities, employ sustainable practices, or contribute to social causes. This provides consumers with a way to align their purchasing decisions with their values and contribute to positive societal change.

The increasing focus on sustainability in e-commerce presents both challenges and opportunities for sellers. Companies must adapt their practices to meet the evolving demands of conscious consumers, prioritizing transparency, traceability, and social responsibility throughout their operations. Platforms, on the other hand, have the opportunity to shape the narrative around sustainable consumption by providing tools and features that empower consumers to make informed and ethical choices.

In this context, personalization in fashion offers a promising strategy to mitigate the negative impacts of fast fashion by focusing on sustainability and waste reduction. When clothing items are personalized, they tend to hold more value for consumers, which can lead to longer usage periods. This extended use could reduce the need for frequent new purchases and lower the volume of clothing that ends up discarded, thereby reducing the environmental footprint of fashion consumption. Besides, the move towards personalization facilitates made-to-order production, addressing the widespread issue of overproduction in the fast fashion industry. By manufacturing garments based on individual customer demands, brands can significantly reduce excess inventory that would otherwise be wasted. Moreover, personalized products that cater to specific preferences and sizes are likely to increase consumer satisfaction, potentially slowing the rapid turnover of clothing items as consumers may prefer to keep and use garments that closely align with their personal needs and tastes.

Personalization also supports the adoption of more sustainable business models, such as on-demand production and circular fashion initiatives, which advocate for the use of sustainable materials and eco-friendly practices. The integration of advanced technologies, such as artificial intelligence (AI) and 3D printing, into personalization processes not only customizes the fashion experience but also improves the sustainability of production methods. For example, 3D printing can significantly cut down on material waste by using only the necessary amount of fabric for each piece of clothing.

Additionally, personalization encourages a shift towards slow fashion, creating a deeper connection between the consumer and their garments. This approach promotes a culture that values quality, sustainability, and ethical production, contrasting with the rapid consumption model typical of fast fashion. Broadly, personalization in fashion leads to more sustainable and thoughtful consumption patterns. By emphasizing individuality and minimizing waste, it aligns with the principles of the circular economy and offers a practical solution to the challenges posed by fast fashion.

Circular economy

The concept of a circular economy has been evolving since the 1970s, with the 2002 'Cradle to Cradle' theory emphasizing the importance of closing resource loops through both biological and technical recycling (McDonough and Braungart, 2002; Guldmann and Huulgaard, 2020; Geissdoerfer et al., 2017). However, the fashion industry's journey towards circularity gained significant momentum in 2012 with the Ellen MacArthur Foundation report. This report defined a circular economy as 'an industrial system that is restorative or regenerative by intention and design' (EMF, 2012, p. 5; 2017), offering a stark contrast to the environmentally detrimental 'take-make-dispose' model of the traditional, linear economy.

As a result, the inefficient use of clothing and materials within the linear model leads to alarming levels of waste and pollution. In fact, the fashion industry is the world's second largest environmental polluter, producing an estimated 20 per cent of the total global water waste and accounting for 10 per cent of all carbon emissions (UN Environment Programme, 2018). While the fashion industry has increasingly become a platform for self-expression and a symbol of cultural, social, and personal identity, this popularity has also fuelled the rise of 'fast fashion', which faces relatively little consumer scrutiny despite its significant environmental impact.

Origins of the circular economy

Though originally coined in the eighteenth century for sustainable forest yields, definitions of sustainability have evolved greatly. While Harwood (1990) views it from an agricultural and environmental lens, others emphasize individual well-being. Subsequently, the Brundtland Report established economic growth, environmental protection, and social equity as interdependent pillars of sustainable development. This emphasis on interconnectedness ensures that environmental concerns are not addressed in isolation. While environmental sustainability is a primary concern for implementing a circular economy within the fashion industry, it is not without careful consideration of the potential benefits for the economy and society. In fact, a circular economy that causes a significant decline in either economic or societal well-being would have failed to create an improved sustainable system, regardless of environmental progress (Kirchherr et al., 2017; Ryberg et al., 2020).

'Limits to growth'

Boulding's (1966) work was prophetic in predicting the Earth's need to transition from the unsustainable 'cowboy economy' of relentless extraction and limitless resource assumptions to a 'closed economy' characterized by circularity and resource efficiency. His 'spaceman economy' metaphor, envisioning our planet as a spaceship with finite resources, became a catalyst for much subsequent ecological thought.

The 'Limits to Growth' theory (Meadows et al., 1972) built upon Boulding's ideas by presenting predictions of societal collapse in 2100 if current consumption patterns continued. While their extreme projections faced criticism for being unrealistic and excessive, the theory highlighted the interconnectedness of resources, pollution, and societal well-being. Critics like Wallich (1982) argued against halting growth, advocating for technological solutions. Despite challenges, 'Limits to Growth' ignited a crucial debate about planetary limitations and the need for sustainable practices, leaving a lasting impact on environmental discourse.

Shifting paradigms: From growth to steady state

A compelling alternative proposed by Daly (1993) acknowledges the environmental limitations of our current 'natural growth' economic model. He envisions a transition to a 'steady-state economy', where both population and the total stock of physical capital remain constant. This model posits that the current focus on endless growth disregards the true value of production when comparing it to the ecological damage caused by unsustainable resource extraction and material use.

While some voices, resonating with critiques of the 'limits to growth' theory, suggest that technological innovations could uncouple economic expansion from resource consumption, the belief in a 'tech-fix' solution might be excessively optimistic. Blomqvist et al. (2013) suggest that, while resource efficiency improvements can play a role, a complete decoupling might be unlikely or insufficient to fully address environmental concerns. Therefore, Daly's steady-state framework remains a relevant proposition for considering alternative economic models that prioritize ecological sustainability alongside human well-being.

Booming fashion, unsustainable growth

The fashion industry has seen considerable expansion in the twenty-first century, driven by various factors. The growth of the global population and a rise in average income levels have certainly contributed. Evidence supporting this includes data indicating that textile production and consumption have doubled in the past decade (Shirvanimoghaddam et al., 2020).

While Souchet (2019) attributes the industry's ecological impact primarily to 'fast fashion', a response to increased demand, a more nuanced perspective is necessary. Accenture (2019) argues that both population growth and rising living standards contribute to the phenomenon, but highlight the influence of social media as a key driver. These platforms expose consumers to constant information about trends, often through influencers and personal networks, creating a strong social pressure to stay stylish and embrace new looks. This fuels demand for the rapid cycle of production and consumption characteristic of fast fashion (Todeschini et al., 2017; Sorensen, 2019; Cachon and Swinney, 2011). Furthermore, social media provides fashion brands with real-time insights into trend fluctuations, prompting them to quickly develop and release new products to capitalize on fleeting fads (Jackson, 2001). This further perpetuates the fast fashion cycle.

Fashion's wasteful reality: A call for change

The fashion industry faces significant environmental challenges. Water consumption is a major concern. Manufacturing a single shirt and pair of jeans requires an estimated nineteen thousand litres of water (Claudio, 2007). This highlights the importance of business models that prioritize extending garment life cycles and reducing overall production (Pedersen et al., 2019).

Land pollution is another issue. Dickson et al. (2009) report that 85 per cent of textiles end up in landfills each year. This, along with the fashion industry's contribution to 10 per cent of global carbon emissions (UN Environment Programme, 2018), underscores the urgent need for drastic change. Population growth further magnifies these challenges. The United Nations (2015) predicts that with current consumption patterns, we may need the resources of nearly three planets to sustain our lifestyles. This scenario underscores the critical role of the fashion industry in reversing environmental damage.

Transitioning to a circular economy could provide a solution. This model emphasizes resource recovery and reuse, minimizing waste and pollution. The latest ideas in the circular economy are diverse and innovative, focusing on waste-to-resource initiatives and employing technology for more sustainable practices (Stahel, 2019).

Fast fashion: Popularity amidst environmental concerns

The fashion industry bears significant responsibility for environmental damage, but fast fashion stands out as a major culprit due to its rapid, resource-intensive production cycle. This short life cycle, leading to mountains of textile waste, has drawn increasing criticism from consumers (Todeschini et al., 2017; Gopalakrishnan and Matthews, 2018). However, the allure of fast fashion persists. The paradox of fast fashion lies in its undeniable environmental impact juxtaposed with its enduring popularity. Understanding the factors driving its appeal, from affordability and trendiness to a responsive supply chain, is important for addressing the industry's challenges and exploring potentially sustainable alternatives.

The ever-shrinking fashion cycle

The vast and growing apparel industry compels players to constantly adapt to evolving consumer demands just to stay afloat. This competitive pressure not only influences pricing strategies but also fuels the need for frequent product updates, leading to an inflated number of 'seasons' offered by retailers (Dissanayake and Sinha, 2015). To cater to this rapid churn, clothing production and consumption must keep pace, resulting in a dramatically shortened fashion life cycle. This cycle encompasses the journey of a garment from design innovation to peak popularity, decline, and eventual obsolescence (Armstrong et al., 2014; Buttle et al., 2013).

While it appears like clothing production solely drives consumer behaviour, the relationship is more nuanced. Increased seasonality and product offerings undoubtedly influence consumer choices, encouraging impulse purchases and faster wardrobe turnover. However, the initial surge in production is ultimately driven by the ever-shifting landscape of consumer desires, making the two entities inextricably linked (Hirscher et al., 2018; Kozlowski et al., 2018).

As the environmental costs of fast fashion become increasingly evident, technological innovations are emerging as essential tools for mitigating these impacts. Advances in recycling technology, AI-driven personalization, and sustainable production methods are reforming how the fashion industry approaches waste reduction.

Fast fashion firms and their business strategies

Fast fashion firms and their digital partners have generally perfected a rapid response strategy to fashion trends, enabling them to move designs from concept to store shelves in just a few weeks. This agility in their supply chain allows for frequent updates to their product lineup, keeping their offerings fresh and aligned with current trends (ING, 2020; Mukendi et al., 2020). For example, H&M and Zara employ advanced supply chain strategies to minimize lead times and costs (Ghemawat and Nueno, 2006). This includes closely integrating with suppliers, optimizing logistics, and leveraging technology for efficient inventory management. These practices enable them to rapidly respond to fashion trends, rotate stock frequently, and introduce new products to the market efficiently, maintaining their competitive edge in the fast fashion industry.

On the other hand, Forever 21 and Gap leverage economies of scale and global sourcing to minimize production costs. By ordering large quantities of materials and products, they can negotiate lower prices with suppliers. Moreover, their global sourcing strategy allows them to manufacture products in countries where labour and materials are more cost-effective, further reducing expenses and enabling them to offer competitive prices to consumers. Fashion Nova uses social media and influencer partnerships by collaborating with a wide range of influencers and celebrities to promote their products. This strategy helps them reach a vast audience and enhances brand visibility, especially on platforms like Instagram, where fashion and lifestyle content are highly consumed.

Despite their success, these companies have encountered criticism and challenges related to their business practices. For example, Gap has faced controversies related to the working conditions in their supply chain, with reports highlighting issues such as gender-based violence and poor labour practices in factories located in Asia. These issues have been linked to the fast fashion industry's demands for quick production turnarounds and low costs, leading to challenging working environments for factory workers. On the other hand, Fashion Nova has faced criticism for the quality of their products, with some customers reporting that the items they received did not meet their expectations in terms of material and construction. Concerns have been raised about the durability and fit of the clothing, suggesting that while the items may be trendy and affordable, they might not offer the best value in terms of long-term wear and quality (Gueye, 2021; EMF, 2017).

Integrating circular economy practices

In terms of the specific circular economy innovations, several fast fashion and apparel companies are adopting these practices to reduce their environmental impact and promote sustainability:

H&M is a notable example in the fast fashion industry, making significant strides towards sustainability. The company is redesigning its product development life cycle to align with circular economy principles, aiming for all its materials to be recycled or sustainably sourced by 2030. They have implemented garment collection initiatives in their stores and are working towards reducing water consumption in their supply chain. H&M's approach includes optimizing resource use, developing new sustainability business models, and demonstrating corporate social responsibility leadership through investments in start-ups that advance technology for sustainable supply chains.

Levi Strauss is addressing the wasteful nature of the fashion industry through various strategies. Their Authorized Vintage collection allows customers to have pre-worn jeans repaired, resized, or restyled by in-house tailors. The company is also committed to producing new garments from 100 per cent recycled cotton by 2025, promoting the reuse and recycling of clothing. Adidas has developed innovative solutions to the challenge of recycling footwear, a typically difficult task due to the mixed materials and glues used. They have created a running shoe made from a single recyclable material without any glue, allowing the shoes to be easily recycled into new pairs. This initiative is part of a broader effort to ensure that used garments and footwear can be turned into new products, avoiding downcycling and landfill.

These examples describe the diverse ways in which companies in the fast fashion and apparel sectors can integrate circular economy practices into their digital operations, from product design and materials sourcing to end-of-life recycling and reuse. Similarly, prominent brands such as Nike, Levi's, and Hugo Boss are adopting personalization strategies to address the environmental concerns associated with fast fashion. Nike's 'Nike By You' platform allows customers to customize their footwear, Levi's offers tailored jeans through their 'Tailor Shop', and Hugo Boss has introduced tech-integrated fashion that links physical items with digital identities, enhancing the user experience in the metaverse. These approaches not only deepen customer engagement but also aim to minimize waste and foster sustainable practices within the fashion industry.

Neglected driver: Consumer choices in the circular fashion economy

While discussions on the circular economy often prioritize manufacturing transformations, the vital role of consumer behaviour remains largely underexplored. This oversight poses a significant threat to the model's success, as Hobson et al. (2016) aptly point out: radical shifts in consumption patterns are crucial for maintaining material lifecycles and preventing waste.

Wastling et al. (2018) provide a useful framework by outlining three key stages where consumer behaviour impacts the circular loop. Firstly, the acquisition stage requires a preference for purchasing used clothing over new items, alongside increased engagement with rental services. However, ING's (2020) report throws a wrench into this initial step, revealing that 72 per cent of consumers are only willing to participate in sustainable practices if they involve no additional effort compared to conventional shopping. This suggests the need for seamless and convenient alternatives for second-hand acquisition and renting.

Secondly, during the consumption stage, extending garment life cycles through repairs becomes instrumental. Vogtlander et al. (2017) reinforce this point, emphasizing that the circular economy hinges on encouraging behaviours that support remanufacturing and reselling. This necessitates encouraging proper garment care and readily accessible repair services. Finally, the disposal stage completes the loop by promoting second-hand selling or free exchanges. This aligns with Vogtlander et al.'s (2017) assertion that neglecting consumer-driven disposal pathways jeopardizes the entire circular model.

A worrying trend within the discourse is the overemphasis on technological advancements as the sole solution to sustainability challenges. This techno-centric approach risks overlooking the critical role other stakeholders, like consumers, play in developing a circular fashion industry. The past decade has witnessed a surge in environmental consciousness, shaping consumer attitudes and influencing their buying decisions. This shift is not accidental. It arises from a growing awareness of the environmental degradation plaguing our planet, fuelled by human activities.

Consequently, corporate environmental responsibility has ascended corporate agendas worldwide, as businesses seek to align with increasingly eco-conscious consumers.

Online strategies to influence consumer behaviour

We need to deepen our understanding of consumer behaviour in the online realm. For instance, examining how social commerce utilizes virtual communities to meet specific transactional objectives can provide valuable insights. Similarly, the role of user-generated content (UGC) in shaping how consumers develop relationships with companies and brands warrants further exploration. These elements are central to developing more environmentally sustainable relationships between companies and customers. As consumers become more aware of the environmental impact of their fashion choices, the role of technology in supporting sustainable practices has become increasingly vital. From AI-driven personalization to advanced recycling techniques, technology offers powerful solutions to help reduce waste and promote more ethical consumption. Consequently, businesses are likely to pay greater attention to the demands of circular economies. Moreover, there is a pressing need to explore the psychological mechanisms that influence consumer behaviours to achieve desirable social outcomes. As observed in the fast fashion industry, consumers play a significant role in driving trends. To meet circular economy goals, it is vital to use online strategies such as virtual communities and UGC to influence consumer behaviours towards sustainable consumption in fast fashion and similar sectors.

Although many companies are making significant strides towards sustainability by implementing recycling programmes and promoting eco-friendly products, consumer responsibility remains equally important. Without a corresponding change in consumer behaviour, even the most progressive corporate initiatives may fail to achieve their full potential. While businesses are rethinking their strategies to prioritize sustainability, consumers hold considerable influence over the fashion industry. As demand for transparency and ethical practices grows, companies are being compelled to adapt their models to meet these evolving expectations.

Why social commerce relies on virtual communities

Social commerce can leverage virtual communities and social media platforms to reshape how consumers engage online. While traditional research on online purchasing emphasizes trust in websites and sellers, virtual communities introduce a critical new element: social knowledge (Leal et al., 2014; Porter and Donthu, 2008). In these communities, members engage in sharing experiences, recommendations, and insights about products, contributing to a collective repository of information that guides purchasing decisions. This shared knowledge enables consumers to make informed and thoughtful decisions, significantly influencing their intent to purchase.

Beyond knowledge sharing, the reputation and content quality of the virtual community itself play a significant role. Both positive and negative feedback ripple through the network, directly influencing potential consumers' perceptions and purchase decisions. This shows the critical role of community management in fostering trust and promoting responsible information sharing. Community trust positively influences online word-of-mouth, directly affecting purchase intentions; moreover, positive interactions among members foster trust and loyalty, ultimately leading to enhanced purchasing behaviour. This broader perspective illuminates the complex ecosystem within virtual communities that shapes consumer decision-making.

The power of connection: How virtual communities thrive

Virtual communities hold immense potential for businesses, particularly in the circular economy sector, offering valuable platforms for user engagement and information exchange. Porter and Donthu (2008) explain the unique composition of virtual communities – anonymous internet users united by shared hobbies and interests. This leads to a certain homogeneity in content, often governed by community norms that guide and restrict user behaviour. Synthesizing these insights, we can distil several key characteristics of virtual communities:

They break down geographical constraints, allowing for a global reach and openness. Within these communities, member identities often maintain a certain level of anonymity.

Communication is diverse, extending beyond just text to include images, videos, and audio, enhancing the richness of the shared experiences and underscoring the platforms' role in facilitating information exchange.

Socialization occurs within the digital environment, where members partake in interactions and community-driven activities, fostering a sense of belonging and social engagement, albeit virtually.

The 'Little Red Book'

The digital revolution has empowered smartphones as the undisputed driving force behind the surging social commerce market. This change is not confined to purchases; a significant portion of social media and news consumption has migrated to mobile platforms, making them fertile ground for targeted product placements. Platforms like Instagram, with its focus on visual content sharing, exemplify this trend. Influencers leverage its reach to create authentic and engaging content, effectively recommending products to a vast audience. Similarly in China, RED, known as the 'Little Red Book', has emerged as a powerhouse in social commerce.

Launched in 2019, RED quickly amassed over three hundred million registered users, capturing a 46 per cent market share. Initially positioned as a cross-border shopping app, it provided premium content for consumers seeking international brands. However, facing stiff competition, RED pivoted in 2018, amplifying its social features and downplaying cross-border shopping.

Today, RED thrives as a hybrid platform, seamlessly blending a vibrant virtual community with an online marketplace. Users forge connections based on shared interests, brands, and even stores, fostering a dynamic environment for information exchange. High-quality content is the lifeblood of this ecosystem, with engaging text, pictures, and video notes dominating UGC. RED actively incentivizes content creation through new user support initiatives, ensuring an ever-flowing stream of valuable information for potential buyers.

This focus on UGC is not merely for engagement; it directly influences the RED Mall's product selection. Popular items from the community find their way to the storefront, creating a symbiotic relationship between the virtual space and the online store. Users discover products through community posts, compare options seamlessly, and ultimately complete the purchase cycle within the platform, making RED a self-contained 'closed loop' for consumption. This unique blend of social networking and e-commerce distinguishes RED from traditional online retailers. While studying user behaviour in conventional e-commerce platforms has yielded valuable insights, RED's social attributes introduce new and exciting complexities. Understanding how community dynamics and UGC influence purchase decisions in this rapidly evolving landscape presents a thrilling frontier for research and innovation.

Monitoring and responding to online conversations

Monitoring and responding to conversations about their offerings is a challenge for many organizations. The concept of the 'connected consumer' suggests that consumers are no longer passive recipients of information; instead, their online activity and content contributions have become valuable tools for marketers (Chevalier and Mayzlin, 2006; Chintagunta et al., 2010). Online reviews, a form of electronic word-of-mouth and UGC, are now central sources of information where customers can infer feedback about products and services (Moe and Trusov, 2011). Firms that enhance their online review platforms can improve market performance, as research shows online reviews significantly influence customers' purchase intentions and have measurable impacts on sales and customer acquisition (Guo et al., 2020).

Many companies are using online reviews as a marketing tool (Gour et al., 2021). For instance, TripAdvisor.com has become a leading information hub in tourism, collecting extensive customer travel experiences through reviews. Similarly, Amazon.com features robust peer-evaluated review systems for its products (Banerjee et al., 2017). The way information is consumed and what information is consumed are critically important in the context of products and services.

Research on online reviews has explored the influence of perceived usefulness, credibility, and risk on purchase intentions (Guo et al., 2020; Sussman and Siegal, 2003). Scholarly work on online reviews has largely focused on valence and volume attributes, with valence being a core sentimental metric. Studies indicate that the valence of online reviews directly impacts the sales of products and services such as movies, books, beauty products, and video games (Chintagunta et al., 2010; Moe and Trusov, 2011).

Why UGC matters

In the current era, where information is abundant, people often depend on recommendations from both their personal networks and online communities. UGC, which includes everything from comprehensive product reviews to brief social media updates, plays a significant role in influencing consumer decisions. This range of content, from detailed analyses to casual updates, has a notable impact on purchasing behaviours. Studies, such as those by Ayeh et al. (2013), Guo et al. (2020), and Moe and Trusov (2011), affirm this influence. Furthermore, research by Leal et al. (2014) identifies two primary factors that affect the impact of UGC: informational influence, which derives from the trust consumers place in the shared insights and experiences of others, and normative influence, which relates to the inherent human desire to align with the behaviours and norms of one's social group, as also discussed by Banerjee et al. (2017) and Petty and Cacioppo (1986).

The practice of advertising is also evolving, with a marked shift towards valuing authentic stories from real people. UGC is at the forefront of this change, with platforms like Instagram and YouTube becoming hubs where product reviews and unboxing videos do more than just inform; they significantly shape purchasing decisions. A key feature of UGC is the quality of information it offers (Chintagunta et al., 2010; Gour et al., 2021). UGC is also characterized by its interactive nature, moving away from the static, one-way communication of traditional media to create a dynamic space where users not only gather information but also share their views and engage in conversations. This interactivity goes beyond simple search functionality, embracing real-time feedback and peer discussions, thus breaking free from the limitations of traditional media formats.

Litvin et al. (2008) find an interesting nuance regarding the influence of the platform on which UGC is shared, suggesting that the platform itself does not significantly affect trust levels. Instead, personalized recommendations and curated collections of UGC seem to have a stronger impact on consumer trust. This insight points to the potential of platforms that apply AI and other technologies to customize and highlight pertinent UGC, thereby amplifying its persuasive power. In essence, the strength of UGC lies in its synthesis of high-quality information, interactive engagement, and system usability (Cheung and Thadani, 2012). It not only delivers authentic and pertinent content but also encourages active participation and ensures a seamless user experience. This amalgamation of features makes UGC a powerful factor in personalized selling, significantly affecting consumer behaviour and buying patterns.

Understanding the consumer mind

Today's well-informed customers, who are adept at conducting online research before making purchases, necessitate that companies adopt innovative business strategies. This is especially critical in the fast fashion and circular economy sectors, where a deep understanding and strategic use of consumer psychology in content and sales strategies are essential. We will now explore key aspects of consumer psychology and how they can be integrated into content creation to effectively engage these savvy consumers.

The role of emotions in content use strategies

Emotions significantly influence how individuals engage with content, impacting not just logical reasoning but also subconscious feelings and motivations that drive behaviour. This effect is supported by research, which highlights the profound impact emotions have on cognitive processes and decision-making. Various theoretical models, such as Ekman's classification of six basic emotions or Beck's four-factor model, offer different perspectives on categorizing emotions, yet all acknowledge their critical role in shaping user interactions.

Positive emotions, in particular, are key in content strategy. Evidence suggests that content that elicits positive responses such as joy, amusement, or wonder tends to attract more attention, encourage sharing, and enhance user engagement (Berger and Milkman, 2012). For instance, content that includes laughter or images of smiling people can stimulate endorphin release, fostering relaxation and creating positive associations with the content (Jackson, 2016).

Beyond happiness: Exploring the power of sadness in content strategies

Conventional wisdom often associates positive emotions with viral content and successful marketing. However, sadness, frequently overlooked in content strategies, may hold immense potential for creating impactful experiences. While negative emotions are indeed less common in viral content (Libert and Tynski, 2013), research suggests they can uniquely drive engagement and memorability. Key arguments for incorporating sadness in content strategies are as follows:

Fostering empathy and action: Sadness can trigger empathy in viewers, leading them to connect with the message on a deeper level. This connection can motivate action, such as sharing the content, supporting a cause, or seeking solutions (Vos, 2015).

Enhancing recall: Studies indicate that negative emotions are often more memorable than positive ones (Libert and Tynski, 2013). This increased recall translates to a longer-lasting impact, ensuring the message remains with viewers long after exposure.

Creating unforgettable experiences: Sadness can evoke vulnerability and intimacy, allowing brands to connect with audiences on a personal level. This vulnerability can lead to more authentic and memorable experiences, strengthening consumer loyalty and trust. Positive emotions often drive the success of viral content and marketing efforts, yet the impact of sadness in content strategies might be underappreciated. Despite being less prevalent in viral content, negative emotions such as sadness can significantly influence engagement and leave a lasting impression.

Sadness has the power to stir empathy in viewers, drawing them closer to the message's core. This emotional bond can motivate individuals to share the content, advocate for a cause, or seek out solutions. Moreover, negative emotions are typically more memorable than positive ones, ensuring that the message resonates with the audience for an extended period. Furthermore, sadness can foster a sense of vulnerability and intimacy, creating a more profound and personal connection. This genuine engagement can enhance loyalty and trust, making the experiences shared through the content truly unforgettable.

Beyond positivity: The impactful potential of fear, surprise, and anger in content

Content strategies frequently lean towards positive emotions to drive engagement and influence. Yet, incorporating a broader spectrum of emotions, including fear, surprise, and anger, can be equally or more effective in resonating with audiences and prompting action (Clough, 2016). For example, fear, when applied judiciously, can captivate viewers by creating a sense of urgency and focus, enhancing message retention and spurring action, especially when coupled with actionable solutions. Environmental documentaries, for instance, might use fear to highlight urgent threats and galvanize support for conservation initiatives.

Surprise acts as a catalyst for engagement by disrupting expectations and sparking curiosity (Johansson, 2017). This can facilitate the introduction of new ideas or viewpoints, fostering a conducive environment for learning and comprehension. Educational materials that incorporate surprising elements or unexpected facts can grab students' attention and improve memory retention. Anger, though requiring careful handling, can be a powerful motivator for social change and collective action. Content that channels anger towards injustices or societal issues can build a sense of unity, drive communal efforts, and heighten the call for reform. Investigative pieces and exposés often harness this emotion to highlight wrongdoings and inspire demands for justice.

Consequently, while positive emotions have their place in content creation, exploring the dynamics of fear, surprise, and anger can open new avenues for impactful communication. By skilfully navigating these emotional terrains, creators can produce content that not only engages but also inspires meaningful change.

The power of belonging: How social identity shapes content and consumers

As social beings, identity and purpose are significantly shaped by the groups to which individuals belong. These affiliations, each with its unique norms and values, have a considerable impact on decisions, including purchasing behaviour. Harnessing the concept of social identity in content creation can substantially boost audience engagement and inspire action. Social identity theory suggests that the self-concept is shaped by affiliations with various groups, leading to the adoption of behaviours and attitudes in line with the group's standards (Goffman, 1967; Tajfel and Turner, 1979). This quest for belonging and shared identity is a fundamental driver of actions and choices (Deaux, 1997; Cooley, 1902).

Against this backdrop, content creators can devise strategies that resonate with audiences:

Targeted messaging: Understanding the social identities of audiences enables the crafting of content that aligns with collective values and aspirations. The use of language, imagery, and references that mirror communal experiences and cultural nuances can increase relevance and connection.

Authentic representation: Featuring spokespeople or influencers who reflect the social identities of the audience can enhance trust and rapport. Seeing one's reflection in content strengthens feelings of inclusion and engagement.

Group-specific storytelling: Stories that highlight the unique challenges and victories of the intended audience can foster a sense of community, heightening the feeling of group affiliation. Such narratives can evoke emotional responses and motivate actions aligned with the desired outcomes.

Recognizing the role of social identity enables content creators to establish deeper relationships with audiences, fostering significant engagement and positioning themselves as trusted figures within the community.

The power of 'don't lose out': Harnessing loss aversion in content

Studies highlight a fascinating aspect of human psychology: we often perceive losses more acutely than gains (Kahneman and Tversky, 1979; Thaler, 2017). The discomfort of missing out on an opportunity or the departure from what's familiar can impact us more significantly than the allure of potential benefits (Brenner et al., 2007; Erev et al., 2008; Harinck et al., 2007). This phenomenon, known as 'loss aversion', heightens our sensitivity to potential risks, prompting a strong desire to circumvent them.

Yet, the ethical application of this insight is paramount. Overuse of fear-based tactics can lead to adverse outcomes, such as increased distrust and irritation among the audience (Harley, 2016). Moreover, not all scenarios or products are suited to strategies centred on loss aversion. The effectiveness of such approaches hinges on a deep understanding of the audience's particular concerns, achieved through meticulous research. Content that thoughtfully addresses these worries, presenting solutions that offer real benefits, can gently steer individuals towards taking beneficial actions.

Therefore, employed with care, loss aversion can be a potent mechanism for enacting positive change. It is not about manipulating fears but about empathetically addressing genuine concerns with meaningful solutions. Through this approach, content can assist individuals and organizations in realizing their objectives, nurturing trust, and cultivating rewarding relationships in the process.

Building lasting connections through reciprocity in content

Reciprocity, a fundamental human principle, is essential in forging successful relationships. This concept, emphasized by Cialdini (2009), illustrates our innate inclination to reciprocate favours, making it an influential factor in shaping behaviour. In the realm of content creation, grasping the essence of reciprocity can pave the way for establishing enduring bonds with an audience. The essence of an effective strategy is to give before expecting anything in return, for example, providing audiences with valuable, empowering information that enhances their knowledge and understanding. This gesture of goodwill, sharing expertise and insights without immediate demands, activates the natural tendency towards reciprocation.

Audiences, feeling a sense of gratitude, are more likely to develop loyalty and a favourable view of the brand. This approach is akin to sowing seeds of trust; the enriching content serves as nourishment, developing an environment conducive to ongoing engagement and future partnerships. This method transcends the conventional marketing focus on discounts or promotions, cultivating authentic connections by addressing a deep-seated human desire to be acknowledged and supported.

In conclusion, social commerce has evolved significantly from its origins in social media. Today, companies are not merely posting content and waiting for engagement; instead, they actively pursue various strategies to create interactive experiences. These not only enhance sales but also help cultivate loyal communities. Such interactive experiences are important for gaining deeper insights into consumer participation in online activities and understanding the psychological motivations behind their actions. This understanding is particularly vital, as circular economy objectives, including the development of sustainable fast fashion consumption, can be more effectively achieved by incorporating consumer psychology into content and communication strategies.

9

FinTech: Revolutionizing the financial landscape

Freelance marketer Rachel, based in Toronto, struggled with managing payments from international clients. Traditional banking, with its high fees and slow processing, created a bottleneck in her business operations. She discovered a FinTech solution that promised to simplify her financial management. Setting up was quick and easy, providing Rachel with a global payment gateway within minutes. This allowed her to invoice clients in their local currency, reducing costs and simplifying transactions for both parties.

Real-time transaction tracking eliminated the need for anxious waiting. Rachel could now see the status of every transaction instantly, offering much greater transparency than traditional banking. The FinTech service also offered significantly lower fees, especially for international transfers. This resulted in substantial cost savings for Rachel over time. An integrated invoice system further streamlined her workflow. Rachel could create, send, and manage invoices directly through the platform, saving time and providing clients with a seamless payment experience, which enhanced her professional image.

The most significant benefit, however, was the suite of financial management tools. These tools allowed Rachel to categorize transactions, track income and expenses, and gain valuable insights into her financial health through detailed reports and dashboards. This comprehensive overview empowered her to make informed decisions, plan for the future, and identify opportunities for growth. Adopting FinTech payment and cash transfer services wasn't just about convenience; it was about efficiency, cost savings, and gaining greater control over her finances. This change streamlined Rachel's business processes, allowing her to focus on her core work and spend less time on administrative tasks. Ultimately, this contributed to the growth and success of her business.

Financial technology (FinTech) organizations are changing the way that people and businesses manage their finances. Just like Rachel's experience with streamlining payments, millions of individuals and businesses are now turning to FinTech solutions to simplify their financial lives, as technologies like blockchain and AI continue to evolve. By using technology to automate and streamline financial processes, FinTech companies are making financial services more accessible and affordable for many individuals. For example, PayPal is an online payments system and a worldwide electronic digital currency that supports online money transfers and serves as an electronic alternative to traditional paper methods like checks and money orders. It is owned by PayPal Holdings, Inc., a subsidiary of eBay, Inc., and is the world's largest internet payment processor by total payment volume. PayPal allows users to send and receive money online using a variety of payment methods, including credit cards, debit cards, bank accounts, and PayPal balances. PayPal also offers a variety of other services, such as online shopping checkout, bill pay, and money transfers.

PayPal promotes personalized selling through various strategies to enhance the customer experience. The company exploits customer data, such as past purchases and browsing history, to generate product recommendations. For example, customers interested in travel might receive suggestions for travel insurance or currency exchange services. PayPal sends customized messages through emails and social media, reflecting the user's previous interactions and interests. Moreover, PayPal's customer service is tailored to individual needs, with representatives having access to specific account details and purchase history to offer more effective support.

Another prominent example of a FinTech company is that of Chime, which is a mobile-only bank that offers a variety of banking services, including checking accounts, savings accounts, and debit cards. Chime is known for its low fees and its focus on mobile banking. Chime was founded in 2013 and launched its mobile banking app in 2014. Chime has over fourteen million active users and over $30 billion in deposits. Chime is a good choice for people who are looking for a low-cost bank with a focus on mobile banking. Chime offers a variety of features that are designed to help people save money, such as a high-yield savings account and a fee-free overdraft programme.

Chime incorporates a range of data points to customize its selling strategies effectively. By analysing customer demographics like age, location, and income, Chime can segment its selling messages and product offerings to cater specifically to various customer groups. Similarly, by monitoring customer behaviour, including spending patterns and how they use their accounts, Chime identifies opportunities to introduce customers to additional products and services that may benefit them. Furthermore, Chime actively seeks feedback from customers through surveys to understand their preferences and needs better. This feedback is crucial for Chime to adjust its product development and promotional efforts, ensuring that the offerings align closely with what customers are looking for. Chime is just one example of a broader movement in the FinTech industry, where mobile-first solutions are becoming the norm, catering to an increasingly digital-savvy customer base.

Lastly, Square is a financial services and digital payments company that provides mobile payment processing software and hardware to businesses. It also offers a variety of other financial services, such as loans and payroll processing. Square was founded in 2009 by Jack Dorsey, who is also the co-founder and CEO of X (Twitter). Square's mission is to 'economically empower everyone'. The company does this by providing businesses with the tools they need to start, run, and grow their businesses. Square's products and services are used by millions of businesses around the world, including small businesses, retailers, restaurants, and service providers. Square is known for its innovative products, such as the Square Reader, which allows businesses to accept credit and debit card payments using their smartphones or tablets. Moreover, Square's diverse pricing models cater to a broad spectrum of business sizes and needs, enabling businesses to choose plans that align with their budget and operational requirements.

FinTech also encompasses broader technological trends in financial services, such as Decentralized Finance (DeFi) and algorithmic trading. DeFi is a new financial system that is built on blockchain technology. DeFi applications allow users to lend, borrow, trade, and invest assets without the need for intermediaries such as banks or brokers. This is disrupting the traditional financial services industry, which has long been dominated by a small number of large institutions. Decentralized autonomous organizations (DAOs) are another new type of organization that is enabled by blockchain technology.

DAOs are governed by smart contracts, which are self-executing contracts that are stored on a blockchain. This makes DAOs more transparent and democratic than traditional organizations, as all members have an equal say in how the organization is run. Another example of FinTech innovations in the financial industry is the rise of algorithmic trading. This type of trading utilizes computers to automatically execute trades based on pre-defined rules, and it now accounts for a significant portion of the trading volume on many stock exchanges (EY, 2019; Aitken, Cumming, and Zhan, 2023).

Emerging FinTech solutions

Customers increasingly demand convenient and efficient online banking services. This trend, coupled with the emergence of tech-savvy FinTech start-ups, has compelled traditional financial institutions to adapt and develop more digital offerings. FinTech leverages technology to innovate financial products, services, and processes, enhancing efficiency, convenience, speed, security, reducing costs, and better meeting user needs (Haddad and Hornuf, 2019; Feyen et al., 2021). FinTech addresses the limitations of traditional financial services, where technological expertise, organizational culture, outdated service concepts, or restrictive regulations hinder innovation.

The younger generation, in particular, prefers digital channels over traditional branch-based interactions (Ouimet and Zarutskie, 2014), making them a key target market. Today's FinTech businesses are evolving artificial intelligence (AI) from basic chatbots into intelligent personal financial assistants with deep learning capabilities (Mogaji, 2021). This advancement will empower AI to provide personalized financial guidance, transcending the traditional role of simply retrieving bank information or answering basic questions. As AI continues to transform the financial services, its ability to provide real-time insights and predictive analytics is becoming a game-changer, not only in fraud detection but also in personalizing financial advice and services.

FinTech thus represents a dynamic and rapidly evolving ecosystem encompassing a range of technologies designed to enhance and transform traditional financial services with innovative solutions (Anan et al., 2023). This sector spans applications from mobile banking and peer-to-peer payment platforms to blockchain and cryptocurrency trading. The primary aim of FinTech is to streamline, optimize, and democratize financial services, making them more accessible, faster, and cost-effective.

Efforts include simplifying payments, providing transparent investment services, and delivering advanced data analytics for better risk management and decision-making. FinTech employs cutting-edge technologies such as AI, machine learning, Big Data, and blockchain to make financial processes more efficient and secure (Gupta et al., 2021). AI and machine learning enhance algorithmic trading, credit scoring, and fraud detection, increasing accuracy and reducing costs (Aitken, Cumming, and Zhan, 2023).

Broadly, FinTech enhances existing financial services and opens new avenues for economic engagement, such as financial inclusion initiatives that integrate unbanked populations into the formal economy. As a result, FinTech has evolved into a key factor in shaping the future of finance, making it more inclusive, efficient, and resilient.

Digitalization in the financial services industry

The rapid growth and expansion of the digital economy worldwide necessitate that all market participants make appropriate adjustments to their operations. Traditional banking models, characterized by cash transactions, extensive branch networks, in-person customer service, face-to-face loan interactions, and large-scale operations monitoring, are directly at odds with the demands of the emerging digital society. This new era prioritizes speed, flexibility in payments, automation through AI, and reduced reliance on human labour, leading to a leaner workforce.

The twenty-first century ushers in a new economic era where the highest quality of banking services takes precedence, achieved through two major pillars:

1. Physical separation of users: Users can interact with banks and lenders digitally, establishing a contactless business collaboration.
2. Robotization of banks: Unattended technologies can potentially drive extensive robotization within banks, automating many traditional banking processes.

This move towards digitalization and automation is fundamentally changing the financial services industry at its core, providing customers with unprecedented levels of convenience, efficiency, and personalization (Haddad and Hornuf, 2019). As FinTech continues to evolve, it will be crucial for traditional banks and new FinTech players to adapt and embrace these technological advancements to remain relevant and competitive in the ever-changing financial sector.

FinTech employs advanced digital technologies and data analytics to set new benchmarks in the financial industry. This change has led to the emergence of disruptive FinTech start-ups that, through their focus on customer needs, are gradually gaining market share from established banks. The success of FinTech firms lies in their ability to offer convenient and customized financial services, which are reshaping consumer habits. This new norm of digital convenience and personalized offerings has elevated consumer expectations throughout the retail service sector.

There is a diverse toolkit that AI offers to banks and other financial institutions, highlighting a range of applications beyond the core functionalities discussed above.

Combatting fraud with machine learning

Banks are increasingly using machine learning algorithms to detect fraudulent activity and protect their customers. These algorithms identify patterns in vast data sets, surpassing human capabilities in recognizing suspicious transactions and client behaviour. AI-powered fraud detection models can combat threats like phishing attempts, stolen cards, counterfeit fraud, and irregular transactions. This technology reduces operational costs, enhances security, and potentially increases transaction approval rates by minimizing false positives.

Loan and credit decisions

AI is transforming loan and credit decisions in banking by analysing vast amounts of data to assess borrower creditworthiness. Research suggests a positive correlation between AI and the quality of loan decisions. AI-powered underwriting systems using Belief-Rule-Based (BRB) models combine AI's analytical power with the explainability of traditional rule-based systems, providing accuracy and transparency in loan approvals and rejections. This empowers banks to make data-driven decisions while maintaining clear reasoning behind each outcome, fostering trust and transparency in lending.

AI-powered insights for better decisions

Banks are applying AI for advanced data analysis and portfolio optimization (Gupta et al., 2021). AI can automate data analysis, uncover hidden patterns, and generate predictive insights to inform critical business decisions. This empowers banks to optimize investment strategies, maximize portfolio returns, and provide personalized advice to customers regarding savings and investment decisions.

Streamlining operations with RPA and NLP

Robotic Process Automation (RPA) software is another valuable AI tool used in banking (Villar and Khan, 2021). RPA mimics basic human tasks, eliminating errors and freeing up staff to focus on more complex activities. Deutsche Bank's successful implementation of RPA exemplifies its cost-saving benefits. Combined with Natural Language Processing (NLP), RPA can automate entire workflows previously managed by humans. NLP enables AI to understand and process human language, expanding its automation capabilities.

What is FinTech?

FinTech is widely recognized as the integration of technology into financial services, offering alternatives to traditional methods (Thakor, 2020; Feyen et al., 2021). A more elaborate definition from the Financial Stability Board positions FinTech as a set of technological advancements in financial services capable of altering business models, workflows, and offerings, potentially affecting financial markets and long-standing financial institutions directly (FSB, 2021). This perspective views FinTech not just as a part of financial innovation but as a distinct innovation itself. With its growing application across various sectors like investment management, insurance, and payments, FinTech is not only competing with but also stimulating innovation within traditional financial services (Milian et al., 2019; Yao et al., 2018; Anan et al., 2023).

At its core, FinTech involves using specialized software or algorithms to improve financial services for businesses and consumers alike. What began with computer technology has now extended to a variety of electronic devices, notably smartphones. FinTech now encompasses a range of emerging financial products, services, and models powered by advanced technology. New methods of delivering traditional financial services are also emerging, such as the advent of branchless financial intermediaries like neobanks and the increasing use of online financial services (Rocchi, 2021). Furthermore, disruptive technologies like crowdfunding and peer-to-peer insurance platforms have surfaced as alternatives to conventional financial institutions and insurance companies. These innovations have opened up access to finance, enabling individuals to engage in financial activities that were once exclusive to institutional investors.

According to Ernst and Young's 'Global FinTech Adoption Index 2019' report (EY, 2019), FinTech adoption is surging worldwide. The report highlights China and India as the frontrunners, boasting an impressive consumer adoption rate of 87 per cent, significantly exceeding the global average of 64 per cent. This surge in FinTech adoption reflects a broader trend of industry growth. Statista (2024) reports that the number of FinTech companies globally has skyrocketed, jumping from 12,131 in 2018 to 29,955 in 2024. This exponential rise is further underscored by a 2019 report by PricewaterhouseCoopers (PwC) which revealed that 82 per cent of financial services companies planned to increase FinTech partnerships within the next three to five years (PwC, 2019). This trend towards collaboration continues to hold true, highlighting the growing recognition of the benefits of FinTech integration.

The FinTech sector thrives in environments that embrace a start-up mentality, characterized by companies eager to refine an idea into a marketable product or service, assess customer reactions, and then adapt as necessary. This agile approach allows start-ups to navigate changes swiftly, unlike the slower processes often found in larger, more established organizations. Given their dynamic nature, start-ups typically face fluctuating periods of growth and challenge. Consequently, they tend to employ younger individuals who bring new knowledge and technical skills suited to the company's demands (Ouimet and Zarutskie, 2014). Moreover, younger workers are often a source of innovative ideas, an invaluable trait within the start-up culture, especially in an industry like FinTech, which is continuously influenced by rapid technological advancements (Lazear and Gibbs, 2009).

Mishkin (1999) was an early advocate for the idea that technology could fundamentally change the financial industry by lowering transaction costs and addressing information asymmetries. According to Alt et al. (2018), the rise of the digital information and communication era has greatly accelerated the move towards a digital financial landscape. The digitization of financial services has now spread beyond conventional banking, affecting various industries and sectors across the banking value chain. Jarvis and Han (2021) regard FinTech as a pivotal force, reshaping the entire financial ecosystem with advancements in technologies like AI, blockchain, Big Data, cloud computing, and social media. FinTech is seen as the future trajectory of the traditional financial sector, emerging as a natural progression following the rapid growth of the internet industry.

The rise of FinTech has spurred the ongoing transformation of global financial services from traditional models, covering areas such as payment systems, insurance management, investment management, and deposits. However, FinTech encompasses more than merely technology-driven innovations in business models for service delivery; it also signifies digital innovation within the financial domain. Consequently, the expansion of FinTech is gradually blurring the lines between different sectors, fostering strategic disintermediation, widening investor access to financial services, and altering the way financial institutions conceive their products and services (Philippon, 2016).

As the intersection of technology and finance continues to be a focus for an increasing number of industry experts and researchers, the understanding of FinTech is becoming more refined. FinTech broadly covers financial services enhanced by cutting-edge technologies and the innovative business models that emerge from these services (Mention, 2019). In essence, FinTech represents a vibrant ecosystem, a term that encapsulates technologies aimed at enhancing traditional financial services through innovative technological solutions.

Beyond convenience: How personalization is transforming FinTech

Personalization is increasingly recognized as essential for the success of FinTech companies. By customizing services and products to meet individual user needs, FinTechs can enhance user engagement, increase customer satisfaction, and improve financial outcomes for both users and the company. According to Dynamic Yield's personalization maturity survey, 72 per cent of consumers consider personalization highly important in the financial sector. The pressure to personalize is intensifying due to competitors seeking a competitive edge and internal stakeholders aiming to future-proof their organizations (Santeralli, 2023). We briefly discuss below the benefits of personalization in FinTech.

Enhanced customer experience: Personalization enables FinTech companies to provide a customer experience adapted to the individual's financial behaviour and preferences. By using data analytics to understand each customer's spending habits, investment behaviours, and financial goals, FinTechs can deliver personalized financial advice, product recommendations, and alerts. For instance, if a user frequently sends money overseas, the FinTech app could offer them better rates on international transfers or introduce them to related services like multi-currency accounts.

Improved user engagement: Personalized services encourage deeper user engagement with the FinTech platform. Custom notifications about unusual spending or investment opportunities keep users informed and cared for, increasing their trust and dependence on the platform. This can lead to higher active user rates and longer session times, key metrics for success in digital platforms.

Increased conversion rates: Personalization leads to more effective marketing and sales strategies. By segmenting customers based on financial needs and behaviours, FinTech companies can target specific groups with offers that are more likely to be accepted. For example, a personalized loan offer with pre-approved amounts and tailored interest rates can be more attractive than a generic offer, increasing the likelihood of acceptance.

Risk management: Personalization is critical in risk assessment and management. By analysing personalized data, FinTechs can better understand a user's risk profile and tailor their offerings accordingly. For instance, understanding a user's financial transactions and credit history allows a FinTech company to offer credit products that match the user's repayment capacity, thereby minimizing defaults and reducing risk.

Customer retention: Personalization fosters stronger relationships with users, enhancing customer loyalty and retention. Tailored experiences make users feel valued and understood, a significant advantage in the competitive FinTech market. Furthermore, personalized financial insights and advice help users achieve their financial goals, reinforcing their loyalty to the platform.

Operational efficiency: Personalization allows FinTechs to optimize their operations. By understanding user preferences and behaviours, companies can streamline operations, allocate resources more effectively, and automate routine customer interactions. This not only reduces operational costs but also enables FinTechs to scale their services efficiently.

Product innovation: Insights from personalized data can inform product development and innovation. Understanding detailed customer needs and identifying gaps in existing offerings can lead FinTechs to develop new products or enhance existing ones, ensuring they remain competitive and relevant in the market.

Ultimately, personalization in FinTech is not just about marketing efficiency or sales growth; it is about fundamentally enhancing the way financial services are conceived, delivered, and experienced by users. As technology evolves and more data becomes available, the scope for personalization in FinTech is likely to expand further, driving the next wave of innovations in the sector.

FinTech's integration into commercial banking

FinTech holds the promise of overcoming the challenges faced by traditional banking systems. By incorporating information technology, it has the potential to break down the information silos that are common in commercial banking, thus mitigating problems associated with information asymmetry. In addition, FinTech could improve a bank's resilience against unexpected crises, indirectly strengthening its risk management strategies. This suggests that traditional banks could harness FinTech to improve service quality, refine their offerings, and undergo internal changes, which could lead to a decrease in risky behaviours.

FinTech, characterized by its diversity, adaptability, and disruptive nature, also has the capability to challenge the traditional banking sector's core operations (Haddad and Hornuf, 2019). By externalizing the design, production, and risk management aspects of conventional financial products, FinTech enhances financial functions and broadens access to financial services, promoting financial inclusion. Besides, FinTech plays an important role in facilitating financial disintermediation and liberalization, while also elevating the efficiency and quality of financial services. Technologies such as Big Data and distributed ledgers are pivotal in applications like asset security, supply chain finance, and trade finance.

Can commercial banks digitally transform?

The rise of FinTech presents both challenges and opportunities for commercial banks. While FinTech solutions often boast improved efficiency, convenience, and cost-effectiveness, particularly in areas like payments (PwC, 2019), traditional banks struggle with legacy systems and higher operating costs. This makes them vulnerable to FinTech start-ups that prioritize agility and lean operations (Vives, 2018). As FinTech disrupts traditional banking sectors like payments, financing, and credit, banks are increasingly turning to technological innovation to bridge the gap (Wang and Sui, 2020; Chen et al., 2021). This strategic response highlights how FinTech can act as a catalyst, pushing banks to modernize their services and embrace new technologies to not only survive but thrive in the evolving financial landscape. As a result:

First, commercial banks are increasingly engaging with and investing in the FinTech sector as part of their strategic response to the growing trend. This involvement not only includes heightened investments in FinTech and information technology but also a focused emphasis on the adoption and integration of FinTech solutions within their operations. The surge in FinTech presents an opportunity for technological innovation, allowing banks to immerse themselves in the FinTech arena by acquiring expertise and technologies. This proactive approach enables them to swiftly partake in the ongoing evolution of the FinTech industry.

Second, large commercial banks are increasingly initiating collaborations with major internet companies, recognizing the inherent advantages these tech giants hold in product management and online distribution channels. Unlike traditional financial institutions, internet companies excel in leveraging Big Data analytics and AI to conduct detailed customer profiling and segmentation, allowing for a more precise alignment of financial products with customer needs. The integration of internet and finance, often referred to as the 'internet + finance' model, has become deeply ingrained in everyday life, especially with the arrival of FinTech and the swift ascendancy of third-party payment platforms like PayPal and Wise. These developments have not only enhanced customer convenience by expanding the scope of payment services but also enabled these third-party platforms to secure a significant portion of the market share rapidly.

Third, commercial banks are increasingly facing competition from FinTech firms that provide analogous services. FinTech companies implement cutting-edge technology to innovate products and services traditionally offered by the financial sector, enhancing efficiency and significantly reducing operational costs. Historically, the domain of payment and settlement was dominated by merchant banks, which used a global network of outlets and various settlement tools, often relying on traditional communication methods like telephone and fax, to manage these transactions. This set-up allowed merchant banks to invest heavily and profit from transaction fees.

However, the rapid rise of FinTech entities, offering services such as digital wallets and third-party payments, has disrupted this traditional model. These FinTech services have gained widespread consumer acceptance due to their ability to provide continuous service, charge minimal transaction fees, and simplify the transaction process. As a result, the stronghold of banks as the primary channel for payment and settlement has been notably weakened, challenging their role in the financial ecosystem.

Fourth, FinTech is enhancing commercial banks' customer bases, particularly by broadening credit access for small and medium-sized enterprises (SMEs), which presents new opportunities. Traditionally, SMEs have faced significant challenges in securing credit, largely due to information asymmetry between these enterprises and commercial banks. However, the innovation of virtual banks, which are more inclined to extend credit to SMEs, is changing this dynamic. The integration of FinTech capabilities such as Big Data and cloud computing allows for a more accurate and comprehensive assessment of an SME's credit behaviour and history. This technological advancement addresses the issue of information asymmetry by providing banks with a clearer understanding of SMEs' creditworthiness, thereby mitigating credit risk.

As a result, the traditional banking sector is currently navigating the dual impact of FinTech, which includes both collaboration and competition. While FinTech can disrupt existing business models of banks and introduce a competitive landscape, it also offers opportunities to enhance operational efficiency through technical support and innovation in business practices. This interaction with FinTech has the potential not only to alter the profitability models of commercial banks but also to improve their approaches to risk management and prevention, marking a significant shift in the banking industry's dynamics.

The impact of FinTech on the financial industry

The impact of FinTech on the traditional financial sector has elicited varied perspectives in academic research (Milian et al., 2019). Some studies posit that FinTech could have a beneficial effect on commercial banks and their approach to risk management (Wang et al., 2021; Oskar and Pawel, 2020). For example, the competitive pressures from internet finance may encourage commercial banks to hasten mergers and restructurings, thereby fostering a survival-of-the-fittest environment. This could lead to enhanced business capabilities among surviving banks, resulting in improved overall efficiency. Similarly, Xia, Liu, and Zhang (2024) propose that FinTech, through advanced technologies like cloud computing and Big Data, could enable banks to more effectively identify and mitigate risks, thus reducing the likelihood of insolvency.

Contrary to the positive outlook, it can also be argued that the pervasive presence of internet finance across the financial market intensifies market competition. The infusion of advanced technology into finance intersects directly with traditional banking operations like savings and lending, heightening the rivalry between FinTech firms and commercial banks. This competition diminishes banks' monopoly profits, devalues their franchises, and erodes their monopolistic edge (Pierri and Timmer, 2020). Echoing this sentiment, Qiao et al. (2018) observe that FinTech's allure for talent indirectly undermines banks' innovation and competitiveness, impairs their ability to mitigate monetary policy effects, and escalates their risk-taking tendencies.

Empirical evidence corroborates the notion that heightened competition compels banks to alter their business models and engage in riskier behaviours (Wang et al., 2021). Moreover, the rise of FinTech has spurred the growth of shadow banking systems. Buchak et al. (2018) found that these shadow banks, utilizing superior technology, can offer consumer services at significantly lower costs than traditional banks, rapidly securing a dominant market position. This development poses a formidable challenge to commercial banks, presenting them with a scale of competition they have not previously encountered.

Streamlined transactions: The rise of social payments

The conventional online shopping experience, often plagued by complex checkout processes and high cart abandonment rates, is evolving with the integration of payment features on social media platforms. This innovation simplifies the purchasing process by eliminating the need to switch tabs and fill out lengthy checkout forms. The introduction of one-click purchasing and smooth integration with digital wallets has made shopping more seamless, reducing abandonment rates and encouraging spontaneous buying.

Beyond convenience, social payments offer significant advantages. They allow companies to collect user data during the checkout process, providing valuable insights into customer preferences and buying patterns. This information is essential for tailoring product suggestions, refining marketing strategies, and boosting sales. Critically, social payments enhance community and trust within social platforms by enabling peer-to-peer payments and group buying, which promote social interaction and deepen brand loyalty. These trends highlight how FinTech has democratized financial services, making them more accessible and affordable for a broader population, including those previously excluded from traditional financial systems. Furthermore, FinTech has fostered a culture of innovation within the financial industry, driving the development of new products, services, and business models (Yao et al., 2018; Wildau, 2016).

Wise, established a decade ago, has significantly disrupted the international money transfer industry with its innovative business model. Their mission to make cross-border transactions affordable, equitable, and straightforward distinguishes them within the FinTech sector and underpins their success. Unlike traditional banks that typically impose a fee of 3–4 per cent per transaction, Wise maintains a substantially lower average fee of just 0.35 per cent. Additionally, Wise incentivizes frequent transactions with a tiered discount system, reducing fees for subsequent transactions – starting from 0.35 per cent for the first transaction to 0.25 per cent for the next, and potentially lower for further transactions.

Wise's commitment to transparency and user-friendliness is exemplified by their online fee calculator, allowing customers to estimate monthly transaction costs effortlessly. This level of clarity and convenience starkly contrasts with practices of other money transfer services like Remitly, which lacks upfront fee estimates, and Western Union, whose fees are higher at 0.95 per cent. Wise employs a peer-to-peer model to execute international money transfers, a method that bypasses traditional cross-border financial flows. For example, if a customer in the United States wishes to send $1,000 to Estonia, they deposit the $1,000 into Wise's US bank account. Wise then transfers the equivalent amount in Euros from its Estonian bank account to the recipient's account in Estonia. This innovative approach means that the funds do not physically cross borders. This system operates by aligning transactions in opposite directions. If a customer wants to exchange $1,000 to Euros, Wise finds another customer looking to transfer a similar amount from Euros to dollars. By pooling these funds, Wise facilitates international transfers without the need for money to physically move between countries.

Much like Wise in the money transfer space, FinTech start-ups are now challenging traditional banking systems across every financial service sector, from loans to insurance, restructuring the competitive landscape.

FinTech in the retail banking sector

Paradoxically, the financial crisis of 2008 sparked the latest period of transformation within the financial sector and the emergence of FinTech. This crisis triggered significant regulatory reforms in the banking industry, leading to the implementation of new frameworks and heightened scrutiny. However, the recession also eroded public confidence in traditional banks. The public's almost universal loss of confidence and change in expectations forced banks and their technology providers to re-evaluate their approach to the retail sector, leading to the emergence of new business models and guarantees (Feyen et al., 2021). The retail banking sector is now witnessing the transformative effects of FinTech, with these forward-thinking companies expanding the scope of retail banking services beyond traditional boundaries. This expansion has facilitated the introduction of novel products and business models, significantly enhancing the customer experience in the process.

The market has seen a surge in start-up digital banks such as Chime, Starling Bank, and Revolut. These pioneering FinTech firms aim to rectify the limitations of traditional banking by providing digital-first, user-centric, and often fee-free services that meet the changing demands and expectations of today's consumers. The inherent agility and flexibility of these technology-driven companies allow for rapid adaptation and the integration of new technologies to improve their services. On the other hand, traditional financial institutions, often encumbered by outdated systems and regulatory challenges, struggle to keep up with the rapid pace of innovation that technology companies set. This disparity in agility has enabled tech companies to seize a significant market share, especially in the realm of payment processing.

As a result, the retail banking sector is experiencing intensified competition due to the influx of IT and digital technologies, which enable FinTech competitors to venture into the domain traditionally held by established banks. This is amplified by the increasing hesitancy of younger generations, especially millennials and Generation Z, to use traditional banking services. These digitally savvy consumers show a greater openness to technology-based banking solutions, like those provided by Monzo and various other FinTech start-ups.

Revolut: A FinTech disruptor

Revolut, a FinTech company founded in 2015 by Nikolay Storonsky and Vlad Yatsenko, emerged in a market dominated by traditional banks. Its initial focus was on simplifying and reducing the cost of spending money abroad. Through a mobile app and an associated card, users could exchange currencies at interbank rates, a significant advantage over traditional banks' fees. This user-centric approach quickly gained traction, propelling Revolut's initial growth and challenging the status quo in the financial services industry.

Revolut has since transformed into a comprehensive financial platform. The freemium model offers a basic account with features like mobile payments and budgeting tools. Paid tiers like Revolut Premium and Revolut Metal provide additional benefits such as higher ATM withdrawal limits, overseas medical insurance, and access to multiple cryptocurrencies. Beyond its initial currency exchange services, Revolut now encompasses checking accounts, stock trading, cryptocurrency exchange, and even insurance options. Technology is a core pillar of Revolut's success. The company leverages advanced algorithms for security, including real-time fraud detection. In addition, the app offers budgeting and analytics tools, allowing users to track spending and set financial goals directly within the platform.

Revolut has expanded to serve millions of customers worldwide in regions like Europe, Australia, Singapore, Japan, and the United States. Navigating diverse regulatory environments is key for achieving such global reach. In the European Union, Revolut secured a European banking licence, allowing insured deposit accounts and broader financial services. The company operates under an e-money licence in the UK while pursuing a full UK banking licence. Revolut's rapid growth has presented challenges. The company has faced scrutiny regarding regulatory compliance, customer service issues, and workplace culture. In response, Revolut has invested in regulatory technology and improved customer support. Looking ahead, Revolut aims to become a one-stop-shop for all financial needs – a financial super app. The company will continue expanding globally, introducing new products, and navigating complex regulatory environments. Revolut's story reflects a broader trend in FinTech, where technology is used to disrupt traditional financial institutions by offering user-friendly, accessible, and cost-effective financial solutions.

As we have seen, FinTech companies like Wise and Revolut are challenging traditional banks with more efficient, customer-friendly services. However, the true impact of FinTech extends beyond just competition—it is also about how these innovations are influencing regulatory frameworks and financial inclusivity.

The evolution of FinTech

Understanding the three stages of FinTech is essential for grasping its full impact on the economy and day-to-day transactions, which we briefly describe below.

FinTech 1.0 (1866–1967): This period laid the groundwork, with the financial sector heavily reliant on analogue technologies despite its close ties to innovation. Think early calculators, credit card machines, and the rise of telegraphs for communication.

FinTech 2.0 (1967–2008): This era witnessed a digital revolution. The development of personal computers, the internet, and digital communication channels like ATMs and online banking transformed how financial services were delivered.

FinTech 3.0 (2008–present): This period is characterized by the convergence of technologies, the rise of FinTech ecosystems, and the increasing focus on regulatory compliance. This phase is also marked by the emergence of new FinTech subsectors, such as InsurTech and RegTech. FinTech 3.0 is characterized by two fundamental changes:

Shifting providers of financial services: Technology companies and start-ups are displacing traditional banks as the primary providers of financial services, offering specialized solutions to consumers, businesses, and even banks themselves.

Accelerated pace of development: A change in consumer perceptions regarding who possesses the expertise and legitimacy to offer financial services has been accompanied by an unprecedented pace of development and growth. This rapid innovation is driven by the convergence of emerging technologies, the rise of FinTech ecosystems, and the increasing focus on regulatory compliance.

FinTech 3.0 represents a transformative phase in the financial services industry, challenging traditional business models and empowering new players to shape the future of finance. FinTech encompasses a broad spectrum of innovative financial solutions, including both the development of new financial products and services and the application of technology to enhance existing financial processes. Consequently, Arner et al. (2015) categorize FinTech into five key areas:

1. Financial management and investing: FinTech extends beyond alternative financing methods like peer-to-peer lending to encompass technology in financial activities, such as algorithmic trading and crowdsourcing campaigns. Additionally, FinTech is expanding its presence in sectors like robo-advisory services.
2. Management of internal financial resources and risk: Financial institutions have invested heavily in developing robust compliance systems, making internal resource management and risk management key drivers of FinTech adoption. For instance, engineers comprise approximately one-third of Goldman Sachs' thirty-three thousand employees.
3. Payment and physical infrastructure: Payments have garnered significant regulatory attention since the 1970s, leading to the establishment of both local and international electronic payment systems. Infrastructures for securities trading and settlement, as well as over-the-counter derivatives trading, also play an important role. Information technology and telecommunications companies are actively exploring opportunities to disintermediate traditional financial intermediaries in these markets.

4. Data protection and monetization: The digitalization of the financial sector has increased its vulnerability to cybercrime and industrial espionage attacks. Data protection and monetization remain significant concerns for government officials, policymakers, regulators, industry participants, and customers alike. However, FinTech innovation is also evident in the use of Big Data to enhance the effectiveness and availability of financial services.
5. Interaction with customers: Internet companies can utilize their existing customer bases to introduce new financial products. The customer interface represents the most promising area for competition with the traditional financial industry.

FinTech challenges

While FinTech has introduced several benefits, including reduced costs, improved service quality, and increased efficiency, it has also presented potential challenges for financial institutions. For instance, the widespread adoption of cloud services has led to a reliance on centralized cloud computing platforms for remote access and interaction between users, computers, and financial institutions. This centralization raises concerns about data security, as sensitive information, including personal details and transaction data, is stored and processed on centralized servers. This centralized approach poses vulnerabilities to security breaches and data leaks. Moreover, the lack of transparency in information processing makes it difficult for customers to monitor and control their data, potentially leading to privacy concerns.

The application of peer-to-peer (P2P) technology in the financial industry has enabled direct transactions between individuals without the involvement of intermediaries (Haddad and Hornuf, 2019). While this approach promotes financial inclusion and accessibility, it also raises credit risk concerns, particularly in the context of online P2P lending. Without the oversight and risk assessment typically provided by intermediaries, P2P lenders face increased exposure to loan defaults and potential losses.

Blockchain technology, with its decentralized, distributed, and cryptographic features, has emerged as a promising solution to address these challenges. Blockchain's decentralized nature eliminates the need for a single point of control, reducing the vulnerability to security breaches and data leaks. More importantly, its transparency and immutable nature enhance accountability and trust in transactions.

Bitcoin and cryptocurrency

The inception of Bitcoin traces back to 2008 when Satoshi Nakamoto unveiled a groundbreaking concept in a paper, proposing a peer-to-peer electronic cash system (Nakamoto, 2008). Nakamoto's vision was for a decentralized digital currency, named Bitcoin, which would be safeguarded through cryptography. This novel system presented a set of key advantages over existing digital currencies. It eliminated the need for third-party intermediaries such as banks, offered significantly lower transaction costs, ensured user anonymity, and was designed to be immune to issues like double-spending and counterfeiting that plague both traditional and digital currencies.

Following the theoretical groundwork laid out in Nakamoto's paper, 2009 marked the practical birth of Bitcoin with the release of its open-source software. This pivotal moment attracted a burgeoning community of enthusiasts and developers who collaboratively tackled the technical challenges, refining and debugging the code. A distinctive feature of the Bitcoin system, as described in subsequent analyses, was its pre-set limit of twenty-one million bitcoins, introducing a scarcity akin to natural resources, which was a deliberate design to prevent inflation and enhance value over time (Low and Teo, 2017). Bitcoin operates on a foundational technology known as blockchain. This technology is a decentralized ledger that records all transactions across a network of computers, ensuring security and transparency without the need for a central authority.

The unique blend of anonymity and transparency in Bitcoin transactions quickly attracted a wide user base. By 2014, the burgeoning interest in Bitcoin sparked significant investment in related start-ups, amplifying its global stature. Bitcoin facilitates the purchase of goods and services, allowing users to exchange it for conventional currency through specific channels. Transactions are conducted using various wallet software options, such as Exodus, Electrum, and Mycelium, as per Bitcoin.org's 2021 report.

Blockchain technology as a disruptive force

Blockchain technology is a distributed ledger technology that has the potential to revolutionize the financial industry. By eliminating the need for intermediaries, blockchain can streamline transactions, improve security, and reduce costs. This could have a significant impact on traditional financial institutions, which rely on intermediaries to process transactions and manage risk.

A prime example of this is the use of smart contracts, heralded as major innovations in the financial industry. Smart contracts have gained considerable attention for their ability to operate autonomously without the need for centralized oversight, further underscored by their integral role in Ethereum, one of the most prominent smart contract-based cryptocurrencies. These contracts, once deployed on the blockchain, are immutable and self-executing, ensuring that terms are automatically fulfilled upon meeting pre-defined conditions. For instance, in a betting context, a smart contract could securely escrow the stakes from both participants and autonomously allocate the winnings to the victor. This approach underscores the goal of minimizing reliance on centralized intermediaries and showcases the revolutionary capability of smart contracts to simplify and secure financial transactions.

Furthermore, in the healthcare sector, blockchain technology is envisioned to enhance the management and exchange of patient data. It promises to bolster the security, privacy, and interoperability of medical records, as noted by McGhin et al. (2019). The potential for blockchain to provide immediate access to a patient's medical history across borders could be life-saving. Traditional methods, which often involve hospitals communicating directly to exchange information, could be streamlined by blockchain, reducing delays and minimizing human errors. In the context of supply chain management, especially within consumer goods industries, blockchain technology is employed to enhance transparency and accountability (Kshetri, 2018). It enables the verification of each step in the supply chain before proceeding to the next, allowing for a more seamless and reliable process. This capability to trace products back through each stage of the supply chain can help identify the origins of defects or damage, thereby potentially reducing the rates of returns and improving overall quality control for businesses.

Finance and the wider implications of blockchain technology

Blockchain technology has the potential to reform the banking sector by streamlining cross-border payments, reducing settlement costs, and enhancing transparency. Blockchain-based systems can eliminate the need for intermediaries, such as correspondent banks, significantly reducing transaction fees and processing times. Historically, cross-border transactions were slow and expensive, but blockchain technology is now radically changing this by eliminating intermediaries and reducing costs, creating opportunities for more efficient global financial systems. Likewise, the immutability of blockchain records can enhance transparency and auditability, reducing the risk of fraud and errors. Blockchain technology can also transform stock exchanges by enabling faster, more secure, and transparent trading. By replacing centralized clearinghouses with decentralized blockchain networks, exchanges can achieve real-time settlement and reduce the risk of counterparty failure.

Blockchain-based systems can also facilitate fractional ownership of assets, opening up new investment opportunities for retail investors. Likewise, blockchain technology can reshape the insurance industry by enhancing fraud prevention, streamlining claims processing, and enabling new insurance products (Brophy, 2019). Smart contracts, self-executing contracts embedded in the blockchain, can automate claims processing, reducing costs and improving efficiency. Moreover, blockchain-based systems can facilitate the development of parametric insurance products, which pay out based on predetermined triggers, such as weather data or sensor readings.

In the healthcare industry, blockchain technology is significantly impacting industry practices by transforming the storage and sharing of medical data. Its decentralized, secure, and immutable features offer numerous benefits, enhancing efficiency, data security, and collaboration among healthcare providers, researchers, and patients. One key application is in medical record storage. Blockchain provides a secure, tamper-proof platform for medical records, addressing issues such as incompatible formats and privacy concerns. It enhances interoperability among healthcare providers, enabling seamless data exchange and comprehensive patient care. Cryptographic algorithms ensure the privacy and confidentiality of sensitive medical data, protecting it from unauthorized access.

Blockchain also simplifies and streamlines the insurance claims process. It reduces administrative burdens and accelerates reimbursements for patients, leading to a more efficient and user-friendly experience for both patients and insurance providers. Real-time data synchronization ensures that insurance companies have the most current patient information, facilitating prompt and accurate processing of claims and minimizing delays and errors associated with outdated or incomplete data.

Besides, blockchain empowers patients to take control of their own health information, promoting greater patient engagement and informed decision-making. Patients can securely store their medical records on a decentralized platform, granting them full ownership and control over their data. Blockchain enables selective sharing of healthcare information with providers, researchers, or clinical trials, facilitating personalized care and contributing to medical research and advancements. This integration makes patients active participants in the broader healthcare ecosystem.

In the developing field of autonomous technology, the concept of autonomous vehicles (AVs) emerged in the early 1920s, gained recognition in the 1980s, and saw a surge in interest with Google's self-driving car project. By July 2016, Google's AVs had driven 1 million miles, with most of the fourteen minor accidents attributed to human error. The Society of Automotive Engineers (SAE) categorizes driving automation into six levels, from Level 0 (no automation) to Level 5 (full automation). Current vehicles feature Levels 0–2, including Automated Cruise Control (Bagloee et al., 2016). Achieving full automation (Levels 4 and 5) could lead to safer, more efficient, comfortable, and sustainable transportation, reducing overall costs and revolutionizing mobility for young people, the elderly, and individuals with disabilities.

Widespread AV adoption could significantly transform transportation and urban landscapes (Wang et al., 2020). AVs might reduce the need for parking and enable smaller car sizes, allowing urban planning to prioritize pedestrians, cyclists, and public spaces. However, despite the potential benefits, AVs face challenges such as technical limitations in handling unexpected situations, ethical decision-making dilemmas, and job displacement in the transportation sector.

Blockchain technology presents solutions to some of these challenges through its decentralized nature, which distributes data across a network rather than relying on a single entity (De La Torre et al., 2020). This decentralization fosters trust via consensus mechanisms that validate and secure data entries. Blockchain also ensures data privacy and tamper-proof security through cryptography. When paired with smart contracts – self-executing agreements that remove the need for intermediaries – blockchain can streamline transactions. Integrating blockchain with AVs could thus herald a new era of intelligent and efficient transportation.

10

Beyond ownership: The rise of the sharing economy

Throughout the nineteenth and twentieth centuries, the global landscape was reshaped by the rise of capitalism. This system, characterized by private ownership of production resources (Scott, 2006), fundamentally altered social and economic structures, particularly in North America and Western Europe. One of its most profound impacts was the transformation of purchase behaviour, giving birth to a dominant consumer culture driven by individualism and material desires.

Industrialization played a crucial role in this shift. Mass production, while increasing availability, also ignited a thirst for novelty, fuelling a sense of 'keeping up with the Joneses'. Sophisticated marketing, wielding powerful tools like aspirational advertising and celebrity endorsements, further stoked this desire. The growth of disposable income and the availability of easy credit, such as instalment plans, made even larger purchases more attainable.

This potent cocktail transformed society's relationship with material goods. What were once basic necessities – clothing, food, shelter – morphed into symbols of identity and social status. People began to define themselves through their possessions, embracing a materialistic world view. The focus shifted from acquiring necessities to accumulating desires, driven by the promise of happiness and social acceptance. This cultural shift had widespread effects, influencing various aspects of life. It affected urban development, leading to the expansion of suburbs and shopping malls designed for those relying on cars. It also contributed to environmental issues, as the drive for more consumption resulted in the overuse of resources and increased pollution. Furthermore, the focus on acquiring material goods exacerbated social inequalities, further separating the affluent from the less privileged.

The legacy of capitalism and its impact on consumer culture is complex and multifaceted. It paved the way for technological advancements, increased standards of living and economic growth. However, it also came at a cost, leaving us with environmental challenges, social inequalities, and a sense of emptiness driven by endless consumption.

Belk (1988) earlier proposed that ownership of physical goods serves as a building block for self-identity, forming an individual's 'extended self'. This perspective, prevalent for much of the twentieth century, is now being challenged by the emergence of alternative economic and consumption models in the twenty-first century. These models, also championed by scholars like Botsman and Rogers (2010), Scott (2006), and Cheng (2016), prioritize access to shared resources over private ownership. The growth of conscious consumerism, driven by increased awareness and growing access to information, presents an opportunity for positive change. The focus is shifting towards ethical and sustainable practices, with individuals seeking alternative models like the sharing economy and the circular economy.

Understanding the sharing economy

Why pay exorbitant prices for products when you can rent them affordably from strangers online? This mindset has propelled the proliferation of online services that allow individuals worldwide to share their commutes through Uber, outsource handyman tasks to TaskRabbit, and engage in a multitude of other collaborative endeavours. These individuals actively engage in the Sharing Economy, a sector that has rapidly grown from a niche market into a significant industry, increasingly recognized as a mainstream social movement. With the increasing scarcity of natural resources, the period characterized by plentiful and inexpensive resources is approaching a conclusion. The trend of excessive consumption, driven by large business companies and major fashion retailers, is diminishing. Concurrently, a culture centred around sharing is beginning to take shape.

Sharing is an innate human behaviour, rooted in our evolutionary history and evident in our ability to cooperate with strangers. This inclination is predicated on our trust in the benevolence and competence of others. For millennia, humans have hunted in packs, and today, roads, hospitals, and schools are all considered part of our commons. The sharing economy aims to rejuvenate these age-old practices by empowering consumers to access what they need with lower economic and environmental costs.

The sharing economy thus distinguishes itself as an impactful economic structure. Its potential ramifications extend to altering consumer patterns, reshaping age-old industries, and boosting the competitive dynamics of retail business structures. Furthermore, technological and commercial progress in recent times has facilitated the sharing economy's leap from the digital domain, such as platforms for sharing music, films, and knowledge, to tangible sectors including hospitality and transportation, broadening its scope and impact (Lamberton and Rose, 2012; John, 2013).

Driven by information technologies like mobile connectivity and online payments (Belk, 2014), it has gained popularity for its affordability, diversity, and environmental benefits. Platforms like Airbnb (accommodation) and Uber (transportation) exemplify this innovation. The sharing economy has fundamentally changed consumption patterns, enabling rapid person-to-person transactions through online platforms. It has transformed consumer lifestyles (Tussyadiah and Pesonen, 2016) and exerted a considerable influence on established business models (Lamberton and Rose, 2012). By offering convenience and enjoyment, the sharing economy has demonstrably improved the lives of many (Belk, 2014; Lamberton and Rose, 2012; Tussyadiah and Pesonen, 2016).

The concept of sharing economy originated with Felson and Spaeth's (1978) idea of collaborative consumption (CC), which focused on reallocating underutilized resources for mutual benefit (providers and consumers). Belk (2009), an early proponent, viewed the sharing economy as the act of sharing personal goods or obtaining them from others for temporary use. Botsman and Rogers (2010) subsequently offered a more systemic perspective, defining it as a method to activate underused assets through models and marketplaces, promoting efficiency and wider access. In 2015, the Oxford Dictionary formalized a widely accepted definition: an economic system where assets or services are shared between individuals, typically facilitated by the internet, for free or for a fee (Heo, 2016).

The emergence of the sharing economy has significantly changed traditional views on ownership. From 1978 to 2008, the sharing economy gradually gained momentum, though it remained under the radar due to a prevailing emphasis on the importance of owning possessions (Guttentag, 2013). The financial crisis of 2008, however, catalysed a shift in perspectives, with an increasing number of people valuing access and experiences over outright ownership. This change in priorities has been instrumental in propelling the swift global spread of the sharing economy around 2008, and its continued growth thereafter. Spanning various sectors, including shared consumption and finance, the sharing economy has now evolved into a novel business framework, challenging conventional notions of ownership and use.

According to Botsman and Rogers (2010), the sharing economy is an economic and social system that allows people to share products that are not being used or are unwanted. They describe this economy as including the redistribution of underutilized assets, systems wherein individuals pay to utilize products (known as product service systems, or PSS), and collaborative lifestyles that involve the sharing of resources. This approach helps reduce waste and improves the use of resources that would otherwise remain idle. Sharing economies can be categorized into four main types (Botsman and Rogers, 2010):

1. Asset sharing: Platforms facilitate the sharing of underutilized assets like housing, workspace, or transportation between providers and consumers for financial gain. The focus here is on using, not owning, these assets.
2. Skill and service sharing: Providers offer their skills, time, or other intangible resources to meet the demands of others.
3. Product redistribution: This model involves the exchange, purchase, or sale of second-hand goods.
4. Collaborative consumption: Users leverage social platforms to share resources and experiences within their social circles, promoting a CC model.

Hamari et al. (2015) further describe the sharing economy as activities organized through online community services, focusing on sharing and using goods or services together. Owyang et al. (2013) identify economic (access to income, financial flexibility), technological (social networks, payment systems), and social factors (social needs, sustainability) as key drivers of the sharing economy. Belk (2014) and Lamberton and Rose (2012) also emphasize its ability to dissolve social barriers and build reputation through shared consumption.

Decentralized marketplaces

In certain contexts, the term 'sharing economy' colloquially refers to disruptive organizations that function within decentralized marketplaces, posing a challenge to traditional providers of goods and services across established sectors through a peer-to-peer (P2P) framework that enhances efficiency and democratizes resource access (Benjaafar et al., 2019). This concept is reinforced by the empirical findings of Zervas et al. (2017), which through a case study in the sharing economy sector highlighted the significant economic repercussions sharing economy entities have on established companies. Although the sharing economy facilitates direct connections between individuals or businesses, promoting democratic interactions, it also includes a diverse array of enterprises that unsettle traditional industries, thereby prompting established companies to adapt and innovate.

In this vein, Acquier et al. (2017) propose a framework for understanding the sharing economy based on three main components: access-based economy (focusing on gaining access to underutilized resources), digital platform economy (highlighting the role of digital platforms in facilitating transactions), and co-creation value economy (emphasizing the importance of trust and social connections).

Driven by the above factors, there are four different sharing economy practices (Schor, 2016), covering both nonprofit and for-profit. The first is recirculation of goods, which has the widest range of applications. The second scenario is one in which companies such as Airbnb, Didi ride-sharing services, or bike-sharing increase the use of durable assets such as houses or cars through rentals. The third type of service exchange is a company such as Task Rabbit, which provides services to consumers; this type of service exchange is used to meet the needs of both supply and demand. The final type is the sharing of productive assets, which also includes sharing business resources.

The growth rate of sharing system development demonstrates that it can create enormous economic value. The three leading types of sharing services include home sharing, ride-sharing, and office sharing, often known as co-working. The global ride-sharing market is projected to expand by over 133 per cent from 2022 to 2028 (Statista, 2024). In 2022, the ride-sharing market's global valuation stood at US$96.9 billion and is anticipated to reach approximately US$226 billion by 2028. PwC (2015) estimates that the sharing economy industry will generate $335 billion in revenue by 2025.

Access-based economy

Some academics suggest that the sharing economy is better described as an access-based economy (Acquier et al., 2017; Wiprächtiger et al., 2019). Denning (2014) argues that since the birth of the internet, people have begun to prefer access to ownership, hailing a new 'Access Economy' in which ownership is replaced with temporary access. Bardhi and Eckhardt (2015) bolster such a claim by pointing to the success of firms such as Uber, that promote financial benefits rather than others, such as Lyft, that promote social benefits. Therefore, the sharing economy is better described as an access economy that focuses on lowering costs and increasing convenience.

The sharing economy has profoundly influenced various sectors, notably hospitality, financial services, and transportation and infrastructure, largely due to innovative business models introduced by companies such as Airbnb and Uber (Belk, 2014). This model promotes P2P sharing of resources and services, posing challenges to established business paradigms. The widespread acceptance and rapid expansion of the sharing phenomenon are driven by specific shifts in societal and economic paradigms. The foundational elements of the economy – capital, goods (or services), and assets – are in a state of flux. Likewise, the social context is evolving, with the lines between production and consumption becoming increasingly indistinct, a phenomenon described as the creation of shared value (van Dijck et al., 2018). The capabilities and ongoing enhancement of digital platforms play an important role in bridging connections between previously disparate participants in the economic ecosystem, marking a significant transformation.

Prosper is a P2P lending platform that enables borrowers to secure personal loans from individual and institutional investors. Established in 2005, Prosper is one of the oldest and largest P2P lending platforms in the United States, boasting over 1 million active borrowers and more than $10 billion in originated loans. The platform allows borrowers to use loans for various purposes, such as debt consolidation, home improvements, and medical expenses. Unlike secured loans, Prosper loans do not require collateral.

Prospective borrowers begin by completing an online application that includes details about their credit history, income, and expenses. Prosper reviews these applications and assigns a credit grade, which influences the interest rates and loan amounts offered to the borrower. Higher credit grades generally result in lower interest rates. Approved borrowers list their loan request on the Prosper website, where investors can review and choose to fund loans that align with their investment criteria. Prosper loans typically have terms ranging from three to five years.

Once a loan is fully funded, the borrower receives the funds and is responsible for making monthly repayments to Prosper, which then distributes these payments to the investors who funded the loan. Prosper is known for offering competitive interest rates that often undercut those of traditional banks and credit unions. The platform also provides flexibility in terms and rapid funding, often within days of application approval. However, using Prosper also has its drawbacks. The platform enforces stricter credit requirements than some other P2P lending services, potentially limiting access for certain borrowers. Additionally, Prosper charges an origination fee on all loans, which increases the borrowing cost. There is also the risk of loan default; if a borrower fails to meet their repayment obligations, investors risk losing their capital.

Sharing economy effectiveness

The sharing economy is built on two essential elements: (1) trust and (2) digital technology. This contrasts with traditional e-commerce, which mainly focuses on mitigating financial risks, as the sharing economy also involves potential physical risks. This aspect leaves consumers more vulnerable, thereby elevating the importance of trust to unprecedented levels. Consequently, the trust factor in the sharing economy is even more pivotal than in traditional e-commerce due to its distinct nature. Unlike transactional models such as eBay, where ownership of items is transferred, the sharing economy typically revolves around temporary access or rentals, necessitating a heightened degree of mutual trust among participants (Fraiberger and Sundararajan, 2015).

This higher level of trust is a key area of research. Bente et al. (2012) used an experimental approach to study the impact of sharer avatars and reputation on consumer trust, finding that both significantly influence trust, though their interaction does not have a substantial effect. Lusch and Nambisan (2015) argue that the sharing economy often involves service exchange (rather than just goods exchange) and usually necessitates close interaction between participants. The sharing economy thus depends on the services or goods offered by providers, with consumers placing their trust in these providers' reliability and the quality of their offerings to conduct transactions on sharing economy platforms. Given the absence of pre-existing relationships between providers and consumers, the platforms within the sharing economy are instrumental in promoting trust, serving as the foundational element for successful interactions and exchanges.

For example, the shared accommodation market, despite its potential, faces challenges like inaccurate listings, inadequate facilities, and safety concerns, creating significant trust barriers for potential renters compared to other sharing options. Trust is thus essential for visitors choosing shared accommodation, and the level of trust they have in the platform offering online booking services directly affects the success of transactions between hosts and visitors. By fostering trust through stricter listing verification and user reviews, shared accommodation platforms can address the current trust hurdle hindering wider adoption in the tourism accommodation market.

The internet also endows the sharing economy with a distinct value proposition: the capability to swiftly and efficiently align countless demands with available resources. The advent of the internet (Web 2.0) has led to a surge in the number of individuals generating and sharing content and information for online consumption. This has, in turn, given rise to social online communities and P2P platforms, facilitating a new form of online-based CC, where products and services are shared through the internet (Hamari et al., 2016). Ukkonen and Hamari (2015) thus highlight the simplified and cost-effective nature of sharing tangible and intangible goods and services through the development of convenient and flexible information systems.

Mobile devices further amplify the sharing economy by enabling seamless access to the internet and advanced digital systems. Smartphones allow individuals to access P2P platforms anytime and anywhere, contributing significantly to the sharing economy's success. Uber, for instance, exemplifies an innovative sharing economy business model that integrates a GPS system with its digital platform services, available through both web and mobile applications, to connect users (drivers and passengers) based on their needs. In this case, the company and its platform act as intermediaries, facilitating sharing between unfamiliar users.

At its core, the sharing economy is centred on the use of digital platforms to efficiently integrate large amounts of idle and surplus resources to meet the diverse needs of consumers. These platforms act as service mediators or intermediaries between internet users, enabling customer-to-customer or business-to-customer interactions (Hamari et al., 2016). Examples include Couchsurfing, a platform for sharing lodging, Wikipedia, and Pinterest, a platform for sharing information and interests.

This economic model has now grown beyond its original realms of accommodation and transportation to encompass solutions for a multitude of everyday needs, making the term 'sharing economy' synonymous with any service that operates through an online platform. The sharing of consumer goods represents another facet of the sharing economy, with emerging start-ups like Peerby in Europe and Fat Llama in the UK illustrating the growing trend of shared consumer goods. This movement is expected to gain further momentum as environmental consciousness and concerns about climate change continue to heighten.

A critical aspect of multi-sided sharing economy platforms is their ability to offer personalized experiences to users. By analysing user preferences and behaviour, platforms provide recommendations and services, creating more meaningful and customized interactions.

Personalization: The engine driving growth in the sharing economy

Digital platforms such as Couchsurfing and Peerby demonstrate the intrinsic connection between the sharing economy and personalization. Particularly in industries such as accommodation, travel and hospitality, and carpooling, these platforms use technology to offer personalized services that cater to individual preferences. This not only enhances the customer experience but also optimizes resource utilization (Abdar and Yen, 2020; Lutz and Newlands, 2018).

In the accommodation sector, platforms like Airbnb use user data, including past bookings, search preferences, and reviews, to offer personalized accommodation suggestions. These recommendations are aligned with the user's preferences, such as location, type of property, amenities, and price range. Personalization not only enhances the user experience but also helps property owners match with the right guests, optimizing occupancy rates and ensuring a better fit between the host's offerings and the guest's needs.

In travel and hospitality, platforms like TripAdvisor personalize travel recommendations and experiences by exploiting data from user behaviours, preferences, and social interactions. These platforms can suggest personalized travel itineraries, dining options, and activities that align with the traveller's interests and past experiences. This level of personalization not only enhances the travel experience but also encourages users to rely on the platform for future travel planning, thereby supporting the various businesses featured on the platform.

Carpooling services like BlaBlaCar enhance the sharing economy experience by matching drivers and passengers based on shared routes and personal preferences. Users can specify their preferences, such as departure times, smoking or non-smoking, preferred conversation levels (hence the name 'BlaBlaCar'), and pet policies. This ensures that the carpooling experience is tailored to the comfort and compatibility of the users, leading to a more enjoyable and personalized journey.

In each of these examples, personalization not only improves the user experience by aligning services more closely with individual needs and preferences but also fosters a sense of community and trust among users, which are key components of the sharing economy.

Sharing economy motivations

To deepen our understanding of the sharing economy, it is important to explore the motivations behind individuals' participation in CC (Si et al., 2020). The motivations for participating in the sharing economy extend beyond convenience and access. Economic, social, and environmental factors all play an important role in shaping consumer behaviour within the sharing economy. Various factors prompt people to engage in the sharing economy, and these can be grouped into four principal categories.

Economic motivations

Economic incentives are the primary drivers of participation in the sharing economy, attracting individuals with the prospects of saving money, earning extra income, or accessing goods and services more affordably. Social economy platforms reduce transaction costs for both buyers and sellers, leading to mutual cost benefits and increased engagement. Belk (2014) shows that this sharing approach often involves the temporary use of underutilized products or services, enhancing the use of existing assets through the internet. Lamberton and Rose (2012) identify the anticipated risk of product scarcity, cost and utility considerations, and familiarity with sharing practices as key motivators, while Hamari et al. (2015) find that motivations for CC are linked to sustainability, enjoyment, and financial gains. Furthermore, Sundararajan (2016) argues that the sharing economy's momentum is driven by mobile technology use, internet advancements, widespread internet access, digital technology evolution, substantial revenues for sharing-based companies, and inefficiencies in certain service sectors.

Social motivations

Social motivations significantly drive participation in the sharing economy. People are attracted to opportunities for meeting new individuals, forming connections and networks, sharing common interests, and joining communities. Social influence, such as seeing friends and family use sharing economy platforms, further encourages participation. Trust within sharing communities, bolstered by rating and review systems, is crucial in reducing perceived risks and promoting platform adoption. Success stories like Uber and Airbnb highlight the sharing economy's impact, which has also inspired the development of co-working spaces and shared living environments (Dezeen, 2021). In co-living, this takes the form of shared amenities and living spaces, alleviating the burden of ownership while simultaneously creating new value for residents.

The sharing economy also addresses the desire for convenience. Convenience is a top priority for Millennials seeking housing, with a study finding that convenience supersedes cost as a priority. This indicates that Millennials are willing to pay a premium if it means living in a more convenient location or having amenities like cleaning handled for them, as is often the case in co-living spaces (Dezeen, 2021; McLaren and Agyeman, 2015). Most co-livings recognize these growing trends by adopting and promoting a sustainable brand and mentality that resonates with their primary target audience. This is evident in the co-living's embrace of the sharing economy, its emphasis on providing a sustainable solution to the housing market's need for more single-occupancy rooms, and the sense of purpose and belonging that residents derive from living in a community.

Environmental motivations

Today's society is characterized by heightened social and environmental consciousness. Sustainability is gaining increasing importance in public perception, and self-awareness is more valued and recognized than ever. Millennials are found to be the generation most concerned about sustainability and the most likely to spend more on products labelled as sustainable (Ciulli and Kolk, 2019; McLaren and Agyeman, 2015). The sharing economy addresses the issue of resource overcapacity and overexploitation by repurposing unused resources in more efficient ways, thereby reducing the need to purchase new goods (Acquier et al., 2017; Heinrichs, 2013). This aspect of reducing and solving environmental problems has contributed to the growth of the sharing economy. Environmental concern has also further motivated sharing economy participation, as sharing behaviours align with anti-consumption principles, promoting sustainable development (Cheng, 2016; Lamberton and Rose, 2012).

For example, the sharing economy can promote sustainable business models, such as carpooling or ride-sharing, which decreases the number of cars on the road and CO_2 emissions. It creates environmentally friendly positions by optimizing existing product value. Similarly, companies like ThredUp in the fashion industry promote sustainability by encouraging consumers to purchase second-hand clothing. Therefore, environmental concerns are a motivating factor for sharing economy involvement. Lee et al. (2018) identify three factors consumers are drawn to the sharing economy: sustainability, but only if they already care about CC; enjoyment of the activity; and economic gains.

Technological motivations

Technological innovations have made it significantly easier and more convenient for individuals to access products and services through sharing economy platforms. With just a few taps or clicks on their devices, users can connect to a wide array of offerings. This ease of access, provided by digital systems, draws people towards using sharing economy services. Consequently, technology plays a pivotal role in driving the adoption of sharing economy platform services. For instance, digital platforms facilitate CC by building trust via interactive communication channels like rating and review systems, which enhance user confidence and reliability (Dredge and Gyimóthy, 2015).

These motivating factors often overlap, with individuals being driven by a blend of reasons. For instance, a person might engage in the sharing economy to save money (economic motivation), meet new people (social motivation), and contribute to waste reduction (environmental motivation).

Collaborative consumption

The waning interest in ownership has facilitated the emergence of new socioeconomic models that prioritize collaboration and streamlined access to goods and services via digital platforms. A central feature of these models is CC, a concept particularly prevalent within the sharing economy framework, as previously mentioned.

CC can be broadly described as the use of technology to transform traditional market activities like renting, lending, swapping, sharing, bartering, and gifting, making them scalable and feasible in ways that were not possible before the internet (Botsman and Rogers, 2010). Influenced by social, economic, and technological shifts, sectors and markets previously untouched by CC are now beginning to adopt this approach (Belk, 2014). Belk's (2014) updated definition of CC, which highlights 'people coordinating the acquisition and distribution of a resource for a fee or other compensation', captures the monetized aspect of this economic model.

Product service systems

The transition from a product-based to a service-based economy began in Western societies in the 1960s and accelerated with the advent of IT systems and the internet in the early 1990s. This shift has led to increased scholarly focus on PSS, which affects various industries such as business management, IT, and engineering, making it a multidisciplinary topic. Tukker (2015) identifies three aspects of PSS: product-oriented (focusing on the physical product), use-oriented (emphasizing the benefits of product use), and results-oriented (focusing on outcomes achieved through product use).

Product-oriented PSS is criticized for resembling conventional ownership models, while use-oriented PSS, such as car sharing, is supported by urbanization and increased population density, which create higher demand for access-based models. Environmental benefits initially incentivized PSS adoption due to potential reductions in consumption through product dematerialization. However, for PSS to be truly environmentally beneficial, they must be designed and implemented with eco-efficiency in mind. A potential drawback is the 'rebound effect', where the lack of ownership may lead to careless consumption, potentially negating the environmental benefits.

Car sharing as a PSS

The convergence of several factors, particularly the advent of digital platforms, has turned car sharing into a sustainable and profitable global business model. Car sharing services' emergence as one of the most popular forms of PSS was predicted by Mont (2004), who asserted that expensive products with minimal use were more likely to succeed as PSS. With an average 8 per cent daily utilization rate, personal vehicles and the mobility sector were ripe for disruption (Sacks, 2011).

Car sharing transportation platforms provide individuals with opportunities to monetize their idle vehicles by acting as online hailing drivers. Customers, on the other hand, can conveniently book rides to their destinations through smartphone apps. This innovative model benefits both parties: drivers can earn money by employing their available resources, while customers enjoy more affordable fares compared to traditional taxis. Several prominent online car sharing platforms have emerged and gained global recognition, including Uber and DiDi. In addition to these multinational platforms, many countries have their own successful local online car sharing companies.

As an integral part of collaborative consumption, the car sharing industry exemplifies the sharing economy's ability to maximize the use of underutilized assets. Let's now explore the different models of car sharing services, such as round-trip and point-to-point car sharing, which provide consumers with flexible and convenient mobility solutions.

Business models in car sharing market

Within the car sharing market, there exists a variety of commercial business models, each offering distinct benefits to end-users, making proper categorization essential. While some studies classify up to seven theoretical car sharing models (Remane et al., 2016), two dominant models are widely recognized in the current commercial landscape: round-trip and point-to-point.

1) Round-trip car sharing: This is the most established car sharing model commercially. Consumers are required to return the vehicle to the exact location from which they accessed it. The vehicles are centrally owned by a business organization and payment is due from the time the car is accessed to the time it is returned. Reservations for this access are made in advance by the consumer. Zipcar is the world's largest car sharing provider who operates using this model (Polak et al., 2014).
2) Point-to-point car sharing: This model offers greater flexibility for consumers than the round-trip model. Within the point-to-point system, users can access a vehicle in one location and return the vehicle to a different location at the end of usage. Consumption within this system is largely spontaneous, with near-instant bookings. The fleet remains centrally owned by a commercial entity. There are two prevalent implementation methods of point-to-point car sharing: station-based and free-floating. Station-based requires the return of the vehicle to a number of permitted locations, while free-floating allows the consumer to leave the vehicle in any legal location. Notable commercial organizations operating this system include Share Now GmbH (for the free-floating method) (Polak et al., 2014).

Round-trip car sharing models represent a natural progression from traditional car rental services and have the potential to be particularly disruptive. This is evidenced by the traditional rental sector's response to such innovative businesses; for example, in 2013, the car rental conglomerate Avis acquired the leading car sharing company Zipcar in a transaction valued at $500 million (Kell, 2013), underscoring the significant impact of car sharing models on the industry.

Lyft is a notable player in the sharing economy, similar to Uber but with a distinct approach and community-focused ethos. Launched in 2012, Lyft facilitates P2P ride-sharing by connecting individuals who need a ride with car owners willing to provide one, all through a user-friendly mobile app. This setup has opened new avenues for individuals to earn income by utilizing an asset they already own – their vehicle – providing significant benefits for those seeking flexible work schedules or additional sources of income.

Lyft has also expanded transportation options, particularly in urban areas, by offering a convenient and reliable alternative to traditional public transit or taxi services. This proves especially beneficial during times when other transportation options are scarce, such as late nights or in less serviced areas. Individuals with a car who meet Lyft's requirements can sign up to become drivers. After passing a background check and vehicle inspection, approved drivers can use the Lyft app to accept ride requests, giving them the flexibility to choose when and where they work. Those in need of transportation can use the app to book a ride, which provides details like estimated arrival time, fare, and information about the driver and their vehicle. Riders can choose from various service options, including shared rides for cost efficiency or luxury cars for a premium experience.

Lyft emphasizes a positive community among its users with features like in-app tipping for drivers and a mutual rating system to foster trust and safety within the Lyft community. Lyft's entry into the ride-sharing market has spurred healthy competition, leading to service improvements and innovations across the industry. This competition benefits consumers through more choices, enhanced services, and often lower prices.

Overall, Lyft exemplifies the principles of the sharing economy by enabling efficient use of personal vehicles, encouraging community engagement among users, and providing flexible economic opportunities for drivers, all while enhancing the diversification and accessibility of urban transportation options.

Beyond transportation, the sharing economy has expanded into various sectors through decentralized marketplaces. These multi-sided platforms facilitate peer-to-peer interactions, allowing individuals and businesses to share a wide range of goods and services, often bypassing traditional intermediaries.

Impact on traditional businesses

The sharing economy is challenging established businesses in multiple ways, notably through competitive pricing and brand management. Sharing economy platforms typically incur lower overhead expenses, enabling them to offer services at more affordable rates, thus intensifying price competition for traditional businesses. Furthermore, the sharing economy complicates the management of brand image and reputation for conventional enterprises. Platforms within the sharing economy often feature customer review systems, which can significantly influence a company's public perception.

Despite the various motivations driving participation in the sharing economy, it is important to consider that the repercussions of this evolving business model may entail diverse costs. This issue is particularly evident in the context of Airbnb's impact on the traditional accommodation sector. Airbnb is a quintessential example of the sharing economy, embodying the essence of the concept by enabling individuals to offer their private residences as accommodations for visitors.

Airbnb: The impact of sharing economy platforms on boutique hotels

The shared accommodation industry began in the United States, with significant players like HomeAway (founded in 2005) and Airbnb (2008). Airbnb connects hosts with spare space to guests seeking accommodation. Established in San Francisco, Airbnb has become the world's largest online marketplace for vacation rentals, with over five million hosts worldwide. In 2023, Airbnb bookings exceeded 448 million, nearly doubling from five years earlier, and its global revenue approached US$10 billion (Statista, 2024).

Airbnb has redefined travel accommodation by providing an alternative to traditional hotels and hostels. It enables property owners to earn extra income by renting out unused spaces, particularly benefiting residents in high-tourism areas. The platform offers travellers a unique experience by staying in residential neighbourhoods and interacting with hosts, promoting a more authentic travel experience. Airbnb thus supports sustainable travel by utilizing existing spaces, reducing the need for new hotel constructions and their environmental impacts (Yang et al., 2019). While hosting strangers can be daunting due to security and privacy concerns, Airbnb has implemented trust-building measures like user reviews and verification systems. Despite occasional trust issues, Airbnb offers unique accommodations and the opportunity to connect with locals worldwide.

Airbnb's rapid growth, such as an 800 per cent increase in services in 2011, has significantly impacted the hospitality industry, influencing traditional hotels and prompting new regulations for short-term rentals. Shared accommodation appeals particularly to younger demographics, offering personalized and diverse experiences compared to standardized hotel rooms. It is often more cost-effective, with platforms like Airbnb providing easy property listings for landlords and competitive pricing for guests. This model efficiently connects fragmented rental supply with potential renters. Unlike traditional hotels, shared accommodation platforms operate as a two-way street where hosts can decline booking requests. Research shows that factors like guest gender and age influence host acceptance decisions, with women and older adults generally viewed more favourably (Zervas et al., 2021).

Economy level

The sharing economy generates uncounted economic gains for many users. While the income earned by service providers on these platforms is often documented, additional unreported earnings are common (Schor, 2016). The concept extends beyond monetary transactions to other forms of value exchange, such as sharing facilities without financial exchange, resulting in economic benefits not captured in traditional metrics. Fraiberger and Sundararajan (2015) argue that significant value generated by the sharing economy is not included in gross domestic product (GDP). Despite some benefits not being reflected in GDP calculations, individuals can augment their income and purchase other goods and services.

The rise of sharing economy companies raises concerns about their impact on employment, traditional companies, and national economies. A major concern is whether sharing economies increase earning opportunities for more people (Fraiberger and Sundararajan, 2015). There are arguments that sharing economy companies may displace traditional companies. For instance, Sundararajan (2016) and Zervas et al. (2017) suggest that Airbnb negatively affects the hospitality sector by causing job losses, reducing revenues, and promoting unfair competition. While the sharing economy is said to increase revenues for its users, critics argue that it also causes unemployment (Sundararajan, 2016). Airbnb, for example, can reduce demand for traditional hotel services, leading hotels to cut jobs (Zervas et al., 2017). Some traditional companies may become irrelevant due to the widespread prevalence of sharing economy practices. Although Airbnb negatively impacts low-end hotels, Zervas et al. (2017) note that the marginal impact decreases as the sharing economy grows. Conversely, the sharing economy can generate new jobs by attracting more tourists with low accommodation costs, providing a shared economic benefit.

Industry level

The sharing economy is reshaping various economic sectors, including hospitality. Traditionally, the hotel sector faces high barriers to entry, significant initial investments, and substantial fixed costs, making financial management complex. According to Fraiberger and Sundararajan (2015), the hotel's structure makes it susceptible to profit losses even with minor demand decreases. Guttentag (2013) shows that reduced hotel revenues directly impact profitability. Research highlights the pivotal role of service quality in hotel performance, with customer-focused strategies driving profitability. The sharing economy, with its emphasis on user-centric services, poses a considerable challenge to traditional providers like hotels. A study by Zervas et al. (2017) on Airbnb's impact on Texas hotels found that a 1 per cent increase in Airbnb listings led to a 0.05 per cent reduction in hotel revenues, demonstrating significant revenue implications for the hotel sector.

Industries increasingly recognize the potential impact of the sharing economy on their operations and future growth. This awareness has led many companies to adapt by formulating new strategies and developing sharing-based business models to maintain competitiveness. Such efforts by established players can disrupt traditional operations and potentially undermine the entire industry. Both established businesses and start-ups should pay close attention to the evolving sharing economy landscape and adjust their strategies accordingly (Matzler et al., 2015).

Firm level

The sharing economy's impacts are not limited to the economy and industry. It has also had significant impacts at the firm and user levels. From a hotel management perspective, P2P platforms pose a different type of competition than that between traditional hotels (Park and Tussyadiah, 2020). Guttentag (2013) reveals that P2P platforms like Airbnb have almost zero marginal costs. This means that they can add or remove rooms with minimal overhead costs. Airbnb is therefore able to scale supply quickly and easily to meet demand. In contrast, hotels need to build new rooms to increase their capacity, which is a more expensive and time-consuming process. This puts hotels at a disadvantage when competing with Airbnb. In addition, Airbnb can offer a wider range of services and products than traditional hotel companies (Zervas et al., 2015). For instance, Airbnb allows users to rent entire houses or apartments, which traditional hotels often do not offer. This makes Airbnb more attractive to some users.

User level

Studies show that the sharing economy is creating huge value for its users in general – both monetary and non-monetary value. Users who act as renters of services benefit by earning from assets that would otherwise remain idle (Hamari et al., 2015). For instance, Airbnb allows individuals with extra rooms that they are not using to earn from them by renting them to other individuals. In short, the sharing economy creates earning opportunities for individuals and also allows individuals to share their financial resources by providing them with affordable services and products. In terms of a broader social impact, the sharing economy promotes the general well-being of people. It improves users' satisfaction and reduces resource wastage. However, it also creates unemployment in some sectors of the economy (Schor, 2016).

Developing effective collaboration strategies

The sharing economy holds immense potential yet presents challenges to both emerging and established businesses. Particularly within the fluid environment of today's evolving economy, conventional business models in many traditional sectors, such as retail, struggle to adapt to current market needs and drive their own growth. The sharing economy has the capacity to disrupt the operational frameworks of some of the world's leading firms, posing a challenge to traditional business practices and existing institutional frameworks (Rifkin, 2014; Priporas et al., 2017).

First, the sharing economy will impact on the traditional passive business philosophy of commercial companies, as it breaks down the barriers between production and consumption. From the previous model that consumers can only passively accept goods provided by companies, it has changed to the mode of C2C (consumer-to-consumer) or even C2B (consumer-to-business). This has had a huge impact on the otherwise closed management mindset of the commercial industry, which has had to start looking at its traditional business philosophy in a new light.

Second, the sharing economy has changed the traditional management model of the retail industry. Retail is typically an asset-heavy management model with high transaction costs. Nevertheless, the sharing economy allows for increased mobility of resources and goods, allowing businesses and individuals to access them as needed. This mobility brings new ways for companies to use their existing resources – sharing, temporary access, reducing the size of their assets. For instance, amid the Covid-19 pandemic, the sharing economy presented alternative employment opportunities for restaurants and medium-sized enterprises, diverging from traditional models. Through collaborative platforms, these businesses could sustain operations and mitigate unemployment. Third, the technological advancements spurred by the sharing economy have transformed the service paradigm in retail and commerce. While traditional retail models offer the benefit of in-store services, the evolving consumer preferences highlight the sharing economy's ability to deliver more personalized and relevant products and services.

The increasing demand for personalized consumer experiences, accentuated by the long-tail effect, is setting higher service expectations that traditional retail's standardized service models fail to meet (Chen et al., 2016). If traditional businesses cannot keep pace with the swift evolution of business models or are slow to launch new ventures, the sharing economy stands ready to supplant these conventional sectors with alternative industry types. Faced with such pressures, these enterprises are compelled to explore innovative business models to sustain their competitive edge, enhance their economic performance, and navigate their challenges effectively.

These enterprises may also consider how personalization greatly amplifies the positive impact of the sharing economy by enhancing user satisfaction and reducing resource wastage, which in turn promotes the general well-being of individuals. This becomes particularly evident in sectors such as shared accommodation, where, despite its advantages, there are notable challenges such as misleading listings, subpar facilities, and concerns over safety. Similarly, the broader sharing economy faces significant hurdles, including supply and demand imbalances, technical constraints, and often inadequate legal frameworks that struggle to keep pace with the rapid evolution of this sector (Cheng, 2016; Ert and Fleischer, 2019).

Personalization addresses these issues by providing a deeper understanding of user behaviour, which is critical for the efficiency of sharing economy platforms. This targeted approach allows platforms to more accurately match users with third-party providers. For instance, by analysing user feedback and interaction data, platforms can identify and correct misleading listings, improve the quality of the facilities offered, and enhance safety measures, thereby aligning services more closely with user expectations and needs.

Moreover, personalization helps balance supply and demand more effectively. Platforms can predict peak times and locations for services, allowing them to suggest adjustments to providers or offer dynamic pricing to balance user demand with available supply. This not only maximizes efficiency but also ensures a smoother operation of services, which can lead to increased trust and reliability in the sharing economy. Additionally, by exploring detailed insights from user data, sharing economy platforms can advocate for more informed and supportive legal frameworks that recognize the unique dynamics of this sector. This could include policies tailored to protect both providers and consumers while fostering an environment that supports innovation and growth.

By enhancing match accuracy and improving service quality, personalization not only enriches the user experience but also serves as a decisive factor in addressing systemic inefficiencies and conflicts within the sharing economy. This contributes to a more robust, reliable, and sustainable economic model that better serves the needs of its participants.

In conclusion, the sharing economy has fundamentally altered the way individuals and businesses interact with goods and services. Through collaborative consumption, access-based models, and peer-to-peer platforms, consumers have embraced a shift from ownership to access. Personalization has played a critical role in facilitating these interactions, driving convenience and efficiency. As the sharing economy continues to evolve, its economic, social, and environmental impact will likely grow, making it an important component of the future global economy.

11

Gig economy: Emerging employment and work institutions

The gig economy is a burgeoning employment trend that encompasses short-term work arrangements across diverse industries. It leverages online platforms and applications to establish a marketplace that facilitates swift and mutually advantageous employment opportunities for both work seekers and companies requiring short-term labour. This alternative to traditional employment arrangements is gaining increasing favour, particularly among the Millennial generation, individuals born between the 1980s and 1990s, who currently comprise 40 per cent of the gig economy workforce (Fountain, 2024).

Uber's 137 million monthly customers demonstrate the significant impact of the global gig economy on broad segments of society and the economy (Iqbal, 2024). Data from DDIY indicates that the worldwide freelance workforce currently stands at 1.57 billion, out of a total global workforce of 3.38 billion people (Fountain, 2024). In the United States alone, the freelancer count reached 73.3 million in 2023, with projections suggesting a rise to 76.4 million by the end of 2024. These figures reflect the significant role of independent workers in global employment, emphasizing the growing demand for flexible working conditions. To understand how these trends manifest in real-world applications, we turn to key platforms driving the gig economy.

TaskRabbit serves as a prime example of the gig economy, distinguishing itself from ride-sharing services such as Uber and Lyft. Established in 2008, TaskRabbit connects people who need help with various tasks to 'Taskers' – individuals ready to complete those tasks for a fee. The platform covers a wide range of services, including home repairs, moving assistance, errands, and cleaning, effectively turning an individual's available time and skills into valuable resources.

Individuals wishing to offer their skills and services can sign up to become Taskers. After a vetting process that includes a background check, they can list their services, set their rates, and indicate their availability on the platform. Those in need of services can use TaskRabbit to find suitable Taskers. Clients can browse through categories of tasks, view Tasker profiles including ratings and reviews, and select someone who fits their requirements for the job. Transactions are conducted through the TaskRabbit platform, facilitating a secure and cashless payment process. Upon completion of the task, both clients and Taskers can leave reviews, helping to maintain trust and quality within the community.

TaskRabbit offers significant economic opportunities for individuals by enabling them to monetize their skills and time. This is particularly beneficial for those seeking flexible work arrangements or supplemental income. For clients, TaskRabbit provides convenient access to a broad array of services that might otherwise be difficult to find, offering substantial value to those who lack the time, ability, or tools to complete specific tasks themselves.

The rise of the gig economy: Friend or foe?

The growth of the gig economy has introduced significant disruptions to conventional business models and labour management practices (Healy et al., 2017). With gig work spreading across different economic sectors and becoming a part of everyday life, it has ignited discussions around the nature and perception of gig economy employment (Vallas and Schor, 2020; Etter et al., 2019).

The gig economy stands distinct from traditional employment paradigms and contingent labour frameworks due to its reliance on online platforms and apps that instantaneously link consumers with specific service providers (Tran and Sokas, 2017; Vallas and Schor, 2020). This real-time connection has become an invaluable resource for a diverse array of users including companies in need of specialized skills on a temporary basis, entrepreneurs, small business proprietors, freelancers, and individuals with varying availability (Todolí-Signes, 2017). Digital platforms in the gig economy also do more than facilitate interaction between consumers and workers; they notify about new tasks, monitor completed assignments and any modifications, and handle payments, further underscoring the sector's dependency on digital technologies (Huws et al., 2017). As a result, gig economy platforms offer substantial benefits, including flexibility and low entry barriers.

The emergence of digital platforms has thus been instrumental in driving substantial economic changes in recent years, serving as a bridge between consumers and service providers by efficiently aligning the demand and supply of flexible labour (Van Dijck et al., 2018; Koutsimpogiorgos et al., 2020; De Stefano, 2015). This move towards a more contingent workforce, with an increased tendency towards outsourcing and labour market flexibility for independent contractors, marks a significant trend in employment practices (Estlund, 2018; Stanford, 2017). Leading gig economy entities include Uber for ride-sharing, TaskRabbit for miscellaneous tasks, Deliveroo and UberEats for food delivery, Helpling for cleaning services, and Upwork for specialized tasks such as translation and programming (Koutsimpogiorgos et al., 2020). The gig economy also involves intricate interactions among multiple stakeholders. Platform companies develop customized applications and websites through which they offer a diverse range of goods and services across various industries (Puschmann and Alt, 2016).

Digital platforms as intermediaries

Digital platforms in the gig economy, though not formal employers, often assume roles similar to a 'shadow employer' by overseeing the work process (Kenney and Zysman, 2016; Berg et al., 2018). Nevertheless, their core role is to act as intermediaries, facilitating the interaction between gig workers and clients. This digital mediation transforms both the transactional procedures and the nature of relationships between service providers and consumers (Prassl, 2018). This viewpoint is supported by Kuhn and Maleki (2017), who emphasize the pivotal role of technology and software in shaping the interactions between workers and clients in the gig economy.

Many management tasks traditionally handled by human supervisors in the gig economy are now managed by algorithms developed by platform companies (Rosenblat, 2018). Multi-sided gig economy platforms differ fundamentally from traditional hierarchical organizations in how tasks are assigned to workers. These platforms undertake various managerial functions, including recruiting workers, providing access to work opportunities, and setting compensation, largely through algorithmic methods (Wood et al., 2019). This form of management is particularly common in app-based work settings, described by Lee et al. (2015) as 'algorithmic management'. This involves using algorithms to allocate, optimize, and evaluate work tasks (Cheng and Foley, 2019). Uber serves as a key example, with algorithms handling several operational aspects: distributing work tasks (decision-making), pinpointing areas of high demand (informational), and assessing service quality via customer ratings (evaluative).

Gig economy platforms serve as significant drivers of value creation, exhibiting characteristics similar to natural monopolies that inherently attract large consumer bases. However, the primary source of this value creation is the work of independent contractors, as opposed to traditional employees (Zipperer et al., 2022). Moreover, the enduring and implicit contracts typically found in conventional employment relationships are largely missing between workers and firms in the gig economy. As these platforms bring forth new market dynamics and forms of organization, they spark considerable debate over appropriate regulatory measures (Malos et al., 2018). Given that the complexities and uncertainties associated with regulating the gig economy are often heightened by the digital nature of these businesses (Etter et al., 2019), it underscores the imperative for gig economy enterprises to adopt comprehensive and clear ethical and social responsibility strategies.

What is the gig economy?

The term 'gig work' has roots in the 1920s jazz scene, describing freelance musicians playing clubs. Bands like the Beatles embraced this concept, seeking creative freedom and a break from traditional employment structures (Nunberg, 2016). As Harvey et al. (2017, p. 20) note, the term originally held positive connotations, reflecting the flexibility and independence inherent in musicians' work. However, Friedman (2014) highlights how, over the years, its meaning has broadened significantly. Initially specific to musicians hired per performance, 'gig work' now encompasses a wider range of employment arrangements.

While the concept itself is not new, gig work gained renewed popularity after the financial crisis when securing permanent jobs became more challenging. This resurgence coincided with technological advancements, with companies like Uber leveraging gig workers to fuel rapid expansion. Consequently, the term 'gig economy' has become widely used in recent years to describe this growing trend of temporary and flexible work structures. In the gig economy, three distinct groups with sometimes competing interests coexist. Workers prioritize the flexibility of setting their own schedules, but often lack job security and benefits. Customers seek the convenience of food deliveries, rides, and various services available at the touch of a button. Companies strive to sidestep the costs associated with professional development, management, and other expenses typical of conventional employment, which can put pressure on worker compensation.

Gig workers are often found in sectors like transportation, delivery, and various services. The unique nature of the gig economy, with its unconventional work characteristics and business models, has made it challenging for scholars to agree on a definitive definition. It is frequently discussed interchangeably with terms such as 'sharing economy', 'crowdwork', and 'platform economy' (Huws et al., 2017). Botsman (2015) views the gig economy as a system where decentralized networks and marketplaces unlock the potential of underutilized assets by aligning supply and demand without the need for traditional middlemen. Moreover, Todolí-Signes (2017) characterizes the gig economy from an industry perspective as a labour market dominated by short-term jobs and a preference for hiring freelancers over full-time employees.

Disrupting traditional work models

The gig economy, characterized by its digital middlemen, disrupts traditional work models and redefines worker-customer interactions. Platforms like Uber and Fiverr connect a vast pool of freelance talent – plumbers, graphic designers, and everything in between – with customers seeking specific services. These platforms act as efficient matchmakers, streamlining the process for both sides (Berg et al., 2018). Customers can browse, select, and pay through user-friendly apps, while workers can find gigs with a few clicks. This immediacy and convenience are transformative, reshaping expectations for both parties. The traditional in-person interaction, like a plumber meeting a homeowner, is replaced by short-term, digital encounters. Workers build their reputation through online profiles, with customer choice heavily influenced by ratings and reviews. This creates a performance-driven culture where feedback directly impacts a worker's credibility and future opportunities.

However, the gig economy's convenience comes with trade-offs. While workers can enjoy flexibility and control over their hours and workload, concerns arise regarding job security and benefits (Aloisi, 2015). Furthermore, the digital platform, despite facilitating connections, might contribute to a sense of detachment and impersonality in these worker-customer relationships. The model thus necessitates a reconsideration of core concepts: what constitutes employment, and how value is exchanged in the service industry.

Matching needs and wants: How personalization fuels the gig economy

Personalization in the gig economy can significantly enhance the experiences of both service providers and consumers by adapting services to match individual preferences, leading to greater efficiency and higher satisfaction levels. This concept is prominent in various sectors, such as independent work tasks, travel, and online food delivery, where personalization influences the interaction and fulfilment processes.

On platforms like TaskRabbit, which connects freelancers with people needing tasks done, personalization is an important factor in enhancing efficiency and effectiveness. Freelancers can list their unique skills and preferences, while consumers can search for services tailored to their specific needs. The platform's algorithms then match consumers with the most suitable freelancers based on these personalized profiles, past reviews, and work history. This level of personalization ensures that tasks are completed by the most qualified individuals, thereby enhancing service quality and customer satisfaction.

In the travel sector, ride-sharing platforms like Uber and Lyft offer extensive personalization options. Users can select the type of vehicle that best suits their needs, from economical to luxury options. The apps also remember preferred routes, pickup locations, and other travel preferences, making future bookings more convenient and customized for individual users. For drivers, these platforms can provide personalized job opportunities based on their location, preferred working hours, and vehicle type, optimizing their earnings and work-life balance.

Online food delivery platforms such as Uber Eats and DoorDash excel in personalization by recommending restaurants and dishes based on a user's past orders, search history, and dietary preferences. This not only simplifies the ordering process but also helps users discover new favourites that align with their tastes. For gig workers, these platforms can offer personalized job suggestions based on their location, preferred working hours, and delivery mode (e.g. car, bike), enhancing their efficiency and job satisfaction.

In each of these examples, personalization within the gig economy helps align services more closely with individual needs and preferences, improving the overall user experience for both service providers and consumers. For service providers, personalization can lead to more relevant job opportunities, better earnings, and increased job satisfaction. For consumers, it means receiving services that are more closely customized to their specific needs. By effectively implementing personalization, gig economy platforms can create a more responsive, efficient, and user-friendly ecosystem.

Gig economy employment

The rise of the gig economy is driven by two main factors: technological advancements and an increasing demand for flexibility. Advances in technology have transformed the way we connect, making it simpler for individuals to find and take on gig work. Apps and platforms facilitate the matching process for both job seekers desiring flexible schedules and locations, and businesses in need of temporary expertise. This is evidenced by data indicating that around 162 million people in the United States and Europe are engaged in the gig economy (Huws et al., 2017; Bughin et al., 2018). However, the autonomy that gig workers enjoy is frequently constrained by the algorithms that manage their work. These algorithms dictate task assignments, monitor performance, and ultimately control many aspects of a worker's experience on the platform.

The surge in temporary employment opportunities is a direct result of this digital revolution. These platforms streamline the hiring process, enabling companies to swiftly hire short-term employees, while allowing individuals to quickly secure work through digital means (Tran and Sokas, 2017). This dynamic benefits both sides: companies obtain prompt access to workforce resources, and individuals find an easier path to flexible work options. However, the gig economy's deviation from conventional employment standards presents challenges, including a lack of legal safeguards for workers, which leads to job insecurity and unpredictable work availability (Huws et al., 2017). While much of gig work is managed by technology, the human element remains central. Gig workers must manage intricate relationships with platforms and customers, often enduring the emotional and physical toll of unstable work conditions.

Despite these disadvantages, the engagement in the gig economy has increased immensely over the last decade, representing new global employment opportunities in ways and in industries that were not possible before (Huws et al., 2017). This mode of employment is particularly popular among Millennials, those born in the 1980s and 1990s, who make up 40 per cent of the gig workforce and are projected to become the predominant demographic in the near future (Coen, 2018). Millennials are often seen as the key catalysts for the expanding gig economy trend, as the demand for alternative employment frameworks increases (Friedman, 2014; Adkins, 2016). With gig workers coming from a wide range of backgrounds, platforms have the potential to adapt their services to meet these varying needs, offering personalized job recommendations, flexible schedules, and more targeted support.

Non-standard employment relationships

The non-standard employment form in the gig economy and its associated issues remain central to the discourse surrounding this sector. Accurately measuring the extent of gig employment thus poses significant challenges. Employee status may hinge partly on control over work hours (Harris and Krueger, 2015). However, work hours in the gig economy are difficult to quantify, as workers are compensated for completing short-term tasks rather than adhering to a set schedule. The time spent waiting for or searching for tasks further blurs the lines of work time. This uncertainty in determining work hours contributes to the difficulties in defining the labour status of gig workers. Understanding labour status is thus critical, as it dictates eligibility for various benefits and protections mandated by social and legal frameworks. These can include minimum wage requirements, overtime pay, parental leave, sick leave, disability insurance, protection from harassment, social security contributions, and taxation.

Some gig organizations position themselves solely as technology companies providing software rather than labour services, often classifying their workers as independent contractors or business partners. This approach, on the one hand, allows gig organizations to reduce labour costs, potentially enhancing company value and attracting more investment. On the other hand, it enables them to circumvent employment law, which may be considered regulatory arbitrage. According to Prassl (2018), the working patterns observed in the gig economy demonstrate a deliberate evasion of employment law, shifting the burden of fluctuating demands onto workers who should not be responsible for such risks. To mitigate the risks of misclassification, organizations may employ deceptive tactics, such as incorporating clauses of representation and warranties, to assert that no employment relationship exists between platforms and workers (De Stefano, 2015; Davis and Hoyt, 2020).

Given the changing technological environment, the use of semi-automated algorithmic management practices allows gig organizations to sidestep liability, prompting questions about who is responsible for the well-being of workers. When multiple parties are involved in the transaction process and employment relationships are obscured, the identification of the responsible party for specific actions becomes ambiguous, particularly in trilateral arrangements (De Stefano, 2015). This practice employed by gig organizations also contributes to the externalization of worker-related costs. Driven by a profit-maximization motive, these organizations strive to minimize labour costs. However, this cost-cutting approach may ultimately be borne by society, such as the cost of controlling environmental pollution, which should ideally be shouldered by the relevant transportation companies (Prassl, 2018).

Despite these concerns, some platform companies have taken steps to provide benefits for their workers. For instance, Lyft drivers have the option to participate in a company-sponsored retirement savings programme.

Classification of gig workers

The concept of an 'employee' in the gig economy differs from traditional industries, as gig workers are typically considered independent contractors who engage in various jobs (or 'gigs') through online platforms to connect with service consumers (Stanford, 2017). These workers are often classified by platforms as self-employed, freelancers, or independent contractors, highlighting the absence of a traditional employment relationship. However, Friedman (2014) argues that while platforms define these workers as independent contractors, they exhibit characteristics of both traditional employment and freelancer contracts. Workers are subject to some degree of management and control by the platforms, suggesting a traditional employment relationship, but they also have the flexibility to choose when, where, and how much they work, implying independent contractor status. This creates a grey area where gig workers do not fit neatly into the categories of traditional employees or independent contractors.

Recognizing this gap, scholars have proposed various approaches to ensure gig workers receive appropriate rights and benefits. Some advocate for classifying them as employees, while others suggest a new category – dependent contractors – to address their unique circumstances (Taylor, 2017). Harris and Krueger (2015) earlier proposed a new categorization called 'independent workers', which falls between the employee and independent contractor designations. However, De Stefano (2015) cautioned that this new classification might be challenging to implement, as it could be used as a cheaper alternative to employee status, potentially hindering gig workers' pursuit of full employment status.

As the notion of short-term 'gig work' is applicable across a wide range of roles in numerous industries and businesses, it is distinguished by several unique characteristics that define gig employment:

On-demand work with no guarantee of continuous engagement: Gig workers are typically hired on an as-needed basis, with no assurance of ongoing employment.

Irregular work patterns: Due to fluctuating demand for their services, gig workers often experience unpredictable work schedules.

Piecework payment: Gig workers are typically compensated based on the completion of individual tasks or projects rather than receiving a fixed monthly salary.

Self-provision of capital equipment and workspace: Gig workers are responsible for providing their own tools, equipment, and workspace, often bearing the associated costs.

Online platform or app-based job organization: Gig work is primarily organized and mediated through online platforms or apps, creating a three-sided connection between the worker, the customer, and the digital intermediary.

In addition to these general features, there are two distinct labour dimensions within the gig economy (Mehta and Kumar, 2020):

1. Crowdsourcing: In crowdsourcing, workers perform tasks through online digital platforms, allowing the job to be completed anywhere in the world. Amazon Mechanical Turk is a prime example of a crowdsourcing platform, where clients can post 'Human Intelligence Tasks' for completion, such as writing reviews, conducting surveys, online tutoring, graphic design, building databases, and more.
2. On-demand work via apps/internet: In on-demand work via apps/internet, the client and the performer are matched online, but the task must be carried out locally or in-person. Uber, for instance, acts as a matching platform connecting clients with drivers and facilitating payment and customer satisfaction evaluation.

Grubhub drivers in the gig economy

Grubhub, a pioneer in the online food delivery industry, operates by connecting customers with local restaurants through its platform. Central to Grubhub's model are its drivers, who deliver orders while navigating the complexities of the gig economy. Founded in 2004, Grubhub has grown to become one of the leading food delivery services in the United States. The company relies on a network of independent contractors who use their own vehicles to make deliveries, embodying the flexibility and independence characteristic of gig work.

Grubhub drivers come from diverse backgrounds, each drawn to the role for various reasons, such as the need for a flexible work schedule or supplemental income. The platform allows drivers to choose their hours and, to some extent, their delivery zones. Drivers receive order notifications through the Grubhub app, which provides details about pickup and drop-off locations, estimated earnings, and delivery time frames. Grubhub drivers earn money per delivery based on factors like distance, time, and order size. They also retain 100 per cent of customer tips. Earnings can fluctuate daily, influenced by factors such as demand, weather, and competition from other drivers.

Grubhub drivers exemplify the broader trends and challenges within the gig economy, balancing the autonomy of independent contract work with operational and financial uncertainties. As the food delivery market continues to evolve, so too will the experiences of Grubhub drivers, underscoring the need for supportive policies and innovative solutions to ensure sustainable and equitable gig work environments.

The experiences of Grubhub drivers show how companies such as Uber Eats, DoorDash, and Grubhub have become integral to daily life, connecting consumers with local eateries through a vast network of freelance delivery personnel. The online food delivery industry, driven by mobile technology and evolving consumer habits, has experienced explosive growth. Drivers, often using their own vehicles, form the backbone of this service, ensuring meals arrive promptly.

However, the gig economy presents a double-edged sword for drivers. While they enjoy flexibility in setting their schedules, earnings fluctuate significantly based on location, time of day, and company policies. Incentives for peak hours or completed deliveries might exist, but income remains unpredictable. Drivers shoulder their expenses – fuel, vehicle maintenance, and insurance. Furthermore, their work depends on app-based algorithms that assign deliveries. This streamlines operations but also leaves drivers at the mercy of technology. They have minimal control over order volume or app-related issues.

Beyond these challenges, gig work offers limited benefits and protections. Drivers, classified as independent contractors, lack health insurance, paid leave, and job security. Low entry barriers can oversaturate the market, making it difficult to secure enough deliveries for a sustainable income. The Covid-19 pandemic further underscored the health risks associated with frequent interactions and handling goods (Cherry and Rutschman, 2020).

Task-based work features in the gig economy

Task-based short-term work is a fundamental aspect of the gig economy. Unlike traditional permanent jobs, work in the gig economy is segmented into smaller tasks that gig workers complete on a 'gig' basis, moving from one task to another. The transitory and fragmented nature of gig work facilitates one-off transactions and gives rise to so-called on-demand workers. This allows workers to provide services for multiple employers simultaneously for relatively low piece-rate pay.

This short-term work offers the kind of flexibility frequently linked to the gig economy in various studies (Petropoulos, 2016). Unlike traditional jobs, gig work allows individuals to choose their own hours and work locations, providing unparalleled flexibility. This adaptability is a key reason many choose to enter the gig economy. In certain types of online crowd work, this flexibility can also create an environment that encourages creativity and the generation of new ideas.

However, some argue that flexibility in the gig economy is illusory and paradoxical (Prassl, 2018). Several factors contribute to the perception of limited flexibility in gig work:

Unpredictable customer demand: The inconsistency and unpredictability of customer demand can challenge workers' ability to dictate their own schedules, particularly if they depend financially on gig work. This may result in extended periods spent searching or waiting for the next job, somewhat curtailing their flexibility. For example, Uber drivers might endure unpaid waiting times for their next ride, while workers on platforms like AMTurk might stay glued to their computers searching for preferable tasks, with some even setting up alerts for available work.

Time-constrained tasks: The presence of tasks that must be completed within a specific time frame can further restrict worker flexibility, an issue compounded by time zone and geographical variances.

Platform work control: The degree of control exerted by certain platforms over the work can also impinge on worker flexibility.

Task brevity: The short duration of many gig tasks can limit the worker's ability to make decisions during the work process, further affecting their autonomy and flexibility.

Thus, the predominantly one-sided nature of flexibility can render the seemingly ideal flexible schedule in the gig economy elusive (Prassl, 2018). Nonetheless, freelancers or professionals with high skills might experience greater flexibility compared to other gig economy workers. Conversely, the transient nature of gig assignments contributes to an absence of sustained commitment between employers and employees, subjecting gig workers to different levels of job instability and unpredictability. This can be particularly challenging for those who depend on gig work as their main source of income or lack alternatives, as they may find themselves caught in a cycle of unpredictable highs and lows.

Technology-enabled roles

As mentioned earlier, digital platforms operate as digital intermediaries, simplifying interactions and assuming managerial functions. Their primary aim is to facilitate efficient connections between service providers and consumers, ensuring a swift and effective match for their respective needs. Platforms such as Uber, Deliveroo, and Lyft focus on specific services like transportation or delivery, where algorithms and extensive data analysis play a key role in aligning supply with demand. On the other hand, platforms that cater to a broader range of services, including Amazon Mechanical Turk, Upwork, and TaskRabbit, place a higher emphasis on aligning with consumer preferences. As intermediaries between service providers (workers) and service requesters (customers), these platforms facilitate smooth transactions, acting as efficient matchmakers who address user needs promptly (Prassl, 2018).

Uber: Operating in a new digital environment

The digital platform business model has experienced significant growth in the past decade, propelling digital ride-sharing companies like Uber to surpass traditional taxi services and establish themselves as the industry's new, innovative leaders in a remarkably short period. However, Uber's path to astronomical success and growth has been inextricably intertwined with a multitude of scandals and tribulations that have drawn widespread condemnation from its stakeholders. Despite the company's turbulent history marked by executive misconduct, there are arguments that reforming the company's practices could rejuvenate the disruptive taxi-hailing app.

For instance, there are substantial gaps in outdated employment laws regarding employment classification that encourage gig companies like Uber to exploit their workers to gain a competitive advantage (Berger et al., 2019). A clear disparity exists in the levels of protection provided to employees, who enjoy the full scope of rights from anti-discrimination laws to unfair dismissal protection, and the self-employed, who are left to fend for themselves. Uber vehemently denies employee status for its drivers, attempting to leverage their flexible work model to shirk responsibility and deprive their drivers of the traditional benefits included under employment contracts, such as sick pay, holiday entitlement, or parental leave.

These employment policies, or lack thereof, have led to various social repercussions, including Uber's susceptibility to ongoing protests around the globe. Disgruntled drivers are likely to seek alternative employment opportunities where more comprehensive policies regarding employee welfare are prevalent. With only 4 per cent of drivers remaining on Uber's platform after one year, rather than committing millions to driver acquisition campaigns and employee status lawsuits, Uber's employment strategies should primarily focus on increasing retention rates and fostering driver relationships, loyalty, and experience by expanding employment rights and introducing comprehensive rewards systems and incentives.

Despite being one of the most successful start-ups, Uber has been exposed for its history of a pervasive culture of alleged sexual harassment, discrimination, and potentially illegal managerial activities. Human resources reportedly often ignored serious claims of misconduct and shielded top performers from accountability so as not to hinder the performance of the organization. This perennial crisis involving systematic failure of Uber management underpins their historical inability to foster a positive organizational culture. Leaders at Uber should collaborate with stakeholders across the business to re-evaluate their company culture and create a strategic plan (Calo and Rosenblat, 2017).

How Uber manages worker performance

The term 'technology of production and organization of work' reflects how advancements in task coordination impact company policies. Take, for example, companies with isolated workforces. These organizations struggle to monitor employee output traditionally. Uber, with its millions of geographically dispersed delivery drivers, exemplifies this challenge. To address the lack of physical proximity, Uber relies on semi-automated and algorithmic systems to manage worker performance. These sophisticated algorithms power a two-way rating system for both customers and drivers. This creates a continuous feedback loop that allows Uber to remotely monitor driver performance against key metrics. If a driver's rating falls below a specific threshold (often around 4.6), they risk automatic deactivation. Conversely, consistently high ratings can unlock benefits like fuel purchase rebates.

This approach aligns with the 'Hawthorne Effect', which suggests that workers monitored electronically might adjust their behaviour to appear more productive. In Uber's case, the constant awareness of being evaluated (through ratings) and the potential rewards for good performance are expected to incentivize positive behavioural changes in drivers. However, concerns have been raised that impersonal, data-driven decisions made through these methods can erode trust between employers and workers. Algorithmic management can also undermine the role of traditional HR departments by dehumanizing their processes and dismantling employment relationships. Moreover, rating systems are highly susceptible to customer biases, providing a platform for consumers to directly assert their prejudices in ways that companies are legally prohibited from doing.

Social repercussions of the gig economy

While gig organizations contribute to economic growth, they also induce various negative impacts, such as social inequality through uneven wealth distribution (Prassl, 2018) and encouraging unfair competitive practices. The efficiency in matching supply with demand, by reducing market friction, facilitates immediate transactions, generating significant value for gig organizations. Nevertheless, due to the reliance on an external workforce, this generated value tends to be disproportionately allocated to investors rather than gig workers, exacerbating wage disparities within the gig economy. Consequently, the gig economy is likely to aggravate social inequalities. Furthermore, in a manner akin to the effects of outsourcing, leading gig economy firms heighten competition among individual workers while diminishing it among gig organizations themselves. This dynamic can lead to monopolistic conditions that disadvantage traditional businesses.

New organizational form

Since the early twentieth century, organizational hierarchies and internal labour markets have been built with clearly defined organizational boundaries. In the late twentieth century, due to increased pressure from capital markets, leading companies were compelled to adjust their strategies to gain more market share and attract more investors. This led to the emergence of external workforces and fissured workplaces. As prevalent business strategies in the 1980s, sub-contracting and outsourcing allowed lead corporations to focus on their core competencies while trimming or outsourcing peripheral departments and activities, such as janitorial services, cleaning, or even the personnel department. Similarly, in the gig economy, organizational boundaries are blurred through the use of an external workforce, reflecting a hybrid of labour market and hierarchy. Gig organizations also focus on the core functions that generate profits and shed those that increase costs. Therefore, the gig organizational form is not entirely new but has historical roots.

Furthermore, as we saw in the case of Uber, gig organizations use rating and reputation systems to manage workers' performance, reflecting the technological control inherent in this model. Instead of relying on human supervisors, performance appraisal in the gig economy primarily hinges on the algorithmic calculation of 'soliciting feedback' from customers through numerical metrics or five-star rating systems. Gig organizations set expectations based on outcomes while also influencing the manner in which work is executed. According to Rosenblat and Stark (2016), rating systems serve as a tool for organizations to cultivate the desired attitude and manner of workers.

Platform companies employ performance protocols to ensure that work is carried out to a high-quality standard. For instance, Handy offered workers suggestions on how to listen to music, including using headphones and requesting the customer's permission. Lyft recommended the 'fist bump' as a way to greet customers (Lee et al., 2015). Furthermore, some platforms have incorporated terms in their 'participation agreement' to prohibit workers from contacting customers outside the platforms. In Uber, the performance protocol enforces a 'zero tolerance' policy for interactions outside the platform. In addition, based on specific work standards, gig organizations utilize technology to conduct highly strict remote supervision to ensure work quality, a practice described as 'permanent probation' by Prassl and Risak (2015). For example, Uber used GPS, gyrometers, and acceleration sensors to track and monitor drivers' real-time location and speed. In Upwork, customers can check workers' work diary, including counting keystrokes and snapshots.

Impact of client ratings and reputation systems

Client ratings and reputation systems are key in the gig economy, especially under algorithmic management, where work assignments often depend on customer feedback. Kuhn and Maleki (2017) suggest that these assignments are typically based on algorithmic assessments or a combination of platform and client decisions. On app-based platforms, where work allocation is controlled by the platform, workers with higher ratings may access more desirable tasks (Duggan et al., 2020). On crowd-based online platforms, those with top customer ratings might be given priority or prominent placement in search results. For instance, high-reputation workers on Wonolo could enjoy early access to opportunities, and on some platforms, like

Handy, payment rates may correlate with customer ratings and task volume (Kuhn and Maleki, 2017).

Conversely, rating systems function as the main performance evaluation method, and workers not meeting the expected standards could face platform-imposed penalties, such as restricted access to lucrative tasks. For instance, Uber might penalize drivers for not meeting acceptance rate thresholds or exceeding cancellation rate limits (Rosenblat and Stark, 2016), even reserving the right to deactivate drivers' accounts without explanation, potentially dismissing those in the lowest performance bracket. This dismissal authority might suggest an employer-like status for gig platforms, contingent on the level of control they maintain.

Algorithm transparency and non-transparency

Although platforms such as Upwork may take into account the fairness of client feedback, the transparency of their algorithms continues to be a concern (Kuhn and Maleki, 2017; Wood et al., 2019). Many Airbnb hosts have expressed concerns about the transparency and clarity of its algorithms. Due to the non-transparency of algorithmic assignment, more experienced workers may have an advantage over novices by identifying patterns or errors in the algorithm (Lee et al., 2015). For instance, experienced Uber drivers may develop workaround strategies to avoid undesirable tasks while maintaining an acceptable rating. Similarly, Lyft drivers intentionally log in and out of the platform since the time spent online may influence work assignment. Since gig organizations have sole access to data and control over platform procedures and rules, privacy concerns arise. However, app organizations cannot disclose algorithm design, as it may be considered proprietary information.

Motivational impact and reputation lock-in

As gig workers accumulate tasks, the threshold for maintaining their ratings escalates, rendering a single poor review relatively inconsequential to their overall standing. This situation could lead to a lack of concern for maintaining high-quality work, thereby reducing the long-term motivational impact of ratings (Lee et al., 2015). Furthermore, strategies that lock workers into their reputations can hinder their ability to switch between platforms, effectively confining them to a specific platform. For instance, Upwork implements a 'lifetime billing strategy' where a worker's commission decreases over time, making it financially unattractive to start anew on another platform (Prassl, 2018). While Donovan et al. (2016) argue that the prestige of a company's brand could bolster a worker's reputation and draw in customers, such reputational benefits are often confined to the gig economy and may not translate to broader professional recognition outside of it.

Algorithmic management in the gig economy uses psychological insights to subtly influence human behaviour. This method allows for a form of indirect oversight of workers without overt coercion, employing techniques like behavioural nudges (Duggan et al., 2020). Such psychological strategies are woven into the platform interfaces via 'choice architecture', effectively influencing worker actions, as observed in platforms like Uber (Rosenblat and Stark, 2016). For instance, adaptive pricing mechanisms like Uber's 'surge pricing' or Lyft's 'Prime Time' modify rates in response to real-time demand (Lee et al., 2015), and heat maps direct drivers to areas with heightened demand. These psychological approaches enable gig companies to subtly guide drivers in making decisions about when, how long, and where to work (Scheiber, 2017).

Reforming the system

Gig economy platforms have developed sophisticated management systems that prioritize aligning customers' interests with those of the platform, often at the expense of the workers. These platforms often employ opaque labour practices, a notable example being the secrecy surrounding the workings of their algorithmic management systems. By keeping the details of these algorithms hidden, gig platforms maintain control over how work is distributed, how workers are evaluated, and how disputes are resolved, all while optimizing their profits and public image. This lack of transparency and the focus on customer and platform benefits create challenges for gig workers, who often seek more clarity and fairness in how they are managed and compensated (Tan et al., 2021; Stewart and Standford, 2017).

There is thus a growing recognition of the need to rethink and redesign these algorithmic management systems. The goal would be to create a more balanced approach that not only serves the interests of the customers and the platforms but also fairly addresses the needs and rights of gig workers. This could involve developing more transparent algorithms, offering workers greater control over their schedules, and providing clearer criteria for performance evaluations and dispute resolutions. Personalizing these systems to benefit both customers and gig workers could lead to more equitable, sustainable, and mutually beneficial outcomes in the gig economy, encouraging a healthier work environment and improving service quality for customers.

Personalization within gig platforms can also be pivotal in enhancing the overall user experience, both for workers and customers. By increasing transparency, these platforms can address the issue of information asymmetry, allowing customers to have a clear understanding of the pricing structure of the services they are using. This involves breaking down the costs associated with a service, such as the base price, any additional fees, and how much of their payment goes directly to the gig worker. By providing this level of detail, customers can make more informed decisions, appreciating the value of the service and the work that goes into it, rather than just seeing a lump sum at the end of a transaction.

This approach can gradually change customer perceptions, helping them understand that fair compensation for gig workers is essential, and that gig services should not be expected to be free or extremely low cost. It emphasizes the principle that gig work, like any other form of labour, deserves fair remuneration that at least meets a living wage standard. Setting service prices to reflect this standard ensures that gig work is sustainable and equitable, contributing to a healthier gig economy where workers are compensated fairly for their efforts and customers are aware of and value the true cost of the services they consume.

Achieving this fair outcome is also contingent on gig economy platforms developing more personalized services that cater to the specific needs of all participants involved, including both gig workers and customers. Personalization can dramatically enhance the overall experience by ensuring that services are more accurately aligned with individual expectations and requirements.

For gig workers, personalized services might include matching them with tasks that align with their skills, availability, and preferred geographical locations. This approach not only maximizes their productivity but also boosts job satisfaction by providing them with opportunities that are best suited to their professional capabilities and personal circumstances. Furthermore, platforms can offer flexible scheduling tools that allow workers to select shifts that fit their lifestyle, enhancing work-life balance. Evidence suggests that platform workers under the tight control of algorithms often engage in customer-directed deviant behaviour. To mitigate the discontinuous intent of gig workers, platform companies tend to employ algorithmic systems. Algorithmic management, when designed appropriately, can serve as an effective tool by reducing gig workers' perceived work intensification, thereby decreasing their intention to discontinue in a boundaryless organizational context. Moreover, algorithmic management can provide essential support for gig workers with limited positive cognitive resources, such as uncertainty tolerance. By further personalizing the gig work experience, platform companies can thus create more stable relationships with their workers.

For customers, personalization involves tailoring the user experience to meet their specific preferences and needs. This could include offering recommendations based on previous interactions, such as suggesting favourite or frequently ordered items, which simplifies the decision-making process and enhances convenience. Besides, platforms can provide adjustable service parameters, such as specifying the desired time for a task to be completed or choosing preferences for service interaction, which can significantly enhance customer satisfaction.

Beyond individual customization, these platforms can apply data analytics to continuously learn from user interactions, thereby refining the accuracy of the matches and recommendations over time. This ongoing optimization ensures that both gig workers and customers receive increasingly relevant and satisfying service engagements. Ultimately, by embedding advanced personalization features into their systems, gig economy platforms can create a more equitable and enjoyable environment. This not only leads to higher retention rates among gig workers by acknowledging and accommodating their needs but also builds loyalty among customers who feel that their preferences are understood and valued. Such an approach encourages a sustainable and thriving ecosystem where the interests of all parties are balanced and protected.

Part 3

Personalization: Challenges and opportunities

The personalization approach offers a nuanced understanding of the decision-making processes that govern participation in digital marketplaces. At its core, this model recognizes that the decisions of buyers and sellers are interdependent, with each party's choice to engage significantly influenced by their expectations of the other's participation. This interdependency creates a formidable challenge for nascent digital platforms. These entities are not merely facilitators; they are de facto market architects and operators, tasked with the complex mission of initiating and sustaining a delicate equilibrium between supply and demand.

As elaborated in this part of the book, the key to navigating this challenge lies in the continuous refinement and deployment of personalization strategies. These strategies transcend basic algorithmic recommendations; they are sophisticated mechanisms designed to enhance the quality and relevance of interactions between sellers and buyers (involving also third parties and complementors). By adapting experiences, products, and services to individual preferences and behaviours, these platforms aim to create a virtuous cycle. Sellers find more targeted avenues for their offerings, while buyers discover products and services that resonate more deeply with their needs. This heightened alignment fosters trust, engagement, and, ultimately, a self-sustaining marketplace ecosystem.

However, the power of personalization brings with it profound responsibilities. In this section, we pivot to a critical examination of what constitutes responsible artificial intelligence (AI) – a concept that underpins effective and ethical personalization. We posit that the success of personalization is inextricably linked to the development and implementation of robust AI governance frameworks. These frameworks must address a multitude of concerns, from data privacy and algorithmic bias to transparency in decision-making. We examine approaches ranging from self-regulation and industry consortia to more formal legislative and regulatory frameworks. The goal is not to stifle innovation but to channel it responsibly, ensuring that the benefits of personalization are not overshadowed by unintended harms.

In concluding our discussion on personalization, we elevate the conversation to a macro perspective. We argue that personalization, when implemented responsibly, transcends being a mere business strategy; it becomes a fundamental mechanism for organizing modern economies. By facilitating more efficient exchanges of goods and services, personalization has the potential to reduce waste, increase consumer satisfaction, and create more resilient, adaptive economic systems.

Moreover, as AI and digital platforms become more adept at understanding and predicting human behaviour, they could play a pivotal role in addressing global challenges. Imagine personalized interventions in healthcare, education, or resource allocation, designed not just for individuals but for communities and even nations. The potential is vast, but so too is the responsibility. In essence, the future of our economies may well hinge on our ability to harness the power of personalization while rigorously upholding ethical standards. It is a delicate balance – one that requires continuous dialogue among technologists, policymakers, ethicists, and the public. By getting this balance right, we can unlock a new era of economic organization: one that is not only efficient and innovative but also equitable, transparent, and aligned with our highest human values.

12

Responsible AI and personalization

Consumers today face a barrage of online choices, coupled with concerns about security, privacy, and the ethical implications of artificial intelligence (AI). This scepticism can hinder trust in both online commerce and AI-powered solutions.

Imagine a busy professional constantly juggling work, family, and personal commitments. Finding time for leisurely shopping trips is a challenge. However, they discover a personalized online shopping platform powered by AI. Initially, the individual is apprehensive about using the platform. They are unsure how AI will understand their preferences and worry about potential data misuse. How will the platform address these concerns?

The platform addresses potential concerns by providing clear explanations about how AI personalizes recommendations and ensures user control over data sharing. This includes the ability to adjust preferences and provide feedback, allowing the AI to learn and adapt to evolving needs. Furthermore, the platform implements robust security measures to protect user data and prioritizes responsible AI development. Over time, this transparency, user-centric approach, and commitment to security lead to positive user experiences, with the platform delivering relevant product suggestions based on past purchases, browsing history, and stated preferences. This, in turn, fosters trust and confidence in AI-powered recommendations.

This suggests that building trust in AI and online commerce requires a multifaceted approach. By prioritizing transparency, user control, security, and positive experiences, firms can create an environment where consumers feel confident and empowered to embrace the benefits of AI-powered solutions. We now turn our attention to examining the foundations of these approaches, considering the potential challenges they may face in implementation.

Digital marketplace dynamics

The personalization approach represents a paradigm shift in our understanding of digital marketplace dynamics. At its heart lies the recognition that the traditional economic model of rational, independent actors making decisions in isolation is inadequate in the context of digital platforms. Instead, this approach posits a more nuanced, interdependent decision-making process that more accurately reflects the complexities of modern digital commerce.

Central to this model is the concept of 'expectation interdependence'. In traditional markets, buyers and sellers might make decisions based primarily on their own needs, resources, and constraints. However, in digital marketplaces, each party's decision to participate is profoundly influenced by their expectations of the other's behaviour. A seller, for instance, might decide to list their products on a platform not just because it is user-friendly or has low fees, but because they believe a sufficient number of buyers will be present. Similarly, a buyer might choose a platform not just for its product range or prices, but because they expect to find reliable, responsive sellers.

This interdependence creates a classic 'chicken-and-egg' problem for new digital platforms. Sellers would not join a platform without buyers, and buyers would not engage without sellers. It is a Catch-22 that has stymied many promising start-ups. However, it is precisely this challenge that elevates these platforms from mere intermediaries to what we might call 'market architects'. The term 'market architect' encapsulates the multifaceted role these platforms must play. They are not passive conduits for transactions but active creators and shapers of economic ecosystems. Their task is not just to build a platform but to orchestrate a complex, living marketplace that includes third-party service providers, complementors, and affiliate organizations. This involves a range of responsibilities:

Market design: Platforms must design rules, incentives, and structures that encourage participation on both sides. This might include offering promotional deals for early adopters, implementing rating systems to build trust, or creating algorithms that prioritize new sellers to give them a fair chance.

Liquidity management: Just as a central bank manages money supply, platforms must manage the 'liquidity' of their marketplace – ensuring there are enough buyers and sellers at any given time to facilitate transactions. Too few of either, and the market stalls.

Trust and safety: In physical markets, trust is often built through face-to-face interactions and local reputations. Digital platforms must replicate this through mechanisms like verified reviews, secure payment systems, and clear dispute resolution processes.

Data-driven optimization: Platforms continuously gather and analyse data on user behaviour, using these insights to refine their market design. For example, they might notice that buyers in a certain region prefer products with next-day delivery and adjust seller requirements accordingly.

Network effect cultivation: The value of a platform increases exponentially with each new user, a phenomenon known as the network effect. Platforms must strategically nurture these effects, often by targeting influential users or integrating with other platforms.

The personalization approach argues that success in these roles hinges on a platform's ability to create personalized experiences. It is not enough to have buyers and sellers; you need the right buyers for each seller and the right sellers for each buyer. This is where AI and data analytics come into play. By analysing user data, platforms can create detailed profiles of both buyers and sellers. For a buyer, this might include past purchases, browsing history, location, and even time of day they typically shop. For a seller, it could include product categories, customer service ratings, shipping speeds, and peak sales periods. Armed with this data, sharing economy or gig economy platforms can:

Personalize product discovery: Instead of overwhelming buyers with every available product, platforms can curate a personalized 'storefront' based on the buyer's interests. This reduces choice overload and increases the likelihood of a purchase.

Optimize seller visibility: Rather than a one-size-fits-all approach, platforms can prioritize sellers in search results based on how well they match a buyer's preferences. A buyer who values fast shipping might see local sellers first, while a buyer focused on unique items might see artisanal sellers.

Targeted notifications: Instead of spamming all users with generic promotions, platforms can send personalized alerts. A seller might be notified when a high-value buyer in their niche joins, or a buyer might be alerted when a favourite seller restocks.

Predictive inventory management: By analysing buyer behaviour, platforms can help sellers predict demand, reducing the risks of overstocking or stockouts.

Dynamic pricing: Platforms can suggest optimal pricing strategies for sellers based on factors like competitor prices, time of year, and individual buyer price sensitivity.

Through these personalized interactions, platforms create a virtuous cycle. Buyers find products they like more easily, increasing their satisfaction and platform loyalty. Sellers find more qualified leads, improving their sales and encouraging them to list more products. This positive feedback loop strengthens the platform's market position, attracting even more users.

In essence, the personalization approach reframes digital platforms not just as marketplaces but as intelligent matchmakers. Their success depends not on the volume of transactions they facilitate, but on the quality and relevance of each interaction. By understanding and catering to the unique needs of each participant, they transform the abstract concept of a 'market' into a personalized, responsive ecosystem.

This approach has profound implications beyond individual platforms. It suggests that in the digital age, economic efficiency is less about optimizing supply chains or production processes (though these remain important) and more about optimizing human connections and experiences. The most successful economies may be those that best harness technology to understand and fulfil the unique needs of each individual. Moreover, this model challenges traditional economic assumptions about competition. In a personalized marketplace, the winner is not necessarily the platform with the most users or the lowest prices, but the one that creates the most value through relevance and trust. This changes the competition from a race to the bottom on price or a rush to accumulate users, to a more nuanced contest based on data intelligence and user experience.

Broadly, the personalization approach offers a compelling framework for understanding and navigating the complexities of digital marketplaces. It recognizes that in an age of information abundance, the scarcest resource is not goods or even buyers and sellers – it is attention and relevance. By mastering the art of personalization, digital platforms do not just facilitate transactions; they create ecosystems of value that align with the unique contours of each participant's needs and aspirations. In doing so, they are not just changing how we buy and sell; they are redefining the very nature of economic interaction in the digital age.

The evolving role of AI

AI is rapidly gaining relevance in modern society, with new applications of this innovative technology emerging at an unprecedented pace, particularly in digital marketplaces. Despite AI's current distance from the human-like creations often depicted in science fiction, algorithms capable of comprehending language or replicating certain aspects of human intelligence are widely implemented (Vetrò et al., 2019; Montes and Goertzel, 2019). Of the major areas of AI, machine learning has recently received an overwhelming share of investment compared to other categories. The AI industry is now widely recognized as holding immense significance for the future of the global economy, with healthcare, finance, automotive, and retail industries already employing AI applications to enhance efficiency, often using digital platforms as a key vehicle for these advancements.

While the potential social benefits of AI technology are plentiful, the risks associated with algorithmic decision-making are also well-documented. AI programmes inherently reflect the biases of their developers, both in how they frame the problem to be addressed and how they select, utilize, and prioritize the data to be processed. Moreover, the ability of AI technology to discern connections and patterns across disparate data sets that would be undetectable by humans poses a significant threat to our privacy and reputation rights.

In this context, business ethics is crucial for understanding corporate responsibility, emphasizing the importance of ethical business operations and production in building trust with stakeholders and users. Defined as a system of policies and practices that uphold a corporation's legal and moral responsibilities, business ethics typically encompass principles such as personal responsibility, corporate responsibility, loyalty, respect, trust, fairness, community, and environmental responsibility (Werhane and Freeman, 1999). Ethics in business is seen as an ongoing process of debate over moral choices, highlighting the need for companies to maintain ethical practices to strengthen stakeholder relationships and foster trust. The intersection of AI and business ethics involves assessing the ethical impacts and potential drawbacks of implementing AI in business operations.

The rise of human-machine teams: AI's expanding role in businesses

The way companies interact with AI has evolved significantly. It all began with automating repetitive tasks, but now AI is moving towards case-by-case augmentation and even substitution of human activities (McLennan et al., 2022). Initially, AI took over administrative burdens like data entry and processing (Lee, 2020). As AI matured, organizations explored its potential for more strategic applications – decision-making support, virtual customer service agents, and talent management with predictive analytics (Benbya et al., 2020).

This advancement was not solely driven by technology. Both evolving AI capabilities and shifting organizational goals played a role. Easier access to vast data sets and advancements in AI algorithms allowed for more complex applications. Facing competition, companies sought efficiency gains and innovation through AI. Today, AI is no longer just a tool for streamlining operations; it is a strategic lever for transformation. As AI redefines job roles, workflows, and even the very nature of work, it presents both opportunities and challenges for company organization. While personalization has transformed digital platforms, its implementation must navigate complex challenges, particularly around AI governance, which we explore next.

Challenges to AI adoption

While AI promises significant benefits, its widespread adoption faces hurdles. A major concern lies in its far-reaching impact on stakeholders, many of whom may not fully understand AI's capabilities. Companies need a clear picture of how AI will affect employees, customers, and partners, yet data on these impacts is often limited, leading to understandable apprehension. Another barrier is corporate culture. Embracing AI often requires significant organizational changes, which can be met with resistance. To unlock AI's full potential, companies need robust IT infrastructure capable of handling the complex data processing involved. This translates to additional investments and potentially a major overhaul of existing systems. Furthermore, recent concerns about social media manipulation and algorithmic bias raise red flags about the responsible use of AI. Companies must tread carefully to avoid data and algorithmic manipulation that could have unintended societal consequences. Failure to do so could lead to a cascade of negative outcomes, including bad press, customer loss, financial decline, and regulatory sanctions.

As indicated above, the implementation of AI also carries significant ethical implications that can impact businesses and society at large. When AI systems fail to fulfil their intended purposes, they create uncertainty and erode stakeholder trust, potentially leading to detrimental outcomes for organizations. Ensuring that AI makes correct and ethical decisions necessitates robust ethical design frameworks; without them, erroneous judgements by AI can disrupt business operations and harm reputations. Key ethical concerns surrounding AI include algorithmic bias, where pre-existing prejudices in data or programming lead to unfair disadvantages for certain groups, undermining equality and justice (Green, 2018). Similarly, the widespread adoption of AI poses risks of increased unemployment, as machines replace human labour, thereby exacerbating socioeconomic inequalities and potentially hindering economic growth, especially among lower-income populations.

In sensitive sectors like healthcare, AI usage raises issues related to privacy breaches and the possibility of critical errors affecting patient outcomes. These concerns highlight the importance of implementing stringent governance and regulatory measures to oversee AI development and deployment. Effective regulations should address moral considerations, safeguard privacy, and establish clear accountability to ensure that AI technologies contribute positively and ethically to society.

Diversity, non-discrimination, and fairness

While AI offers incredible potential for personalization, it also poses significant ethical challenges, particularly around bias and accountability. Discrimination and bias pose a significant threat when implementing automated decision-making systems. Machine learning algorithms are susceptible to bias at various stages, from design to training (Green, 2018; ACM, 2017). For example, using historical data lacking diversity can perpetuate discrimination against minorities in areas like hiring or loan approvals. Besides, relying on seemingly neutral data like postal codes or magazine subscriptions might indirectly discriminate by acting as proxies for protected characteristics like race or gender (Montes and Goertzel, 2019). The emphasis on efficiency in AI can exacerbate these risks, disproportionately impacting marginalized groups.

While algorithmic bias is often discussed, it is important to recognize the root cause: human prejudice, both conscious and unconscious. Achieving complete transparency in automated decisions remains a challenge, but it is worth noting that human decision-making is often equally opaque. Interestingly, research suggests that AI might one day surpass humans in consistently upholding legal, fair, and transparent principles (ACM, 2017). This could lead to a future where human decisions are reviewed by AI for bias, flipping the current script where humans review automated systems.

The ethical tightrope: Balancing AI adoption with employee privacy

As personalization becomes more sophisticated, the need for responsible AI is paramount. Integrating AI into workplace processes thus requires careful consideration of ethical and privacy concerns. Many AI systems rely heavily on vast data sets, often containing sensitive employee information, to function effectively. This raises critical questions about employee consent, data security, and the potential for employee surveillance. Additionally, the lack of transparency in AI decision-making processes generates concerns about accountability and fairness, particularly during performance reviews or recruitment.

Human-machine collaboration introduces its own set of challenges, including communication, trust, and the division of decision-making responsibilities (Allison et al., 2021). While AI excels at processing massive amounts of data and identifying patterns beyond human capabilities, it lacks the intuitiveness and adaptability of human judgement (Lee, 2020). This can create difficulties in situations requiring both human intuition and AI expertise. In this context, overreliance on AI for decision-making could diminish the value of human expertise, potentially leading to its decline.

Accountability, technological flaws, and human agency

Businesses implementing AI face a critical question: who is accountable when things go wrong? Current legal frameworks treat AI as a tool, but as AI capabilities advance, this might need to change. The lack of a universal code of ethics for AI development further complicates the issue (Iphofen and Kritikos, 2019; McLennan et al., 2022). Historically, society has found ways to regulate new technologies, and AI should be no exception (Perri, 2001). However, pressure needs to be placed on the tech industry to establish clear ethical guidelines. While some, like Floridi and Sanders (2004), argue that currently only humans can bear moral responsibility, the lines blur with the introduction of advanced AI. They propose that in the future, AI itself might hold some level of moral accountability. This raises an important question: what level of intelligence or moral awareness does an AI need to be held responsible for its actions, rather than its creators or those controlling the data it uses?

Despite impressive advancements, AI still lacks the critical thinking skills of adult humans. Even with ethical programming, AI struggles with social nuances and learning from mistakes. This raises concerns about granting AI autonomous decision-making power in complex social situations. Human oversight also faces hurdles. AI systems often incorporate third-party data with privacy limitations or use opaque machine learning models resistant to explanation. The General Data Protection Regulation's (GDPR) emphasis on human intervention might not translate perfectly to fully autonomous AI. The potential of AI is undeniable, but its workplace integration demands a measured approach. The gap between rapid development and effective regulation poses a challenge. We need clear boundaries – innovation must respect worker rights and job security. Regulators face the delicate task of promoting beneficial AI applications while ensuring ethical use. This necessitates global collaboration between companies, governments, and researchers to establish a robust and adaptable regulatory framework.

Rapid AI advancements are creating a wave of anxiety among workers, with the American Psychological Association's 2023 survey reporting increased stress, anxiety, and burnout related to job displacement fears (APA, 2023). Renowned figures like Stephen Hawking and Elon Musk have also voiced concerns about the potential for AI to surpass human capabilities and even pose an existential threat. Some experts paint a dystopian future where AI widens the gap between the haves and have-nots, threatening democracy itself. Others argue that responsible development and governance can mitigate these risks, allowing the benefits of AI – like increased efficiency and innovation – to outweigh the downsides (Lee, 2020; Allison et al., 2021). The pessimists' vision of machines replacing human decision-making entirely might not be the inevitable outcome. History offers a potential counterpoint. The Industrial Revolution, another transformative era, ultimately led to job creation in new sectors. Similarly, AI might not spell widespread unemployment, but rather a shift in the types of jobs available.

To navigate this new world, both businesses and workers need to adapt. Companies can play an important role in easing employee anxieties. Prioritizing upskilling programmes equips workers with the skills needed to thrive alongside AI, while open communication addresses job security concerns and fosters a collaborative environment where humans and AI work together.

Moreover, HR practitioners must carefully balance the adoption of technological advancements with a commitment to maintaining a human-centric approach. AI's increasing role in HR often relies on extensive employee data collection and analysis, raising significant privacy and security concerns. Preventing unauthorized access, data breaches, and the misuse of personal information is paramount. Implementing stringent data protection protocols that comply with regulations like GDPR is essential. Open and transparent communication with employees about how their data is used and protected is vital for building trust in this evolving landscape.

Can AI be ethical?

Traditionally, the ethical implications of AI fall on its developers and users. But what if AI could be inherently ethical? Vetrò et al. (2019) argue that AI should go beyond narrow, task-driven goals. They propose that AI should contribute to a more just and equitable society. A collaborative effort to explore the ethical and social implications of AI could guide responsible and inclusive design. Expanding on this idea, Floridi and Sanders (2004) explore the concept of AI as a moral agent. They compare AI development to human development, where children aren't considered morally responsible until adulthood. Similarly, at what stage would AI reach a level of development where it could be considered a moral agent? This raises the intriguing question: can AI ever be truly self-sufficient in its ethical decision-making, or will it always rely on the moral framework instilled by its creators?

The idea of 'mind-less morality' – where AI can exhibit ethical behaviour without true sentience – is gaining traction as we approach an advanced information age. This theoretical perspective holds promise, but it's important to acknowledge the limitations of current AI capabilities. A key obstacle is the gap between AI and adult human intelligence. As Oravec (2018) and Brundage (2014) point out, AI systems often lack the ability to understand the full impact of their actions. Since they cannot grasp the consequences of their choices, attributing praise or blame in the traditional sense becomes difficult. Therefore, while 'mind-less morality' offers an intriguing avenue for future AI development, it might be premature to consider ethical autonomy for current AI systems. The focus for now should likely be on ensuring AI are programmed with strong ethical guidelines and operate within well-defined parameters.

The regulation of automated decision-making

As we delve into the ethical implications of AI, it is important to consider how platforms can maintain user trust while using AI for personalization. Linked to earlier discussion, the use of guidelines to ensure the responsible use of AI is necessary, particularly given that the law may not be ready to tackle such issues. Many academics and companies have created frameworks to regulate the actions of artificially intelligent automata. However, defining the 'right' moral framework for AI decisions is complex. Allen et al. (2000) show the limitations of various theoretical approaches. Embedding complex moral theories into algorithms might be computationally infeasible, and some methods could lead to flawed systems.

The authors suggest a multi-pronged approach might be required to balance these limitations. Ideally, an 'ethical AI' would be intelligent enough to understand the consequences of its actions on living beings, enabling it to make morally sound decisions (Allen et al., 2000). However, given current limitations, the responsibility for governing AI actions might fall primarily on humans for the foreseeable future. In this context, Anderson and Anderson (2015) propose a framework for ethical AI development: the case-supported principle-based paradigm. This approach leverages ethical theory to guide the behaviour of autonomous systems.

The paradigm offers a two-step process:

1. Verification and application of ethical principles: The framework helps identify and apply ethical principles relevant to specific situations. These principles can then be used to justify the system's actions.
2. Overarching control mechanism: The principles act as a control mechanism to prevent unintended or unethical behaviour by the AI system.

However, implementing this approach is not without challenges. Developing and applying these principles can be complex, requiring new tools and methodologies (Anderson and Anderson, 2015). Sharkey (2017) highlights three key hurdles:

1. Difficulty and cost: Developing and implementing these principles can be expensive and time-consuming.
2. Defining ethical relevance: Reaching agreement on which features of an AI system are ethically relevant can be challenging.
3. Ethical consensus: There may not be universal agreement on what constitutes an ethical outcome in every situation.

Despite these challenges, Anderson and Anderson's paradigm offers a valuable framework for building ethical AI systems. Many other frameworks exist (e.g. Montes and Goertzel, 2019; ACM, 2017; EY, 2018), although all appear to cover the same basic concepts: awareness/transparency, access and redress, accountability, explanation of processes, data provenance, auditability, and validation and testing. Below, we briefly describe the OECD Principles on AI and the EU's AI Act 2024.

The OECD Principles on AI were adopted in May 2019 by OECD member countries, establishing a framework for AI that is innovative, trustworthy, and respectful of human rights and democratic values. These principles, updated in 2024 to address new developments in general-purpose and generative AI, include recommendations for public policy and strategy. They emphasize AI's role in promoting inclusive growth, sustainable development, and well-being, ensuring AI systems are transparent, explainable, robust, secure, safe, and accountable. The OECD AI Principles outline five core values-based principles for responsible AI stewardship:

1. AI should benefit people and the planet by promoting inclusive growth, sustainable development, and well-being.

2. AI systems should respect the rule of law, human rights, democratic values, and diversity, incorporating appropriate safeguards.
3. AI systems should be transparent and explainable.
4. AI systems should be robust, secure, and safe.
5. AI systems should be accountable.

The EU's AI Act 2024 categorizes AI systems based on their risk levels, imposing obligations on providers and users accordingly. Unacceptable risk AI systems, such as those manipulating behaviour or using real-time biometric identification without consent, are banned. Specifically:

AI systems deemed a threat to people will be banned, including: cognitive behavioural manipulation of vulnerable groups (e.g. voice-activated toys encouraging dangerous behaviour in children); social scoring based on behaviour, socioeconomic status, or personal characteristics; biometric identification and categorization, including real-time and remote facial recognition; exceptions may exist for law enforcement, particularly for serious cases requiring court approval.

High-risk AI systems, affecting safety or fundamental rights, are subject to stringent assessment and registration requirements. Specifically, AI systems impacting safety or fundamental rights are considered high risk and fall into two categories:

1. AI in products under EU product safety legislation (e.g. toys, aviation, cars, medical devices, lifts)
2. AI in specific areas requiring EU database registration, such as critical infrastructure management, education, employment, public services, law enforcement, migration, and legal assistance

These high-risk systems must be assessed before market release and throughout their life cycle. Complaints can be filed with designated national authorities.

Furthermore, the Act mandates transparency for generative AI, requiring disclosure that content was AI-generated, and compliance with EU copyright laws. This legislation aims to promote innovation while ensuring AI systems are safe and trustworthy. Specifically:

Generative AI, like ChatGPT, must meet transparency standards and comply with EU copyright law, including: disclosing AI-generated content; preventing the generation of illegal content; publishing summaries of copyrighted data used for training. High-impact AI models, such as GPT-4, must undergo thorough evaluations and report serious incidents to the European Commission. AI-generated or modified content (e.g. deepfakes) must be clearly labelled to inform users.

In summary, responsible AI entails the ethical, transparent, and accountable development and deployment of AI systems. It emphasizes fairness, safety, and societal benefit by aligning AI with ethical principles and respecting human rights. Key components include reducing biases, protecting privacy, and ensuring AI systems are explainable. Organizations must be accountable for AI outcomes, establishing clear guidelines and governance to manage AI's impact effectively. Ensuring fairness involves a strong focus on bias reduction, while protecting user privacy requires robust data security measures. AI should be designed to be safe, secure, and human-centric, enhancing human capabilities while maintaining user control and understanding. Furthermore, responsible AI considers environmental sustainability by promoting eco-friendly development practices. By building trust and minimizing risks, responsible AI seeks to make a positive contribution to society.

User data and accountability

Digital platforms, unlike traditional businesses, flourish on the strength of interconnected user networks, dynamic ecosystems, and user empowerment, encouraging organizational resilience and adaptability (Srnicek, 2017). By treating data as an intangible asset, these platforms can transform it into a significant resource in multiple ways: selling anonymized data allows companies to offer valuable insights into user behaviour, aiding marketing or research efforts of other organizations. Moreover, exploiting user data to develop new products or services presents novel opportunities for offerings or revenue models previously untapped.

Digital platforms can also apply user data to customize information and content, subtly influencing public opinion through algorithmic filtering. Social media and search engines personalize user feeds with algorithms, selecting specific content to promote while downplaying others, thereby shaping the narrative and affecting users' views on different subjects. Similarly, by employing user data, businesses can deliver customized advertisements or messages that resonate with individuals' beliefs and biases, swaying undecided users or reinforcing existing viewpoints. However, this personalized strategy can lead to the creation of echo chambers, where users predominantly come across information that reinforces their pre-existing beliefs. This can restrict exposure to a range of perspectives and impede the development of critical thinking skills.

In some scenarios, companies may leverage user data to restrict access to information or services. They could implement personalized pricing strategies, varying the cost of identical products or services based on an individual's perceived ability to pay, potentially narrowing options for certain consumers. Although crucial for maintaining a safe online environment, entities with extensive user data might filter out content that contradicts their viewpoints or jeopardizes their interests, thus limiting the spectrum of available opinions and possibly infringing on free speech. Besides, businesses may limit access to specific features or services contingent on a user's profile or activities. For example, a financial institution could restrict access to particular investment choices for individuals deemed 'high risk' based on their data analysis.

The market dominance and lock-in effects

The market dominance and lock-in phenomena show how a company with a large user base and detailed user data can secure a market position that is difficult for competitors to challenge and for users to abandon (Coyle, 2018; Srnicek, 2017). Network effects come into play, for instance, with a social media platform; as it gains users, its value to new users increases because they can connect with a wider network. This creates a feedback loop where the platform with the most users continues to grow in appeal, making it hard for new competitors to emerge. This situation is akin to a telephone network: the utility of a single phone is minimal, but as more people own phones, the network's overall value soars for everyone involved.

Switching costs may arise as users personalize their platform experience, which can include:

Data integration: Essential data such as photos, contacts, and transaction history are stored on the platform, so moving to a competitor could mean losing this data or having to replicate it.

Network effects at a personal level: The likelihood of switching diminishes if a user's close contacts predominantly use one platform, as moving to another platform may mean losing easy connectivity with them.

Learned behaviour: Users become familiar with a platform's interface and features, making the switch to a different platform a daunting task that requires learning an entirely new system.

Such switching costs create entry barriers for newcomers, as users might hesitate to switch platforms due to the potential loss of their data and connections. This allows the dominant platform to maintain its market share, even in the absence of continual innovation or the best features. The combined impact of network effects and switching costs strengthens the position of dominant platforms. The more data a company has on its users, the better it can customize the user experience, further reinforcing network effects and switching costs. This self-reinforcing cycle entrenches the leading platform's position, making it increasingly difficult for new entrants to make inroads.

Addressing market dominance in digital platforms thus requires a multifaceted approach (Helberger, 2020; Coyle, 2018): Updating antitrust laws for the digital era could redefine market power, tackle self-preferencing behaviours, and make it easier for small companies to challenge larger ones. It is also vital to scrutinize mergers and acquisitions among major tech companies to prevent further market concentration and ensure a dynamic competitive environment. Incentives such as research grants or tax breaks for start-ups can encourage the emergence of new platforms, challenging the status quo.

Simplifying platform switching for users through straightforward data transfers and interactions can lessen barriers to service changes. Furthermore, mitigating network effects by requiring dominant platforms to fairly share data with smaller competitors can level the playing field; enabling users to transfer their data freely across platforms can also reduce switching costs and boost user autonomy; mandating clearer disclosures by platforms on their data practices can aid users in making informed privacy decisions. Stricter data privacy laws can curb the misuse of user data and reduce platforms' ability to manipulate user behaviour.

It is important to recognize that there is no standard solution. Tackling market dominance effectively might need a blend of the discussed strategies to cultivate a competitive and equitable digital environment. Moreover, this subject is part of an ongoing dialogue with continually evolving aspects:

Balancing competition and innovation: Achieving an optimal balance between stimulating competition and encouraging innovation in the tech sector is critical. Excessive regulations could stifle innovation, while too little oversight might solidify market dominance.

Global regulatory challenges: Developing regulations that effectively apply across borders poses a substantial challenge due to the international nature of many digital platforms.

Empowering consumers: Educating consumers about their data rights and encouraging informed decisions about their platform usage is fundamental.

The design processes underpinning coordination and control technologies such as digital platforms, big data analytics, and AI are also key to effective governance. To fully comprehend the impact of these technologies on organizations, markets, and work, it is essential to examine the designers' agendas, ideologies, and power dynamics, along with the organizational context of the design process. A nuanced understanding involves exploring the interplay between design and use, tackling data and access challenges, and identifying key theoretical frameworks for AI and platform governance.

Through a comprehensive strategy and ongoing dialogue, policymakers and industry stakeholders can work towards a more balanced digital ecosystem that aligns competition, innovation, and consumer protection. The move towards intangible assets and external value generation presents new challenges for businesses, particularly in safeguarding intellectual property, protecting data, and complying with regulatory mandates. This change also encourages critical reflections on the sustainability of digital business models in the face of rising data privacy concerns, worries about platform monopolies, and the implications of the gig economy on worker rights.

Effective platform governance is vital for the health and sustainability of platform ecosystems. It establishes clear rules, norms, and structures that shape interactions among users, developers, and the platform itself. Good governance balances competing interests, fosters innovation, builds trust, and supports long-term growth. It addresses key issues such as data privacy, content moderation, intellectual property, and value distribution, creating a fair and transparent environment that mitigates risks and promotes collaboration. Strong governance protects the platform's integrity and reputation, which are required for attracting users and partners, and helps manage risks associated with rapid technological change. Ultimately, platform governance is about enabling platform success by driving innovation, enhancing user experiences, and ensuring resilience in dynamic markets.

As discussed, digital giants like Alibaba and Amazon are rapidly expanding their platform ecosystems by harnessing advanced data analytics, disrupting the long-standing dominance of brick-and-mortar retailers. However, this digital transformation poses risks of unfair exploitation for complementors and customers due to the power of AI and big data analytics wielded by these platform companies. Safeguarding the well-being of consumers and complementors is essential for maintaining a healthy ecosystem. An ideal ecosystem should be characterized by inclusivity, customer orientation, non-predatory practices, mutual benefit, and commercial viability. A harmonious platform ecosystem can be built on everyday digital technologies to orchestrate consumer networks and co-create value with every ecosystem member, leveraging sophisticated tools like AI and personalization. This approach offers a multi-stakeholder and ecosystem-wide perspective that enriches the platform ecosystem and AI practice.

Conclusion

AI is bringing in a new era, brimming with potential to transform businesses and society. However, this exciting future is tempered by concerns about potential risks. One major concern lies in the tension between AI systems and existing legal frameworks. Data protection laws, designed for a pre-AI world, may struggle to handle the complexities of AI data collection and use, raising privacy and ethical concerns. Additionally, the potential for algorithmic bias to discriminate against minority groups necessitates careful consideration.

The risks posed by AI demand a complex response. Current AI systems lack the moral compass to govern themselves, necessitating external oversight for responsible use. While the debate between legal and ethical frameworks rages on, legal systems may struggle to keep pace with AI's rapid evolution. Therefore, ethical frameworks, even if not universally adopted, remain a crucial stopgap. Organizations can either tailor existing frameworks to their industry or leverage those developed by AI experts. The onus of mitigating risks and preventing unethical AI use lies in a collaborative effort. Engineers, academics, and policymakers must work together to develop robust and adaptable governance strategies.

The promise of AI advancements is undeniable, but so are the potential downsides related to privacy, bias, and social justice. To navigate these challenges, we need a new generation of professionals. These 'AI Ethicists' will require an interdisciplinary skillset, blending knowledge of technology, ethics, and critical thinking. Their focus will be ensuring AI is deployed safely and ethically – which encompasses legal, ethical, technical, and security considerations. Security in this context means safeguarding AI systems from malicious attacks. On the legal and ethical front, ensuring unbiased and socially responsible AI development is paramount. Industries also have a critical role to play. Just like responsible product stewardship, they must take ownership of the AI systems they create and manage them with care. The onus is on creators and data controllers to mitigate risks and negative impacts. Ultimately, trust is the key to unlocking AI's full potential. By promoting responsible development and deploying AI with human well-being in mind, we can ensure this technology serves as a force for good.

On the other hand, privacy regulations are in a constant state of flux around the world (Walters and Novak, 2021). This reflects the growing importance of data privacy in our increasingly online lives. As we rely more on digital platforms for education, finance, and work, governments face pressure to safeguard citizen data. This includes personal information, financial records, and communication details. The complexities of the digital world, with its constant evolution, necessitate ongoing legislative efforts. Robust data protection measures are essential to ensure our privacy is protected in this evolving environment.

13

Social media and platform governance

The Cambridge Analytica scandal, which came to light in early 2018, revolves around the misuse of Facebook user data during the 2016 US presidential election. Cambridge Analytica, a UK-based political consulting agency, obtained the personal information of numerous Facebook users without their permission. This information was purportedly utilized to craft and disseminate political ads aimed at influencing voter behaviour.

The sequence of events started with Aleksandr Kogan, a researcher who developed a Facebook app named 'This Is Your Digital Life'. Although only about two hundred and seventy thousand individuals engaged with the app, it managed to collect data from not just these users but also their network of Facebook friends, ultimately impacting an estimated eighty-seven million users. This extensive data collection was facilitated by the permissive data-sharing policies of Facebook at the time.

Kogan then transferred this data to Cambridge Analytica, which employed it to construct voter profiles. The company asserted its capability to create detailed models for predicting and swaying electoral decisions. Among its clients was the Donald Trump presidential campaign, which used these insights for targeted political advertising leveraging the acquired data.

This incident illustrates Facebook's significant influence on the digital realm as a dominant force in social media. However, its substantial presence has been marred by ongoing allegations and verified instances of user privacy violations: by 2022, Meta, Facebook's parent company, incurred fines nearing 1 billion euros from the Irish Data Protection Commission for data privacy breaches, plunging the platform into a whirlwind of public distrust and negative sentiment. This situation highlights the complex legal challenges that other digital platforms, such as Amazon, must also navigate.

For instance, despite substantial investments in data encryption and firewalls to comply with Europe's General Data Protection Regulation (GDPR) of 2018, Amazon faced a record-breaking fine of €746 million in 2021 for failing to adhere to general data processing regulations. Moreover, the US Federal Trade Commission (FTC) and the Justice Department imposed a $25 million penalty on Amazon related to its Alexa voice assistant for alleged violations of the Children's Online Privacy Protection Act (US Department of Justice, 2023).

The FTC also filed an antitrust lawsuit against Amazon in 2023, blaming it for engaging in monopolistic practices, taking advantage of both sellers and consumers by forcing sellers to use its platform, warehouses, and delivery services, thus inflating costs. The FTC pleaded to the court to contemplate obligating the e-commerce giant to sell assets/part of its business with the aim of dismantling the giant's market dominance (Bartz, 2023). Regulators have also noticed a subtler level of activity that skews the authenticity of product reviews and rankings on online shopping platforms such as Taobao and Pinduoduo. This manipulation is primarily conducted through click farms, which are operations that use automated software or large numbers of hired individuals to create fake accounts. These accounts are then used to generate artificial interactions with a seller's products or services, such as likes, views, reviews, and purchases.

While the Cambridge Analytica case highlights the misuse of data in political contexts, the Amazon case illustrates the economic consequences of platform dominance. Historically, similar monopolistic concerns prompted legislative actions in the early twentieth century, a trend we are now seeing again in the digital platform era. The Cambridge Analytica scandal, along with other instances of online misconduct, has underscored the urgent need for robust data protection legislation and ethical guidelines for managing personal data (Polanski, 2018; Confessore, 2018; Zuboff, 2019). These incidents have ignited broad discussions on the substantial power held by major tech corporations, emphasizing the need for increased transparency and accountability in the digital realm. For example, platforms must maintain user trust amid increased attempts to manipulate the system, such as the issue of fake reviews (Mayzlin et al., 2014). As production moves beyond traditional internal operations, the growing importance of third-party contributions, freelance workforces, and collaborations with affiliates in value creation necessitates new governance and policy models to address challenges like ensuring quality control, managing intellectual property rights, and encouraging fair labour practices across these external networks.

Platform enterprises and new ethical challenges

Digital platforms, which encompass a wide range of apps and services, occupy a unique role in the modern economy by acting as intermediaries in multi-sided markets. They exhibit characteristics of both traditional businesses and online marketplaces like Facebook Marketplace. These platforms enable buyers to access a diverse selection of products from various sellers while allowing sellers to reach a broader customer base (van Dijck et al., 2018). As a result, digital platforms have significant control over online marketplaces, influencing the distribution and sales of third-party products and services.

While early platforms like MySpace had limited control over data, today's platforms like Facebook and Google wield immense power over user data and require far more stringent regulatory oversight. Platforms such as Google and Baidu manage user interactions through technical interfaces, data-driven algorithms, and proprietary terms of service that align with their business models (Plantin et al., 2018; Cusumano, Gawer, and Yoffie, 2019). This often involves promoting the exchange of personal information, which becomes a valuable commodity. These platforms typically monetize this data through targeted advertising campaigns or other strategies (Dencik and Kaun, 2020). Likewise, the content industries have been shaped by successive waves of vertical integration, whether through direct ownership or strategic contracts. This traditional model often meant that a relatively small cadre of major players controlled content distribution channels, limiting the diversity and accessibility of content. The onset of the digital era, however, has ushered in a transformative shift, radically expanding the horizons of content-related industries.

Digital platforms have thus emerged as pivotal agents of change, creating an unprecedented level of content discovery. Through mechanisms like curation, crowdsourcing, and the facilitation of global distribution, these platforms have significantly broadened the scope for innovation in content creation and dissemination. At the heart of this revolution is the ability of digital platforms to harness collective intelligence and fine-tune their offerings to reflect consumer preferences more accurately, guiding audiences towards more targeted and engaging content experiences.

Yet, this democratization of content discovery and reliance on crowdsourced information come with significant challenges. As Mayzlin et al. (2014) note, maintaining user trust is vital in an environment increasingly vulnerable to the manipulation of reviews and ratings. As platforms evolved from simple social networks to economic powerhouses, the challenges they faced also transformed, particularly in terms of managing competition and consumer data. Platforms must therefore carefully navigate these complexities to preserve the integrity of the mechanisms that have enabled their transformative impact on content industries. This new business model, often referred to as 'platformization', brings with it a range of ethical challenges that threaten its long-term sustainability.

Platform ecosystem

Platform ecosystems represent complex networks where various stakeholders interact under the orchestration of platform enterprises, which serve as the pivotal entities at the core of these interactions (Foerderer, 2020). These platform companies do not operate in isolation; rather, they function within a broader system that includes complementors such as third-party service providers, consumers, and governmental bodies. Each of these actors plays a crucial role in shaping the ecosystem's dynamics and contributes to its overall health and success.

In these ecosystems, platform enterprises must meticulously manage the balance between individual and collective interests. They strive to create an environment where the contributions of complementors enhance the platform's value, while also ensuring that consumer needs are met and regulatory requirements are adhered to. This balancing act is vital for maintaining the stability and sustainability of the ecosystem. The role of complementors, often third-party developers or service providers, is particularly significant (Rietveld et al., 2019). They extend the platform's functionality and enrich the user experience by providing additional services and features. This symbiosis not only enhances the platform's attractiveness and utility but also stimulates innovation and diversity within the ecosystem.

Through collaboration, platforms introduce new features and services, expanding value for all ecosystem participants. However, the distribution of this value often becomes contentious. Complementors seek to maximize their share based on contributions, while platforms aim to retain the majority. This dynamic, characterized by interdependent yet competing interests, can hinder value capture for platforms if complementors are not effectively managed. Platforms like TikTok exemplify this complex interplay between value creation and capture. Key mechanisms, including complementarity, internalization, algorithmic enhancements, and personalization, influence how platforms balance these competing forces. Similarly, contemporary theories on ecosystem firms often overlook the potential for emerging practices in which users or complementors disrupt the benefits enjoyed by an ecosystem orchestrator. Ecosystem firms are typically driven by network effects, learning, and economies of scale. However, factors such as product perishability, flexibility of use, and demand elasticity can further amplify this disruptive effect, especially in platform ecosystems.

Consumers, for their part, benefit from a wide array of choices and an enhanced experience facilitated by the integration of various services. Their feedback and engagement are important for continuous improvement and adaptation of the platform to meet evolving needs. Government interaction with platform ecosystems can range from regulatory oversight to partnership. This relationship is crucial as it helps ensure that the operations within the platform ecosystem adhere to legal and ethical standards, protecting the interests of all parties involved, especially the end-users.

Platformization effect

Platformization describes the growing dominance of digital platforms, such as social media sites, e-commerce platforms, and various online services, in both economic and social realms (Just, 2018). This trend involves platforms expanding into various sectors, impacting business operations, communication methods, content consumption, and service provision (Barwise and Watkins, 2018). Spulber (2011) termed this change a 'Business Revolution', noting that it transforms various aspects of life similarly to how the Industrial Revolution reshaped factories.

Platformization is characterized by the integration of platform infrastructures and governance models into different sectors, including media, education, and healthcare (Hovenkamp, 2019; Poell et al., 2019). Driven by network effects, the increasing quantification of information (datafication), and the digitalization of interactions, this phenomenon alters market dynamics, social behaviours, and the balance of power between businesses and consumers (Yi et al., 2023; McIntyre and Srinivasan, 2017). Furthermore, platformization contributes to the concentration of gatekeeping authority among leading platforms, granting them substantial power over data circulation, access to information, distribution mechanisms, and the conduct of competitors and users alike (Evens and Donders, 2018). Despite critiques of their dominance and potential to stifle competition, social media platforms now play a central role in facilitating public discourse and can even support civic engagement and activism (Jackson et al., 2020; Iosifidis and Andrews, 2019). This multifaceted nature highlights concerns that extend beyond mere market dynamics, including issues related to privacy, data rights, and the ethical considerations surrounding political communication on these platforms.

The success of social media and online marketplaces hinges on how these platforms employ personalization to refine and enhance user experiences by adapting content and recommendations to align with individual preferences and behaviours. This personalization is achieved through sophisticated algorithms that process vast amounts of data, including browsing history, purchase records, and social interactions, to predict user preferences and suggest relevant content. For example, an e-commerce platform might suggest products based on a user's previous searches and purchases, while a social media platform might curate a feed that reflects the user's interests and interactions.

The dynamic ecosystems created by such personalized experiences are beneficial for both users and businesses (Iosifidis and Andrews, 2019; Foerderer, 2020). Users enjoy a more targeted online experience that feels uniquely suited to their needs, potentially leading to higher satisfaction and engagement levels. For businesses and content creators, personalization can lead to increased visibility for their products and services, higher conversion rates, and more effective targeting of their marketing efforts. However, the reliance on personalization raises several concerns. Privacy issues emerge as platforms collect and analyse vast amounts of personal data to fuel their personalization algorithms. Users may not always be aware of the extent of data collection or how their information is being used, leading to potential breaches of privacy. Another concern is the potential for platform lock-in, where users become so integrated and comfortable with a platform's personalized ecosystem that switching costs, both perceived and real, become prohibitively high. This can limit competition and innovation, as users might be less inclined to explore alternative platforms or services, leading to a consolidation of power among a few dominant platforms.

The digital platform market thus introduces distinct challenges for competition policy. Aspects such as network effects, economies of scale, and the customization of services through data analysis create substantial barriers for new entrants, thereby stifling competition (Katz, 2019). These dynamics call for a rethinking of traditional concepts of 'competition' and 'market power' within the realm of digital platforms. The debate surrounding the influence of platforms touches on both their control over the market and their impact on political discourse, which are critical considerations in developing effective regulatory strategies. How platform power is perceived – whether as a concern related to market dynamics or political discourse – greatly affects the direction of regulatory measures (Popiel, 2020). For instance, in the United States, there is a growing perception that antitrust laws could be a viable solution for curbing the market dominance of these platforms.

Given the complexity of maintaining privacy and ethical standards, how can platforms ensure compliance without stifling innovation? In the next section, we explore potential regulatory frameworks that balance these concerns. As user manipulation becomes increasingly prevalent, regulatory bodies are proposing stricter guidelines for data management to safeguard user privacy and trust.

Market power and antitrust

Lina Khan, as chair of the FTC, has expressed significant concerns about Amazon's business practices, particularly focusing on issues related to market power and antitrust. Khan argues that Amazon leverages its dominant positions in online retail and cloud computing to suppress competitors, drawing parallels to historical monopolies such as the railroad industry. She points out that Amazon may engage in predatory pricing strategies, initially setting low prices to drive out competition, followed by price hikes. Additionally, Khan criticizes Amazon's dual role as both a retailer and a marketplace platform, which she believes could disadvantage independent sellers.

Khan also challenges the adequacy of using consumer prices alone as a measure of competition, arguing that this narrow focus fails to consider the broader impacts on innovation and market dynamics. She is concerned about Amazon's potential to stifle innovation over the long term and the reinforcing effect of its extensive consumer data collection on its market dominance. To address these issues, Khan advocates for a revision of antitrust laws to reflect the wider effects on competition and innovation, not just immediate pricing impacts. She also calls for a more stringent enforcement of existing antitrust laws to prevent potential abuses of market power by large corporations like Amazon (Khan, 2017; 2019; Popiel, 2022).

Addressing market dominance in digital platform markets involves various strategies, including regulation and antitrust enforcement, promoting competition, and enhancing user empowerment and data privacy:

Regulation and antitrust enforcement: Updating antitrust laws to address the distinctive challenges posed by digital platforms could involve establishing new standards for evaluating market power that extend beyond traditional market share metrics (Delrahim, 2019). This update could also focus on curbing platforms' self-preferencing practices and enhancing the capacity of smaller players to challenge the dominance of larger platforms. Moreover, conducting detailed reviews of mergers and acquisitions within the tech industry is important to prevent further market consolidation and ensure healthy competition.

Promoting competition: Supporting the development of new platforms to compete with established entities, potentially through government research and development funding or start-up incentives, is vital. Making it easier for users to switch between platforms by guaranteeing data portability and interoperability is highly desirable. Furthermore, levelling the playing field for smaller platforms by requiring dominant platforms to share data fairly and under regulated conditions can help counteract network effects.

User empowerment and data privacy: Empowering users to easily move their data between platforms, requiring platforms to be transparent about their data practices, and implementing stronger data privacy regulations to safeguard user information and limit the ability of platforms to shape user choices are essential measures. Addressing market dominance demands a multifaceted approach, adapted to the changing digital environment. Important ongoing considerations involve balancing the promotion of competition with the support of innovation in the technology sector, developing regulations that work globally given the international nature of digital platforms, and raising awareness among consumers about their data rights to encourage more informed choices regarding platform use.

A comprehensive, collaborative approach, involving continuous dialogue among policymakers and stakeholders, is essential for developing a digital ecosystem that balances competition, innovation, and user rights.

Digital platforms and ecosystems have now become a linchpin of the global economy, generating unprecedented value while simultaneously introducing novel forms of market failure. As regulators navigate this new landscape, traditional industrial organization economics is proving increasingly inadequate. To effectively address the unique challenges posed by digital ecosystems, a new framework is necessary to identify and measure firm-inflicted harm. This approach should complement existing economic tools while providing actionable insights for policymakers and regulators.

For example, in a significant legal development on 5 August 2024, US District Judge Amit Mehta ruled that Google has illegally maintained its monopoly in online search and advertising. After a ten-week trial, the US Department of Justice successfully argued that Google's exclusive agreements with device manufacturers like Apple and Samsung hindered competition by making Google the default search engine on most devices. Judge Mehta determined that these agreements effectively prevented rival search engines from gaining traction and user data, thus unlawfully perpetuating Google's dominance. While Google plans to appeal the decision, the ruling could lead to substantial changes in the company's operations, including potential limitations on its ability to secure exclusive default search agreements.

Examining the ethical landscape of platforms

Platforms like online marketplaces harness the power of personalization to significantly refine and enhance user experiences, customizing content and recommendations to closely align with individual preferences and behaviours. This process involves the sophisticated use of algorithms that analyse vast amounts of data to accurately predict user preferences and offer content that is most relevant to each individual. For instance, an e-commerce platform may use this data to recommend products that a user is likely to buy based on their previous searches and purchases, while a social media platform might tailor a user's feed to include posts that align with their past interactions and stated interests.

Within this broader ecosystem, roles such as independent marketplaces and third-party transactions become crucial. These elements enhance the personalization process by offering additional data points and interaction opportunities, further enriching the user experience and broadening the range of options available. They not only facilitate the integration of diverse services and products but also contribute to a more connected and responsive environment.

This dynamic ecosystem, enriched by personalized experiences, is mutually beneficial for both users and businesses, including complementors like app developers, advertisers, and independent sellers. Users benefit from an online experience that feels uniquely tailored to them, which can lead to increased satisfaction and higher levels of engagement. For businesses and third parties, personalization drives greater visibility of their products and services. This targeted visibility often results in higher conversion rates and more efficient marketing, as ads and products are directed towards users who are most likely to be interested in them, based on analysed behavioural data. Moreover, the continuous feedback loop provided by user interactions and preferences allows platforms and businesses to refine their algorithms and strategies continually. This ongoing refinement not only improves the accuracy of personalized content but also ensures that the ecosystem adapts to changing consumer behaviours and market conditions, keeping the digital environment vibrant and competitive.

Platform governance thus requires a reimagined approach that takes into account its distinct organizational structure, user demographics, content limitations, and accountability framework (Haggart, 2020; Yi et al., 2023; Bakhtiar et al., 2023). Unfortunately, the platform ecosystem often suffers from a lack of governance and accountability, resulting in unethical business practices, user exploitation, and collusion among platform operators, which ultimately erodes user trust.

Embracing a proactive and cooperative approach to platform governance and accountability can lead to a more sustainable and ethical platform economy, prioritizing user welfare and fostering long-term trust and development. Governing platform ecosystems, given their hybrid nature, requires a wide-ranging approach. This extends traditional accountability to include strategies for the unique challenges and opportunities they present. Effective management requires understanding how platform dynamics influence stakeholder interactions, competition, and the market as a whole. This ensures platform responsibility becomes ingrained in operations. This two-pronged approach is essential for platforms to flourish economically and contribute positively to society.

Platform governance

Research on platform governance has been steadily gaining momentum, exploring who and how it should be governed (Ghosh, 2019; Just, 2018). Traditionally, scholars have focused on identifying key stakeholders involved, including governments, platforms, users, the public, and even media outlets. They have typically suggested various governance frameworks, including meta-governance, market-driven mechanisms, self-regulation, networked strategies, and collaborative efforts involving multiple parties. However, a critical gap remains: understanding how the collective decision-making of multiple stakeholders influences platform governance and accountability. While studies on traditional governance mechanisms with limited rationality offer valuable insights, the platform context presents a unique challenge due to its complex ecosystem (Katz, 2019).

The governance of artificial intelligence (AI) and digital platforms thus represents one of the most pressing challenges of our digital age. As these technologies become increasingly central to our economic, social, and political lives, the need for effective oversight grows ever more urgent. Our exploration of governance strategies is motivated by the unique operational landscape of digital platforms – a landscape that upends traditional notions of business responsibility and accountability.

At the heart of this challenge lies the multi-sided nature of digital platforms (Foerderer, 2020). Unlike a traditional retailer that interacts primarily with suppliers and customers, platforms like Amazon, Uber, or Airbnb create complex ecosystems involving buyers, sellers, workers, content creators, advertisers, and a host of third-party service providers. Each interaction within this ecosystem is mediated by AI algorithms that personalize experiences, recommend products or services, and even influence pricing.

This intricate web of relationships, coupled with the opacity of AI decision-making, creates a governance quagmire. Consider a few scenarios:

1. An AI-driven recommendation on a social media platform promotes divisive content to boost user engagement, unintentionally fuelling social unrest. Who is accountable? The content creator? The platform? The AI developers?
2. A ride-sharing app's algorithm favours drivers with higher ratings, unintentionally discriminating against drivers from certain neighbourhoods due to biased user feedback. How do we ensure fairness in such a system?
3. An e-commerce platform uses past purchase data to personalize prices, leading to some users paying more for the same product. Is this illegal price discrimination or legitimate market segmentation?
4. A job-matching platform's AI favours candidates with certain keywords in their resumes, inadvertently perpetuating gender or racial biases in hiring. How do we make these systems equitable?

Each of these scenarios highlights the complex interplay between AI-driven personalization, user behaviour, and broader societal impacts. They underscore fundamental questions:

Accountability: In a world where decisions are increasingly made by algorithms, who bears responsibility for unintended consequences? The platform? The AI developers? The users whose data trains the AI?

Fairness and non-discrimination: How do we ensure that personalization algorithms, which by definition treat users differently, do not cross the line into illegal or unethical discrimination?

Transparency: Given the 'black box' nature of many AI systems, how can users, regulators, or even platform operators truly understand how decisions are being made?

Privacy: Personalization relies on vast amounts of user data. How do we balance the benefits of data-driven personalization with fundamental rights to privacy?

Market power: As platforms become more personalized and 'sticky', they can create network effects that lead to monopolistic power. How do we promote innovation without allowing digital giants to stifle competition?

These questions demand a new approach to governance – one that is as adaptive and multifaceted as the technologies it seeks to regulate. Our examination reveals several emerging strategies:

Self-regulation and ethical frameworks: Many tech companies, recognizing the reputational and legal risks of unchecked AI, are developing internal ethical guidelines. Google's AI Principles, Microsoft's Responsible AI Standard, and the IEEE's Ethically Aligned Design are examples. These frameworks often commit to principles like fairness, transparency, and privacy. However, critics argue that without external enforcement, these are just good intentions.

Industry consortia: Recognizing that many AI challenges transcend individual companies, industry leaders are forming consortia like the Partnership on AI. These groups work to develop best practices, conduct research on societal impacts, and engage with policymakers. The advantage is shared learning and a unified industry voice. The risk is that these groups could become lobbying arms that resist meaningful regulation.

Algorithmic auditing: A growing field of computer scientists and ethicists are developing methods to audit AI systems for bias, fairness, and transparency. IBM's AI Fairness 360 or Google's What-If Tool allow developers to test their algorithms. Some propose that platforms be required to submit to regular third-party audits, much like financial audits for public companies.

Legal and regulatory frameworks: Governments are beginning to step in. The EU's GDPR includes provisions on automated decision-making. The EU's Artificial Intelligence Act 2024 classifies AI systems by risk level and impose stricter requirements on high-risk applications. In the United States, sector-specific laws like the Fair Credit Reporting Act are being reinterpreted for the AI age. The challenge is crafting laws that are specific enough to be effective but flexible enough to keep pace with technology.

User empowerment and digital literacy: Some argue that users themselves must be part of the solution. This could mean clearer data consent processes, 'AI nutrition labels' that explain how an algorithm works, or even user-controlled AI agents that negotiate with platform algorithms on the user's behalf. However, this puts a lot of onus on users and may exacerbate digital divides.

Adaptive regulation: Inspired by approaches in fields like drug approval, some propose 'regulatory sandboxes' where companies can test AI systems in controlled environments. Regulators would work alongside developers, learning about the technology while monitoring for risks. This could lead to more informed, flexible regulation.

Multi-stakeholder governance: Given the global nature of digital platforms, some advocate for international governance bodies akin to those for climate change or nuclear non-proliferation. These would bring together governments, companies, academics, and civil society to develop global norms and enforcement mechanisms.

The goal of these varied approaches is not to impede the transformative potential of AI and personalization. Indeed, personalized platforms have the potential to make markets more efficient, products more satisfying, and even contribute to solving global challenges like healthcare access or resource allocation. Rather, the aim is to channel this innovation responsibly. Effective governance can actually accelerate adoption by building trust. If users believe their data is safe and algorithms are fair, they are more likely to engage. If start-ups have clear rules, they can innovate without fear of regulatory backlash. If society sees AI as a tool for empowerment rather than exploitation, it will embrace rather than resist these technologies. Moreover, governance is not just about preventing harm; it is about actively shaping AI for the public good. Imagine personalized educational platforms that adapt to each child's learning style, or smart city systems that optimize public services based on individual needs. With the right governance, AI could become a powerful tool for equity and social welfare.

The governance of AI and digital platforms is not a peripheral concern but central to the future of our digital economy and society. The multi-sided, AI-driven nature of these platforms creates governance challenges that defy traditional regulatory models. However, through a combination of self-regulation, industry cooperation, technical tools, adaptive regulation, and user empowerment, it is possible to craft a governance framework that is as innovative as the technologies it oversees. If done right, personalization can be harnessed to create an economy that is not just efficient but fair, not just innovative but responsible – an economy where technology amplifies human potential and respects human values. If society falters, it risks a digital dystopia of manipulation, discrimination, and unchecked corporate power. The path chosen will shape not just how people buy and sell but how they live, learn, and interact in the digital age. The governance of AI and digital platforms is, in essence, the governance of our shared digital future.

Governing platform: Embracing digital tools and collaboration

Since the 2018 Cambridge Analytica scandal, platforms have had to re-evaluate their governance structures – a process that continues to evolve. Facebook's response to disinformation during political events, such as the 2016 U.S. election, illustrates the challenges of balancing free speech with the need to combat false information. Despite attempts to flag and remove misleading content, critics argue that Facebook's policies have been inconsistent and reactive. Likewise, YouTube's content moderation policies, particularly concerning harmful or extremist content, demonstrate the challenges of applying AI-based moderation at scale, as automated systems frequently misclassify content, resulting in both under- and over-enforcement.

However, advancements in big data, cloud computing, and 5G technology continue to offer powerful tools for addressing online misconduct. With the help of sophisticated anti-cheating algorithms and tools for detecting fraudulent activities, platforms can quickly identify and rectify instances of irresponsible behaviour. This enhances the efficiency of platform governance, enabling quicker responses and bolstering the integrity of the platform. Implementing a well-defined reward and punishment system is also important (Bakhtiar et al., 2023; Haggart, 2020). Applying user credit scoring systems that flag risks and potential trust issues can serve as an effective preventive measure against misconduct. In addition, refining reward systems with transparent evaluation criteria can encourage both service providers and users to adopt constructive behaviours, contributing to a more secure and trustworthy platform environment.

Building trust and accountability within a platform ecosystem depends on two key pillars:

1. Shared leadership and responsibility: Platform leaders must clearly define their role and take the initiative in establishing a robust governance framework. This framework should promote clear and efficient interactions between all ecosystem members, developing a sense of shared accountability for maintaining a healthy platform environment.
2. Symbiotic collaboration: The ultimate goal is to cultivate a collaborative environment where platform enterprises, complementors (third-party service providers), and consumers work together towards mutually beneficial outcomes. This requires open and transparent communication, establishing shared goals and a collective commitment to responsible platform participation. By developing a sense of partnership, all stakeholders can contribute to a thriving digital ecosystem.

By embracing digital tools and fostering collaboration, platform enterprises can transcend traditional limitations and lead the way towards a more responsible and sustainable ecosystem. This shift from top-down control to collaborative governance holds the promise of a future where platforms not only drive economic growth but also contribute to a healthier and more equitable digital world.

For example, digital platforms in the content industry not only offer their own curated recommendations but also raise questions about their impact on consumer choice and potential antitrust concerns. These concerns can manifest in various ways, such as online resale price maintenance, most favoured nation clauses, or practices like refusals to deal, tying, bundling, and exclusive dealing, all of which could limit competition. The increasing number of enforcement actions taken by governments and private entities against tech platforms is leading to the development of a specialized legal framework customized to the digital environment. Concurrently, there are initiatives to establish proactive regulations for major digital corporations, aimed at defining acceptable practices for these entities (Halaburda and Yehezkel, 2019; Li and Zhu, 2021).

A general governance framework

Governing digital platforms effectively is a complex task that requires a multifaceted approach involving regulation, oversight, and cooperation among various stakeholders, including governments, platforms, and users (Rietveld et al., 2019; Foerderer, 2020). Governments can develop and enforce regulatory frameworks that set standards for fairness, transparency, data protection, and accountability. To prevent monopolistic behaviours and ensure fair competition, governments can apply or adapt antitrust and competition laws to the digital economy. This might include breaking up companies if they become too dominant in a way that harms societal interests or stifles innovation.

The emergence of powerful digital platforms necessitates robust governance strategies to balance competing priorities. One key challenge is ensuring a safe and positive user experience. Platforms need effective content moderation mechanisms to prevent the spread of harmful or illegal material. However, this must be balanced with respecting the right to free speech. This might involve more transparent and accountable moderation policies, along with a combination of AI-powered detection and human oversight.

User data control is another critical aspect of platform governance. Platforms should be required to provide clear information about how user data is collected and used. Users, in turn, should have the right to opt out of data collection practices or request the deletion of their information entirely. Transparency is essential for holding platforms accountable. Requiring platforms to be transparent about their algorithms and business practices can help ensure they are not engaging in discriminatory practices or other harmful behaviours. This could involve independent audits to verify responsible conduct.

We also need to consider platform integration, which combines different platforms' components, as a key factor in driving network effects and establishing platform dominance. However, its impact on complementor engagement remains unclear, particularly in terms of how integration affects knowledge sharing and the balance between contributing to common benefits and protecting private interests. This presents a governance challenge for platform owners: they must support complementor-driven value creation while capturing enough value to sustain their operations. Overly restrictive governance can stifle innovation, while lenient governance risks losing control over value capture. To navigate this, platform owners must efficiently govern complementors' business models by setting incentives, establishing clear contracts, and implementing mechanisms such as revenue-sharing or intellectual property agreements. Good governance also requires monitoring and enforcement to ensure compliance with platform standards, ultimately balancing complementor innovation with value capture to maintain the ecosystem's long-term health and viability.

Multi-stakeholder engagement is thus crucial for addressing the broader social impacts of digital platforms. Bringing together tech companies, government bodies, NGOs (non-governmental organizations), and user groups in collaborative dialogue and decision-making processes fosters a more holistic approach to governance. Empowering users through digital literacy programmes equips them with the knowledge and skills to navigate digital platforms safely, including making informed decisions about their data and privacy. The global nature of digital platforms necessitates international cooperation. Treaties or agreements on key issues like privacy, cybersecurity, and taxation can help ensure consistent and effective governance across borders.

Ethical considerations should be an integral part of platform governance. Encouraging or mandating the development and adherence to ethical guidelines for new technologies deployed on platforms can help mitigate potential risks. User empowerment tools can also play a significant role in regulating platform behaviour. Providing users with more control over their experience through features like refined privacy settings, easier reporting mechanisms, and greater control over content and data can help individuals govern their interactions with these platforms.

Effective platform governance is an ongoing process that requires continuous adaptation as new technologies emerge and societal impacts evolve. It demands ongoing collaboration and dialogue among all stakeholders involved in the digital ecosystem. For example, from a government perspective, ensuring fair competition is equally crucial, especially when platforms dominate multiple markets.

Building trust and collaboration for a thriving ecosystem

Complementors – businesses and individuals who develop products and services that elevate a platform's value proposition – are the backbone of any thriving platform ecosystem (Chung et al., 2023; Iosifidis and Andrews, 2019). They exist alongside the platform, offering functionalities and integrations that enrich the user experience. Their success is essential for the platform's reputation and sustainability (Rietveld et al., 2019). For instance, consider app developers who create games for the Apple App Store. These developers are complementors who contribute significantly to the App Store's value proposition for iPhone users.

To excel within a platform ecosystem, complementors should focus on three key areas: robust quality management systems are essential for building high-quality products and services. This creates consumer trust and loyalty, allowing complementors to stand out and avoid negative publicity. By consistently exceeding expectations, complementors become synonymous with excellence within the platform; protecting consumer data is paramount. Implementing a strong data privacy system safeguards personal information and builds trust with users. This commitment not only protects consumers but also shields complementors from potential legal and ethical issues, allowing them to operate with confidence; responsible behaviour is key to a healthy ecosystem. This includes aspects like transparency in pricing and data practices, fair competition within the platform's guidelines, and a commitment to user safety and ethical marketing practices. By adhering to these principles, complementors contribute to a positive and sustainable environment for everyone involved.

Furthermore, user communities are integral to complementor engagement on co-creation platforms. These platforms act as social hubs and catalysts for open innovation, thriving on active user participation. Successful engagement mechanisms build a strong sense of community identity and personal satisfaction among complementors, motivating sustained contributions. By cultivating a supportive environment, platforms can maximize complementor involvement, driving continuous innovation and platform success.

Championing responsibility in the platform ecosystem

Consumers are the lifeblood of any platform ecosystem, and their role in shaping its ethical governance is nothing short of critical. They can become active agents for positive change: the first step is understanding platform governance and accountability. Educational campaigns and easily accessible information can help consumers become aware of a platform's responsibilities and the impact of their own choices on the ecosystem. Second, shifting from passive bystanders to active participants requires cultivating an 'active consumer' mindset. This means consciously choosing complementors who prioritize ethical and sustainable practices, leaving reviews that highlight responsible behaviour, and engaging in discussions about platform policies. Moreover, consumers can support initiatives that promote platform responsibility and voice concerns constructively.

Third, consumers have a natural talent for identifying issues. By honing their ability to recognize gaps and shortcomings in platform governance, including those of complementors, they become empowered watchdogs of the ecosystem. Fourth, openly communicating concerns and providing thoughtful feedback directly to platform enterprises is clearly important. This two-way communication helps platforms address issues and improve their governance practices. Fifth, when necessary, consumers can leverage social media platforms to raise awareness about platform misconduct or inaction. Public scrutiny can be a powerful tool for driving change.

The critical role of customer feedback in driving value creation within platform ecosystems and its importance in the relationships among platform owners, complementors, and end users cannot be overstated. Customer feedback serves as a key communication tool, offering insights that influence decision-making across the ecosystem. For platform owners, feedback refines features, optimizes user experience, and identifies growth opportunities, ensuring the platform remains competitive. For complementors, it guides innovation and improvement, enhancing their offerings and strengthening their relationship with the platform. End users provide feedback that shapes platform development, aligning it with their needs and expectations. Consequently, customer feedback is a central mechanism that aligns the interests of all participants, driving innovation, enhancing engagement, and supporting the platform's long-term success.

The role of external watchdogs

The platform ecosystem necessitates a dynamic legal framework that can keep pace with rapid technological advancements, with the government playing a key role in crafting new approaches to regulate emerging technologies, such as algorithms (Dencik and Kaun, 2020). This involves tackling concerns like algorithmic discrimination, bias, and privacy breaches with specific laws and regulations. For instance, recent cases of biased algorithms in loan approvals highlight the need for regulations to ensure fairness and transparency. Furthermore, the government should encourage dialogue and collaboration among platform stakeholders, promoting responsible practices and pre-empting potential issues. Given the complexities of data and stakeholder management, the next step is to develop governance structures capable of addressing these challenges. Meanwhile, the media serves as a vital watchdog, holding platform enterprises and complementors accountable for their social practices (Iosifidis and Andrews, 2019; Jackson et al., 2020).

The government can empower the media by encouraging outlets to investigate and report on under-covered social responsibility issues within the platform ecosystem. It can also advocate for responsible journalism that accurately portrays the social responsibility efforts, both positive and negative, of platform actors. This transparency not only motivates these actors to improve their practices but also builds trust with the public. By actively engaging with both the government and the media, platform enterprises and complementors can foster a more responsible and sustainable ecosystem. This collaborative approach ensures that: emerging issues are promptly addressed; new technologies and their potential social impacts are proactively managed; irresponsible behaviour is exposed, holding actors accountable and deterring future misconduct; public scrutiny and fair reporting encourage actors to prioritize ethical practices and make positive contributions to society.

In conclusion, the government and the media are pivotal in shaping the platform ecosystem through the development of legal frameworks and independent reporting. By encouraging collaboration and transparency, they empower all stakeholders to contribute to a more responsible and sustainable digital world. Given the intricate interdependencies and the broad range of interests within platform ecosystems, there is a growing need for nuanced governance structures and accountability mechanisms. Traditional governance models, designed for physical marketplaces, may struggle to keep pace with the rapid innovation and global reach of online platforms. Policymakers and regulators must then recognize the growing importance of third-party contributions, freelance workforces, and collaborations with affiliates in value creation. This requires new governance and policy models to address challenges like ensuring quality control, managing intellectual property rights, and upholding fair labour practices across these external networks.

14

A paradigm shift in production and consumption

We have explored how personalization is fundamentally changing the landscape of production and services. Social commerce stands as a prime example, where personalization thrives due to its dynamic and trend-driven nature, demanding continuous adaptation from companies. Those unable to evolve may fall behind, echoing the concept of survival of the fittest. This movement is driven by the seamless fusion of e-commerce, the accessibility of comprehensive customer data like purchase histories or browsing habits, and the creative use of artificial intelligence (AI), all contributing to more customized and engaging customer experiences. In this concluding chapter, we initiate our examination of these evolving trends against the backdrop of the long-standing debate in market economies: organization versus market.

Organizations versus markets

Ronald Coase (1937) observed that while markets facilitate exchange, their reliance on external mechanisms can incur significant transaction costs. These costs encompass finding reliable partners, negotiating and enforcing contracts, and navigating market inefficiencies. In the real world, imperfect markets with information asymmetries, externalities, and lock-in effects can limit the efficiency of purely market-based transactions. For instance, a buyer may lack critical information about a used car, leading to a disadvantageous purchase. Moreover, market-based transactions can create dependencies on external actors, like relying on a specific supplier, which can limit flexibility and adaptability. Markets also often struggle to address externalities, such as pollution from a factory, which can impose costs on society beyond the market transaction itself.

In contrast, firms, with their inherent structure and access to information, have the potential to overcome these market shortcomings. They possess the ability to efficiently collect and disseminate information, internalize external effects by assuming responsibility for their consequences, and adjust to evolving conditions more adeptly than systems based entirely on market transactions. By rectifying these particular market flaws, organizations present alternative methods of coordination to the market's 'invisible hand' of pricing. They employ strategies such as information sharing, incentives, organizational culture, and hierarchical arrangements.

Organizations can also redistribute risk, moving it from individuals averse to risk to those more willing to accept it within the firm, thus facilitating the creation of distinctive products that defy market standardization. The discretionary decision-making allowed within organizational structures can also tackle the issue of incomplete contracts, reducing dependence on pricing as the sole resolution mechanism. While pricing remains a fundamental element in market transactions, it may not fully reflect the real value of a product or service, considering the wide range of social and emotional factors that influence human behaviour. Additionally, the hierarchical nature of organizations fulfils human needs for structure and leadership, offering individuals the chance to exert influence and work towards common objectives. This aspect, coupled with their capacity to rectify market shortcomings, positions organizations as a meaningful alternative or complement to market mechanisms across various economic and social settings.

Market imperfections, such as monopolies or informational deficits, frequently necessitate that organizations internalize the exchange of goods and services. When markets fail to address issues like externalities or information asymmetries, firms step in to provide more structured solutions through internal hierarchies and coordinated decision-making. However, as discussed in Chapter 2, no organization is flawless. Even in tightly regulated economies like that of Soviet Russia, some form of free, price-controlled trade continued to exist (Milgrom and Roberts, 1992). Moreover, internal labour and capital markets within organizations display their own set of flaws. On the other hand, pure markets are susceptible to issues like cartel formations. Even under seemingly optimal conditions, markets can experience failures. Instances such as the Asian financial crisis of 1997, the 2008 US banking crisis, and recent economic challenges in Europe highlight situations where governmental intervention was required to support struggling entities, often justified as being in the 'larger public interest'.

Principal-agent models have indeed played an important role in shaping modern capitalism by providing a framework for understanding and addressing the conflicts of interest between owners and managers. The liberalization and privatization policies of the Reagan and Thatcher eras, driven by these models, have profoundly transformed economies by promoting market-oriented reforms and reshaping the landscape of corporate governance. However, the ongoing challenges and limitations of this approach underscore the need for a more nuanced understanding of corporate management and governance.

Behavioural economists challenge the traditional view of markets as purely rational entities. They argue that it is individuals, with all their inherent biases and emotions, who ultimately drive market behaviour. This human element can lead to inefficiencies and potentially justify active intervention. Robert Shiller, a prominent figure in behavioural economics, highlights the concept of 'animal spirits' – the emotional and irrational forces that can influence our financial decisions. These emotions, coupled with our inherent biases, can lead to herd mentality. We may be swayed by market sentiment, collectively pushing prices up or down beyond their true value, potentially leading to bubbles and crashes. This is partly why most economic activities fall somewhere along the spectrum between pure markets and purely centralized organizations. In this context, understanding the interplay between markets and organizations, with their respective strengths and weaknesses, is essential for comprehending the complexities of contemporary economic systems.

This becomes increasingly critical as economic and business ecosystems are constantly changing, particularly in the current competitive climate. In the current twenty-first century, digital activities have permeated businesses worldwide, evidenced by a vast digital network connecting people and communities, transcending time and geographical boundaries. Consequently, consumers' expectations of products and services have also undergone significant changes, particularly in terms of accessibility, convenience, delivery speed, and pricing. Companies are also progressively embracing sophisticated digital technologies to maintain a competitive edge, affecting societies and economies alike. Innovative tools such as social networks, Big Data, and the Internet of Things (IoT) enable them to fundamentally restructure their operational models. In an environment where digital platforms dominate and competition is intense, several factors contribute to a firm's competitive edge. Among these, proprietary complementors, early adoption advantages, and personalization have emerged as key sources of competitive advantage.

These developments frequently require overhauling core operations, adapting products and processes, and updating organizational structures. Broadening the range of functions and features in products and services is central to accommodate the varied preferences of an expanded customer base. Effective management practices are also crucial to navigate these complex transformations (Bloom and van Reenen, 2007). Consequently, businesses find themselves at a pivotal moment where devising innovative strategies to create customer value is imperative, with the personalization of products and content to suit individual preferences emerging as a fundamental tactic. Personalization introduces a novel framework for conducting economic transactions, making the system more efficient and effective by catering to the specific needs of individual users and customers, and simultaneously connecting them to larger communities. This approach signifies broader societal shifts prompted by the rise of digital technologies and the growth of the social economy (van Dijck et al., 2018).

Personalization is essentially embedded within a broader, potent ecosystem transformation. This ecosystem is driven by the exponential growth of online marketplaces and social commerce. These developments have not only redefined consumer behaviours but have also restructured the operational dynamics of businesses across various sectors. For consumers, this evolution translates into an abundance of choices. Online platforms offer unparalleled price comparison capabilities, transparency, and convenience. Concurrently, in the era of Big Data, the capability to process, analyse, and leverage vast data sets has emerged as a critical competitive edge. Firms are now employing sophisticated algorithms and computing power to navigate this wealth of information, discern patterns, and predict consumer behaviours. This capability enables businesses to rapidly adjust to market changes, extensively customize their offerings, and maintain a prominent position in the constantly evolving digital marketplace.

In summary, the evolving dynamics between production and consumption highlight a profound change driven by technological advancements, changing consumer preferences, and an increasing focus on sustainability, all of which are redefining traditional business models and liberal market forces.

Personalization: A simple narrative

Personalization is a straightforward yet impactful concept: it aims to cater to the individual needs and preferences of each person. Driven by digital innovations and data analytics, personalization involves collecting customer data to offer customized recommendations and experiences. Using advanced technology, personalization can create unique offerings for each customer, further enhancing the consumer experience. This method starkly contrasts with the standardized approach typical of Fordism and traditional bureaucratic models, emphasizing instead the value of diversity and customization. Personalization also frequently utilizes economies of scope, valuing adaptability over the rigid efficiency associated with mass production. Companies employ personalization as a strategy to achieve economic advantages, including cost reduction, enhanced convenience, and customization of products and services (Krishnaraju and Mathew, 2013; Okazaki et al., 2020; Athey et al., 2023a).

Personalization thus represents a fresh approach to structuring transactions, moulding products, services, or experiences around the requirements and needs of each customer. Its appeal lies in the tangible benefits it delivers to users. Through content and recommendations specifically adjusted to their interests, users engage in interactions that are not only more pertinent but also more captivating. This also shows how the advent of the internet and digital platforms has given consumers more power, turning them from mere receivers of products into active co-creators of their consumption experiences. They are no longer limited to one-size-fits-all products but can personalize products and services to meet their exact needs.

This change requires a deep reassessment of traditional business models, with a new focus on serving niche markets and emphasizing product differentiation instead of just aiming for large-scale production. This move towards a customer-focused model does not just make things more convenient; it opens up new possibilities for creating value. By addressing the specific needs of market segments or even individual customers, businesses can set themselves apart by offering something truly unique. Various technologies can enable this, including digital twins – virtual representations of physical entities or systems that allow companies to test strategies, optimize operations, and make data-driven decisions. Personalization significantly enhances the utility of digital twins by aligning them with the specific needs of businesses, customers, and unique scenarios. Similarly, Liquid Neural Networks (LNNs) are adaptive AI models that adjust in real-time to evolving data streams, allowing for continuous learning without retraining. LNNs provide companies with AI that dynamically adapts, enhancing performance and accurately reflecting both organizational and product changes.

Personalization beyond monopolies: Democratization in markets

Personalization allows firms to stand out in crowded markets by offering unique experiences that resonate with individual customers. An exciting aspect of personalization thus lies in its broad reach. It is not solely the domain of behemoth corporations or established business organizations. In today's e-commerce environment, individual sellers within marketplaces can also use personalization strategies to meet the unique needs and preferences of their customers. This 'democratization' of personalization empowers micro-entrepreneurs and smaller businesses to compete effectively by employing their niche expertise and agile decision-making capabilities. Furthermore, business organizations, regardless of size, can personalize their offerings to specific market segments based on shared characteristics or behaviours. This allows them to serve diverse populations more effectively, maximizing customer satisfaction and loyalty within each segment. For example, a clothing retailer might offer personalized recommendations and promotions based on customer demographics and purchase history, creating a more targeted and relevant experience for each demographic group.

Ultimately, the power of personalization transcends the limitations of size and structure. From individual sellers in e-commerce marketplaces to established businesses of all scales, personalization tools and techniques present an opportunity to connect with customers on a deeper level, offering customized products, services, and experiences that drive value. This democratization of personalization empowers market participants, large and small, to carve out unique niches and address the needs of diverse audiences, enriching the overall consumer experience in the process.

In this context, personalization may be mistakenly equated with individualization, but they are distinct concepts. While individualization customizes experiences to the specific characteristics of each individual, personalization focuses on meeting broader user needs and goals without imposing rigid authority structures. Personalization provides flexible systems that adapt to different users, empowering them with choices and autonomy. It offers tools and options that help users achieve their goals in a natural way, rather than dictating a specific outcome. This approach encourages a collaborative, user-driven experience, unlike the more prescriptive nature of individualization.

For example, in education, personalization offers students various resources and learning paths aligned with their interests and learning styles, providing guidance and options without imposing a rigid curriculum. This differs from individualization, which creates highly specific plans that may limit student autonomy. In the digital marketplace, personalization is seen in platforms like Amazon, where product recommendations are based on user behaviour patterns, offering relevant suggestions while allowing users the freedom to explore and refine their choices according to their preferences.

Creating contemporary market structures and new forms of organizations

As Girish (2020) states: 'personalized recommendations use data not just to predict but also influence our actions'. Personalization is disrupting modern market structures and leading to the emergence of new organizational forms. By addressing the distinct likes and needs of individual consumers, businesses are transitioning from conventional, uniform approaches to more dynamic, customer-focused models. This change not only alters how companies engage with their customers but also influences their internal operations, marketing strategies, and product development approaches. Moreover, personalization is driving the expansion of niche markets, encouraging companies to specialize and innovate within particular segments. This focus on specialization encourages the development of highly targeted solutions, which, in turn, requires organizations to be agile and adaptable.

The integration of technology, particularly AI and machine learning, plays a pivotal role in enabling personalization at scale. Companies are leveraging these technologies to understand customer behaviours, predict preferences, and deliver experiences seamlessly. This technological underpinning necessitates a culture of continuous learning and adaptation within organizations, further influencing their structure and operations. Personalization is thus catalysing significant changes in market structures and the way organizations are formed, marked by a heightened focus on customer needs, operational flexibility, and a strong dependence on technology and data. This movement towards more engaging, agile, and innovative practices is defining the new norms in business operations.

Personalization: Managing transactions

As organizations increasingly adopt technologies like AI and machine learning to automate existing processes, innovators are going a step further by radically reimagining work architecture to maximize the synergy between human and machine capabilities. This groundbreaking approach is not just about efficiency; it is about reinventing how work is structured and executed, leveraging the strengths of both humans and machines. Such pioneering work architecture aims to complement human skills with machine precision and endurance, resulting in a collaborative environment where each contributes its best. This can lead to the creation of new roles where human workers oversee, manage, and complement automated systems, turning their attention to tasks that require creativity, emotional intelligence, and strategic thinking – abilities that machines have yet to master.

Consequently, personalization impacts the internal dynamics of organizations, particularly as companies embrace more agile and adaptable organizational frameworks. This flexibility is achieved through flatter hierarchies, cross-functional teams, and a culture that encourages innovation, experimentation, and rapid iteration. Such teams collaborate closely to quickly develop and adapt products and services. Decision-making in these organizations is predominantly data-driven, relying extensively on advanced analytics and customer insights to shape strategies and actions. These practices allow companies to pivot quickly in response to market trends, customer feedback, or new technological advancements, ensuring they remain competitive and relevant in a fast-evolving digital environment.

Furthermore, personalization can lead to operational efficiencies by automating routine tasks, improving workflow processes, and optimizing resource allocation. This not only reduces costs but also frees up employees to focus on more strategic and creative tasks, further driving innovation and growth. We can thus argue that personalization equips businesses with the tools and mindset needed to thrive in the digital economy, by both enhancing the customer experience and building a more responsive and efficient organizational model.

AI-driven personalization: The engine of economic growth in the digital age

Just as Coase's theory of the firm sought to explain the role of organizations in reducing transaction costs, modern AI-driven personalization tools extend this idea by enabling firms to predict customer needs and streamline transactions more efficiently. Personalization is thus reshaping the economy, affecting not only the structure and strategies of individual firms and entire industries but also the dynamics of platform ecosystems. This transformation is rooted in the ability to adapt products, services, and user experiences to individual preferences using vast amounts of data and sophisticated analytics.

Firms across various sectors are applying data analytics and AI to understand consumer behaviours and preferences at an unprecedented granular level. For firms and industries, personalization marks a departure from standardized approaches, pushing companies towards offering bespoke solutions. This change is apparent in sectors ranging from retail, where online platforms recommend products based on browsing and purchase history, to healthcare, where treatments and wellness plans are increasingly tailored based on personal health data. The push for personalization compels firms to rethink their value chains, marketing strategies, and customer engagement models, prioritizing data acquisition and analytics capabilities to understand and anticipate consumer needs.

Personalization also impacts the organization of industries. Traditional industry boundaries are blurring as companies integrate vertically or horizontally to capture and utilize consumer data effectively. For example, tech companies might enter the healthcare sector, using wearable devices to offer personalized health recommendations. This convergence leads to the emergence of new business models and revenue streams, such as subscription models that offer personalized experiences or products regularly. Whereas traditional firms operated within fixed hierarchies, today's digital platforms are breaking down these barriers by allowing businesses to leverage external contributors and third-party providers, creating more decentralized and adaptive business models.

In the realm of platform ecosystems, personalization is equally transformative. Platforms connecting various users – whether consumers, content creators, or service providers – are harnessing personalization algorithms to enhance user engagement and satisfaction (Foerderer, 2020; Parker et al., 2017). For instance, social media networks and content streaming services use personalization to curate feeds and recommend content, thereby creating highly satisfying user experiences. This not only increases platform stickiness but also amplifies the network effects essential for the growth and competitiveness of these platforms.

Simultaneously, production is increasingly moving from internal firm operations to external environments, where third-party contributions, complementors, and affiliate organizations significantly enhance value creation (Chung et al., 2023; Rietveld et al., 2019). In this model, companies rely on external partners, freelancers, and other third-party entities to perform tasks and services traditionally handled in-house. This can range from manufacturing components to providing digital services like software development or content creation. The rationale behind this shift includes

Table 4 Free Market Exchange, Bureaucratic Structure, and Personalization

Feature	Free market exchange	Bureaucratic structure	Personalization
Definition	A vibrant marketplace where vendors and customers negotiate process based on supply and demand.	A formal organization with established procedures and regulations guiding transactions.	Adaptive transactions aim to meet individual consumer preferences and needs through the use of data and technology, while simultaneously connecting them to wider communities.
Key characteristics	Competition, negotiation, price flexibility	Standardization, set rules, competence, accountability	Customization, data-driven, technology-enabled
Focus	Balancing supply and demand to determine transactions	Adhering to established rules and procedures	Aligning offerings with individual customer needs and desires
Process	Arm's length trade	Direction and control	Collaborative relationship
Interaction	Direct negotiation between vendors and customers.	Transactions follow formal, predefined procedures.	Engaged, often digital, interactions tailored to the individual.
Flexibility	High flexibility in prices and offerings based on market conditions.	Limited flexibility, with transactions bound by rules and regulations.	Highly flexible with third-party and affiliate involvement.
Outcome	Output-based outcomes; efficiency; limited access	Input-based outcomes; limited access	Output-based outcomes; democratization of access
Example	A farmer's market where process may vary based on demand and negotiation.	A government agency where services are provided based on standardized criteria.	A streaming service recommending shows based on viewing history.

cost reduction, increased flexibility, access to specialized skills, and the ability to scale quickly in response to market demands.

Digital platforms thus operate across multiple sectors, blending competition with cooperation – a concept known as 'co-opetition'. This complexity, along with the influence of network effects and multi-sided markets, exposes the limitations of traditional economic theories, underscoring the need for new models to better understand and explain the dynamics of modern digital economies. Unlike traditional firms, digital platforms rely on network effects, where the platform's value increases as more users join. The dynamics of these platforms require an understanding of how value creation and distribution occur in a multi-sided market, where the platform connects different groups of users. This challenges the conventional wisdom of supply and demand in linear markets, where firms produce goods or services that are directly consumed by customers.

In conclusion, personalization is steering the economy towards a more data-driven and user-centric paradigm, significantly influencing the strategies of firms and the evolution of platform ecosystems. This change underscores the growing importance of data as a strategic asset and the need for robust frameworks to manage the implications of personalized experiences.

Having discussed the three production and consumption models – free market exchange, bureaucratic structure, and personalization economy – we can now compare these different approaches (see Table 4):

Free market exchange: Imagine a market where vendors compete for customers, negotiating prices until both sides are satisfied. This is the classic free market, where supply and demand dictate transactions.

Bureaucratic structure: Think of a formal organization with established procedures and regulations. Transactions follow set rules, prioritizing fairness and accountability over individual customization.

Personalization: Personalization refers to a method of organizing transactions such that they are aligned with the individual preferences and needs of consumers. Personalization leverages data and technology to create unique and relevant experiences adapted to individual preferences and needs, concurrently fostering connections to broader social communities.

The idea that 'the market knows best' is a central argument for free market thinkers. While there may be some truth to this in specific situations, the inherent imperfections of markets often create challenges. For example, the invisible hand describes how free markets can lead to optimal societal outcomes in terms of resource allocation. In essence, while personalization and the invisible hand come from different domains (economic organization/technology and neoclassical economics), both touch upon the idea of processes leading to beneficial outcomes – one through data-driven customization of experiences and the other through individual self-interested actions in a market. However, unlike the free market approach, personalization often makes the processes leading to beneficial outcomes, as well as the outcomes themselves, more visible. Personalization thus represents a forward-thinking method for organizing economic exchanges, creating a system that enhances productivity by catering to the distinct needs of individual users and customers and simultaneously connecting them to larger communities.

In summary, Weberian bureaucracy embodies a traditional, mass-production approach, prioritizing efficiency. In contrast, personalization, a modern, customer-centric approach, leverages technology to deliver desired products and services. Personalization thrives on adaptability and flexibility, essential in today's dynamic market. Driven by digital technologies and the service economy, personalization signifies a fundamental shift in how we conceive, create, and deliver goods and services. This move from mass production to personalization aligns with the broader transition from an industrial economy to a post-industrial or information-based economy. The move away from Weberian bureaucracy and Fordism reflects these larger economic and technological changes, particularly the rise of digital technologies and the service economy.

How personalization is changing the organization of the economy

Personalization is transforming both the organization of firms and industries as well as influencing platform ecosystems. Driven by extensive data utilization and intellectual property innovation, personalization is giving rise to a new class of businesses and market configurations that rely heavily on strategic assets such as Big Data and communication technologies. This change is particularly noticeable within e-commerce marketplaces and the dynamic sphere of production, where the involvement of external third parties in generating value is becoming more significant (Foerderer, 2020; Rietveld et al., 2019). As businesses increasingly adopt personalization, the underlying market structures are also evolving in response to changing consumer behaviours.

In this economic environment, data is not merely an asset but a cornerstone of competitive advantage. Firms that excel in collecting, analysing, and leveraging consumer data can offer highly personalized products and services, distinguishing themselves in the marketplace. This capability has improved the traditional value proposition, with companies like Amazon and Alibaba using consumer data to tailor the shopping experience, recommend products, and even predict future purchases. Consequently, a significant portion of these firms' value derives from strategic assets such as data, algorithms, brand equity, and customer relationships, rather than physical assets. Moreover, the realm of intellectual property, especially in data analytics and personalization algorithms, has become a critical asset class, often surpassing the value of physical assets. The investment in developing unique algorithms that can decipher consumer behaviour, streamline logistics, or adapt content is substantial. These proprietary technologies, protected as intellectual property, are major contributors to a firm's market value, as seen in tech giants like Google and Facebook, whose high valuations are primarily based on their data-centric business models.

The personalization phenomenon is thus reshaping the structure of markets and production processes. E-commerce platforms, acting as intermediaries that link consumers with a vast network of third-party sellers, exemplify this trend. These platforms use data to match buyers with sellers, facilitate transactions, and offer targeted advertising services, creating an ecosystem where much of the value is generated by external participants. This model enables platforms to scale rapidly without significant physical assets, as production and fulfilment are largely handled by third parties (Rietveld et al., 2019; Chung et al., 2023). Personalization also significantly impacts the dynamics of platform ecosystems (Parker et al., 2017; Foerderer, 2020). Platforms that facilitate interactions among various users, such as consumers, complementors, and content creators, are increasingly integrating personalization algorithms to enhance user experience and engagement. This not only improves the relevance of services provided to each user but also strengthens network effects, as a more engaged user base attracts more content creators and service providers, further enriching the platform.

This trend towards an open model of production, where external contributors play a vital role in value creation, is evident across various sectors. For example, in the software industry, open-source initiatives and third-party developers are essential to the ecosystem, enhancing the value of platforms such as Android and GitHub. In the gig economy, companies like Uber and Airbnb rely on independent providers for transport and lodging services, deriving their value more from the data and networks they manage than from physical assets.

Personalization is also important for enabling digital platforms to effectively aggregate and allocate resources, which can be used to address societal challenges. By adapting services and content to meet the unique needs and preferences of users, platforms can optimize resource distribution and enhance the efficiency of their operations. This targeted approach allows platforms to address specific societal issues more directly and effectively, from enhancing accessibility to promoting inclusive economic growth. In essence, the use of data and intellectual property in personalization is not only creating a new type of firm and market dynamics but also shifting the locus of value creation from internal production to external ecosystems. This transition highlights the growing importance of strategic assets and the need for innovative management and regulatory approaches to navigate the complexities of the new emerging economic system.

How personalization is impacting the business ecosystem

To better understand how personalization is revolutionizing modern business models, let's explore how social commerce integrates these principles into digital marketplaces. In previous chapters, we have discussed in detail how personalization is changing the business ecosystem. For example, social commerce is a rapidly growing e-commerce trend exploiting social media platforms as direct sales channels. It integrates purchasing with the social media experience, enabling users to acquire products without departing from their chosen platform. This strategy capitalizes on user-generated content, online communities, and social interactions to fuel product discovery, engagement, and, eventually, sales. We now briefly review how personalization impacts not only social commerce but also other aspects of the business ecosystem. For example, FinTech represents a vibrant ecosystem, a term that encapsulates technologies aimed at enhancing traditional financial services through innovative technological solutions.

(1) Social commerce is evolving beyond mere transactional interactions, embracing a model centred on community engagement within digital marketplaces. In this transition, sellers move from simply presenting products to developing dedicated online spaces where consumers can connect, share experiences, and actively participate in the journey. This community-driven approach offers a unique blend of social interaction and product discovery, blurring the lines between traditional marketing and peer-to-peer influence.

Several key factors contribute to the rise of community-driven commerce, which offers numerous benefits to consumers. It grants access to a wealth of authentic user-generated content such as reviews, comparisons, and styling tips, which can empower consumers to make informed decisions and alleviate purchase anxiety. Furthermore, these communities create a sense of belonging and shared experience, enabling consumers to connect with others who have similar interests and values, and to discover products that truly resonate with them. Besides, the aspect of community engagement can be rewarding, with gamification elements and exclusive content introducing a level of enjoyment and excitement to the experience.

Social commerce also empowers consumers to actively participate in the creation of products and services, a process known as co-creation. This collaborative approach involves engaging customers through various social media platforms by implementing tools like surveys, polls, and discussion forums to gather their input and preferences. Beyond general feedback, co-creation can be used to design personalized offerings that specifically address individual customer needs. For instance, a company might allow customers to select their preferred attributes, such as design, colour, and features, thereby adapting the product to their personal tastes and requirements. This method not only enhances customer satisfaction but also cultivates a deeper connection between the brand and its consumers. The foundation of social commerce's success lies in its adept use of personalization techniques. These techniques extend beyond simple customization by diving deep into user preferences, behaviours, and interactions within social platforms to craft a personalized experience. This level of personalization is achieved through sophisticated data analytics that sift through vast amounts of social interactions, purchase history, and user-generated content to identify patterns and preferences.

By harnessing this rich data, social commerce platforms can offer product recommendations, promotions, and content that resonate with individual users. This not only makes the purchasing experience more engaging and relevant but also streamlines the path to purchase by aligning offerings with the user's specific needs and interests. The result is a more intuitive and satisfying customer journey, which in turn enhances user engagement and conversion rates. Similarly, personalization in social commerce fosters a sense of community and connection among users. By integrating social features such as likes, shares, and reviews, coupled with personalized content, social commerce platforms create a dynamic and interactive environment. This environment encourages users to engage not only with the platform but also with each other, sharing opinions, experiences, and recommendations. This social interaction adds a layer of trust and authenticity to the shopping experience, which traditional e-commerce often lacks.

Therefore, the application of personalization in social commerce is transforming how customers discover, interact with, and purchase products in social marketplaces. It is not just about selling products; it is about creating an immersive and personalized social shopping experience that leverages the power of community and connectivity. This approach significantly contributes to the enhanced performance and effectiveness of social commerce platforms, setting a new standard for how commerce can be seamlessly integrated into the social fabric of the digital age.

(2) Commercial banks have consistently been a key player in the market as a crucial institution within the economy. Traditional banks are facing increasing pressure

> from newcomers to the market, particularly technology companies. These tech giants, viewing the financial services sector as a natural extension of their existing core businesses, are posing a significant threat to traditional banking institutions. This pressure has forced banks to innovate at an accelerated pace, seeking new methodologies to stay ahead of the curve.

Traditional banks, mirroring the diversification strategies of tech companies, are now extending their service range beyond traditional limits to preserve their market share. They aim to respond to the evolving consumer expectations for personalized, accessible, and technologically advanced financial solutions. The emergence of FinTech represents a time of both opportunities and challenges for the banking sector. Financial technology has unsettled the traditional banking model by popularizing online investments, mobile payments, and other digital financial services. These advancements pose a challenge to the conventional revenue and service models of established banks, heightening competition and pressure. However, FinTech also offers solutions to age-old problems such as high transaction costs through the use of efficient online technologies. As a result, commercial banks are progressively integrating FinTech into their operations to boost their performance with innovative products and business strategies. Adapting to the opportunities that FinTech provides is essential for commercial banks in the current economic environment.

To thrive in the future, commercial banks must tap into FinTech's potential to personalize financial products and services, thereby improving their operational efficiency and carving out unique competitive advantages, all while maintaining rigorous risk management. This strategy is in line with the core mission of FinTech: to centre financial services around the consumer's needs. The essence of FinTech's transformative impact lies in its strategic application of advanced technologies such as AI machine learning and Big Data analytics. These technologies empower FinTech solutions to go beyond traditional financial services by deeply understanding and anticipating customer needs, preferences, and behaviours in real time.

AI machine learning algorithms analyse extensive data sets, uncovering valuable insights from patterns not readily discernible to human analysts. Through this analysis, FinTech services adapt their offerings to individual customer needs, ensuring financial products and advice are both pertinent and customized. Big Data analytics further enhances this process by providing the computational power needed to process and analyse the enormous data sets characteristic of the financial industry. This capability allows FinTech companies to deliver predictive insights about market trends, risk assessment, and customer behaviour, enabling more informed decision-making for both the service provider and the consumer.

Moreover, the integration of these technologies facilitates a more dynamic interaction between financial service providers and their customers. For instance, chatbots and virtual assistants, powered by AI, can provide instant, on-demand financial advice and customer support, improving accessibility and customer engagement. This innovative approach not only improves customer satisfaction by providing more personalized and efficient services but also opens up new opportunities for financial inclusion. By applying these technologies, FinTech can reach underserved populations, offering tailored financial products that address specific challenges and needs, such as microloans, personalized insurance plans, and financial literacy tools. Generally, the core of FinTech's revolution in the financial sector is its adept use of AI machine learning and Big Data to deeply understand and meet customer financial needs in a way that is both innovative and inclusive, vastly improving the delivery of financial services.

(3) Since the economic crisis in 2008, people have been increasingly concerned over the value of their underutilized assets and have tried to find a way to gain benefits from these assets in a situation of uncertainty. The trend of consumption has shifted from hyper-consumption to the post-consumer consumption. At the same time, the development of information and communication technology (ICT) has enabled people to form new types of communication, one of which is the new sharing model using digital platforms. Thus, the sharing economy as a new way of consumption has gained interest and recognition worldwide.

The sharing economy has gained traction in many countries, spanning sectors such as hospitality, transportation, and more. It enables people to generate extra income by using idle assets. Furthermore, it has empowered and strengthened people's communities by increasing interaction among them as well as stimulating social norms and practices. From an economic aspect, the sharing economy helps individuals lower their transaction costs, creating opportunities for asset owners to more easily access customers, which in turn enhances the local economy and stimulates national economic growth.

Although the sharing economy has proliferated during the decade, some barriers and challenges impede its success. The legality of the new business model has been questioned, as well as the specific laws or regulations that should govern this new economy. Moreover, the sharing economy has a radical effect on society and raises the question of how to effectively enforce laws and regulations. For example, Uber has rejected responsibility for any liability towards passengers, as the company has positioned itself as an intermediary that provides platform services rather than as the owner of the car. Some countries have banned Uber and Airbnb, as their operations are viewed as illegal and pose a threat to both citizens and traditional businesses in the industry.

Personalization holds the potential to enhance efficiency within the sharing economy. It can assist participants in overcoming various obstacles associated with sharing economy platforms. For providers, including both service and goods providers, challenges such as uncertain income streams and the absence of regulatory protections for workers pose significant deterrents to participation. Consumers, on the other hand, often face hurdles such as unfamiliarity with the platform's technology and concerns about the quality of products and services offered. Personalization can address these issues by refining the practices of sharing economy platforms, making them more user-friendly and trustworthy for all involved. For example, personalization within the sharing economy harnesses the power of advanced data analytics to ensure that services are finely tuned to meet the specific needs and preferences of each user. By analysing a wealth of data points, from past user behaviour and preferences to real-time demand and supply conditions, these analytics enable service providers to offer experiences that resonate more deeply with individuals.

This level of customization not only enhances user satisfaction but also contributes to the efficient use of resources, matching idle assets with those who need them most. For instance, in a car-sharing platform, data analytics can help match a person looking for a vehicle in a specific location with the nearest available car that meets their preferences for size, model, or even eco-friendliness. This precision in service alignment not only elevates the user experience but also maximizes the utility of assets that would otherwise remain underutilized, driving the sharing economy's effectiveness and sustainability.

(4) The gig economy introduces a distinctive blend of hurdles and prospects for companies, legislative bodies, and society at large. As this sector continues to evolve, it becomes imperative to maintain continuous discourse and investigation to ensure that ethical principles guide decision-making processes. The dynamic nature of gig work, characterized by its flexibility and independence, also brings forth questions regarding job security, workers' rights, and equitable compensation. Addressing these issues requires collaborative efforts from all stakeholders to develop frameworks that balance innovation with worker protection.

The rise of the gig economy is not only reshaping traditional labour markets but is also a prime example of personalization in action, as platforms like Uber and Airbnb adapt services to meet the specific needs and preferences of both workers and customers. For businesses, the gig economy opens up avenues for accessing a diverse talent pool without the overheads associated with traditional employment. However, this model also demands new strategies for workforce management, engagement, and retention. Companies must navigate the complexities of integrating gig workers into their operations while ensuring compliance with evolving labour laws and ethical standards. Policymakers play an important role in shaping the regulatory environment that governs gig work. Legislation needs to adapt to the realities of gig employment, offering clarity on the status of gig workers and the responsibilities of platforms. Society as a whole stands to benefit from the opportunities presented by the gig economy, such as increased service availability and entrepreneurial openings. Yet, there is a collective responsibility to address the potential downsides, like the erosion of traditional employment protections and the widening of economic disparities.

For gig platforms, there is significant potential in harnessing advanced personalization techniques. By employing sophisticated algorithms and data analytics, platforms can enhance the efficiency of work allocation, match clients with the most suitable service providers, and strengthen the relationships between workers and platforms. Personalization can lead to better job satisfaction for gig workers by aligning tasks with their preferences and skills, and by providing them with more control over their work schedules. Likewise, improved matching algorithms can enhance customer satisfaction by ensuring that service providers meet their specific needs and expectations. This dual focus on worker and customer satisfaction can foster a more vibrant, equitable, and sustainable gig economy ecosystem.

(5) The shift towards Industry 5.0, marked by the advent of generative AI, is transforming the realms of work and technology. This new era emphasizes the synergistic interaction between humans and machines, spotlighting the need for tailored education and specialized skill acquisition. Personalized learning solutions, such as adaptive learning systems and micro-credentials, can play a central role in equipping the workforce with the intricate skills necessary for leveraging generative AI. These include competencies in data analysis, fostering human-AI partnerships, and navigating the ethical implications of AI deployment.

Addressing the complexities of managing advanced AI systems, ensuring their ethical usage, and smoothly integrating these technologies into current operational processes pose significant challenges. Targeted educational programmes, aimed at addressing individual learning preferences and professional aspirations, equip workers with the necessary expertise to innovate and adapt in this evolving setting. Programmes that enhance both technical and interpersonal skills ready individuals to engage with advanced AI technologies, enhancing their creative, analytical, and problem-solving capabilities. As the journey into Industry 5.0 continues, the focus on individualized learning paths and specific skill enhancement grows ever more important. This focused approach equips the workforce to overcome obstacles, harness the benefits of AI across various sectors, and pave the way for a collaborative and inventive future.

(6) The global financial scene is experiencing a significant change due to the widespread adoption of blockchain technologies. Among the most notable developments arising from this technological advancement is the creation of Decentralized Autonomous Organizations (DAOs). These entities function according to predefined rules, eliminating the necessity for intermediaries or centralized governance. For instance, start-ups are no longer restricted to securing funds from a limited group of wealthy investors or financial institutions. They now have the opportunity to reach out to a global audience, making access to capital more democratic and involving a diverse group of stakeholders from all around the world. Furthermore, DAOs depart from traditional business structures by operating without a standard hierarchical set-up. Decisions within DAOs are made through consensus, considering individual preferences and eliminating the need for traditional managerial roles such as managers or CEOs. While traditional firms have long dominated economic systems through hierarchical management, DAOs represent a move towards more democratized, technology-driven governance models.

The blockchain technology & web 3.0 that underpin DAOs make them accessible to anyone with an internet connection, facilitating collaboration on a global scale.

This has resulted in diverse communities from different corners of the world coming together to work on various projects. Consequently, traditional systems are facing disruptions, particularly in sectors that depend on intermediaries like banking, insurance, and brokerage. DAOs are enabling automation of functions traditionally performed by these intermediaries, leading to more efficient operations and cost reductions. Intellectual property rights are also challenged in a decentralized set-up, making it difficult to enforce copyrights and patents in a DAO-influenced environment. Companies are also adopting new revenue models, moving towards token-based systems where stakeholders receive tokens that may increase in value, deviating from traditional revenue and equity models. DAOs often emphasize community objectives, environmental sustainability, and worldwide collaboration, advocating for a more equitable economic model that extends beyond just profit.

The emergence of DAOs brings forth both challenges and prospects, envisioning a future characterized by a more inclusive, personalized, and globally interconnected economic system. For a smooth transition and to tackle the socioeconomic challenges that accompany this change, it is essential for regulators, entrepreneurs, and educators to collaborate closely. Fundamentally, the digital technologies underpinning DAOs and similar innovations are reshaping the capitalist economy. As with all technological shifts, there will be both advantages and drawbacks. Yet, with strategic planning and international collaboration, the potential benefits for society at large are significant.

Looking ahead

The ascent of personalization marks a significant trend that will shape the future of economic engagement. With technological progress and evolving consumer expectations, the capacity to meet individual and community needs and preferences is becoming increasingly important for business success. Despite the challenges that exist, the potential for personalization to reveal new value and create a more engaging and fulfilling economic environment is unmistakable.

The widespread embrace of personalization signifies a profound change in economic and social dynamics. Driven by technological innovation and a shift towards a service-driven economy, this trend has deep ramifications for the production, consumption, and organization of goods and services. While obstacles persist, the capacity of personalization to meet user requirements and unveil new opportunities presents a vibrant and promising outlook for the future of economic transactions.

Appendix

Recommender systems

In today's information-saturated world, recommender systems (or recommendation systems) have become essential tools for addressing the problem of information overload. The sheer volume of data available, particularly on the internet, often overwhelms users, making it difficult to identify truly valuable information. Online retail businesses like Wiggle benefit significantly from implementing recommendation systems, which enhance the customer shopping experience by offering personalized product suggestions, promoting products effectively, and ultimately driving revenue growth.

The rapid development of the internet has exacerbated the challenge of information overload, with the vast amount of available information surpassing individuals' or systems' ability to process or utilize it effectively. This overload is further compounded by irrelevant and redundant data, which hinders users from extracting the information they seek. Recommender systems have emerged as significant tools to combat this issue, enabling users to make informed decisions in a complex information environment. In e-commerce, recommender systems help users discover items that match their interests and preferences. These systems are particularly effective when users face a vast array of information without clear requirements, mitigating information overload by guiding them to relevant content. From the perspective of information producers, recommender systems highlight pertinent information and capture users' attention, optimizing the flow of information.

Recommender systems serve as a bridge between users and information, assisting users in finding valuable data while presenting content that aligns with their interests. This creates a win-win situation for both information consumers and producers, streamlining the flow of information in an increasingly digital world.

Recommender systems classification

In e-commerce, recommender systems are automated tools designed to help customers find products that match their interests and preferences, thus alleviating the information overload common on many websites. These systems deliver personalized and exclusive recommendations to targeted users, enhancing user engagement and spotlighting products likely to be purchased, thereby boosting retailer revenue.

Recommender systems are generally classified into three main categories:

1. Content-based filtering (CBF): This method analyses the content of items a user has previously interacted with – such as product descriptions, reviews, and browsing history – to recommend similar items.
2. Collaborative filtering: This approach employs the collective behaviour of users with similar preferences to suggest products positively received by those users.
3. Hybrid filtering: This technique combines content-based and collaborative filtering to provide a more comprehensive and personalized recommendation experience.

These methodologies enable recommender systems to adapt to various user needs and preferences, optimizing the shopping experience and improving business outcomes for e-commerce platforms.

Initially, recommender systems functioned similarly to search engines, relying on query-based information retrieval where users entering specific keywords would be presented with relevant items. This process, known as content-based recommendation, matched item attributes without considering user preferences. However, with the evolution of the internet and greater access to customer data, understanding customer behaviours and preferences became possible.

Collaborative filtering, first applied in email filtering systems, emerged as a highly effective method in recommender systems. It predicts user preferences by analysing the preference patterns of a group of existing customers. Today, recommender systems are used across various fields, including social media, e-commerce, and online streaming. Companies are developing hybrid systems that combine different approaches to address specific challenges, distinguishing them from traditional search engines by offering personalized and individualized content.

Content-based recommender system

CBF recommends items to users based on the similarity to items they have positively rated in the past. This approach relies on the content description of the items. For example, in a film recommendation system, if a user enjoys movies with themes of 'fantasy', 'magic', and 'Europe and the United States', CBF might suggest films like *Harry Potter* or *Lord of the Rings*. The system uses item descriptions and user preferences to determine recommendations, leveraging algorithms that calculate item similarity based on overlapping content descriptions, often using keywords. The Term Frequency-Inverse Document Frequency (TF-IDF) method identifies representative keywords to label items, facilitating the similarity calculation and recommendations based on user purchase history.

The CBF process involves three main steps:

1. Item representation: Extracting specific features, such as content descriptions, to represent each item.

2. Learning user profile: Understanding user preferences by analysing the characteristics of items they liked or disliked in the past.
3. Recommendation generation: Comparing user profile characteristics with candidate items to recommend the most relevant set of items to the user.

CBF offers several advantages:

1. User control: Users can influence the recommendation process through their exclusive ratings, allowing the system to build personalized information archives.
2. Transparency: The system enhances transparency by explaining recommendations based on item content similarity, improving user comfort.
3. Cold start problem: CBF can recommend new items that have not been interacted with by any user, addressing the cold start problem for new users or items.

However, CBF also has limitations:

1. Content generation: It can be difficult to generate attributes for items with limited content information, especially in certain domains.
2. Overemphasis: The system might overemphasize specific product aspects, potentially limiting recommendation diversity and personalization.
3. User input: Obtaining explicit user ratings can be challenging, as users typically do not actively provide this information.

Collaborative filtering recommender system

Collaborative filtering hinges on the idea that the best recommendations come from others who share similar tastes. It identifies users with similar preferences and generates a list of recommended items based on predicted ratings. This process unfolds in three stages:

Creation of a user rating matrix: Initially, a matrix is formed by analysing user purchase history and preferences, derived from both explicit ratings – obtained through surveys – and implicit ratings, which include behaviours like website navigation and click-through rates (Breese et al., 2013).

Finding similar users: Using methods like the neighbouring approach or latent factor models, the system calculates user similarities. The neighbouring approach focuses on user-user similarities, while latent factor models, such as matrix factorization (Koren et al., 2009), uncover underlying relation.

Predicting unknown ratings: The system then predicts ratings for items not yet rated by the user, based on the similarities identified in the previous step. Items highly rated by similar users are recommended.

Regarding the processing of the rating matrix in recommender systems, two main approaches are commonly used: the neighbouring method and latent factor models. The neighbouring method calculates the similarity among users, effectively grouping those with similar preferences. On the other hand, the latent factor model, particularly matrix factorization, aims to uncover the underlying relationships between users and items. As detailed by Koren et al. (2009), matrix factorization involves decomposing the user-item interaction matrix R into two lower-dimensional matrices, P (user-factor) and Q (item-factor). The entries in matrix P are derived from user behaviours and purchase history, while matrix Q captures the properties of the items. The product of matrices P and Q estimates the rating R_{ui} – the user's preference for a specific item – as shown in the formula:

$$R_{ui} = P_u^T q_i = \sum_{k=1}^{k} p_{uk} q_{ik}$$

The matrix factorization process is depicted in Figure A.1. One significant advantage of matrix decomposition is its ability to predict a user's preference for an unknown item, which is invaluable for personalizing recommendations. Furthermore, this method can accommodate diverse customer ratings across various dimensions, such as movie genres, directors, and actors. Compared to the content-based approach, matrix factorization does not rely on having analysable content. It works effectively without needing to understand the specific attributes of the items, as noted by Su and Khoshgoftaar (2009). This feature makes it particularly robust and versatile in handling complex recommendation scenarios where item details are sparse or unavailable.

Collaborative filtering can be divided into memory-based and model-based approaches. Memory-based methods focus on calculating similarities between users or items, using metrics like Euclidean distance, Pearson correlation, and cosine similarity. Model-based approaches, on the other hand, employ algorithms like Naive Bayes, SVD, and deep neural networks to tackle issues like data sparsity and scalability (Koren et al., 2009).

Collaborative filtering has several advantages, such as its ability to function without specific domain knowledge, making it especially effective in areas like music and film where user ratings are crucial. Model-based systems within collaborative filtering employ advanced techniques to address data sparsity and scalability issues, enhancing accuracy

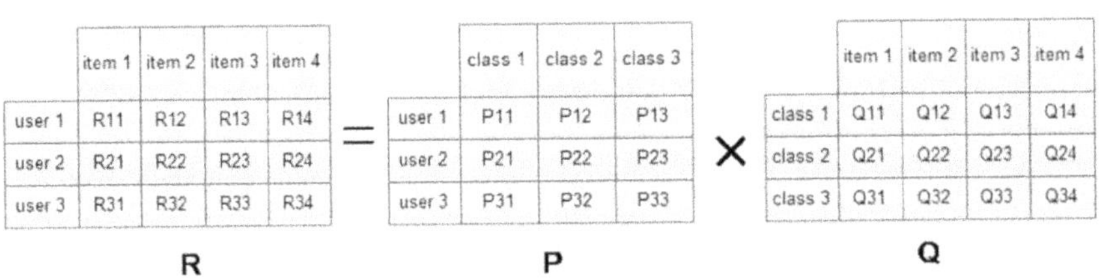

Figure A.1 Matrix factorization explanation.

and performance. Additionally, collaborative filtering offers a broad spectrum of recommendations across various categories. However, it faces challenges like the ramp-up problem, which makes generating precise recommendations difficult with limited initial data. Data sparsity issues arise when it's challenging to compute item similarities due to infrequent ratings. Scalability is another concern, as it requires significant computational power as the user base grows. Moreover, the timeliness factor means that changing user preferences can diminish the relevance of previously gathered data.

Hybrid recommender systems

A hybrid recommendation system combines multiple recommendation techniques to improve performance and address the limitations of individual methods. For instance, content-boosted collaborative filtering merges content-based prediction with collaborative filtering to combat data sparsity (Melville et al., 2002). Furthermore, incorporating data clustering into collaborative filtering helps solve the ramp-up problem by creating a probabilistic model (Kim and Li, 2004). These hybrid systems leverage the broad coverage and speed of content-based methods alongside the depth and accuracy of collaborative filtering.

One challenge in collaborative filtering is the portfolio effect, where the system tends to recommend very similar items, leading to a narrow range of suggestions. Ziegler et al. (2005) proposed a topic diversification method to broaden and diversify recommendations, taking into account the user's varied interests while slightly compromising average accuracy. Hybrid systems can integrate various approaches, from traditional methods like content-based and knowledge-based filtering to advanced techniques like deep neural networks. They might combine different CBF methods or merge content-based with collaborative filtering into a unified model. These systems can be implemented in several ways, falling into three main paradigms: monolithic, parallelized, and pipelined.

Monolithic hybridization involves integrating multiple methods into a single model:

- Feature combination: This technique merges the outputs of different recommendation systems as item features, such as using matrix decomposition to derive item feature factors that are then used in CBF to identify item similarities.
- Feature augmentation: Utilizing clustering methods like k-means, this approach identifies items with similar features and uses algorithms like Apriori to find association rules among items, which then inform subsequent recommendation algorithms.

Parallelized hybridization employs each method independently and combines their results:

- Weighted: Initially, all recommendation methods are equally weighted, with adjustments made based on customer feedback. For example, collaborative filtering might be weighted more heavily when there is consistent item rating.

- Switching: The system switches between methods based on specific situations or phases. Initially, content-based methods may predominate, with collaborative filtering becoming more prominent as data accumulates.
- Mixed: Recommendations from different methods are displayed simultaneously when they all provide feasible results.

Pipelined hybridization uses the output of one method as the input for another:

- Cascade: The initial top-*n* recommendation list from one method is refined by subsequent methods, including re-ranking and pruning, to ensure relevance and prevent the inclusion of low-quality items.
- Meta-level: This approach uses an entire model as the system input, such as a user profile model incorporating textual labels and preferences, upon which collaborative filtering is then applied, effectively addressing data sparsity issues.

In summary, hybrid recommendation systems employ multiple techniques to provide more accurate, diverse, and personalized suggestions, overcoming the challenges faced by single-method systems. The three hybridization paradigms each address different scenarios, varying in their approach to input data and algorithm adaptation. The monolithic paradigm is best suited for simple feature data, requiring minimal modifications to recommender algorithms. In contrast, the parallelized paradigm operates with each algorithm independently, necessitating a balance in the significance of outcomes from different algorithms. The pipelined paradigm, being the most complex and time-intensive, requires that models generated by one method be adjusted to be compatible with subsequent methods. Due to its capacity to integrate diverse types of features, it has the potential for superior performance.

Recommender systems in practice

Companies tailor their recommender systems to suit specific business needs. For example, YouTube employs deep neural networks to create a unified vector space that incorporates both user and item features. By analysing factors like viewing history, search terms, and demographic data, YouTube's system offers personalized content recommendations (Covington et al., 2016). In e-commerce, click-through rates are essential for understanding customer interest, with higher rates indicating a higher likelihood of purchase. Attention mechanisms help evaluate the impact of historical behaviours on these rates, as some past purchases may better predict future buying patterns (Zhou et al., 2018).

Hybrid recommender systems are increasingly integrating machine learning and deep learning techniques to analyse customer behaviour and preferences. Deep learning methodologies, such as multilayer perceptrons, autoencoders, convolutional neural networks (CNNs), and recurrent neural networks (RNNs), are adept at handling complex data models. For instance, RNNs are ideal for sequential behavioural data, while CNNs can process diverse data types, including visual and linguistic information.

References

Breese, J. S., Heckerman, D., and Kadie, C. (2013). Empirical analysis of predictive algorithms for collaborative filtering. arXiv preprint *arXiv*: 1301.7363.

Burke, R. (2002). Hybrid recommender systems: survey and experiments. *User Modeling and User-Adapted Interaction*, 12(4), 331–70.

Covington, P., Adams, J., and Sargin, E. (2016, September). *Deep neural networks for YouTube recommendations*. In Proceedings of the 10th ACM conference on recommender systems (pp. 191–8).

Goldberg, D., Nichols, D., Oki, B. M., and Terry, D. (1992). Using collaborative filtering to weave an information tapestry. *Communications of the ACM*, 35(12), 61–70.

Kim, B. M., and Li, Q. (2004, September). *Probabilistic model estimation for collaborative filtering based on items attributes*. In IEEE/WIC/ACM International Conference on Web Intelligence (WI'04) (pp. 185–91). IEEE.

Koren, Y., Bell, R., and Volinsky, C. (2009). Matrix factorization techniques for recommender systems. *Computer*, 42(8), 30–7.

Melville, P., Mooney, R. J., and Nagarajan, R. (2002). Content-boosted collaborative filtering for improved recommendations. *Aaai/iaai*, 23, 187–92.

Pazzani, M. J., and Billsus, D. (2007). Content-based recommendation systems. In *The adaptive web* (pp. 325–41). Berlin, Heidelberg: Springer.

Su, X., and Khoshgoftaar, T. M. (2009). A survey of collaborative filtering techniques. *Advances in Artificial Intelligence*, 1–19.

Zhou, M., Ding, Z., Tang, J., and Yin, D. (2018, February). *Micro behaviors: A new perspective in e-commerce recommender systems*. In Proceedings of the eleventh ACM international conference on web search and data mining (pp. 727–35).

Ziegler, C. N., McNee, S. M., Konstan, J. A., and Lausen, G. (2005, May). *Improving recommendation lists through topic diversification*. In Proceedings of the 14th International Conference on World Wide Web (pp. 22–32).

Bibliography

Abdar, M., and Yen, N. Y. (2020). Analysis of user preference and expectation on shared economy platform: An examination of correlation between points of interest on Airbnb. *Computers in Human Behavior*, 107, p. 105730.

Abdullah, R., and Fakieh, B. (2020). Health care employees' perceptions of the use of artificial intelligence applications: Survey study. *Journal of Medical Internet Research*, 22(5), p. e17620. doi: 10.2196/17620.

Accenture (2019). The future of circular fashion: Assessing the viability of business models. pp. 1–50. https://d2be5ept72nvlo.cloudfront.net/2019/05/The-Future-of-Circular-Fashion-Report-Fashion-for-Good.pdf.

Acemoglu, D. et al. (2020). *AI and jobs: Evidence from online vacancies*. Cambridge, MA: National Bureau of Economic Research. Doi: 10.3386/w28257.

Acemoglu, D., and Autor, D. (2011). Skills, tasks and technologies: Implications for employment and earnings. *Handbook of Labor Economics*, 4, pp. 1043–1171.

Acemoglu, D., and Restrepo, P. (2019). Automation and new tasks: How technology displaces and reinstates labor. *Journal of Economic Perspectives*, 33(2), pp. 3–30.

Acemoglu, D., H Autor, D., Hazell, J., and Restrepo, P. (2020). *AI and jobs: Evidence from online vacancies*. National Bureau of Economic Research, 28257. doi: 10.3386/w28257.

ACM.org. (2017). USACM statement on algorithmic accountability. www.acm.org/binaries/content/assets/public-policy/2017_usacm_statement_algorithms.pdf.

Acquier, A., Daudigeos, T., and Pinkse, J. (2017). Promises and paradoxes of the sharing economy: An organizing framework. *Technological Forecasting and Social Change*, 125, pp. 1–10.

Adadi, A., and Berrada, M. (2018). Peeking inside the black-box: A survey on explainable artificial intelligence (XAI). *IEEE Access*, 6, pp. 52138–60.

Adkins, A. (2016). *Millennials: The job-hopping generation*. Gallup. https://www.gallup.com/workplace/236474/millennials-jobhopping-generation.aspx.

Adomavicius, G. et al. (2022) Effects of personalized recommendations versus aggregate ratings on post-consumption preference responses, *MIS Quarterly* (46:1), 627–43.

Adomavicius, G., and Tuzhilin, A. (2005). Personalization technologies: A process-oriented perspective. *Communications of the ACM*, 48(10), pp. 83–90.

Adomavicius, G., and Tuzhilin, A. (2005). Personalization technologies: A process-oriented perspective. *Communications of the ACM*, 48(10), pp. 83–90.

Agrawal, A., Gans, J. and Goldfarb, A. (2022) *Power and prediction: The disruptive economics of artificial intelligence*. Cambridge: Harvard Business Review Press.

Aguirre, E. et al. (2015). Unraveling the personalization paradox: The effect of information collection and trust-building strategies on online advertisement effectiveness. *Journal of Retailing*, 91(1), pp. 34–49.

Aitken, M., Cumming, D. and Zhan, F. (2023). Algorithmic trading and market quality: International evidence of the impact of errors in colocation dates. *Journal of Banking & Finance*, 151, 106843.

Akerlof, George A., and Shiller, Robert J. (2009). *Animal spirits: How human psychology drives the economy, and why it matters for global capitalism*. Princeton, NJ: Princeton University Press.

Aksoy, L., Cooil, B., and Lurie, N. H. (2011). Decision quality measures in recommendation agent's research. *Journal of Interactive Marketing*, 25(2), pp. 110–22.

Aksoy, N. C. et al. (2021). A typology of personalisation practices in marketing in the digital age. *Journal of Marketing Management*, 37(11–12), pp. 1091–122.

Albert, E. T. (2019). AI in talent acquisition: A review of AI applications used in recruitment and selection. *Strategic HR Review*, 18(5), pp. 215–21.

Allen, C., Varner, G., and Zinser, J. (2000). Prolegomena to any future artificial moral agent. *Journal of Experimental & Theoretical Artificial Intelligence*, 12(3), pp. 251–61.

Allison, J. P. et al. (2021). Special issue: Artificial intelligence and engineering design. *Journal of Mechanical Design*, 144(2), 020301.

Aloisi, A. (2015). Commoditized workers: Case study research on labor law issues arising from a set of 'on-demand/gig economy' platforms. *Comparative Labor Law & Policy Journal*, 37(3), pp. 653–90.

Alt, R., Beck, R., and Smits, M. T. (2018). FinTech and the transformation of the financial industry. *Electronic Markets*, 28(3), pp. 235–43.

Amazon Staff. (2023). 5 ways Amazon is using AI to improve your holiday shopping and deliver your package faster. https://www.aboutamazon.com/news/operations/amazon-uses-ai-to-improve-shopping.

Anan, L. et al. (2023). *FINTECHS: A new paradigm of Growth*, McKinsey & Company. Available at: https://www.mckinsey.com/industries/financial-services/our-insights/fintechs-a-new-paradigm-of-growth.

Anderson, J., and Rainie, L. (2018). Solutions to address AI's anticipated negative impacts, *Artificial Intelligence and the Future of Humans*, Pew Research Center, https://www.pewresearch.org/internet/2018/12/10/solutions-to-address-ais-anticipated-negative-impacts/.

Anderson, J., Rainie, L., and Luchsinger, A. (2018). Artificial Intelligence and the Future of Human. *Pew Research Center*. https://www.pewresearch.org/internet/2018/12/10/artificial-intelligence-and-the-future-of-humans/.

Anderson, M., and Anderson, S. (2015). Toward ensuring ethical behavior from autonomous systems: A case-supported principle-based paradigm. *Industrial Robot: An International Journal*, 42(4), pp. 324–31.

Anshari, M., Almunawar, M. N., Lim, S. A. and Al-Mudimigh, A. (2019). Customer relationship management and Big Data enabled: Personalization & customization of services. *Applied Computing and Informatics*, 15(2), pp. 94–101.

Antonio, V. (2018). How AI Is changing sales. *Harvard Business Review*. 30 July, hbr.org/2018/07/how-ai-is-changing-sales.

Antorini, Y. M., Muniz, A. M. and Askildsen, T. (2012). Collaborating with customer communities: Lessons from the LEGO Group. *MIT Sloan Management Review*, 53(3), pp. 73–95.

APA (2023). *2023 Work in America survey*, American Psychological Association, www.apa.org/pubs/reports/work-in-america/2023-workplace-health-well-being.

Armstrong, C. M. et al. (2015). Sustainable product-service systems for clothing: exploring consumer perceptions of consumption alternatives in Finland. *Journal of Cleaner Production*, 97, pp. 30–9.

Arner, D. W., Barberis, J., and Buckley, R. P. (2015). *The evolution of FinTech: A New Post-Crisis Paradigm?* Research Paper No. 2015/047, Hong Kong: University of Hong Kong, Faculty of Law. https://dx.doi.org/10.2139/ssrn.2676553.

Arntz, M, Gregory, T., and Zierahn, U. (2016). The risk of automation for jobs in OECD countries: A comparative analysis. *OECD Social. Employment and Migration Working Papers*, 2(189), pp. 47–54.

Arora, N. et al. (2008). Putting one-to-one marketing to work: Personalization, customization, and choice. *Marketing Letters*, 19(3–4), pp. 305–21.

Assiouras, I. et al. (2019). Value co-creation and customer citizenship behavior. *Annals of Tourism Research*, 78, p. 102742.

Athey, S. et al. (2023a). Can personalized digital counseling improve consumer search for modern contraceptive methods? *Science Advances*, 9(40). DOI: 10.1126/sciadv.adg44.

Athey, S., Cole, S. A., Nath, S., and Zhu, S. J. (2023b). *Targeting, personalization, and engagement in an agricultural advisory service.* SSRN. https://ssrn.com/abstract=4536641.

Autor, D. H. (2015). Why are there still so many jobs? The history and future of workplace automation. *Journal of Economic Perspectives*, 29(3), pp. 3–30.

Autor, D., Levy, F., and Murnane, R. J. (2003), The skill content of recent technological change: An empirical exploration. *The Quarterly Journal of Economics*, 118(4), pp. 1279–333.

AWS (2021). What is Amazon personalize? – Amazon personalize. https://docs.aws.amazon.com/personalize/latest/dg/what-is-personalize.html.

Ayeh, J. K., Au, N., and Law, R. (2013). 'Do we believe in TripAdvisor?' Examining credibility perceptions and online travellers' attitude toward using user-generated content. *Journal of Travel Research*, 52(4), pp. 437–52.

Ba, S., Whinston, A. B., and Zhang, H. (2003). Building trust in online auction markets through an economic incentive mechanism. *Decision Support Systems*, 35(3), pp. 273–86.

Bagloee, S. A. et al. (2016). Autonomous vehicles: Challenges, opportunities, and future implications for transportation policies. *Journal of Modern Transportation*, 24(4), pp. 284–303.

Bahtar, A. Z., and Muda, M. (2016). The impact of user–generated content (UGC) on product reviews towards online purchasing–A conceptual framework. *Procedia Economics and Finance*, 37, pp. 337–42.

Bakarich, K., and O'Brien, P. (2020). The robots are coming … but aren't here yet: The use of artificial intelligence technologies in the public accounting profession. *Journal of Emerging Technologies in Accounting*, 18(1), pp. 27–43.

Bakhtiar, M. M. et al. (2023), Social and financial incentives for overcoming a collective action problem, *Journal of Development Economics*, 162, p. 103072.

Balmaceda, F., and Soruco, P. (2008). Asymmetric dynamic pricing in a local gasoline retail market. *Journal of Industrial Economics*, 56(3), pp. 629–53.

Banerjee, S., Bhattacharyya, S., and Bose, I. (2017). Whose online reviews to trust? Understanding reviewer trustworthiness and its impact on business. *Decision Support Systems*, 96, pp. 17–26.

Bang, H., and Wojdynski, B. W. (2016). Tracking users' visual attention and responses to personalized advertising based on task cognitive demand. *Computers in Human Behavior*, 55, pp. 867–76.

Bansal, A. et al. (2023) A study of human resource digital transformation (HRDT): A phenomenon of innovation capability led by digital and individual factors. *Journal of Business Research*, 157, p. 113611.

Bardakci, A., and Whitelock, J. (2004). How 'ready' are customers for mass customisation? An exploratory investigation. *European Journal of Marketing*, 38(11/12), pp. 1396–416.

Bardhi, F., and Eckhardt, G. M. (2015). The sharing economy isn't about sharing at all. *Harvard Business Review*. https://hbr.org/2015/01/the-sharing-economy-isnt-about-sharing-at-all.

Bar-Gill, O. (2019). Algorithmic price discrimination when demand is a function of both preferences and (mis)perceptions. *The University of Chicago Law Review*, 86(2), pp. 217–54.

Baron, R. A., and Tang, J. (2011). The role of entrepreneurs in firm-level innovation: Joint effects of positive affect, creativity, and environmental dynamism. *Journal of Business Venturing*, 26(1), pp. 49–60.

Barro, S., and Davenport, T. H. (2019). People and machines: Partners in innovation. *MIT Sloan Management Review*, 60, pp. 22–8.

Bartz, D. (2023). Amazon faces landmark monopoly lawsuit by FTC. Reuters. https://www.reuters.com/technology/us-sues-amazoncom-breaking-antitrust-law-harming-consumers-2023-09-26.

Barwise, P., and Watkins, L. (2018). The evolution of digital dominance: How and why we got to GAFA. In M. Moore and D. Tambini (eds), *Digital Dominance: The Power of Google, Amazon, Facebook, and Apple* (pp. 21–49). Oxford: Oxford University Press.

BBC (2019). *How computing's first 'killer app' changed everything*. Available at: https://www.bbc.co.uk/news/business-47802280.

Beckert, S (2014). *Empire of cotton: A global history*. New York: Knopf.

Belk, R. (1988). Possessions and the extended self. *Journal of Consumer Research*, 15(2), pp. 139–68.

Belk, R. (2009). Sharing. *Journal of Consumer Research*, 36, pp. 715–34.

Belk, R. (2014). You are what you can access: Sharing and collaborative consumption online. *Journal of Business Research*, 67(8), pp. 1595–600.

Benbya et al. (2020). Artificial intelligence in organizations: Current state and future opportunities. *SSRN Electronic Journal*, 19(4). doi: https://doi.org/10.2139/ssrn.3741983.

Benjaafar, S. et al. (2019). Peer-to-peer product sharing: Implications for ownership, usage, and social welfare in the sharing economy. *Management Science*, 65(2), pp. 477–93.

Bente, G., Baptist, O., and Leuschner, H. (2012). To buy or not to buy: Influence of seller photos and reputation on buyer trust and purchase behavior. *International Journal of Human-Computer Studies*, 70(1), pp. 1–13.

Berg, J. et al. (2018). *Digital labour platforms and the future of work: Towards decent work in the online world*. International Labour Organization. https://www.ilo.org/global/publications/books/WCMS_645337/lang--en/index.htm.

Berger, J., and Milkman, K. (2012). What makes online content viral? *Journal of Marketing Research*, 49(2), pp. 192–205.

Berger, T. et al. (2019). Uber happy? Work and well-being in the 'gig economy. *Economic Policy*, 34(99), pp. 429–77.

Black, J. S., and van Esch, P. (2020). AI-enabled recruiting: What is it and how should a manager use it? *Business Horizons*, 63(2), pp. 215–26.

Blomqvist, L. et al. (2013). Does the shoe fit? Real versus imagined ecological footprints. *PLoS Biology*, 11(11): e1001700.

Bloom, N., and van Reenen, J. (2007). Measuring and explaining management practices across firms and nations, *Quarterly Journal of Economics*, 122(4), pp. 1351–408.

Boden, M., et al. (2017). Principles of robotics: Regulating robots in the real world. *Connection Science*, 29(2), pp. 124–9.

Boerman, S. C. (2020). The effects of the standardized Instagram disclosure for micro- and meso-influencers. *Computers in Human Behavior*, 103, pp. 199–207.

Bond, S. D., He, S. X., and Wen, W. (2019). Speaking for 'free': Word of mouth in free-and paid-product settings. *Journal of Marketing Research*, 56(2), pp. 276–90.

Botsman, R. (2015). Defining the sharing economy: What is collaborative consumption – and what isn't? Fast Company. https://www.fastcompany.com/3046119/defining-the-sharing-economywhat-is-collaborative-consumption-and-what-isnt.

Botsman, R., and Rogers, R. (2010). *What's mine is yours: The rise of collaborative consumption*. New York: Harper Business.

Boudet, J. et al. (2019). *The future of personalization—And how to get ready for it*. McKinsey. https://www.mckinsey.com/business-functions/marketing-and-sales/our-insights/the-future-of-personalization-and-how-to-get-ready-for-it.

Boulding, K. (1966). The economics of the coming spaceship earth. In H. Jarrett (ed.), *Environmental quality in a growing economy, resources for the future*. Baltimore: Johns Hopkins University Press, pp. 3–14.

Bragazzi, N. L. et al. (2020) How big data and artificial intelligence can help better manage the COVID-19 pandemic. *International Journal of Environmental Research and Public Health*, 17(9), p. 3176.

Brenner, L. et al. (2007). On the psychology of loss aversion: possession, valence, and reversals of the endowment effect. *Journal of Consumer Research*, 34(3), pp. 369–76.

Bresnahan, T. (2018). Artificial intelligence technologies and aggregate growth prospects. In G. Zodrow and J. Diamond (eds), *Prospects for economic growth in the United States*. Cambridge: Cambridge University Press.

Bright, L. F., Kleiser, S. B., and Grau, S. L. (2015). Too much Facebook? An exploratory examination of social media fatigue. *Computers in Human Behavior*, 44, pp. 148–55.

Brodley, C. E., and Friedl, M. A. (1999). Identifying mislabelled training data. *Journal of Artificial Intelligence Research*, 11, pp. 131–67.

Brooks, G., Drenten, J., and Piskorski, M. J. (2021). Influencer celebrification: How social media influencers acquire celebrity capital. *Journal of Advertising*, 50(5), pp. 528–47.

Brophy, R. (2019). Blockchain and insurance: A review for operations and regulation. *Journal of Financial Regulation and Compliance*, 28(2), pp. 215–34.

Brougham, D., and Haar, J. (2018). Smart technology, artificial intelligence, robotics, and algorithms (STARA): Employees' perceptions of our future workplace. *Journal of Management & Organization*, 24(2), pp. 239–57.

Brundage, M. (2014). Limitations and risks of machine ethics. *Journal of Experimental & Theoretical Artificial Intelligence*, 26(3), pp. 355–72.

Brynjolfsson, E., and McAfee, A. (2014). *The second machine age: Work, progress, and prosperity in a time of brilliant technologies*. New York: W. W. Norton.

Brynjolfsson, E., and McAfee, A. (2014). *The second machine age: Work, progress, and prosperity in a time of brilliant technologies*. New York: W. W. Norton.

Brynjolfsson, E., Li, D. and Raymond, L. R. (2023). Generative AI at work, NBER. Available at: https://www.nber.org/papers/w3116.

Bryson, J. J. (2019). The past decade and future of ai's impact on society. In *Towards a New Enlightenment? A Transcendent Decade*, vol. 11.

Buchak, G. et al. (2018). Fintech, regulatory arbitrage, and the rise of shadow banks. *Journal of Financial Economics*, 130(3), pp. 453–83.
Buenstorf, G. (2007). Creation and pursuit of entrepreneurial opportunities: an evolutionary economics perspective. *Small Business Economics*, 28(4), 323–37.
Bughin, J. et al. (2018). *Independent work: Choice, necessity, and the gig economy*. McKinsey. https://mck.co/2KJQ0eq.
Bughin, J., Lund, S., and Manyika, J. (2018). *Notes from the AI frontier: Modeling the impact of AI on the world economy*. McKinsey Global Institute.
Bughin, J., Lund, S., and Manyika, J. (2018). *Notes from the AI frontier: Modeling the impact of AI on the world economy*. McKinsey Global Institute.
Bundy, A. (2017), Preparing for the future of Artificial Intelligence. *Journal of Knowledge, Culture and Communication*, 32(2), pp. 285–7.
Buttle, M., Vyas, D., and Spinks, C. (2013), Evaluating the financial viability and resource implications for new business models in the clothing sector, *WRAP Working Together for a World without Waste Research Paper*. http://www.wrap.org.uk/sites/files/wrap/Clothing%20REBM%20Final%20Report%2005%2002%2013_0.pdf.
Cachon, G., and Swinney, R. (2011). The value of fast fashion: Quick response, enhanced design, and strategic consumer behavior. *Management Science*, 57, pp. 778–95.
Cai, J. et al. (2018). Utilitarian and hedonic motivations for live streaming shopping. In *TVX 2018 – Proceedings of the 2018 ACM International Conference on Interactive Experiences for TV and Online Video* (pp. 81–8). https://doi.org/10.1145/3210825.3210837.
Calo, R., and Rosenblat, A. (2017). The taking economy: Uber, information, and power. *Columbia Law Review*, 117, p. 1623.
Calvano, E. et al. (2019). Algorithmic pricing what implications for competition policy? *Review of Industrial Organization*, 55(1), pp. 155–71.
Camerer, C., Loewenstein, G., and Prelec, D. (2007). Predictable choices. *The American Economic Review*, 97(1), pp. 329–64.
Chandler, A. D. (1962). *Strategy and structure: Chapters in the history of the American industrial enterprise*. MIT Press.
Chang, H. H., Wong, K. H., and Shen, Y. A. (2022). Effects of the consumer socialization process on content sharing on SNSs: Social comparison and anticipated emotions as moderators. *Technological Forecasting and Social Change*, 174, p. 121262.
Chang, H.-J. (2010). *23 Things they don't tell you about capitalism*. London: Bloomsbury.
Charlwood, A., and Guenole, N. (2022). Can HR adapt to the paradoxes of artificial intelligence? *Human Resource Management Journal*, 32(4), pp. 729–42.
Chen, C. et al. (2019). Digitally facilitated newspaper consumption and value co-creation. *The Bottom Line*, 32(1), pp. 16–46.
Chen, L. (2017). Measuring algorithms in online marketplaces. *ProQuest Dissertations and Theses*, 149. https://repository.library.northeastern.edu/files/neu:cj82q9886.
Chen, L., Mislove, A., and Wilson, C. (2016). An empirical analysis of algorithmic pricing on Amazon Marketplace. In *Proceedings of the 25th International Conference on World Wide Web—WWW'16* (pp. 1339–49). New York: ACM Press. https://doi.org/10.1145/2872427.2883089.
Chen, X., You, X., and Chang, V. (2021). FinTech and commercial banks' performance in China: A leap forward or survival of the fittest? *Technological Forecasting and Social Change*, 166, p. 120645.

Cheng, M. (2016). Sharing economy: A review and agenda for future research. *International Journal of Hospitality Management*, 57, pp. 60–70.
Cheng, M., and Foley, C. (2019). Algorithmic management: The case of Airbnb. *International Journal of Hospitality Management*, 83, pp. 33–6.
Cheong, H. J., and Morrison, M. A. (2008). Consumers' reliance on product information and recommendations found in UGC. *Journal of Interactive Advertising*, 8(2), pp. 38–49.
Cherry, M. A., and Rutschman, A. S. (2020). Gig workers as essential workers: How to correct the gig economy beyond the COVID-19 pandemic. *ABA Journal of Labor & Employment Law*, 35(1), pp. 11–16.
Cheung, C. M., and Thadani, D. R. (2012). The impact of electronic word-of-mouth communication: A literature analysis and integrative model. *Decision Support Systems*, 54(1), pp. 461–70.
Chevalier, J. A., and Mayzlin, D. (2006). The effect of word of mouth on sales: Online book reviews. *Journal of Marketing Research*, 43(3), pp. 345–54.
Chevalier, S. (2024). Generative AI adoption commerce use worldwide. www.statista.com/statistics/1415436/generative-ai-adoption-commerce-use-worldwide/.
Chevalier, S. (2024). Top channels for product search worldwide 2023. www.statista.com/statistics/1034209/global-product-search-online-sources/.
Chevalier, S. (2024a). Generative AI use in selected commercial cases worldwide 2023. www.statista.com/statistics/1415436/generative-ai-adoption-commerce-use-worldwide/.
Chevalier, S. (2024b). Brands-believed-to-be-doing-an-excellent-job-providing-personalization 2021–2022. www.statista.com/statistics/1415811/brands-believed-to-be-doing-an-excellent-job-providing-personalization/.
Chintagunta, P. K., Gopinath, S., and Venkataraman, S. (2010). The effects of online user reviews on movie box office performance: Accounting for sequential rollout and aggregation across local markets. *Marketing Science*, 29(5), pp. 944–57.
Christensen, C. M., Raynor, M. and McDonald, R. (2015). What is disruptive innovation? *Harvard Business Review*, 93, pp. 44–53.
Christensen, F. (2022). Streaming stimulates the live concert industry: Evidence from YouTube. *International Journal of Industrial Organization*, 85, p. 102873.
Chung, H. D., Zhou, Y. M., and Ethiraj, S. (2023), Platform governance in the presence of within-complementor interdependencies: Evidence from the rideshare industry, *Management Science*, 70(2), pp. 799–814.
Chung, H. D., Zhou, Y. M., and Ethiraj, S. (2023). Platform governance in the presence of within-complementor interdependencies: Evidence from the rideshare industry, *Management Science*, 70(2), pp. 799–814.
Cialdini, R. B. (2009). *Influence: Science and practice* (5th edn). London: Pearson Education.
Ciulli, F., and Kolk, A. (2019). Incumbents and business model innovation for the sharing economy: Implications for sustainability. *Journal of Cleaner Production*, 214, pp. 995–1010.
Claudio, L. (2007). Waste couture: Environmental impact of the clothing industry. *Environmental Health Perspectives*, 115, pp. 448–54.
Clough, M. (2016). 6 Emotions That Will Make or Break Your Content Strategy. https://contently.com/strategist/2016/02/18/6-emotions-that-will-make-or-break-your-content-strategy/.

Coase, R. H. (1937). The nature of the firm. *Economica N.S*, 4, pp. 386–405.
Coen, D. (2018). *Generation Z and Millennials lead the way as more than a third turn to gig economy to supplement primary income.* Alix Partners. https://www.alixpartners.com/media-center/pressreleases/generation-z-and-millennials-lead-the-way/.
Condoor, S. (2004) Importance of teaching the history of technology'. In *Proceedings – Frontiers in Education Conference, FIE.* doi: 10.1109/fie.2004.1408508.
Confessore, N. (2018). *Cambridge Analytica and Facebook: The scandal and the fallout so far, The New York Times.* https://www.nytimes.com/2018/04/04/us/politics/cambridge-analytica-scandalfallout.html.
Conniff, R. (2011). What the Luddites really fought against. *Smithsonian Magazine*, www.smithsonianmag.com/history/what-the-luddites-really-fought-against-264412/.
Cooley, C. F. (1902). *Human nature and the social order.* New York: Scribner.
Coombs, C. R., Hislop, D., Taneva, S., and Barnard, S. (2020), The strategic impacts of Intelligent Automation for knowledge and service work: An interdisciplinary review. *Journal of Strategic Information Systems*, 29(4), pp. 1–30. https://doi.org/10.1016/j.jsis.2020.101600.
Cooper, L. A. et al. (2019), Robotic process automation in public accounting. *Accounting Horizons.* American Accounting Association, 33(4), pp. 15–35.
Coppola, D. (2023). Type of data used to personalize B2B digital experience Europe. www.statista.com/statistics/1384311/type-of-data-used-to-personalize-b2b-digital-experience-europe/.
Coyle, D. (2018). Platform dominance: The shortcomings of antitrust policy. In M. Moore and D. Tambini (eds), *Digital dominance: The power of Google, Amazon, Facebook, and Apple* (pp. 50–70). Oxford: Oxford University Press.
Coyle, D. (2018). Platform dominance: The shortcomings of antitrust policy. In M. Moore, and D. Tambini (eds), *Digital dominance: The power of Google, Amazon, Facebook, and Apple* (pp. 50–70). Oxford: Oxford University Press.
Crandall, D., Cosley, D. Huttenlocher, D. Kleinberg, J., and Suri, S. (2008). Feedback effects between similarity and social influence in online communities. *Proceedings of the 14th ACM International conference on Knowledge discovery and data mining*, pp. 160–8. doi: 10.1145/1401890.1401914.
Cropanzano, R. et al. (2017). Social exchange theory: A critical review with theoretical remedies. *Academy of Management Annals*, 11(1), pp. 479–516.
Cusumano, M. A., Gawer, A., and Yoffie, D. B. (2019). *The business of platforms: Strategy in the age of digital competition, innovation, and power.* HarperBusiness.
Daly, H. (1993). Steady-state economics: A new paradigm. *New Literary History*, 24(4), pp. 811–16.
Daly, R. P. (1956), Integrated data processing with the Univac file computer. In *Proceedings of the Western Joint Computer Conference, AIEE-IRE 1956.* New York: Association for Computing Machinery, pp. 95–8.
Daugherty, P. R., and Wilson, H. J. (2018). *Human + machine: Reimagining work in the age of AI.* Cambridge: Harvard Business Review Press.
Davis, M. E., and Hoyt, E. (2020). A longitudinal study of piece rate and health: evidence and implications for workers in the US gig economy. *Public Health*, 180, 1–9.
Day, H. I., Maynes, F., and Spring, L. (1972). Prior knowledge and the desire for information. *Canadian Journal of Behavioral Science*, 4, 330–7.
De Keyzer, F. et al. (2022) How and when personalized advertising leads to brand attitude, click, and WOM intention. *Journal of Advertising*, 51(1), pp. 39–56.

De La Torre, G., Rad, P., and Choo, K. (2020). Driverless vehicle security: Challenges and future research opportunities. *Future Generation Computer Systems*, 108, pp. 1092–1111.

de Meza, D., and Lockwood, B. (1998) Does asset ownership always motivate managers? Outside options and the property rights theory of the firm. *Quarterly Journal of Economics*, 113(2), pp. 361–86.

De Stefano, V. (2015). The rise of the just-in-time workforce: On-demand work, crowdwork, and labor protection in the gig-economy. *Comparative Labor Law and Policy Journal*, 37, p. 471.

Deaux, K. (1997). Social identification. In E. T. Higgins and A. W. Kruglanski (eds), *Social psychology: Handbook of basic principles* (pp. 777–98). The Guilford Press.

Dell'Era, C., and Landoni, P. (2014). Living lab: A methodology between user-centered and participatory design, *Creativity and Innovation Management*, 23(2), pp. 137–54.

Deloitte (2015). The robots are coming – A Deloitte Insight report. https://www2.deloitte.com/content/dam/Deloitte/uk/Documents/finance/ deloitte-uk-finance-robots-are-coming.pdf.

Deloitte (2023). Connectivity mobile trends survey. https://www2.deloitte.com/xe/en/insights/industry/telecommunications/connectivity-mobile-trends-survey/2023/data-privacy-and-security.html.

Deloitte (2023). Sustainable consumer behaviour and lifestyle. www2.deloitte.com/uk/en/pages/consumer-business/articles/sustainable-consumer.html.

Delrahim, M. (2019). Blind[ing] me with science: Antitrust, data, and digital markets – challenges to antitrust in a changing economy *Harvard Law School*, Cambridge, MA, 8 November 2019. Department of Justice. https://www.justice.gov/opa/speech/file/1217071/download.

Dencik, L., and Kaun, A. (2020). Datafication and the welfare state. *Global Perspectives*, 1(1), 1–8. https://doi.org/10.1525/gp.2020.12912.

Denning, S. (2014). An economy of access is opening for business: Five strategies for success. *Strategy & Leadership*, 42(4), pp. 14–21.

DeSteno, D. et al. (2004). Discrete emotions and persuasion: The role of emotion-induced expectancies. *Journal of Personality and Social Psychology*, 86(1), p. 43.

Dezeen (2021). All together now co-living co-working. www.dezeen.com/2021/06/10/all-together-now-co-living-co-working/.

Dhir, A. et al. (2019). Antecedents and consequences of social media fatigue. *International Journal of Information Management*, 48, pp. 193–202.

Dickson, M., Loker, S., and Eckman, M. (2009). *Social responsibility in the global apparel industry*. New York: Fairchild Books.

Dikstein, L., and Gurwitz, C. (2018). The future of operations-Beyond process automation. https://www2.deloitte.com/content/dam/Deloitte/global/Images/infograp hics/gx-consulting-foo-beyond-process-automation-info.pdf.

Dimov, D. (2007). From opportunity insight to opportunity intention: The importance of person-situation learning match. *Entrepreneurship Theory and Practice*, 31(4), 561–83.

Dinev, T., Hart, P., and Mullen, M. (2008). Internet privacy concerns and beliefs about government surveillance – An empirical investigation. *Journal of Strategic Information Systems*, 17, pp. 214–33.

Dirican, C. (2015). The impacts of robotics, artificial intelligence on business and economics, *Procedia – Social and Behavioural Sciences*, 195, pp. 564–73.

Dissanayake, G., and Sinha, P. (2015). An examination of the product development process for fashion remanufacturing. *Resources, Conservation and Recycling*, 104, pp. 94–102.

Dogan, M., Jacquillat, A., and Yildirim, P. (2024). Strategic automation and decision-making authority. *Journal of Economics Management and Strategy*, 33(1), pp. 203–46.

Donnelly, L. (2018). Robots are better than doctors at diagnosing some cancers, major study finds. *The Telegraph*. Available at: https://web.archive.org/web/20210617013241/https://www.telegraph.co.uk/news/2018/05/28/robots-better-doctors-diagnosing-cancers-major-study-finds/.

Donovan, S. A., Bradley, D. H., and Shimabukuru, J. O. (2016). *What does the gig economy mean for workers*? Congressional Research Service: Report, pp. 1–16.

Duggan, J. et al. (2020). Algorithmic management and app-work in the gig economy: A research agenda for employment relations and HRM. *Human Resource Management Journal*, 30(1), pp. 114–32.

Dushnitsky, G., Piva, E., and Rossi-Lamastra, C. (2022), Investigating the mix of strategic choices and performance of transaction platforms: Evidence from the crowdfunding setting, *Strategic Management Journal*, 43(3), pp. 563–98.

Dutta, D. et al. (2022) Augmented employee voice and employee engagement using artificial intelligence-enabled Chatbots: A field study, *International Journal of Human Resource Management*, 34(12), pp. 2451–2480.

Eckhardt, G., and Bardhi, F. (2012). Access-based consumption: The case of car sharing. *Journal of Consumer Research*, 39(4), pp. 881–98.

Edward, M., and Sahadev, S. (2012). Modeling the consequences of customer confusion in a service marketing context: An empirical study. *Journal of Services Research*, 12(2), pp. 127–46.

Eirinaki, M., and Vazirgiannis, M. (2003). Web mining for web personalization. *ACM Transactions on Internet Technology*, 3(1), pp. 1–27.

Elegido, J. M. (2011). The ethics of price discrimination. *Business Ethics Quarterly*, 21(4), pp. 633–60.

Ellsworth, P. C., and Scherer, K. R. (2003). *Appraisal processes in emotion*. Oxford: Oxford University Press.

EMF (2012). Towards the circular economy: Economic business rationale for an accelerated transition. https://www.ellenmacarthurfoundation.org/towards-a-circular-economy-business-rationale-for-an-accelerated-transition.

EMF (2017). A new textiles economy: Redesigning fashion's future. https://www.ellenmacarthurfoundation.org/assets/downloads/publications/A-New-Textiles-Economy_Full-Report.pdf.

Erev, I., Ert, E., and Yechiam, E. (2008). Loss aversion, diminishing sensitivity, and the effect of experience on repeated decisions. *Journal of Behavioral Decision Making*, 21(5), pp. 575–97.

Ert, E., and Fleischer, A. (2019). The evolution of trust in Airbnb: A case of home rental. *Annals of Tourism Research*, 75, pp. 279–87.

Estlund, C. (2018). What should we do after work? Automation and employment law. *The Yale Law Journal*, pp. 254–326.

Etter, M., Fieseler, C., and Whelan, G. (2019). Sharing economy, sharing responsibility? Corporate social responsibility in the digital age. *Journal of Business Ethics*, 159(4), p. 935.

Evens, T., and Donders, K. (2018). *Platform power and policy in transforming television markets*. Cham: Palgrave Macmillan.
Evie, T. (2020). Siemens' talent team is saving 30% of time with an AI employee, AI Interview Scheduling Tool for Recruiters. https://www.evie.ai/blog/siemens-talent-team-saving-30-time-with-ai-employee.
EY (2019). Global fintech adoption index. Available at: www.assets.ey.com/content/dam/ey-sites/ey-com/en_gl/topics/banking-and-capital-markets/ey-global-fintech-adoption-index.pdf.
EY.com. (2018). How do you teach AI the value of trust? https://www.ey.com/Publication/vwLUAssets/ey-how-do-you-teach-ai-the-value-of-tr ust/$FILE/ey-how-do-you-teach-ai-the-value-of-trust.pdf.
Fan, H., and Poole, M. S. (2006). What is personalization? Perspectives on the design and implementation of personalization in information systems. *Journal of Organizational Computing and Electronic Commerce*, 16(3–4), pp. 179–202.
Felson, M., and Spaeth, J. (1978). Community structure and collaborative consumption: A routine activity approach. *American Behavioral Scientist*, 21(4), pp. 614–24.
Feyen, E. et al. (2021). Fintech and the digital transformation of financial services: Implications for market structure and public policy. *Bank for International Settlement (BIS) Papers, No 117*.
Fisher, M., Gallino, S., and Li, J. (2018). Competition-based dynamic pricing in online retailing: A methodology validated with field experiments. *Management Science*, 64(6), pp. 2496–514.
Floridi, L. (2016). Mature information societies-A matter of expectations. *Philosophy and Technology*, 29(1), pp. 1–4.
Floridi, L., and Sanders, J. (2004). On the morality of artificial agents. *Minds and Machines*, 14(3), pp. 349–79.
Foerderer, J. (2020). Interfirm exchange and innovation in platform ecosystems: evidence from apple's worldwide developers conference, Management Science, 66(10), pp. 4359–4919.
Fountain, C. (2024). *Freelance statistics* (2024 Ed.). www.ddiy.co/freelance-statistics/.
Fraiberger, S., and Sundararajan, A. (2015). *Peer-to-peer rental markets in the sharing economy*. Working Papers 15–19, NET Institute.
Franke, N., and Hader, C. (2014). Mass or only 'niche customization'? Why we should interpret configuration toolkits as learning instruments. *Journal of Product Innovation Management*, 31(6), pp. 1214–34.
Franke, N., and Schreier, M. (2008). Product uniqueness as a driver of customer utility in mass customization. *Marketing Letters*, 19(2), pp. 93–107.
Franke, N., Keinz, P., and Steger, C. J. (2009). Testing the value of customization: when do customers really prefer products tailored to their preferences? *Journal of Marketing*, 73(5), pp. 103–21.
Freedman, S., Lin, H., and Prince, J. (2018). Information technology and patient health: Analyzing outcomes, populations, and mechanisms. *American Journal of Health Economics*, 4(1), pp. 51–79.
Frey, C. B., and Osborne, M. A. (2017). The future of employment: How susceptible are jobs to computerisation? *Technological Forecasting and Social Change*, 114, pp. 254–80.
Friedman, G. (2014). Workers without employers: Shadow corporations and the rise of the gig economy. *Review of Keynesian Economics*, 2(2), pp. 171–88.

FSB (2021). FinTech, Financial Stability Board. https://www.fsb.org/work-of-the-fsb/financial-innovation-and-structuralchange/fintech/.
Fu, S., et al. (2020). Social media overload, exhaustion, and use discontinuance: Examining the effects of information overload, system feature overload, and social overload. *Information Processing & Management*, 57(6), p. 102307.
Ganatra, N., and Pandya, J. (2023). The transformative impact of artificial intelligence on HR practices and employee experience: A review. *Journal of Management Research and Analysis*, 10(2), pp. 106–11.
Geissdoerfer, M. et al. (2017). *The circular economy – A new sustainability paradigm? Journal of Cleaner Production*, 143, pp. 757–68.
Ghemawat, P., and Nueno, J. L. (2006). Zara: Fast fashion. *Harvard Business School Publishing Harvard Business School Case*, 703–497.
Ghosh, D. (2019, 30 May). Don't break up Facebook – treat it like a utility. *Harvard Business Review*. https://hbr.org/2019/05/dont-break-up-facebook-treat-it-like-a-utility.
Gibbons R., and Roberts, J. (2013) *The handbook of organizational economics*. Princeton, NJ: Princeton University Press.
Girish, D. (2020). The social dilemma' review: Unplug and run. *The New York Times*. https://www.nytimes.com/2020/09/09/movies/thesocial-dilemma-review.html.
Girish, D. (2020). The Social dilemma' review: Unplug and run. *The New York Times*. https://www.nytimes.com/2020/09/09/movies/thesocial-dilemma-review.html.
Goffman, E. (1967). *Interaction ritual: Essays in face-to-face behaviour*. Chicago: Aldine Press.
Gomez-Aguilar, A. (2020). *Content bubbles: How platforms filter what we see*. IGI Global.
Gomez-Aguilar, A. (2020). *Content bubbles: How platforms filter what we see*. IGI Global.
Gopalakrishnan, S., and Matthews, D. (2018). Collaborative consumption: A business model analysis of second-hand fashion. *Journal of Fashion Marketing and Management*, 22(3), pp. 354–68.
Gour, A., Aggarwal, S., and Erdem, M. (2021). Reading between the lines: Analyzing online reviews by using a multi-method Web-analytics approach. *International Journal of Contemporary Hospitality Management*, 33(2), pp. 490–512.
Grad, B. (2007). The creation and the demise of VisiCalc. https://www.semanticscholar.org/paper/The-Creation-and-the-Demise-of-VisiCalc-Grad/6287185ed8390cbf88641853df7181a2b76945a3.
Granovetter, M. (1985). Economic action and social structure: The problem of embeddedness. *American Journal of Sociology*, 91(3), pp. 481–510.
Granovetter, M. (1985). Economic action and social structure: The problem of embeddedness. *American Journal of Sociology*, 91(3), pp. 481–510.
Graßmann, C., and Schermuly, C. C. (2020). Coaching with artificial intelligence: Concepts and capabilities. *Human Resource Development Review*, 20(1), p. 153448432098289.
Green, B. P. (2018). Ethical reflections on artificial intelligence, *Scientia et Fides*, 6(2), pp. 9–31.
Grensing-Pophal, L. (2022). The role of AI in retaining top talent. SHRM. https://www.shrm.org/resourcesandtools/hr-topics/technology/pages/the-role-of-ai-in-retaining-top-talent.aspx.
Griliches, Z. (1957). Hybrid corn: An exploration in the economics of technological change. *Econometrica*, 25(4), 501–522.

Groover, M. (2018). Automation, Encyclopedia Britannica. https://www.britannica.com/technology/automation.
Gu, B. et al. (2007). Competition among virtual communities and user valuation: The case of investing-related communities. *Information Systems Research*, 18(1), pp. 68–85.
Gu, X., Kannan, P. K., and Ma, L. (2018). Selling the premium in freemium. *Journal of Marketing*, 82(6), pp. 10–27.
Gueye, S. (2021). The fashion industry can move away from the take-make-waste model – and signs of change are evident. https://www.ellenmacarthurfoundation.org/articles/the-trends-and-trailblazers-creating-a-circular-economy-for-fashion.
Guldmann, E., and Huulgaard, R. D. (2020). Barriers to circular business model innovation: A multiple-case study. *Journal of Cleaner Production*, 243, p. 118160.
Gulliford, F., and Parker D. (2019). AI: the HR revolution. *Strategic HR Review*, 18(2), pp. 52–5.
Guo, J., Wang, X., and Wu, Y. (2020). Positive emotion bias: Role of emotional content from online customer reviews in purchase decisions. *Journal of Retailing and Consumer Services*, 52, p. 101891.
Guo, X. (2019). Research on the transition from financial accounting to management accounting under the background of artificial intelligence. *Journal of Physics: Conference Series*, 1345(4), p. 042031.
Guo, Z. X. et al. (2011). Applications of artificial intelligence in the apparel industry: A review. *Textile Research Journal*, 81(18), pp. 1871–92.
Gupta, M., Semwal, S., and Bali, S. (2021) Financial portfolio optimization: An AI Based Decision-Making Approach. In *Industry 4.0, AI, and Data Science* (pp. 231–40). CRC Press.
Guskova, M. F., and Nepopushcheva, A. O. (2019). The Management and Automation of Manufacturing Processes. In *Proceedings of the 2019 IEEE InternationalConference*, Institute of Electrical and Electronics Engineers Inc., pp. 8–10. doi: 10.1109/ITQMIS.2019.8928326.
Guttentag, D. (2013). Airbnb: disruptive innovation and the rise of an informal tourism accommodation sector. *Current Issues in Tourism*, 18(12), pp. 1192–217.
Gvili, Y., and Levy, S. (2023). I share, Therefore I trust: A moderated mediation model of the influence of eWOM engagement on social commerce. *Journal of Business Research*, 166, p. 114131.
Haddad, C., and Hornuf, L. (2019). The emergence of the global fintech market: Economic and technological determinants. *Small Business Economics*, 53(1), pp. 81–105.
Haenlein, M., and Kaplan, A. (2019). A brief history of artificial intelligence: On the past, present, and future of artificial intelligence. *California Management Review*, 61(4), pp. 5–14.
Haggart, B. (2020). Global platform governance and the internet-governance impossibility theorem. *Journal of Digital Media & Policy*, 11(3), pp. 321–39.
Hajli, N. et al. (2017) A social commerce investigation of the role of trust in a social networking site on purchase intentions. *Journal of Business Research*, 71, pp. 133–41.
Halaburda, H., and Yehezkel, Y. (2019). Focality advantage in platform competition. *Journal of Economics & Management Strategy*, 28(1), pp. 49–59.
Haley, L., (2023). The European Union's proposed artificial intelligence regulation on recruiting and hiring processes, *Scitech Lawyer*, 19(3), pp. 26–30.
Hamari, J., Sjöklint, M., and Ukkonen, A. (2016). The sharing economy: Why people participate in collaborative consumption. *Journal of the Association for Information Science and Technology*, 67(9), pp. 2047–59.

Hann, I. et al. (2005). *Analysing online information privacy concerns: An information processing theory approach. System Sciences* – Annual Hawaii International Conference, 1–10.

Harinck, F. et al. (2007). When gains loom larger than losses: Reversed loss aversion for small amounts of money. *Psychological Science*, 18(12), pp. 1099–110.

Hariri, R. H., Fredericks, E. M., and Bowers, K. M. (2019). Uncertainty in big data analytics: Survey, opportunities, and challenges, *Journal of Big Data*, 6(1), pp. 1–16.

Harley, A. (2016). *Prospect theory and loss aversion: How users make decisions.* https://www.nngroup.com/articles/prospect-theory/.

Harris, S. D., and Krueger, A. B. (2015). *A proposal for modernizing labor laws for twenty-first-century work: The 'independent worker'* (pp. 2015–10). Washington, DC: Brookings.

Harvey, G. et al. (2017). Neo-villeiny and the service sector: The case of hyper flexible and precarious work in fitness centres. *Work, Employment and Society*, 31(1), pp. 19–35.

Harwood, R. (1990). Sustainable agricultural systems. In R. Harwood, ed., *A history of sustainable agriculture* (1st edn). Ankeny: Soil and Water Conservation Society, pp. 3–19.

Hayes, J. L. et al. (2021). The influence of consumer–brand relationship on the personalized advertising privacy calculus in social media. *Journal of Interactive Marketing*, 55(1), pp. 16–30.

He, J. et al. (2019). The practical implementation of artificial intelligence technologies in medicine. *Nature Medicine*, 25(1), pp. 30–6.

Healy, J., Nicholson, D., and Pekarek, A. (2017). Should we take the gig economy seriously?' *Labour & Industry: A Journal of the Social and Economic Relations of Work*, 27(3), pp. 232–48.

Heinrichs, H. (2013). Sharing economy: A potential new pathway to sustainability. *Gaia*, 22(4), pp. 228–31.

Helberger, N. (2020). The political power of platforms: How current attempts to regulate misinformation amplify opinion power. *Digital Journalism*, 8(6), pp. 842–54.

Helberger, N. (2020). The political power of platforms: How current attempts to regulate misinformation amplify opinion power. *Digital Journalism*, 8(6), pp. 842–54.

Heo, C. (2016). Sharing economy and prospects in tourism research. *Annals of Tourism Research*, 58, pp. 166–70.

Herzberg, F., Mausner, B., and Snyderman, B. (1959). *The motivation to work* (2nd edn). Wiley.

Hess, T. (2016). Options for formulating a digital transformation strategy. *MIS Quarterly Executive*, 15(2), pp. 123–39.

Hestad, M. (2013). *Branding and product design: An integrated perspective.* Surrey: Gower Publishing Limited.

Heung, C., Xiao, B., and Liu, I. (2014). Do actions speak louder than voices? the signaling role of social information cues in influencing consumer purchase decisions. *Decision Support Systems*, 65, pp. 50–8.

Hirscher, A. L., Niinimäki, K., and Joyner, J. C. M. (2018). Social manufacturing in the fashion sector: New value creation through alternative design strategies? *Journal of Cleaner Production*, 172, pp. 4544–54.

Ho, S. Y. and Bodoff, D. (2014). The effects of Web personalization on user attitude and behavior. *MIS Quarterly*, 38(2), pp. 497–A10.

Hobson, K., and Lynch, N. (2016). Diversifying and de-growing the circular economy: Radical social transformation in a resource-scarce world. *Futures*, 82, pp. 15–25.

Hoffreumon, C., Forman, C., and van Zeebroeck, N. (2024). Make or buy your artificial intelligence? In search of complementarities in technology sourcing. *Journal of Economics & Management Strategy*, 33(2), pp. 452–79.

Hong, W., Chan, F. K., and Thong, J. Y. (2021). Drivers and inhibitors of internet privacy concern: A multidimensional development theory perspective. *Journal of Business Ethics*, 168(3), pp. 539–64.

Horng, S. M., and Wu, C. L. (2020). How behaviors on social network sites and online social capital influence social commerce intentions. *Information & Management*, 57(2), p. 103176.

Hovenkamp, H. (2019). Platforms and the rule of reason: The American express case. *Columbia Business Law Review*, 2019(1), pp. 34–92.

Hovland, C. I., and Weiss, W. (1951). The influence of source credibility on communication effectiveness. *Public Opinion Quarterly*, 15(4), p. 635.

Huang, H., and Benyoucef, M. (2013) From e-commerce to social commerce: A close look at design features. *Electronic Commerce Research and Applications*, 12(4), pp. 246–59.

Hui, X., Reshef, O., and Zhou, L. (2023). The short-term effects of generative artificial intelligence on employment: Evidence from an online labor market. SSRN: http://dx.doi.org/10.2139/ssrn.4527336.

Huws, U. et al. (2017). *Work in the European gig economy – Research results from the UK, Sweden, Germany, Austria, the Netherlands, Switzerland and Italy*. Brussels: FEPS – Foundation for European Progressive Studies. Available at: https://uhra.herts.ac.uk/bitstream/handle/2299/19922/Huws_U._Spencer_ N.H._Syrdal_D.S._Holt_K._2017_.pdf?sequence=2.

IAPP (2023). IAPP privacy and consumer trust report. https://iapp.org/resources/article/privacy-and-consumer-trust-summary/.

IBM (2023). IBM Consulting. https://www.ibm.com/consulting.

ICAEW (2019). How artificial intelligence will impact accounting. https://www.icaew.com/technical/technology/artificial-intelligence/artificial-intelligence-articles/how-artificial-intelligence-will-impact-accounting.

ING (2020). Learning from consumers: How shifting demands are shaping companies' circular economy transition. https://www.ingwb.com/media/3076131/ing-circular-economy-survey-2020-learning-from-consumers.

Inzelt, G., Szabó, T., and Kriston, A. (2010). The marriage of car sharing and hydrogen economy: A possible solution to the main problems of urban living. *International Journal of Hydrogen Energy*, 35(23), pp. 12697–708.

Iosifidis, P., and Andrews, L. (2019). Regulating the internet intermediaries in a post-truth world: Beyond media policy? *International Communication Gazette*, 82(3), pp. 211–30.

Iphofen, R., and Kritikos, M. (2019). Regulating artificial intelligence and robotics: Ethics by design in a digital society. *Contemporary Social Science*, 16(2) pp. 170–84.

Iqbal, M. (2024). Uber revenue and usage statistics. www.businessofapps.com/data/uber-statistics/.

Jackson, A. (2016). Your content marketing should evoke emotion. http://www.findandconvert.com/2016/06/your-content-marketing-should-evoke-emotion.

Jackson, J. C., Castelo, N., and Gray, K. (2020). Could a rising robot workforce make humans less prejudiced? *American Psychologist*, 75(7), pp. 969–82.

Jackson, S. J., Bailey, M., and Welles, B. F. (2020). *#Hashtagactivism: Networks of race and gender justice*. Cambridge, MA: MIT Press.

Jackson, T. (2001). The process of fashion trend development leading to a season. In *Fashion marketing: Contemporary issues*, ed. T. Hines, and M. Bruce, 121–32. Section 7. Oxford: Elsevier Butterworth-Heinemann.

Jain, G., Paul, J., and Shrivastava, A. (2021). Hyper-personalization, co-creation, digital clienteling and transformation. *Journal of Business Research*, 124, pp. 12–23.

Jarvis, R., and Han, H. (2021). FinTech innovation: Review and future research directions. *International Journal of Banking, Finance and Insurance Technologies*, 1(1), pp. 79–102.

Jensen, M. C., and Meckling, W. H. (1976). Theory of the firm: Managerial behavior, agency costs and ownership structure. *Journal of Financial Economics*, 3(4), pp. 305–60.

Johansson, A. (2017). Surprise Is Your Best Friend in Content Marketing: Here's How to Use It. http://www.coolsiteoftheday.com/surprise-best-friend-content-marketing-heres-use/.

John, N. A. (2013). The social logics of sharing. *The Communication Review*, 16(3), pp. 113–31.

Johnson, J. P., Rhodes, A., and Wildenbeest, M. (2023). Platform design when sellers use pricing algorithms. *Econometrica*, 91(5), pp. 1841–79.

Johnston, E. et al. (2021). The interest, knowledge, and usage of artificial intelligence in accounting: Evidence from accounting professionals. *Accounting & Taxation*, 13 (1), pp. 45–58.

Jones, C. I., and Tonetti, C. (2020). Nonrivalry and the economics of data. *American Economic Review*, 110(9), pp. 2819–58.

Just, N. (2018). Governing online platforms: Competition policy in times of platformization. *Telecommunications Policy*, 42(5), pp. 386–94.

Kahneman, D., and Tversky, A. (1979). Prospect theory: An analysis of decision under risk. *Econometrica*, 47 (March), pp. 263–92.

Kaiser, U., Schreier, M., and Janiszewski, C. (2017). The self-expressive customization of a product can improve performance. *Journal of Marketing Research*, 54(5), pp. 816–31.

Kaneko, K., Kishita, Y., and Umeda, Y. (2018). Toward developing a design method of personalization: Proposal of a personalization procedure. *Procedia CIRP*, 69 (2018), pp. 740–5.

Kang, I. G., Croft, B., and Bichelmeyer, B. A. (2020). Predictors of turnover intention in U.S. federal government workforce: Machine Learning evidence that perceived comprehensive HR practices predict turnover intention. *Public Personnel Management*, 50(4), pp. 538–58.

Karbon (2023). The state of AI in Accounting 2024. https://karbonhq.com/resources/state-of-ai-accounting-report-2024/.

Karimi, J., and Walter, Z. (2015). The role of dynamic capabilities in responding to digital disruption: A factor-based study of the newspaper industry. *Journal of Management Information Systems*, 32(1), pp. 39–81.

Katz, M. L. (2019). Multisided platforms, big data, and a little antitrust policy. *Review of Industrial Organization*, 54(4), pp. 695–716.

Kazim, E. et al. (2021) Systematizing audit in algorithmic recruitment. *Journal of Intelligence*, 9(3), p. 46.

Kell, J. (2013). Avis to buy car sharing service Zipcar. WSJ. Available at: http://facweb.northseattle.edu/zasmulski/BUS101/Avis%20to%20Buy%20CarSharing%20Service%20Zipcar%20-%20WSJ.pdf.

Keller, R. et al. (2019). Affordance- Experimentation- Actualisation Theory in Artifical Intelligence Research: A predictive Maintenance Story. *40th International Conference on Information Systems*, pp. 1–17.

Kennedy, J. (2020, July 23). *Monopoly myths: Do Internet platforms threaten competition?* Information Technology & Innovation Foundation. https://itif.org/publications/2020/07/23/monopoly-myths-do-internet-platforms-threaten-competition.

Kenney, M., and Zysman, J. (2016). The rise of the platform economy. *Issues in Science and Technology*, 32(3), p. 61.

Keynes, J. M. (1930). *Economic Possibilities for our Grandchildren*, Essays in Persuasion, New York: W.W. Norton, 1963, pp. 358–73.

Khan, L. (2017). Amazon's antitrust paradox. *Yale Law Journal*, 126(3), pp. 710–805.

Khan, L. (2019). The separation of platforms and commerce. *Columbia Law Review*, 119(4), pp. 973–1098.

Khan, R., Lewis, M., and Singh, V. (2009). Dynamic customer management and the value of one-to-one marketing. *Marketing Science*, 28(6), pp. 1063–79.

Ki, C., and Kim, Y. (2019). The mechanism by which social media influencers persuade consumers: The role of consumers' desire to mimic. *Psychology & Marketing*, 36(10), pp. 905–22.

Kirchherr, J., Reike, D., and Hekkert, M. (2017). Conceptualizing the circular economy: An analysis of 114 definitions. *Resources, Conservation & Recycling Advances*, 127, pp. 221–32.

Kirzner, I. M. (1973). *Competition and entrepreneurship*. Chicago: University of Chicago Press.

Kirzner, I. M. (1997). Entrepreneurial discovery and the competitive market process: An Austrian approach. *Journal of Economic Literature*, 35(1), pp. 60–85.

Koh, B., Raghunathan, S., and Nault, B. R. (2017). Is voluntary profiling welfare enhancing? *MIS Quarterly*, 41(1), pp. 23–41.

Kokolakis, S. (2017). Privacy attitudes and privacy behaviour: A review of current research on the privacy paradox phenomenon. *Computers & Security*, 64, p. 122.

Konovalova, V., Ashurbekov, R., and Zakharov, D. (2023). Artificial intelligence systems in human resource management: Potential advantages and conditions for their implementation. *Proceedings of Computer Science and Information Technologies 2023 Conference*. doi: 10.51408/csit2023_71.

Konstan, J. A., and Riedl, J. (2012). Recommender systems: From algorithms to user experience. *User Modeling and User-Adapted Interaction*, 22(1–2), pp. 101–23.

Koren, Y. (2010). *The global manufacturing revolution*. Wiley.

Koutsabasis, P. et al. (2008). A descriptive reference framework for the personalization of e-business applications. *Electronic Commerce Research*, 8(3), pp. 173–92.

Koutsimpogiorgos, N. et al. (2020). Conceptualizing the gig economy and its regulatory problems. *Policy & Internet*, 12(4), pp. 525–45.

Kozlowski, A., Searcy, C., and Bardecki, M. (2018). The redesign canvas: Fashion design as a tool for sustainability. *Journal of Cleaner Production*, 183, pp. 194–207.

Kramer, T. (2007) The effect of measurement task transparency on preference construction and evaluations of personalized recommendations, *Journal of Marketing Research*, 44(2), pp. 224–33.

Krishnaraju, V., and Mathew, S. K. (2013). Web personalization research: An information systems perspective. *Journal of Systems and Information Technology*, 15(3), pp. 254–68.

Krishnaraju, V., and Mathew, S. K. (2013). Web personalization research: An information systems perspective. *Journal of Systems and Information Technology*, 15(3), pp. 254–68.

Kshetri, N. (2018). Blockchain's roles in meeting key supply chain management objectives. *International Journal of Information Management*, 39, pp. 80–9. 24.

Kuhn, K. M., and Maleki, A. (2017). Micro-entrepreneurs, dependent contractors, and Instaserfs: Understanding online labour platform workforces. *Academy of Management Perspectives*, 31, pp. 183–200.

Kumar, V., Rajan, B., Venkatesan, R., and Lecinski, J. (2019). Understanding the role of Artificial Intelligence in personalized engagement marketing. *California Management Review*, 61(4), pp. 135–55.

Kummer, M., and Schulte, P. (2019). When private information settles the bill: Money and privacy in Google's market for smartphone applications. *Management Science*, 65(8), pp. 3470–94.

Kwon, K., and Kim, C. (2012). How to design personalization in a context of customer retention: Who personalizes what and to what extent? *Electronic Commerce Research and Applications*, 11(2), pp. 101–16.

Kwon, K., Cho, J., and Park, Y. (2010). How to best characterize the personalization construct for e-services. *Expert Systems with Applications*, 37(3), pp. 2232–40.

Lamberton, C. P., and Rose, R. L. (2012). When is ours better than mine? A framework for understanding and altering participation in commercial sharing systems. *Journal of Marketing*, 76, pp. 109–25.

Lazear, E. P., and Gibbs, M. (2009). *Personnel economics in practice* (2nd edn). Hoboken, NJ: John Wiley.

Le Vine, S., Zolfaghari, A., and Polak, J. (2014). *Carsharing: Evolution, challenges and opportunities*, Centre for Transport Studies, Imperial College London, 22th ACEA Report.

Leahy, J. (2013). Targeted consumer involvement: An integral part of successful new product development, *Research Technology Management*, 56(4), pp. 52–8.

Leal, G. P. A., Hor-Meyll, L. F., and de Paula Pessôa, L. A. G. (2014). Influence of virtual communities in purchasing decisions: The participants' perspective. *Journal of Business Research*, 67(5), pp. 882–90.

Lee, J. (2020). Access to finance for artificial intelligence regulation in the financial services industry. *European Business Organization Law Review*, 21(4), pp. 731–57.

Lee, J. E., and Watkins, B. (2016). YouTube vloggers' influence on consumer luxury brand perceptions and intentions. *Journal of Business Research*, 69, pp. 5753–60.

Lee, J. J. Y. et al. (2014). The financial impact of loyalty programs in the hotel industry: A Social Exchange Theory Perspective. *Journal of Business Research*, 67(10), pp. 2139–46.

Lee, M. K. et al. (2015, April). Working with machines: The impact of algorithmic and data-driven management on human workers. In *Proceedings of the 33rd annual ACM conference on human factors in computing systems*, pp. 1603–12.

Lee, Z. W. Y. et al. (2018). Why people participate in the sharing economy: an empirical investigation of Uber. *Internet Research*, 28(3), pp. 829–50.

Lewis, P. (1988) The executive computer; Lotus 1-2-3 Faces Up. March 13. www.nytimes.com/1988/03/13/business/the-executive-computer-lotus-1-2-3-faces-up-to-the-upstarts.html.

Li, C. (2019). The placebo effect in web-based personalization. *Telematics and Informatics*, 44, p. 101267.

Li, H., and Zhu, F. (2021). Information transparency, multihoming, and platform competition: A natural experiment in the daily deals market. *Management Science*, 67(7), pp. 4384–407.

Li, X., Wang, X., and Nault, B. R. (2024). Is personalized pricing profitable when firms can differentiate? *Management Science*, 70(7) pp. 4167–952.

Liang, T. P., and Turban, E. (2011). Introduction to the special issue social commerce: A research framework for social commerce. *International Journal of Electronic Commerce*, 16(2), pp. 5–14.
Libert, K., and Tynski, K. (2013). Research: The emotions that make marketing campaigns go viral. https://hbr.org/2013/10/research-the-emotions-that-make-marketing-campaigns-go-viral.
Liebowitz, J. (2013). *Big data and business analytics*. Boca Raton, Fl: Crc Press.
Lim, J. S., and Zhang, J. (2022). Adoption of AI-driven personalization in digital news platforms: An integrative model of technology acceptance and perceived contingency, *Technology in Society*, 69, p. 101965.
Lim, W. M. et al. (2022). Past, present, and future of customer engagement. *Journal of Business Research*, 140, 439–58.
Lin, X., and Kishore, R. (2021). Social media-enabled healthcare: A conceptual model of social media affordances, online social support, and health behaviors and outcomes. *Technological Forecasting and Social Change*, 166, p. 120574.
Lin, X., Wang, X., and Hajli, N. (2019). Building e-commerce satisfaction and boosting sales: The role of social commerce trust and its antecedents. *International Journal of Electronic Commerce*, 23(3), pp. 328–63.
Lindecrantz, E., Tjon Pian Gi, M., and Zerbi, S. (2020). *Personalizing the customer experience: Driving differentiation in retail*. McKinsey. https://www.mckinsey.com/industries/retail/our-insights/personalizing-the-customer- experience-driving-differentiation-in-retail.
Lisjak, M., Bonezzi, A., and Rucker, D. D. (2021). How marketing perks influence word of mouth. *Journal of Marketing*, 85(5), pp. 128–44.
Litvin, S. W., Goldsmith, R. E., and Pan, B. (2008). Electronic word-of-mouth in hospitality and tourism management. *Tourism Management*, 29, pp. 458–68.
Liyanaarachchi, G., Deshpande, S., and Weaven, S. (2021). Online banking and privacy: Redesigning sales strategy through social exchange. *International Journal of Bank Marketing*, 39(6), pp. 955–83.
Low, K. F., and Teo, E. G. (2017). Bitcoins and other cryptocurrencies as property? *Law, Innovation and Technology*, 9(2), pp. 235–68.
Lowe-Calverley, E., and Grieve E. (2021). Do the metrics matter? An experimental investigation of Instagram influencer effects on mood and body dissatisfaction. *Body Image*, 36, pp. 1–4.
Lu, B., Fan, W., and Zhou, M. (2016). Social presence, trust, and social commerce purchase intention: An empirical research. *Computers in Human Behavior*, 56, pp. 225–37.
Lusch, R., and Nambisan, S. (2015). Service innovation: A service-dominant logic perspective. *MIS Quarterly*, 39(1), pp. 155–75.
Lutz, C., and Newlands, G. (2018). Consumer segmentation within the sharing economy: The case of Airbnb. *Journal of Business Research*, 88, pp. 187–96.
Ma, L., Krishnan, R., and Montgomery, A. L. (2015). Latent homophily or social influence? An empirical analysis of purchase within a social network. *Management Science*, 61(2), pp. 454–73.
Madden, S. (2012). From databases to Big Data. *IEEE Internet Computing*, 16(3), pp. 4–6.
Maity, S. (2019). Identifying opportunities for artificial intelligence in the evolution of training and development practices. *Journal of Management Development*, 38(8), pp. 651–63.
Makridakis, S. (2017). The forthcoming Artificial Intelligence (AI) revolution: Its impact on society and firms. *Futures*, 90, pp. 46–60.
Malcom, T. (1970). *The luddites, machine breaking in regency England*. New York: Shoken.

Malos, S., Lester, G. V., and Virick, M. (2018). Uber drivers and employment status in the gig economy: Should corporate social responsibility tip the scales? *Employee Responsibilities and Rights Journal*, 30(4), pp. 239–51.

Manyika, J. et al. (2017). *A future that works: Automation, employment, and productivity.* McKinsey Global Institute.

Marr, B. (2019). *Artificial intelligence in practice: how 50 successful companies used AI and machine learning to solve problems.* Wiley.

Martin, K. D., and Murphy, P. E. (2017). The role of data privacy in marketing. *Journal of the Academy of Marketing Science*, 45(2), pp. 135–55.

Marvin, G., Jackson, M., and Alam, M. G. R. (2021). A Machine Learning Approach for Employee Retention Prediction. *EEE Region 10 Symposium (TENSYMP).* pp. 1–8, doi: 10.1109/TENSYMP52854.2021.9550921.

Matthews, R. C. O., Feinstein, C. H., and Odling-Smee, J. (1982). *British Economic Growth 1856–1973.* Oxford: Oxford University Press.

Matzler, K., Veider, V., and Kathan, W. (2015). *Adapting to the sharing economy.* Cambridge, MA: MIT.

Mayer-Schonberger, V. and Cukier, K. (2014). *Big data: A revolution that will transform how we live, work, and think.* New York: Houghton Mifflin Harcourt.

Mayzlin, D., Dover, Y., and Chevalier, J. (2014). Promotional reviews: An empirical investigation of online review manipulation. *American Economic Review*, 104, pp. 2421–55.

McAfee, A., and Brynjolfsson, E. (2012). Big data: The management revolution. *Harvard Business Review*, 90(10), pp. 61–7.

McDonough, W., and Braungart, M. (2002) *Cradle to cradle: Remarking the way we make things.* New York: North Point Press.

McGhin, T. et al. (2019). Blockchain in healthcare applications: Research challenges and opportunities. *Journal of Network and Computer Applications*, 135, pp. 62–75.

McIntyre, D. P., and Srinivasan, A. (2017). Networks, platforms, and strategy: Emerging views and next steps, *Strategic Management Journal*, 38(1), 141–60.

McKinsey (2017). *Jobs lost, jobs gained: Workforce transitions in a time of automation.* McKinsey Global Institute's 2017 report.

McKinsey (2021). Sign up now: Creating consumer and business value with subscriptions. https://www.mckinsey.com/capabilities/growth-marketing-and-sales/our-insights/sign-up-now-creating-consumer-and-business-value-with-subscriptions.

McLaren, D., and Agyeman, J. (2015). *Sharing cities: A case for truly smart and sustainable cities.* Cambridge, MA: MIT Press.

McLennan, S., Fiske, A., Tigard, D., Müller, R., Haddadin, S., and Buyx, A. (2022). Embedded ethics: A proposal for integrating ethics into the development of medical AI. *BMC Medical Ethics*, 23(1), p. 6.

Meadows, D. H. (1972). *The limits to growth; a report for the Club of Rome's project on the predicament of mankind.* New York: Universe Books.

Mehta, B. S., and Kumar, A. (2020). Future of work: The emerging gig economy. *Journal of Development Policy Review*, 1(1), pp. 10–16.

Mention, A. L. (2019). The future of fintech. *Research-Technology Management*, 62(4), pp. 59–63.

Meybaum, H. (2014). *The art of product design: Changing how things get made.* New Jersey: John Wiley.

Milgrom, P., and Roberts, J. (1992). *Economics, organization, and management.* California: Prentice-Hall.

Milian, E. Z., Spinola, M., and de Carvalho, M. M. (2019). FinTechs: A literature review and research agenda. *Electronic Commerce Research and Applications*, 34, Article ID: 100833. https://doi.org/10.1016/j.elerap.2019.100833.

Min, Ji-a (2018). AI recruitment: The future of automated recruiting, ideal. https://ideal.com/ai-recruitment/.

Mishkin, F. S., and Strahan, P. E. (1999). What will technology do to financial structure? NBER working paper, 6892.

Mittelstadt, B. D., and Floridi, L. (2016). The ethics of algorithms: Mapping the debate. *Big Data & Society*, 3(2), pp. 1–21. https://doi.org/10.1177/2053951716679679.

Moe, W.W., and Trusov, M. (2011). The value of social dynamics in online product ratings forums. *Journal of Marketing Research*, 48(3), pp. 444–56.

Mogaji, E., Balakrishnan, J., Nwoba, A. C., and Nguyen, N. P. (2021). Emerging-market consumers' interactions with banking chatbots. *Telematics and Informatics*, 65, p. 101711.

Mokyr, J., Vickers, C. and Ziebarth, L. (2015). The history of technological anxiety and the future of economic growth: Is this time different? *Journal of Economic Perspectives*, 29(3), pp. 31–50.

Moll, J., and Yigitbasioglu, O. (2019). The role of internet-related technologies in shaping the work of accountants: New directions for accounting research. *The British Accounting Review*, 51(6), p. 100833.

Moller, L. et al. (2017). Characterizing digital disruption in the general theory of disruptive innovation. In ISPIM Innovation Symposium ISPIM Conference. https://vbn.aau.dk/ws/portalfiles/portal/261533809/Characterizing_digital_disruption_in_the_ general_theory.pdf.

Mont, O. (2004). Drivers and barriers for shifting towards more service-oriented businesses: Analysis of the PSS field and contributions from Sweden. *The Journal of Sustainable Product Design*, 2(3/4), pp. 89–103.

Montes, G., and Goertzel, B. (2019). Distributed, decentralized, and democratized artificial intelligence. *Technological Forecasting and Social Change*, 141, pp. 354–8.

Montgomery, A. L., and Smith, M. D. (2009). Prospects for personalization on the internet. *Journal of Interactive Marketing*, 23(2), pp. 130–7.

Moran, G. (2012). Sleek design for the stroller set. *Entrepeneur*, 40(12), p. 89.

Mothersbaugh, D. L., Huhmann, B. A., and Franke, G. R. (2002). Combinatory and separative effects of rhetorical figures on consumers' effort and focus in ad processing. *Journal of Consumer Research*, 28(4), pp. 589–602.

Mugge, R., Schoormans, J. P., and Schifferstein, H. N. (2009). Emotional bonding with personalised products. *Journal of Engineering Design*, 20(5), pp. 467–76.

Mukendi, A. et al. (2020). Sustainable fashion: Current and future research directions. *European Journal of Marketing*, 54(11), pp. 2873–909.

Murphy, B. (2023). Jeff Bezos: 'the most important single thing is to focus obsessively on …, Inc. https://www.inc.com/Bill-Murphy-jr/bezos-most-important-single-thing-focus-obsessively-on-customer.html.

Murthi, B. P. S., and Sarkar, S. (2003). The role of the management sciences in research on personalization. *Management Science*, 49(10), pp. 1344–62.

Nagarajah, E. (2018). What does automation mean for the accounting profession? https://www.PwC.com/my/en/assets/press/1608-accountants-today-automation-impact-on-accounting-profession.pdf.

Najafabadi, M. M. et al. (2015) Deep learning applications and challenges in Big Data Analytics. *Journal of Big Data*, 2(1).

Nakamoto, S. (2008). *Bitcoin: A peer-to-peer electronic cash system*. Bitcoin.org.

Naylor, R. W., Lamberton, C. P., and West, P. M. (2012). Beyond the 'like' button: The impact of mere virtual presence on brand evaluations and purchase intentions in social media settings. *Journal of Marketing*, 76, pp. 105–20.

Neisser, H. P. (1942). 'Permanent' technological unemployment: Demand for commodities is not demand for labor. *American Economic Review*, 32, pp. 50–71.

Noy, S., and W. Zhang (2023). *Experimental evidence on the productivity effects of generative artificial intelligence*. SSRN 4375283.

Nunberg, G. (2016). *Goodbye jobs, hello 'gigs': How one word sums up a new economic reality*. NPR.org, 11 January 2016, https://npr.org/460698077/goodbye-jobs-hello-gigs-nunbergs-word-of-the-year-sums-up-a-new-economic-reality.

Oberauer, K., and Lange, E. B. (2008). Interference in verbal working memory: Distinguishing similarity-based confusion, feature overwriting, and feature migration. *Journal of Memory and Language*, 58(3), pp. 730–45.

Odlyzko, A. (2003). Privacy, economics, and price discrimination on the internet. In *Proceedings of the 5th International Conference on Electronic Commerce (ICEC '03)*. New York: ACM, pp. 355–66.

OECD. (2020). *AI and the future of work: Policy implications*. OECD Publishing.

Okazaki, S. et al. (2020). Understanding the strategic consequences of customer privacy concerns: a meta-analytic review, *Journal of Retailing*, 96(4), pp. 458–73.

Onnela, J.-P., and Reed-Tsochas, F. (2010). Spontaneous emergence of social influence in online systems. *Proceedings of the National Academy of Sciences of the United States of America*, 107(43), pp. 18375–80.

Oravec, J. (2018). Artificial intelligence, automation, and social welfare: Some ethical and historical perspectives on technological overstatement and hyperbole. *Ethics and Social Welfare*, 13(1), pp. 18–32.

Oskar, K and Pawel, P. (2020). The rise of fintech: A cross-country perspective. IESEG Working Paper Series 2020-ACF-07. DOI: https://dx.doi.org/10.2139/ssrn.3624456.

Ouimet, P., and Zarutskie, R. (2014). Who works for startups? The relation between firm age, employee age, and growth. *Journal of Financial Economics*, 112(3), pp. 386–407.

Owyang, J., Tran, C., and Silva, C. (2013). *The collaborative economy*. Altimeter.

Pan, Y., and Froese, F. J. (2023). An interdisciplinary review of AI and HRM: Challenges and future directions. *Human Resource Management Review*, 33(1), pp. 1–22.

Pappas, I. O. et al. (2016). Explaining online shopping behavior with fsQCA: The role of cognitive and affective perceptions. *Journal of Business Research*, 69(2), pp. 794–803.

Park, S., and Tussyadiah, I. P. (2020). How guests develop trust in hosts: An investigation of trust formation in P2P accommodation. *Journal of Travel Research*, 59(8), pp. 1402–12.

Parker, G., Van Alstyne, M., and Jiang, X. (2017). Platform ecosystems: How developers invert the firm. *MIS Quarterly*, 41(1), pp. 255–66.

Pedersen, E., Earley, R., and Andersen, K. (2019). From singular to plural: exploring organisational complexities and circular business model design. *Journal of Fashion Marketing and Management*, 23(3), pp. 308–26.

Peng, Y., and Chang, J. S. (2019). An exploration on the problems of replacing accounting professions by ai in the future. *ICIBE 2019*. Available at: http://dx.doi.org/10.1145/3364335.3364345.

Peppers, D., and Rogers, M. (1997). *The one-to-one future*. New York: Double Day Publications.
Perez, S. (2020). Instagram swaps out its 'Activity' tab for 'Shop' in new global test. https://techcrunch.com/2020/07/07/instagram-swaps-out-itsactivity-tab-for-shop-in-new-global-test/.
Perez-Vega, R. et al. (2021). Reshaping the contexts of online customer engagement behavior via Artificial Intelligence: A conceptual framework. *Journal of Business Research*, 129, pp. 902–10.
Perri, 6. (2001). Ethics, regulation and the new artificial intelligence, part II: autonomy and liability. *Information, Communication & Society*, 4(3), pp. 406–34.
Petropoulos, G. (2016). *An economic review on the collaborative economy*. European Parliament. http://www.europarl.europa.eu/RegData/etudes/IDAN/2016/595358/IPOL_ IDA(2016)595358_EN.pdf.
Petty, R. E., and Cacioppo, J. T. (1986). The elaboration likelihood model of persuasion. In: communication and persuasion (pp. 1–24). *Springer Series in Social Psychology*. New York: Springer. https://doi.org/10.1007/978-1-4612-4964-1_1.
Petty, R. E., and Cacioppo, J. T. (1986). The Elaboration Likelihood Model of persuasion. In L. Berkowitz (ed.), *Advances in experimental social psychology*, 19, pp. 123–205.
Pfiffelmann, J. et al. (2020) Personalized advertisements with integration of names and photographs: An eye-tracking experiment, *Journal of Business Research*, 111, pp. 196–207.
Philippon, T. (2016). *The fintech opportunity*, National Bureau of Economic Research, No. w22476, 10.3386/w22476.
Pierri, M. N., and Timmer, M. Y. (2020). *Tech in fin before fintech: Blessing or curse for financial stability*? International Monetary Fund.
Piketty, T. (2014). *Capital in the twenty-first century*. Translated by Arthur Goldhammer. Harvard University Press.
Pittman, M. (2015). Creating, consuming, and connecting: Examining the relationship between social media engagement and loneliness. *The Journal of Social Media in Society*, 4(1) pp. 66–98. doi:10.1207/S15327752JPA6601_2.
Plantin, J.-C. et al. (2018). Infrastructure studies meet platform studies in the age of google and Facebook. *New Media & Society*, 20(1), pp. 293–310.
Poell, T., Nieborg, D., and van Dijck, J. (2019). Platformisation. *Internet Policy Review*, 8(4), pp. 1–13.
Polak, J., Zolfaghari, A., and Vine, S. (2014). *Carsharing: evolution, challenges and opportunities*. Centre for Transport Studies: Imperial College London.
Polanski, P. P. (2018). Some thoughts on data portability in the aftermath of the Cambridge Analytica scandal. *Journal of European Consumer and Market Law*, 7(4), pp. 141–6.
Polanyi, K. (1944). *The great transformation: The political and economic origins of our time*. Farrar & Rinehart.
Popiel, P. (2020). Addressing platform power: The politics of competition policy. *Journal of Digital Media & Policy*, 11(3), pp. 341–60.
Popiel, P. (2022). Regulating datafication and platformization: Policy silos and tradeoffs in international platform inquiries. *Policy & Internet*, 14(1), pp. 28–46.
Porter, C. E., and Donthu, N. (2008). Cultivating trust and harvesting value in virtual communities. *Management Science*, 54(1), pp. 113–28.

Postma, O., and Brokke, M. (2001). Personalization in practice: The proven effects of personalization. *Journal of Database Marketing & Customer Strategy Management*, 9(2), p. 142.

Prahalad, C. K., and Ramaswamy, V. (2004). Co-creation experiences: The next practice in value creation. *Journal of Interactive Marketing*, 18(3), pp. 5–14.

Prassl, J. (2018). *Humans as a service: The promise and perils of work in the gig economy*. Oxford: Oxford University Press.

Prassl, J., and Risak, M. (2015). Uber, taskrabbit, and co.: Platforms as employers-rethinking the legal analysis of crowdwork. *Comparative Labor Law and Policy Journal*, 37, pp. 1–30.

PricewaterhouseCoopers (2019) *82% of banks, insurers, investment managers plan to increase fintech partnerships; 88% concerned they'll lose revenue to innovators*, PwC.

Priporas, C. et al. (2017). Unraveling the diverse nature of service quality in a sharing economy. *International Journal of Contemporary Hospitality Management*, 29(9), pp. 2279–2301.

Purdy, M., Zealley, J., and Maseli, O. (2019). The risks of using AI to interpret human emotions. *Harvard Business Review*. Available at: https://hbr.org/2019/11/the- risks-of-using-ai-to-interpret-human-emotions.

Puschmann, T., and Alt, R. (2016). Sharing economy. *Business & Information Systems Engineering*, 58(1), pp. 93–9.

PWC (2015). *The shift from ownership to access*. PWC. Available at: http://pwccn.com/webmedia/doc/635570221864005413_auto_shift_ownership _access_jan2015.pdf.

PWC (2017). Spotlight: Robotic process automation (rpa) what tax needs to know now. Available at: https://www.pwc.com/gx/en/tax/publications/assets/pwc-tax-function-of-the-future-focus-on-today-robotics-process-automation.pdf.

PWC (2023). Who's afraid of AI? Most employees aren't. https://www.pwc.com/gx/en/issues/c-suite-insights/the-leadershipagenda/who-is-afraid-of-ai-most-employees-arent.html.

Qiao, H., Chen, M., and Xia, Y. (2018). The effects of the sharing economy: How does internet finance influence commercial bank risk preferences? *Emerging Markets Finance and Trade*, 54(13), pp. 3013–29.

Rakowski, J. (2004). Does the consumer have an obligation to cooperate with price discrimination? *Business Ethics Quarterly*, 14(2), pp. 263–74.

Ramos, H. (2019). Review of Elliott, Anthony. 2019. The culture of AI: Everyday life and the digital revolution. *Security Journal*. doi:https://doi.org/10.1057/s41284-019-00220-7.

Remane, G. et al. (2016). *A taxonomy of carsharing business models*. www.academia.edu/28900968/A_Taxonomy_of_Carsharing_Business_Models.

Ren, Q., and Weng, W. (2019). Research on the training method of accounting professionals in the era of artificial intelligence. 2019 *IEEE International Conference on Computer Science and Educational Informatization (CSEI)*,. https://doi.org/10.1109/CSEI47661.2019.8938947.

Reuters (2014). Daimler's car sharing business car2go to quit UK, London a challenge. Reuters. http://www.reuters.com/article/daimler-europcar-carsharingidUSL6N0OE4X420140528.

Ricci, F. et al. (2015). *Recommender systems handbook*. Springer.

Riegger, A. S. et al. (2021). Technology-enabled personalization in retail stores: Understanding drivers and barriers. *Journal of Business Research*, 123, pp. 140–55.

Rietveld, J., Schilling, M A., and Bellavitis, C. (2019). Platform strategy: Managing ecosystem value through selective promotion of complements, Organization Science, 30(6), pp. 1125–1393.
Rifkin, J. (2014). *The zero marginal cost society: The internet of things, the collaborative commons, and the eclipse of capitalism*. St. Martin's Press.
Rizvi, J. (2022). The success of social commerce. https://www.forbes.com/sites/jiawertz/2022/12/31/the-success-of-social-commerce/.
Rocchi, J. M. (2021). Competition between neobanks and online banks in the French retail banking market and reactions from universal banks. In A. Sghari and K. Mezghani (eds), *Influence of fintech on management transformation* (pp. 191–216). IGI Global. DOI: 10.4018/978-1-7998-7110-1.ch009.
Rosenberg, N. (1971). *The economics of technological change*. Harmondsworth: Penguin.
Rosenblat, A. (2018). When your boss is an algorithm. *New York Times*, www.nytimes.com/2018/10/12/opinion/sunday/uber-driver-life.html.
Rosenblat, A., and Stark, L. (2016). Algorithmic labour and information asymmetries: A case study of Uber's drivers. *International Journal of Communication*, 10, pp. 3758–84.
Ross, J. W., Beatch, C. M., and Sebastian, I. M. (2017). How to develop a great digital strategy. *MIT Sloan Management Review*, 58(2), pp. 7–9.
Ross, M. (2023). AI sparks revolution in how much supermarkets charge you for food. www.telegraph.co.uk/money/consumer-affairs/food-cheaper-near-expiry-supermarkets-test-ai/.
Roth, D., and Lomas, K. (2017), *How artificial intelligence is transforming the retail conversation*. The Store WPP in partnership with IBM, pp. 18–32.
Russell, S., and Norvig, P. (2010). *Artificial intelligence: a modern approach*. 3rd edn. New Jersey: Pearson, p. 2.
Ryberg, M. W. et al. (2020). Downscaling the planetary boundaries in absolute environmental sustainability assessments – A review. *Journal of Cleaner Production*, 276, p. 123287.
Sachs, J. D. and Kotlikoff, L. J. (2012). *Smart machines and Long term misery*. Cambridge: NBER working paper 18629.
Sacks, D. (2011). The sharing economy. fast company. https://www.fastcompany.com/1747551/sharing-economy pp. 88–131.
Salesforce (2022). Customer engagement research. www.salesforce.com/news/stories/customer-engagement-research/.
Salonen, V., and Karjaluoto, H. (2016). Web personalization: The state of the art and future avenues for research and practice. *Telematics and Informatics*, 33(4), 1088–104.
Samara, D., Magnisalis, I., and Peristeras, V. (2020). Artificial Intelligence and big data in tourism: A systematic literature review, *Journal of Hospitality and Tourism Technology*, 11(2), pp. 343–67.
Samuel, A. (1959). Arthur Samuel: Pioneer in machine learning, www.infolab.stanford.edu/pub/voy/museum/samuel.html.
Sanders, E. B. N., and Stappers, P. J. (2008). Co-creation and the new landscapes of design. *CoDesign: International Journal of CoCreation in Design and the Arts*, 4(1), pp. 5–18.
Santeralli, E. (2023) Financial services personalization maturity. www.dynamicyield.com/blog/financial-services-personalization-maturity-2023/.
Sarwar, S., Dent, A., Faust, K., Richer, M., Djuric, U., Van Ommeren, R., and Diamandis, P. (2019). Physician perspectives on integration of artificial intelligence into diagnostic pathology. *NPJ Digital Medicine*, 2(1).

Satow, K. L. (1975). Social approval and helping. *Journal of Experimental Social Psychology*, 11(6), pp. 501–9.

Savci, M. et al. (2021). Histrionic personality, 25 narcissistic personality, and problematic social media use: Testing of a new hypothetical 26 model. *International Journal of Mental Health and Addiction*, 19, pp. 986–1004.

Scheiber, N. (2017). *How Uber uses psychological tricks to push its drivers' buttons. New York Times*. https://nyti.ms/2nMmDtc.

Schor, J. (2016). Debating the sharing economy. *Journal of Self-Governance and Management Economics*, 4(3), pp. 7–22.

Schumpeter, J. (1934). *The theory of economic development: An inquiry into profits, capital, credit, interest, and the business cycle*. Cambridge: Harvard University Press.

Schumpeter, J. A. (1934). *The theory of economic development: an inquiry into profits, capital, credit, interest, and the business cycle*. New Brunswick, NJ: Transaction Publishers.

Schwab, K. (2017). *The fourth industrial revolution*. London: Penguin Books.

Schweizer, M., Kotouc, A. J., and Wagner, T. (2006). Scale development for consumer confusion. *Advances in Consumer Research*, 33(1), pp. 184–90.

Sciara, S. et al. (2023). Going public on social media: The effects of thousands of Instagram followers on users with a high need for social approval. *Current Psychology*, 42, pp. 8206–20.

Scott, B. (2006). *The political economy of capitalism*. Available at: http://www.hbs.edu/faculty/Publication%20Files/07-037.pdf.

Seele, P. et al. (2019). Mapping the ethicality of algorithmic pricing: A review of dynamic and personalized pricing. *Journal of Business Ethics*, 170(4), pp. 697–719.

Shane, S., and Venkataraman, S. (2000). The promise of entrepreneurship as a field of research, *Academy of Management*, 25(1), pp. 217–26.

Sharkey, A. (2017). Can robots be responsible moral agents? And why should we care? *Connection Science*, 29(3), pp. 210–16.

Sharma, S., and Crossler, R. E. (2014). Disclosing too much? Situational factors affecting information disclosure in social commerce environment. *Electronic Commerce Research and Applications*, 13(5), pp. 305–19.

Sher, G., and Benchlouch, A. (2023). The privacy paradox with AI. https://www.reuters.com/legal/legalindustry/privacy-paradox-with-ai-2023-10-31/.

Shirvanimoghaddam, K. et al. (2020). Death by waste: Fashion and textile circular economy case. *Science of the Total Environment*, 718, pp. 1–10.

Shrihari, S., and Srinivasan, R. (2012). Social influence effects in online product ratings. *Journal of Marketing*, 76, pp. 70–88.

Si, H. et al. (2020). Understanding intention and behavior toward sustainable usage of bike sharing by extending the theory of planned behavior. *Resources, Conservation and Recycling*, 152, 104513.

Simon, H. A. (2000). Bounded rationality in social science: Today and tomorrow. *Mind & Society*, 1(1), pp. 25–39.

Simonson, I. (2005). Determinants of customers' responses to customized offers: Conceptual framework and research propositions. *Journal of Marketing*, 69(1), pp. 32–45.

Simonson, I. (2005). Determinants of customers' responses to customized offers: Conceptual framework and research propositions. *Journal of Marketing*, 69(1), pp. 32–45.

Skog, D., Wimelius, H., and Sandberg, J. (2018). Digital disruption. *Business & Information Systems Engineering*, 60(5), pp. 431–7.
Smink, A. R. et al. (2020). Shopping in augmented reality: The effects of spatial presence, personalization and intrusiveness on app and brand responses. *Journal of Business Research*, 118, pp. 474–85.
Smith, A. (1776). *An inquiry into the nature and causes of the wealth of nations*. London: Printed for W. Strahan; and T. Cadell, in the Strand.
Sorensen, J. J. (2019). Millennial perceptions of fast fashion and second-hand clothing: an exploration of clothing preferences using Q methodology. *Social Sciences*, 8. p. 244.
Souchet, F. (2019). Fashion has a huge waste problem. Here's how it can change. World Economic Forum. https://www.weforum.org.
Sparrow, B., Liu, J., and Wegner, D. M. (2011). Google effects on memory: Cognitive consequences of having information at our fingertips. *Science*, 333(6043), pp. 776–8.
Spears, L. (2023). Harnessing the power of gamification and AI in learning and development, LinkedIn. https://www.linkedin.com/pulse/harnessing-power-gamification-ai-learning-development-liv-spears/.
Spenner, P., and Freeman, K. (2012). To keep your customers, keep it simple. *Harvard Business Review*. https://hbr.org/2012/05/to-keep-your-customers-keep-it-simple.
Spiekermann, S. (2006). Individual price discrimination – an impossibility? In *International Conference for Human–Computer Interaction*. Workshop on Privacy and Personalization. 47–52.
Spulber, D. F. (2011). Should business method inventions be patentable? *Journal of Legal Analysis*, 3(1), pp. 265–340.
Srnicek, N. (2017). *Platform capitalism*. Cambridge: Polity.
Stahel, W. (2019). *The circular economy: A user's guide*. Routledge.
Stanford, J. (2017). The resurgence of gig work: Historical and theoretical perspectives. *The Economic and Labour Relations Review*, 28(3), pp. 382–401.
Statista (2023). Personalization attitudes consumers worldwide. www.statista.com/statistics/1415507/peronalization-attitudes-consumers-worldwide/.
Statista (2023a). Global retailers ability to use data for personalization. www.statista.com/statistics/1415978/global-retailers-ability-to-use-data-for-personalization/.
Statista (2023b). Types data shared personalized experience United. *States*/www.statista.com/statistics/1379534/types-data-shared-personalized-experience-united-states/.
Statista (2023c). B2B e-commerce personalization methods worldwide www.statista.com/statistics/1413348/b2b-e-commerce-personalization-methods-worldwide/.
Statista (2023d). E-commerce worldwide – statistics & facts. www.stati sta.com/topics/871/ online-shopping/#topicOverview.
Statista (2024). Top 100 companies: Sharing economy. www.statista.com/study/140121/top-100-companies-sharing-economy/.
Statista (2024a). Airbnb statistics & facts. www.statista.com/topics/2273/airbnb/#topicOverview.
Steppe, R. (2017). Online price discrimination and personal data: A general data protection regulation perspective. *Computer Law and Security Review*, 33(6), pp. 768–85.
Steuart, J. (1767). *An inquiry into the principles of political economy*. London: J.B Putnam.
Stewart, A., and Standford, J. (2017). Regulating work in the gig economy: What are the options? *The Economic and Labour Relations Review*, 28(3), pp. 420–37.

Strickland, B. R., and Crowne, D. P. (1962). Conformity under conditions of simulated group pressure as a function of the need for social approval. *The Journal of Social Psychology*, 58, pp. 171–81.

Suk, J. (2023). The impact of AI & automation on workforce development trends, Hurix Digital. https://www.hurix.com/the-impact-of-ai-and-automation-on-workforce-development-trends/

Sundararajan, A. (2016). *The sharing economy: The end of employment and the rise of crowd-based capitalism*. Cambridge, MA: MIT Press, pp. 128–9.

Sunikka, A., and Bragge, J. (2012). Applying text-mining to personalization and customization research literature–Who, what and where? *Expert Systems with Applications*, 39(11), pp. 10049–58.

Sunstein, B. R. (2003). *The megaphone effect: Operating principles for communications in the digital age*. The Communication Yearbook.

Surprenant, C. F., and Solomon, M. R. (1987). Predictability and personalization in the service encounter. *Journal of Marketing*, 51(2), pp. 86–96.

Susskind, D., and Susskind, R. (2015), *The future of the professions: How technology will transform the work of human experts*. Oxford: Oxford University Press.

Sussman, S. W., and Siegal, W. S. (2003) Informational influence in organizations: An integrated approach to knowledge adoption. *Information Systems Research*, 14, pp. 47–65.

Sweller, J., Ayres, P., and Kalyuga, S. (2011). *Cognitive load theory (Explorations in the learning sciences, instructional systems and performance technologies)*. New York: Springer.

Tajfel, H., and Turner, J. C. (1979). An integrative theory of intergroup conflict. In W. G. Austin and S. Worchel (eds), *The social psychology of intergroup relations* (pp. 33–47). Monterey, CA: Brooks/Cole.

Tam, K. Y., and Ho, S. Y. (2006). Understanding the impact of web personalization on user information processing and decision outcomes. *MIS Quarterly*, 30(4), pp. 865–90.

Tan, Z. M., et al. (2021). The ethical debate about the gig economy: A review and critical analysis. *Technology in Society*, 65, p. 101594.

Taylor, M. G. et al. (2017). Good work: The Taylor review of modern working practices. https://www.gov.uk/government/publications/good-workthe-taylor-review-of-modern-working-practices

Thakor, A. V. (2020). Fintech and banking: What do we know? *Journal of Financial Intermediation*, 41, p. 100833.

Thaler, R. H. (2017). Behavioral economics. *Journal of Political Economy*, 125(6), pp. 1799–805.

Thaler, R. H., and Sunstein, C. R. (2022), *Nudge: Improving decisions about health, wealth and happiness*. London: Allen Lane.

Thoumrungroje, A. (2014). The influence of social media intensity and EWOM on conspicuous consumption. *Procedia-Social and Behavioral Sciences*, 148, pp. 7–15.

Todeschini, B. et al. (2017). Innovative and sustainable business models in the fashion industry: Entrepreneurial drivers, opportunities, and challenges. *Business Horizons*, 60(6), pp. 759–70.

Todolí-Signes, A. (2017). The 'gig economy': Employee, self-employed or the need for a special employment regulation? *Transfer: European Review of Labour and Research*, 23(2), pp. 193–205.

Tong, S., Luo, X., and Xu, B. (2020). Personalized mobile marketing strategies. *Journal of the Academy of Marketing Science*, 48(1), pp. 64–78.

Trading Economics (2016). *United Kingdom GDP per capita PPP.*
Tran, M., and Sokas, R. (2017). The gig economy and contingent work. *Journal of Occupational and Environmental Medicine*, 59(4), pp. 63–6.
Treiblmaier, H. et al. (2004). Evaluating personalization and customization from an ethical point of view: An empirical study. In 37th Annual Hawaii International Conference on System Sciences. IEEE.
Tucker, C. E. (2014). Social networks, personalized advertising, and privacy controls. *Journal of Marketing Research*, 51(5), pp. 546–62.
Tukker, A. (2015). Product services for a resource-efficient and circular economy – a review. *Journal of Cleaner Production*, 97, pp. 76–91.
Turiale L., and Scuderi A. (2013). Evaluation *of* social media actions *for the* agrifood system. *Procedia Technology*, 8, pp. 200–8.
Turing, A. M. (1936). On Computable Numbers, with an Application to the Entscheidungs problem. In *Proceedings of the London Mathematical Society*, Series 2 (42), pp. 230–65.
Tussyadiah, I., and Pesonen, J. (2016). Impacts of peer-to-peer accommodation use on travel patterns. *Journal of Travel Research*, 55(8), pp. 1022–40.
Twilio (2023). Global retailers ability to use data for personalization. https://www.statista.com/statistics/1415978/global-retailers-ability-to-use-data-for-personalization/.
Twilio (2023). Online shopping consumers repeat buyers personalized experience. www.statista.com/statistics/1300134/online-shopping-consumers-repeat-buyers-personalized-experience/.
Twilio (2023a). Customer expectations for better personalization worldwide. https://www.statista.com/statistics/1415837/customer-expectations-for-better-personalization-worldwide/.
Twilio (2023a). Success measurement in using AI-driven personalization worldwide-2023. www.statista.com/statistics/1415821/success-measurement-in-using-ai-driven-personalization-worldwide-2023/.
Ukkonen, A. and Hamari, J. (2015). The sharing economy: Why people participate in collaborative consumption. *SSRN Electronic Journal.*
UN Environment Programme (2018). Putting the brakes on fast fashion. https://www.unenvironment.org/news-and-stories/story/putting-brakes-fast-fashion.
United Nations (2015). Goal 12: Ensure Sustainable Consumption And Production Patterns. https://www.un.org/sustainabledevelopment/sustainable-consumption-production/.
Upadhyay, A., and Khandelwal, K. (2018). Applying artificial intelligence: implications for recruitment. *Strategic HR Review*, 17(5), pp. 255–8.
US Department of Justice (2023). *Amazon agrees to injunctive relief and $25 million civil penalty for alleged violations of children's privacy law relating to Alexa.* Office of Public Affairs, United States, Department of Justice. https://www.justice.gov/opa/pr/amazon-agrees-injunctive-relief-and-25-million-civil-penalty-alleged-violations-childrens.
Vallas, S., and Schor, J. B. (2020). What do platforms do? Understanding the gig economy. *Annual Review of Sociology*, 46, pp. 273–94.
van Dijck, J. (2009). Users like you? Theorising agent in user-generated content. *Media, Culture & Society*, 31(1), pp. 41–58.
van Dijck, J., Poell, T., and de Waal, M. (2018). *The platform society: Public values in a connective world.* Oxford: Oxford University Press.
van Esch, P., Black, J., and Ferolie, J. (2019). Marketing AI recruitment: The next phase in job application and selection. *Computers in Human Behavior*, 90, pp. 215–22.

Varian, H. R. (2014). Big data: New tricks for econometrics. *Journal of Economic Perspectives*, 28(2), pp. 3–28.
Verhoef, P. C. et al. (2021). Digital transformation: A multidisciplinary reflection and research agenda. *Journal of Business Research*, 122, pp. 889–901.
Verhoef, P., Kannan, P., and Inman, J. (2015) From multi-channel retailing to omni-channel retailing: Introduction to the special issue on multi-channel retailing. *Journal of Retailing*, 91(2), pp. 174–81.
Vesanen, J., and Raulas, M. (2006). Building bridges for personalization: A Process Model for Marketing. *Journal of Interactive Marketing*, 20, pp. 5–20.
Vetrò, A. et al. (2019). AI: from rational agents to socially responsible agents. *Digital Policy, Regulation and Governance*, 21(3), pp. 291–304.
Villar, A. S., and Khan, N. (2021). Robotic process automation in banking industry: a case study on Deutsche Bank. *Journal of Banking and Financial Technology*, 5(1), pp. 71–86.
Vives, X. (2018). *The impact of Fintech on banking – European econ*omy. European Economy. Available at: https://european-economy.eu/2017- 2/the-impact-of-FinTech-on-banking/.
Vogtlander, J. G. et al. (2017). Combined analyses of costs, market value and eco-costs in circular business models: Eco-efficient value creation in remanufacturing. *Journal of Remanufacturing*, 7(1), pp. 1–17.
Vohs, K. D. et al. (2008). Making choices impairs subsequent self-control: A limited-resource account of decision making, self-regulation, and active initiative. *Journal of Personality and Social Psychology*, 94(5), pp. 883–98.
Vos, L. (2015). Inside out: Why sadness is the key to happy shareable content. https://marketinginsidergroup.com/content-marketing/inside-sadness-key-happy-shareable-content/.
Vrontis, D. et al. (2022). Artificial intelligence, robotic, advanced technologies and human resource management: A systematic review. *The International Journal of Human Resource Management*, 33(6), pp. 1–30.
Waldfogel, J. (2015). First degree price discrimination goes to school. *Journal of Industrial Economics*, 63(4), pp. 569–97.
Wallich, H. (1982). The limits to growth revisited. *Challenge*, 25(4), pp. 36–42.
Walmart (2020). How Walmart embraces Immersive Learning, Strivr. https://www.strivr.com/customers/walmart/.
Walsh, G., Hennig-Thurau, T., and Mitchell, V. W. (2007). Consumer confusion proneness: scale development, validation, and application. *Journal of Marketing Management*, 23(7–8), pp. 697–721.
Walters, R., and Novak, M. (2021). Cyber security. In R. Walters and M. Novak (eds), *Cyber security, artificial intelligence, data protection & the law* (pp. 21–37). Springer Singapore. https://doi.org/10.1007/978-981-16-1665-5_2.
Wang, Q., and Shukla, P. (2013). Linking sources of consumer confusion to decision satisfaction: The role of choice goals. *Psychology & Marketing*, 30(4), pp. 295–304.
Wang, X. (2020). *Research on the Transition from Financial Accounting to Management Accounting in the Era of Artificial Intelligence. 5th International Conference on Mechanical, Control and Computer Engineering (ICMCCE).* http://dx.doi.org/10.1088/1742-6596/1345/4/042031
Wang, Y. et al. (2020). Challenges and Solutions in Autonomous Driving: A Blockchain Approach. *IEEE Network*, 34(4), pp. 218–26.

Wang, Y., and Sui, X. (2020). Can fintech improve the efficiency of commercial banks? – An analysis based on big data. *Research in International Business and Finance*, 55, p. 101338.

Wang, Y., Sui. X., and Zhang, Q. (2021). Can fintech improve the efficiency of commercial banks?—An analysis based on big data. *Research in International Business and Finance*, 55, 101338.

Warren, S. D., and Brandeis, L. D. (1890). The right to privacy. *Harvard Law Review*, 4, pp. 193–220.

Wastling, T., Charnley, F., and Moreno, M. (2018). Design for circular behaviour: Considering users in a circular economy. *Sustainability*, 10, p. 1743.

Wautelet, T. (2017). The impact of digitalization on international companies: A case study of LEGO. 23095.01448. https://www.researchgate.net?publications1319273016.

Waytz, A., and Norton, M. I. (2014). Botsourcing and outsourcing: Robot, British, Chinese, and German workers are for thinking-not feeling-jobs. *Emotion*, 14(2), pp. 434–44.

Weakliem, D. L., and Frenkel, S. J. (2006). Morale and workplace performance. *Work and Occupations*, 33(3), pp. 335–61.

Wedel, M., and Kannan, P. K. (2016). Marketing analytics for data-rich environments. *Journal of Marketing*, 80(6), pp. 97–121.

WEF (2018). *WEF future of jobs report 2018*. World Economic Forum 2018 report. http://www3.weforum.org/docs/WEF_Future_of_Jobs_2018.pdf.

WEF (2020). The future of jobs report 2020. https://www.weforum.org/publications/the-future-of-jobs-report-2020/. The World Economic Forum 2020 report.

WEF (2023). WEF future of jobs 2023.pdf, World Economic Forum 2023 report (weforum.org).

Werhane, P. H., and Freeman, R. E. (1999). Business ethics: The state of the art, *International Journal of Management Reviews*, 1(1), pp. 1–16.

Wildau, G. (2016). *Tencent backs down in mobile payments war with Alibaba. Financial Times*. Available at: https://www.ft.com/content/df82fc8e-0d36-11e6-9cd4-2be89 8308be3.

Williams, A. (2006). Product service systems in the automobile industry: Contribution to system innovation? *Journal of Cleaner Production*, 15(11–12), pp. 1093–1103.

Williams, K. R. (2022). The welfare effects of dynamic pricing: Evidence from airline markets. *Econometrica*, 90(2), pp. 831–58.

Williamson, O. E. (2007). *The economic institutions of capitalism. Firms, markets, relational contracting*. Gabler.

Wilson, C. et al. (2021). Building and auditing fair algorithms, *Proceedings of the 2021 ACM Conference on Fairness, Accountability, and Transparency*. doi: 10.1145/3442188.3445928.

Wilson, H. J., and Daugherty, P. R. (2018). *Human + machine: Reimagining work in the age of AI*. Boston, MA: Harvard Business Review Press.

Wiprächtiger, D. et al. (2019). Access-based business model innovation in frontier markets: Case study of shared mobility in Timor-Leste. *Technological Forecasting and Social Change*, 143, pp. 224–38.

Wood, A. J. et al. (2019). Good gig, bad gig: Autonomy and algorithmic control in the global gig economy. *Work, Employment and Society*, 33(1), pp. 56–75.

Wu, P. H., and Lin, C. P. (2016). Learning to foresee the effects of social identity complexity and 27 need for social approval on technology brand loyalty. *Technological Forecasting and Social Change*, 111, pp. 188–97.

Wu, X., and Zhou, J. (2021). The influential factors of developing better in the global stream media market: An analysis of Netflix. *Advances in Social Science, Education and Humanities Research*, 586(1), pp. 177–83.

Xia, H., Liu, J., and Zhang, Z. J. (2024). Identifying Fintech risk through machine learning: Analyzing the Q&A text of an online loan investment platform. *Annals of Operations Research*, 333, 579–59.

Xu, Z., and Dukes, A. (2019). Product line design under preference uncertainty using aggregate consumer data. *Marketing Science*, 38(4), pp. 669–89.

Yampolskiy, R. V. (2018). *Artificial intelligence safety and security*. CRC Press.

Yang, S. B. et al. (2019). In Airbnb we trust: Understanding consumers' trust-attachment building mechanisms in the sharing economy. *International Journal of Hospitality Management*, 83, pp. 198–209.

Yao, M. et al. (2018). Impact of payment technology innovations on the traditional financial industry: A focus on China. *Technological Forecasting and Social Change*, 135, pp. 199–207.

Ye, G. et al. (2021). The value of influencer marketing for business: A bibliometric analysis and managerial implications. *Journal of Advertising*, 50(2), pp. 160–78.

Yi, J., Li, J., and Chen, L. (2023). Ecosystem social responsibility in international digital commerce. *Journal of International Business Studies*, 54(1), pp. 24–41.

Yorks, L., Abel, A. L., and Rotatori, D. (2022). *Strategic human resource development in practice: Leveraging talent for sustained performance in the digital age of AI*. Cham, Switzerland: Springer (Management for professionals). doi: 10.1007/978-3-030-95775-9.

Zand, D. E. (1972). Trust and managerial problem solving. *Administrative Science Quarterly*, 17(2), pp. 229–39.

Zanker, M., Rook, L., and Jannach, D. (2019). Measuring the impact of online personalisation: Past, present and future. *International Journal of Human-Computer Studies*, 131, pp. 160–8.

Zervas, G., Proserpio, D., and Byers, J. W. (2017). The rise of the sharing economy: Estimating the impact of Airbnb on the hotel industry. *Journal of Marketing Research*, 54(5), pp. 687–705.

Zervas, G., Proserpio, D., and Byers, J. W. (2021). A first look at online reputation on Airbnb, where every stay is above average. *Marketing Letters*, 32(1), pp. 1–16.

Zhang, T., Agarwal, R., and Lucas Jr., H. C. (2011). The value of IT-enabled retailer learning: Personalized product recommendations and customer store loyalty in electronic markets. *MIS Quarterly*, 35(4), pp. 859–81.

Zhang, Y. et al. (2020). The Impact of artificial intelligence and blockchain on the accounting profession. *IEEE Access*, 8, pp. 110461–77. https://doi.org/10.1109/ACCESS.2020.3000505.

Zhang, Z., and Liu, H. (2015). Social recommendation model combining trust propagation and sequential behaviors. *Applied Intelligence*, 43(3), pp. 695–706.

Zhou, F., Ji, Y., and Jiao, R. J. (2013). Affective and cognitive design for mass personalization: status and prospect. *Journal of Intelligent Manufacturing*, 24(5), pp. 1047–69.

Zhou, L., Zhang, P., and Zimmermann, H. D. (2013). Social commerce research: An integrated view. *Electronic Commerce Research and Applications*, 12(2), pp. 61–8.

Zine, P. U. et al. (2014). A framework for value co-creation through customization and personalization in the context of machine tool PSS. *Procedia CIRP*, 16, pp. 32–37.

Zipperer, B. et al. (2022). *National survey of gig workers paints a picture of poor working conditions, low pay*. Economic Policy Institute. Available at: ww.epi.org/publication/gig-worker-survey/.
Zivnuska, S. et al. (2019). Social media addiction and social media reactions: The implications for job performance. *The Journal of Social Psychology*, 159(6), pp. 746–60.
Zuboff, S. (2019). *The age of surveillance capitalism: The fight for a human future at the frontier of power*. New York: Public Affairs.

Websites

Airbnb, www.airbnb.com
Amazon, www.amazon.com
Chime, www.chime.com
Etsy, www.etsy.com
Grubhub, www.grubhub.com
Lyft, www.lyft.com
Netflix, www.netflix.com
Nike, www.nike.com
Paypal, www.paypal.com
Prosper, www.prosper.com
Revolut, www.revolut.com
Spotify, www.spotify.com
Square, https://squareup.com
TaskRabbit, www.taskrabbit.com
Twitch, www.twitch.tv
Uber, www.uber.com
Wise, https://wise.com

Index

www.ingramcontent.com/pod-product-compliance
Ingram Content Group UK Ltd.
Pitfield, Milton Keynes, MK11 3LW, UK
UKHW020240290926
15470UKWH00002B/641

9 781350 444416